NONE A STRANGER THERE

NONE A STRANGER THERE

England and/in Europe on the Early Modern Stage

Edited by
SCOTT OLDENBURG
and MATTEO PANGALLO

THE UNIVERSITY OF ALABAMA PRESS
TUSCALOOSA

The University of Alabama Press
Tuscaloosa, Alabama 35487-0380
uapress.ua.edu

Typeface: Scala Pro

Cover image: "*Europa Prima Pars Terrae In Forma Virginis* (Europe in the Shape of a Queen),"
Heinrich Bunting, Hanover, c. 1581
Cover design: Sandy Turner Jr.

Cataloging-in-Publication data is available from the Library of Congress.
ISBN: 978-0-8173-2213-7 (cloth)
ISBN: 978-0-8173-6173-0 (paper)
E-ISBN: 978-0-8173-9533-9

To the strangers everywhere, then and now.

Contents

Acknowledgments   ix

Introduction: Reading Early Modern Drama after Brexit
  SCOTT OLDENBURG AND MATTEO PANGALLO   1

1. "The Uncertainty of This World": Shakespeare in "Unprecedented" Times
  MARGARET TUDEAU-CLAYTON   37

2. Profiting in Babylon: Transnationalism and Typology in the Biblical
  Drama of the English Traveling Theater
  KEVIN CHOVANEC   64

3. Astonished and Amazed: Early Modern English Black Christianity and
  Respectability Politics in Middleton and Munday's *The Triumphs of Truth*
  JAMIE PARIS   86

4. The Nation Embarrassed: Shameful Memories in the Henriad
  JOHN S. GARRISON AND KYLE PIVETTI   107

5. Building a Wall around Tudor England: Coastal Forts and Fantasies of
  Border Control in *Friar Bacon and Friar Bungay*
  TODD ANDREW BORLIK   131

6. The Brut, the Bruce, and Brexit: Scottish Independence in *The Valiant
  Scot* (1637), *The Outlaw King* (2018), and *Robert the Bruce* (2019)
  VIMALA C. PASUPATHI   153

7. English Imperialism and Staff Fighting in *Mucedorus*
  MATT CARTER   180

8. "Let Burnt Sack Be the Issue": Immigrants as Threat and Remedy in
  William Shakespeare's *The Merry Wives of Windsor*
  HEATHER BAILEY   198

9. "Thou Hast Incurred the Danger": Shylock, Brexit, and Urban Citizenship
  WILLIAM CASEY CALDWELL   216

Bibliography   245

Contributors   269

Index   273

Acknowledgments

This volume would not have been possible without the intellectual generosity, persistence, and diligence of our dedicated contributors. We are grateful to them for all they did over the course of three years to make this collection as strong as possible and for sharing their scholarship and their ideas with us and our readers. We are also grateful to Daniel Waterman, editor-in-chief of the University of Alabama Press, Michelle Dowd, director of the Hudson Strode Program in Renaissance Studies, and the entire editorial board at the University of Alabama Press for their guidance, support, and professionalism, as well as their enthusiasm for this project. Finally, we are also thankful for the timely and thoughtful feedback shared with us by the volume's two anonymous reviewers, whose suggestions and critiques helped strengthen the collection.

Matteo would like to thank Scott for being such a crucial part of this project and for his attentive, expert, and supportive work as a coeditor and for providing a wealth of guidance drawn from his deep knowledge of early modern drama, history, and the England-Europe relationship. He is also grateful to the scholars with whom he has discussed aspects of this project over so many years and whose suggestions and encouragement have helped bring it to fruition, including Arthur Kinney, Adam Zucker, Pamela Allen Brown, Joshua Eckhardt, Peter Kirwan, and the VCU undergraduates of his senior seminar Immigrants in Early Modern Drama. Finally, as always, he is thankful for Nettie, Atticus, and Tobias, whose love, support, and patience make everything possible.

Scott in turn thanks Matteo, who initially conceived of the volume and whose persistence, creativity, and insight made its completion possible. Some of Scott's thinking on the issues covered here stems from a lively 2017 Shakespeare Association of America seminar, "Shakespearean Migrants, Immigrants, Immigrants, Exiles, and Refugees" with Kevin Chovanec, Ton (AJ) Hoenselaars, Michael Shumway, and Amy Lou Smith. He also thanks Michelle for her love, support, and patience.

NONE A STRANGER THERE

Introduction

Reading Early Modern Drama after Brexit

Scott Oldenburg and Matteo Pangallo

"Quelle catastrophe, le Brexit!" AD libs Jonathan Cullen as Dr. Caius in Fiona Laird's 2018 Royal Shakespeare Company (RSC) performance of William Shakespeare's *The Merry Wives of Windsor*. The line elicits laughter—for once in the play not entirely at the doctor's expense, whose French pronunciation of English is a running joke throughout the play. Brexit, the UK's 2016 referendum on leaving the European Economic Union and thereby limiting immigrant labor in the nation, provides an uncomfortable context for the production, with Falstaff donning a Union Jack vest and, as Peter Kirwan rightfully objects, Black actors cast only as servants.[1] Laird herself appears to have been ambivalent (at best) about Brexit. In a 2016 blog posting she compared the vote to the plebian protest at the outset of *Coriolanus* and to the storming of the Bastille, while also lamenting the lack of resolve held by key Brexit proponents— then-UK prime minister David Cameron, UK members of Parliament Boris Johnson and Michael Gove, and member of the European Parliament Nigel Farage.[2] The Brexit context of this production of *The Merry Wives of Windsor* highlights how, like Cameron, Johnson, Gove, and Farage, the play wants it both ways: to evoke anti-immigrant sentiment and to flee from the implications of xenophobia by hiding behind the claim that in the end it was only a joke to be laughed "o'er by a country fire."

Such Shakespearean images of an inclusive communal hearth in a Brexit context stand in stark contrast to the way the Brexit vote fueled an increase in anti-immigrant and especially anti-Muslim acts of violence in the UK, "a country fire" turned conflagration.[3] Indeed, Brexit prompts Brodie Wadell to examine the unfortunate resonance of the major anti-immigrant riot of the sixteenth century, Evil May Day, with present day anti-immigrant violence and Joseph Campana to reflect on the precarity of sovereignty itself.[4] And Laird's production of *The Merry Wives of Windsor* was certainly not the only Shakespeare play to be influenced by the new context of Brexit. For example, L. Monique Pittman reads the BBC *Hollow Crown* series (based on Shakespeare's first and second tetralogies) in terms of Brexit and neonationalism more broadly conceived; Marina Gerzic considers Rupert Goold's 2016 production of *Richard III* as reflecting the political turmoil amid the Vote Leave campaign; Stephen O'Neill notes several evocations of *King Lear* in commentaries on Brexit and declares, "*King Lear* is Shakespeare's Brexit play," basing this observation largely on the play's depiction of nihilism and a fragmented realm; and in her readings of performances of *A Midsummer Night's Dream* and *Much Ado About Nothing*, Bridget Escolme examines the role nostalgia plays in performance and the ideology underpinning Brexit.[5] Outside of Shakespeare studies, Kevin A. Quarmby describes Cheek by Jowl's 2019 production of Francis Beaumont's *The Knight of the Burning Pestle* as a "Brexit-spattered romp through destructive populism," while in his review of Fiona Buffini's production of Thomas Middleton's *The Revenger's Tragedy*, Ben Haworth suggests that "the preposterous portrayal of power in the hands of the morally bankrupt cannot fail but resonate with modern audiences reeling from the post-Brexit political pantomime."[6] Finally, as Anna Blackwell summarizes, there was considerable media attention given to the rather glib Brexit question, "Which way would Shakespeare vote?"[7]

None a Stranger There builds on these accounts of recent productions of early modern drama, noting significant points of connection between the development of early modern English nationhood, as expressed in many of the period's plays, and Brexit's neonationalist orientation. Just as early English nationhood was founded in part on the break with Rome and Roman Catholicism, so Brexit's neonationalism stems from the break with Europe and the European Union.[8] Early modern English national identity relied in part on a founding myth that suppressed Celtic origins; the neonationalism of Brexit deployed a vague nostalgia for English preeminence and imagined cultural homogeneity while ignoring the violence that accompanied English colonialism.[9] Worries over immigration and assimilation as well as implicit and overt racism appear both in the rhetoric of early modern English nationalism and Brexit's neonationalism. Early modern English nationhood developed in tandem with an increasingly centralized state leaning toward absolutism; as a modern nation-state, the UK naturally has a highly centralized government, but the Leave vote appears to correspond to an increased trust in authoritarianism.[10] In most senses,

Brexit's neonationalism appears as an intensification of the factors that fueled early modern English nationhood. Edmund Spenser's call for "a kingdom of our own language" thus comes back with a vengeance as post-Brexit linguaphobia.[11]

As she covered a pro-Brexit march by the xenophobic English Defence League (EDL), reporter Afua Hirsch was told by one of the leaders of the right-wing extremist group, "You're OK . . . You speak English properly. You know our ways. You're like us. It's the others we have a problem with."[12] Hirsch notes the way such linguaphobic demands for assimilation amount to "a chilling and insidious form of racism" that posits English culture (as though it were a coherent monolith) as superior and makes inclusion contingent on the degree immigrants can mimic Englishness. The EDL's primary target has been Muslims; the Islamophobic group's demand for assimilation, then, is not merely that immigrants learn English but rather that they abandon their most deeply held beliefs so that white English citizens might feel comfortable. Englishness itself is varied and elusive, so many immigrants find themselves striving toward an imaginary ideal of Englishness impossible to achieve.

This premium on assimilation is nothing new to England, of course. During the Peasant Revolt of 1381 rebels reportedly executed any Flemings who were judged to pronounce the words "bread and cheese" inadequately.[13] The mockery of Dr. Caius and Parson Evans in *Merry Wives* based almost entirely on their imperfect English is a comic expression of the same antipathy to difference. A similar dramatization of linguistic assimilation is found in Sir Thomas Salusbury's 1641 Twelfth Night masque staged at Knowsley House for James Stanley, Lord Strange, and his wife. The performers included the Stanley's daughter, the household staff, and several members of the local community, including French apothecary Abraham L'Anglois, who was cast as the Prologue because, as Salusbury noted at the start of his manuscript, he spoke "very broken English."[14] Later in the masque, when Christmas describes the gifts he will bring to the various members of the Knowsley community, Salusbury again singled out L'Anglois to make comic use of his accent. With a joking reference to the sacrament of anointing with oil, Christmas declares that, among the gifts for L'Anglois, he will include "some quantity of English honey to anoint his tongue, that he may be understanded."[15] Christmas's promise of linguistic assimilation would, of course, paradoxically erase the very aspect of L'Anglois's performance that his casting as the Prologue was meant, for comic purposes, to emphasize. This paradox speaks to the conflicted process by which English culture attempted to define itself: not merely by rejecting what was alien but also exploiting it and ultimately incorporating it.

No extant evidence reveals who L'Anglois was, or why or when he arrived in England or at Knowsley, though his name resembles the kind of wordplay many immigrants used to signal affinity for their adopted home. David George suggests "he may have been a Huguenot who came to England in the train of Lord Strange's wife, Charlotte de la Trémoille," whose father, Claude de La Trémoille, Duke of Thouars, had been a Protestant leader since 1587.[16] If L'Anglois was a Huguenot, he likely bristled at a joke about being subjected to Holy Unction—the Catholic-derived sacrament of healing that the Church of England still practiced but Calvinists, including the Huguenots, rejected. Christmas's promise then seems to signal not only a desire for L'Anglois's linguistic assimilation but his religious conversion as well.

As with the EDL today, then, rendering immigrants' speech more "English" was just one of many demands for assimilation in early modern England. In 1571 a petition complained that the strangers who had settled in England to flee the violence of the Wars of Religion on the Continent comprised "a common wealth unto themselves," and in 1593 a debate about immigrants ensued in the House of Commons, with Nicholas Fuller complaining, "This is to be noted in these Strangers, they will not converse with us, they will not marry with us, they will not buy any thing of our Country-men."[17] The conversion of Irish and Romani characters in Ben Jonson's masques might reasonably be read as wish fulfillment of these demands for assimilation as the rustic aliens shed their otherness upon encountering the monarch.

Ultimately, this premium on assimilation appears disingenuous, particularly when race is a factor. In what has come to be known as the "Windrush scandal," in 2018 at least eighty British-born citizens of Caribbean descent were deported and others denied basic benefits of British citizenship. Their parents or grandparents had arrived in the UK as part of the Windrush generation, subjects of British colonies who settled in the UK after being made de facto citizens by the British Nationality Act of 1948. The matter should have been settled by, among other things, the 1608 case of Robert Calvin, a Scottish-born subject of King James who had been treated as an alien when it came to inheriting English land. The court ruled in Calvin's favor, contributing to the legal precedent of jus soli: citizenship by birth.[18] Despite being raised in England, however, many of the British-born descendants of the Windrush generation were wrongly treated as undocumented immigrants amid the anti-immigrant fervor of Brexit. The primary reason? They were not white.[19] As Adrian Favell puts it, Brexit "opened a Pandora's box of old-style racism and xenophobia."[20]

Racism and xenophobia were never really boxed away in England, however, and many premodern critical race studies (PCRS) scholars have pointed to the continuities between premodern and contemporary racism, especially anti-Black racism. While specific iterations of race-making change over time, Margo Hendricks notes that from the mid-sixteenth century on the term "race" "became increasingly associated with a colour-based taxonomy ('black race' or 'white race')."[21] Imtiaz Habib's observation that the term "blackamoore," designating difference in race and religion, first appears in the historical record in 1547 provides a substantial instance of precisely the shift Hendricks sees in the period.[22] Kim F. Hall sees the emergence of this kind of race-making as tied to the development of early English national identity.[23] And Ian Smith notes the convergence of economic, political, and social factors in the sixteenth and seventeenth centuries that gave rise to anti-Black racism in England as "a strategy to protect and defend its own national reputation."[24] One might reasonably tie the increased visibility of racism surrounding Brexit to a similar anxiety around English national identity in the twenty-first century.

Here Jonson's masques provide English fantasies of specifically racial assimilation. Jonson's first masque, *The Masque of Blackness* (1605), features Queen Anne and her ladies performing in blackface and exotic dress as the Daughters of Niger. Having learned about European standards of beauty, the moon, here named Aethiopia, tells the Daughters of Niger that a place ending in—*tania* will transform their complexions. After trying Mauritania, Lusitania, and Aquitania, Niger and his daughters come upon an unknown land. Oceanus explains, "This land, that lifts into the temperate air / His snowy cliff, is Albion the fair," and within moments Aethiopia enters to explain that this is indeed the place she wanted them to find, Britannia, and that its ruler, King James I, can "blanch an Æthiop, and revive a corse." The issue of race is overdetermined here: the focus on the White Cliffs of Dover and the name Albion links the land to the whiteness desired by the Daughters of Niger and naturalizes James's alleged whitening power. The whiteness of Britannia is coupled in Aethiopia's description with a kind of English exceptionalism: she explains that "the triple world admires" Britannia and at the same time it is "a world divided from the world," part of and apart from European Christendom. The daughters are instructed to bathe in rosmarine and seafoam every full moon for a year. Pragmatically this gives Queen Anne and her ladies more than enough time to remove the blackface they donned for the masque, but the bathing in what Aethiopia calls "that purer brine" also appears to be a kind of prolonged secular baptism. While Dennis Austin Britton has found that English Protestant writers tended to reject Catholic romance motifs of baptism-as-racial-transformation, the magical space of the masque allows for a fantasy of complete assimilation, or as Britton puts it in his description of Catholic versions of the romance motif, "to transform and then incorporate that which is different but desirable."[25] *The Masque of Blackness* then resonates strongly with the chauvinist English exceptionalism and demand for assimilation made more visible amid Brexit.

While resonances between early modern and neonational England open interpretive possibilities for understanding early modern England's emergent nationhood, the study of early modern nationhood helps make sense of elements of current neonationalist trends. This is not to indulge in a facile anachronism. Rather, we understand present events as rendering visible certain aspects of the past. It is no coincidence that the performance or theatricality of power (particularly that of Queen Elizabeth) was a theme among several New Historicists writing during the Reagan era, characterized as it was by an actor who became president of the United States.[26] Looking at *Cymbeline* in light of Brexit, David J. Baker evokes the term "Brexiternity," referring to the way an event (or epoch) like Brexit causes us to rethink the prehistory of the event, inviting a sense of "temporal indeterminacy, with before shading into after into now."[27] Without abandoning historicism, then, the analyses of the past in this volume are similarly present- and future-oriented. As Paolo Freire puts it, "To the degree that the historical past is not 'problematized' so as to be critically understood, tomorrow becomes simply the perpetuation of today."[28]

Not all the contributions to this volume are historicist in orientation, however. Contemporary performances of early modern plays necessarily speak to the present. Even attempts at "authentic" reconstructions of early modern theater necessarily compel audiences to grapple with aesthetics and politics in the present. "Original practices" productions of Shakespeare—those using an all-male cast, a prosthetic nose for Shylock, blackface for Othello—make claims to "authenticity" but those practices carry with them the weight of histories of misogyny, anti-Semitism, and anti-Black racism.[29] Audiences (and readers) inevitably bring their own aesthetic expectations and political contexts to early modern texts. Whether historicist or presentist, the chapters that follow see the rise of neonationalism in general and Brexit specifically as significant frames through which to read early modern drama.

None a Stranger There explores how political and cultural debates in the 2010s and 2020s catalyzed in England by Brexit, in the United States by the Trump administration's anti-immigration policies, and by similar neonationalist efforts in other countries reflect, but also importantly differ from, debates about national identity, immigration, and borders in the early modern period. The contributors to this collection consider how such issues manifested themselves in English plays, masques, pageants, and other forms of cultural expression. The individual chapters speak to how notions about Englishness, identity, and difference intersected with the developing sense of Europe as a concept as much as a physical geographic unit, as well as with debates in the period about England's relationship to Europe—debates that, in many ways, seem remarkably prescient for our current moment. If the early modern period was one of emergent English nationhood, how can the ways it dramatized that experience inform the ways we think about the emergent neonationhood of our own time? That is, how can dramatic culture's responses to the early modern moment of nation-formation help us better understand our own modern moment of neonationalism? In many important ways, of course, it cannot. To demand too much of these plays, to declare every parallel prophetic or cautionary, is to ignore crucial historical distance and incongruities between these periods. Such positivist anachronism risks glossing over the insurmountable political, social, cultural, intellectual, and economic differences between our periods. But in other ways, *None a Stranger There* takes as its premise that there is much we can understand about crises in own time by looking to how the past engaged with, negotiated around, overcame, or failed to overcome similar crises. There may, in fact, be a greater risk in ignoring what the past has to tell us than there is in not asking it to speak at all.

Like the rise of neonationalism in our own time, enmeshed within early modern debates about English identity in relation to the nations around it, and how those debates were represented in the drama of the period, were ongoing negotiations about race and ethnicity, national sovereignty, language, religion, economic relationships, and the broader nature of transnational cultural contact and exchange. As in our own historical moment, notions of what constituted Europe, and the idea of a "European" identity, were contested in the early modern period, or, as Andrew Hiscock noted in 2022, as societies in the sixteenth and seventeenth century attempted to define what constituted "Europe" and being "European," "considerations of cultural origination and difference exercised early modern Europe as much as they have more recent political debate."[30] While the idea of Europe as a geographical unit dates to the Roman era—if not earlier—the idea of "European" as an identity started to take form in the sixteenth century, though even then who precisely was included in that designation was unclear.[31] Starting in the mid-sixteenth century, the adjective "European" began to be deployed to delineate those who "belonged" to particular traditions of the West, and the idea of being "European" began to form around what Gerard Delanty terms "an idea and an identity" rather than just "a region and polity."[32] Nonetheless, what exactly that "idea" and that "identity" encompassed—let alone what constituted Europe's physical borders—was never fully clear in the period. While Robert Bartlett traces the origins of the idea of "Europe" to the period of Frankish dominance in the eleventh and twelfth centuries, and Norman Davies goes back even further to the start of the Gallic uprisings against Rome in the fourth to ninth centuries, John Hale argues that between 1450 and 1620, "the word Europe first became part of common linguistic usage and the continent itself was given a securely map-based frame of reference, a set of images that established its identity in pictorial terms, and a triumphal ideology that overrode its internal contradictions."[33] In what is apparently the first use of the word "Europe" in print in English, in Richard Eden's 1555 translation of the Italian historian Pietro Martire d'Anghiera's 1530 Latin work, *De Orbe Novo* (given the title in English of *The Decades of the Newe Worlde or West India*), the term is used to characterize the "Precopites," a people living in the area of what is today Poland and Ukraine and who were, according to d'Anghiera, "European Tartars."[34] Here the adjective distinguishes the Precopites from their adversaries beyond the outer line of what constituted "Europe," in the land of "Russia," but the adjective also calls attention to how the Precopites actually straddled the border themselves, being not only "European" but also, like the Russians, "Tartars." A city such as Venice, with its history of transnational trade, multiculturalism, and ethnic pluralism, not surprisingly provided another point for contesting the idea of "European" as a fixed identity: the 1601 English translation of Giovanni Botero's *The Travellers Breviat* reports Venetians as saying "that they [that is, Venetians] have two eies; the people of Europe, one; the residue of the [other] nations, none" and that they only "give this good report of the Europeans" due to their global trading relationships with the Portuguese and Spanish. This text is notable for being one of the earliest uses in print of "European" not as an adjective but as a proper noun for a particular group of people.[35] The implication of the proverb, of course, is that Venetians themselves, with their two eyes, are not the same group of people as those who are "European." This idea of Venice as a place separate from Europe is implied in the anonymous 1625 play *The Knave in Grain*, when Chrisipus recalls the Venetian merchant Franciscus as "a milder, better tempered Gentleman, *Venice* nor *Europe* yielded"—a phrase that simultaneously situates Venice within Europe (expanding geographically from the city to the continent, with the city inside the continent) but also, paradoxically, implies its distinction from Europe (the city as equivalent to, or alongside, the continent but not necessarily within it).[36] These deviations from the idea of Europe as an undifferentiated political, cultural, or geographic whole point to what Delanty refers to as the "myth of unity": "As the use of the word Europe increased in the sixteenth and seventeenth centuries, the continent became more divided than ever before."[37] David Blanks likewise notes that, apart from particular members of the "educated classes," in the period, "most 'Europeans' did not see themselves" as European but, rather "as part of a particular family or clan, or perhaps, in broader terms, as coming from a specific place, or maybe simply as Christians."[38] As Roberto Dainotto cautions, "The homogenizing assumptions of the term ['European'], in fact, run the perpetual risk of obliterating the interior borders and fractures of European hegemony."[39]

Not surprisingly, then, most early modern English references to "Europe" are vague and amorphous in meaning; typically, the word is used simply to designate difference from the other major parts of the world, particularly Asia, Africa, and the Americas. In Thomas Campion's masque for the Earl of Somerset's marriage in 1613, for example, "Europe" appeared as one of the "foure parts of the earth"—Europe, Asia, Africa, and America—summoned to dance together "in a strange kinde of confusion"; each of the realms wore clothing emblematic of their general cultural identity: Europe was dressed "in the habit of an Empresse, with an Emperiall Crowne on her head," Asia wore "a Persian Ladies habit with a Crowne on her head," Africa was "like a Queene of the Moores, with a crown," and America was in "a skin coate of the colour of the juyce of Mulberies, on her head large round brims of many coloured feathers, and in the midst of it a small Crowne."[40] Europe was not again personified in an English entertainment until John Tatham's mayoral show for Richard Chiverton's installation as lord mayor of London in 1657, when "Europe" and the other parts of the world (Asia, Africa, and America again) appeared in a chariot, all "answerable to the nature of their several Countreys," though none speaking or otherwise performing.[41] What Tatham meant by "the nature" of their countries is unclear, but it likely referred to costuming and possibly skin color. Certainly there was an assumption in the period that the different geographic regions of the world could be aligned with different "types" of people—in the anonymous 1613 *Treasurie of Auncient and Moderne Times*, for example, the author confidently asserts that "natuarally the people of *Europe* are more magnanimous and warlike, then they of *Asia*."[42] Tatham, however, may have been interested less in character types than in *racialized* types grouped by regions of the world. Just two years after Tatham's mayoral show, Richard Flecknoe used a similar device in his spectacle *The Marriage of Oceanus and Brittania*, but in Flecknoe's masque the dance of the "four parts of the World" was explicitly racialized in terms of both clothing and skin color: "*Asia* in *Turkish* habit, *Affrica* in Moorish, and all black, *America*, swarthy in a featherd garment; and *Europe* fair and richly clad."[43] Importantly, Europe was separate from the figure of Brittania in Flecknoe's entertainment; indeed, she was also subservient to Brittania: Europe—like the other parts of the world—danced before Brittania's throne and was summoned by Oceanus for an act of symbolic imperialism in which Brittania extracted resources from the other parts of the world: "Come *Europe*," Oceanus sings, "swarthy *Affrica*, / Rich *Asia* and *America* / Bring your treasures all away / Tribute to pay / Unto *Brittanias* Throne."[44] As they obediently "deliver their riches" to Brittania, Oceanus sings of them—including Europe—as "vassals all" to Brittania, bringing "presents" to his beloved, including silk from Asia, fruit from Europe, and generic "wealth" from Africa and America.[45]

Flecknoe's song and dance extravaganza clearly presented Britain as a differentiated entity, and, implicitly, identity, from Europe, but the meaning of "Europe" itself was a point of contention throughout the period, not least because the geographic unit of "Europe" and the identity category of "European" were not always seen as necessarily coterminous. As Florian Kläger and Gerd Bayer aptly put it, "Europe" served as a useful signifier not because it carried a clear, fixed meaning but "precisely by virtue of its emptiness [and availability] as an alternative to religious, geographical, national, partisan, or other conceptions" of identity.[46] A sense of using the identity of "European" to distinguish, or, rather, exclude a group of people regardless of their position in relation to the borders of the geographic unit of "Europe" is found in Thomas Brightman's 1611 *A Revelation of the Apocalyps*, in which the theologian claims that the end of days will be signaled "not [by] the utter decay of the truth among the *Europeans*, but of such a renewing among the *Jewes*."[47] Implying that one could not be both Jewish and European, Brightman, like so many others in the period, understood "European" as a function not of national identity or geographic residence but, rather, religious identity and ethnicity. But even this reflection of what Kläger and Bayer describe as the medieval notion of "Europe" as "the *communitas Christiana*" and what Roberto Dainotto refers to as the "clerical map" of the idea of Europe, became, in the early modern period, problematized and destabilized as the organizing principle for what constituted "Europe."[48] In the same vein as Brightman, but reflecting the early modern fracturing of the idealized "Christian" monolithic identity of (Catholic) medieval Europe, Richard Bernard in 1626 distinguished "the European" church from "the Russian, Greeke, and Abyssine Churches."[49] The anonymous playwright of the 1608 *The Merry Devil of Edmonton* jokingly plays with the alignment of "European" with "Christian" when Smug responds to Bilbo's assertion that he "maist serve the Duke of Europe" by agreeing that he will indeed "serve the Duke of Christendom."[50] A similar phrase is used mockingly in Thomas Randolph's 1627 *Hey for Honesty, Down with Knavery*, where the pope is described as "the Shepheard of all *Europe*," creating a correlation between the geographic unit of "all" Europe and the religious identity of Catholicism.[51] But others deployed the term in precisely the opposite way: Sir Thomas Roe, for example, in describing the possibility of a civil war within Turkish-occupied Poland, noted that, should one occur, "this *European* part had beene in danger to have beene torne away by the division."[52] Despite being part of the Muslim empire, Poland was still, in Roe's view, "*European*," due to its geographic contiguousness and no doubt its historical identity prior to Ottoman occupation. Samuel Purchas similarly divided the Ottoman Empire into a "*European* part of the Empire, and another of the *Asian*."[53] For some in the period, then, despite being "occupied" by a Muslim superpower, those lands still constituted part of "Europe"—though perhaps, as Dainotto puts it in notably loaded terms, an "other Europe" that appeared to those in the West as "dark, threatening, and quite Oriental."[54]

Other writers in the period looked beyond confessional identity for markers of collective "Europeanness" that transcended nations' geographic borders. Thomas Dekker, for example, aligns the idea of shared identity with socioeconomic, and specifically laboring, status in his 1599 *The Shoemaker's Holiday* when Simon Eyre triumphantly declares "the Gentle trade" to be "a living for a man through Europe, through the world" and demonstrates

as much by consenting to his workers' demands for transnational class solidarity by hiring "Hans," the Dutch "brother of the Gentle Craft" (actually the Englishman Lacy in disguise).[55] Indeed, anxieties about labor
as a transnational identity underwrote many of the early modern English
state's attempts to cordon itself off from the states on the Continent. W.
Mark Ormrod, for example, observes that a suitable historical analogy for
Brexit may be found as early as 1484, when Richard III and his parliament
instituted the "first comprehensive legislation restricting immigration at
a national level" and imposed severe restrictions on foreign labor, ostensibly in an effort to combat what was perceived to be the loss of English
jobs to foreign workers, but really to guard against what was feared to be
the ensuing "social breakdown" caused by the movement, and potentially
cooperation, of laboring classes across borders.[56] Not surprisingly, and not
unlike events after Brexit, Richard's immigration restriction resulted in a
break with Europe that had profoundly negative economic effects on the
very same English people whom it was supposed to help.

Religion and class were just two categories for what constituted "European" identity. As noted, Flecknoe and Tatham conceived of "European"
as a racial category, and even earlier, for Sebastian, in Shakespeare's 1611
The Tempest, there is a notional idea of "European" as a racial group distinct
from—and which should, he implies, be *kept* distinct from—the racial group
of "African" when he rebukes Alonso because the king "would not blesse
our Europe with your daughter, / But rather loose her to an Affrican."[57]
Sebastian's choice of the pronoun "our" to characterize Europe speaks to
both the character's idea of Italy as part of Europe but also—in a play
that is, to use Crystal Bartolovich's phrase, "singular in its insistent spatial ambiguity" about geography and often reminds the audience of its
Englishness (as in Trinculo's famous desire to capture Caliban and put
him on display in England)—the broader idea of England as a part of "our
Europe" as well.[58] Despite Brexiteers' frequent citing of Shakespeare—
particularly John of Gaunt's exhaustively requoted "sceptr'd isle" speech
from *Richard II*—Shakespeare's own views about the relationship between
England and Europe are impossible to discern. In his plays, Shakespeare
sometimes presents England as a part of the European community and
sometimes implies its separation, depending on the perspective of the
character speaking. For example, in *1 Henry VI*, the Duke of Bedford vows
to "make all Europe quake," which seems to suggest he views England
as distinct from Europe; at the same time, in *3 Henry VI*, King Edward
IV praises the English Duke of York as "the flower of Europe," and in *2*

Henry IV, the English Falstaff identifies himself as the most "active fellow in Europe," both of which statements explicitly identify the Englishman as a European. For many in the period, there was never any question that England was, and had been since time immemorial, part of Europe and that being "English" meant also being "European." In his triumphant—and clunky—ode "Palae Albion," at the start of his 1621 *The History of Great Britanie*, William Slatyer acknowledges as much by titling the third canzone "European Nations, and especially the Britons originall, with all deserved praises in their honor."[59] Shakespeare, unfortunately, never offers such a clear statement of his own position on the question.

While it is in Shakespeare's history plays that he most frequently and fully engages with ideas about England in relationship to Europe, a similar engagement sits at the core of other plays as well. In *King Lear*, for example, the reckless fragmentation of the British state, with its ensuing personal and political traumas, only resolves through the intervention of a hybrid Anglo-Continental military force—French soldiers led by an exiled English princess. But perhaps it is in *Cymbeline* that Shakespeare most carefully dramatizes the nuanced tension defining England's place in or alongside Europe. Reading this late play for what it suggests about the Anglo-European relationship (coded in the play as the Britannic-Roman relationship) reveals a trajectory that begins with justifications for a full Brexit-style break with the Continent, followed by qualifications of those justifications, and finally a resolution that implies a reciprocal partnership between two equals and the establishment of a new political order.

While residing in Rome, the heart of the pan-European political body, Posthumus earns the ethnicized nickname "the Briton Reveller" because, as Iachimo reports, "none a stranger there [is] / So merry and so gamesome."[60] It is in Rome, then, not England, where the "strangers" from across the continent gather, drawn as if by gravity to Europe's governmental and administrative center of power. Peripheral Britain's relationship with that center becomes, of course, the primary point of conflict in the play's political plot when, like the Brexiters' objections to the UK contributing financially to the EU budget, Cymbeline refuses to continue paying his country's tribute to the empire. Britain's vassalage, the king declares to the Roman ambassador, was unjustly and unwisely ceded: "Till the injurious Romans did extort / This tribute from us, we were free."[61] Rather than continue bowing to Roman military power, Cymbeline cites the ancestral pedigree of Britain's independent monarchy, which "Ordained our laws, whose use the sword of Caesar / Hath too much mangled."[62] The idea of replacing the threat of conquest by the continental power with the rule of law by ancient British right is such a fundamental concept that even the foolish Cloten understands it, asserting with pride that "Britain's a world / By itself, and we will nothing pay / For wearing our own noses."[63] Cloten's obviously xenophobic and implicitly racialized remark—a swipe, apparently, at the stereotypically large Roman nose—aims at both essentializing and embodying the construct of British exceptionalism.

Despite the centrality of this concept to England's separation from Rome—a separation Shakespeare's audience may have read as foreshadowing the Henrician Reformation—the play does not come to endorse fully such an extreme isolationist view. Articulated in Innogen's consideration of escaping her homeland, for example, there is a contrasting understanding of Britain as distinct but still part of a larger world:

> Hath Britain all the sun that shines? Day, night,
> Are they not but in Britain? I'th' world's volume
> Our Britain seems as of it but not in't,
> In a great pool a swan's nest. Prithee, think
> There's livers out of Britain.[64]

The reasonable Innogen adopts the same rhetorical figure as the foolish Cloten—Britain as/in a "world"—but in her perspective Britain, while an elegant "swan's nest," is still nonetheless part of the global community of humanity. Her sense of displacement, which leads her to weigh the benefits of becoming a refugee, frames her home country as distinct from the world not because it is *politically* separate or superior, as Cloten (and the queen and, ultimately, Cymbeline) presume, but because it is, for her, as for so many refugees, suddenly made strange. Innogen's experience leads her to the conclusion that Britain is an isolated space or, more precisely, a place of isolation and estrangement, where she is no longer welcome; but with that despair also comes the recognition that one's life need not be delimited to Britain alone. There are people living, and lives to be lived, beyond Britain as well as within it.

By the end of the play, Britishness becomes embodied in the almost mythical figures of the Cambrian outlaws, Guiderius and Arviragus and their kidnapper, Belarius, who, like Innogen, refused to separate himself from Britain when he was banished from his homeland. Rather, he remained and, along with Guiderius and Arviragus, became instrumental in Britain's own separation from the Continent by prevailing in the war with Rome. They are, as Cymbeline puts it when he knights them, "the liver, heart, and brain of Britain, / By whom, I grant, she lives."[65] Innogen herself, in her disguise as the page boy serving the Roman general Lucius, is also distinguished as being emblematic of Britishness: the boy should be spared punishment by Cymbeline because, Lucius points out, he is "a Briton born" and "hath done no Briton harm, / Though he have served a Roman"; notably, the page's moral qualities seem to emblematize the virtues that signal "Britishness" ("so kind, so duteous, diligent, / So tender over his occasions, true, / So feat, so nurse-like").[66]

But even this sense of a clear and discrete difference between British and Roman is collapsed in the play's resolution, for even though Britain has won the war and thus achieved the opportunity to establish the political independence for which it went to war in the first place, Cymbeline ends the play by choosing to return to the imperial fold. "Although the victor, we submit to Caesar," the king pledges in his penultimate speech. "And to the Roman empire, promising / To pay our wonted tribute."[67] By electing to pay the tribute, Cymbeline reveals that what was objectionable to paying it before was not the fact of paying tribute but the means by which the tribute was required: if it had not been compelled, Britain would have apparently agreed to the obligation freely and spared both sides the loss of life caused by the war. Unity between Britain and Europe comes about, then, not by force or threat but by mutual respect. The "harmony of this peace" foreseen by the soothsayer (and thus projected forward indefinitely in time to Shakespeare's, and even our own, moment) is not one of either division or dependence but of partnership:

> our princely eagle,
> Th' imperial Caesar, should again unite
> His favour with the radiant Cymbeline,
> Which shines here in the west.[68]

Cymbeline himself confirms this sense of unification between Britain and Europe in the play's final speech: "Let / A Roman and a British ensign wave / Friendly together."[69] In its resolution, the play enacts a reconciliation of Britain to the Continent from which it sought, violently, to disentangle itself. To this end, it is no coincidence that the nurse who years ago kidnapped the infant British princes Arviragus and Guiderius—an act for which Belarius married her—and thus made possible that reconciliation was named Euriphile, that is, "Lover of Europe."

Cymbeline dramatizes a conceptual shift from Britain as a component of a larger European whole, to Britain as an entirely separate political space, and finally to Britain joined with Europe in an entirely new political relationship. In the play's ultimate calculus of the relationship between England and Europe, the two are neither separate nor conflated but paired in a willing and voluntary bond of amity forged through a pseudo-republican act of choice. Caesar remains ruler, but only because Cymbeline elects to allow him that role. The play's political arc depicts England debating separation from the larger European community to which the country feels it has been unjustly tied, but in the end, and on England's own terms, choosing—to use Brexit terminology—to Remain.[70] Given this arc, it was not surprising that in the lead-up to the referendum in spring 2016, the RSC staged a Brexit-pointed version of *Cymbeline*. Melly Still's production was, according to Rachel Ellen Clark, "overtly political" in the warning it sought to convey about the consequences of the referendum succeeding; the production portrayed post-Brexit Britain as "a postapocalyptic wasteland, standing in stark contrast to a vibrant, multicultural Italy," and emphasized "the fundamental lack of logic behind Leave votes."[71] As Lisa Hopkins notes, Still's Britain "had lost its place in the world" as a result of its decision to break with Europe.[72]

The RSC's 2016 *Cymbeline* was merely the most recent in a long history of productions of the play that contextualized the political arc of England's separation from and reunification with Europe against modern political events, such as the Washington, DC–based Arena Stage's 1982 production (Britain's choice to return to the European community as a step toward multilateral nuclear disarmament), the Stratford Festival's 1986 production (Britain's choice to return to the European community as the salvation of Europe during World War II), the California Shakespeare Festival's 1990 "totalitarian nightmare" production (Britain's choice to return to the European community as a model of liberty for Eastern Europe), the San Diego Repertory Theatre's 1990 production (Britain's choice to return to the European community as a reflection of European reunification after the fall of the Berlin Wall), and the Chicago-based Shakespeare Repertory Theater's 1993 production (Britain's choice to return to the European community as an exemplar of peace for the war-torn Middle East).[73] Such political messaging can be traced earlier, even as far back as the 1682 production of Thomas D'Urfey's adaptation of *Cymbeline*, titled *The Injured Princess, or, The Fatal Wager*, a Restoration-style celebration of the reestablishment of royal authority through the return of the rightful heir to the English throne. When we reflect on how *Cymbeline*, or any of the many other plays examined in the following chapters, continues to speak to national identity and nationalism in our own political moment (or how our own political moment can speak to the plays) we are participating in a longer history of creative and scholarly reflection and reimagining about the connections between cultural expression and the concept of the nation. Brexit and our other contemporary conflicts over national affinity and alienation are modern versions of many of the same questions that animated early modern playwrights, writers, and thinkers. What is the nation? What is the relationship between nations? Between the people of a nation and those of other nations? Must the borders between nations be also borders between people? Or is it possible to, like Innogen, recognize that the sun shines on us all without regard to borders—to envision a world where none are strangers? Or perhaps we can at least settle for a world that heeds Hamlet's advice to Horatio, when the latter remarks on the "wondrous strange" appearance of the ghost of Hamlet's father: "And therefore as a stranger give it welcome."[74]

Early modern English dramatists besides Shakespeare, of course, engaged with the question of Europe, Europeans, and "European" identity and England's relation to all three. Those engagements, however, were also varied and often contradictory and, to borrow Ellen Welch's apt description, "highlight the artificiality of the idea of Europe in the early modern period"; as Welch notes, in performance culture, the "idea of Europe" was "far from a static concept [because] it could be manipulated by artists and patrons to respond to shifting political conditions. . . . 'Europe' appears here as a performative category, reinvented with each reiteration on the stage."[75] Just as the idea of Europe was malleable across performance contexts, so too were dramatic expressions of the idea of England's relationship to Europe. One of the earliest of those dramatic expressions appears in Robert Wilson's ca. 1581 *The Three Ladies of London*, when Usury praises England by noting that there "was not in Europe and the whole world beside" a better "place for Lucar to bide," thus explicitly identifying England as component to Europe.[76] More than any other playwright of the time, Christopher Marlowe especially invokes Europe by name, typically in terms of the geographic expanse of the continent and its determinate borders—as when Queen Isabella, in the circa 1592 *Edward II*, pledges that she will flee "even to the utmost verge / of *Europe*," which she identifies with "the shore of *Tanaise*," that is, the river Tanais (now the Don), flowing from just south of Moscow down to the Sea of Azov and widely referenced in the period as (one) theoretical boundary for Europe.[77] Ben Jonson draws upon the idea of European boundaries for comic purposes in his 1599 *Every Man Out of His Humor* when the foolish, unworldly Sogliardo praises Shift as "the tallest man living within the walls of *Europe*," to which the witty fool Carlo Buffone rejoins, "The walls of *Europe*! take heed what you say Signior, *Europe*'s a huge thing within the walls."[78] For Thomas Heywood, however, a key aspect of European identity, derived from its mythological origins, was the transcendence of such exclusionary walls: in the dedicatory epistle for the first part of his ca. 1612 *The Iron Age*, Heywood notes that "two [of] the rarest Phœnixes in *Europe*, namely *London* and *Rome*" rose from the ashes of that "illustrious . . . Citty" Troy, "although it were scituate in *Asia*."[79] The phoenix imagery suggests that Heywood understands London and Rome—both Protestant and Catholic Europe—as not merely *coming from* Asian origins but, in fact, the great city of Asia reborn on Europe's soil.[80]

References in early modern English drama specifically to England's relationship to Europe often imply that the country was a part (usually, in the view of English playwrights, an essential part) of what was perceived as some form of continental community. In the anonymous 1594 *True Tragedie of Richard the Third*, the tyrant—facing defeat at Bosworth—draws upon the image of an outward-expanding series of concentric circles in his vow to "joyne England against mee with England, Joyne Europe with Europe, come Christendome, and with Christendome the whole world, and yet I will never yeeld but by death onely."[81] A reverse trajectory is mapped by Valerio at the end of George Chapman's 1601 *All Fools*, when he zooms in geographically to observe that cuckoldry "is universall over the face of the world, general over the face of *Europe*, and common over the face of this Countrey. What Cittie, what Towne, what Village, what Streete? nay, what House can quit it selfe of this prerogative?"[82] Dekker likewise categorizes England as one of the principal parts of Europe in his 1599 *Old Fortunatus*, when Fortunatus catalogues "England, Fraunce, Spaine, and welthy Belgia / And all the rest" as "Europs blessed daughters."[83] So too does Philip Massinger, in his 1621–22 *The Maid of Honour*, celebrate England as "the Empresse of the European Isles," because she is also "the Mistresse of the Ocean" and King Henry, in John Ford's 1623–34 *Perkin Warbeck*, praises England as sustaining Europe because the country's "charge / Flowes through all *Europe*," making it a "steward" of the whole continent "against the creeping Cankar of Disturbance."[84] England, and specifically London, is the triumph of Europe in Dekker's 1604 entertainment welcoming King James, Queen Anne, and Prince Henry into the capital, as the "Genius" of

London identifies the city as not just the "Jewell of the Land; *Englands right Eye*" but as "this little world of men; this precious Stone, / That sets out *Europe*."[85] The transnational political connotations of the Genius's welcome situated the capital city of the new Scottish monarch of England as the literal jewel of Europe and prefaced the subsequent pageants that were staged, as the title page puts it, "as well by the English as by the Strangers," that is, the resident immigrants, of the cosmopolitan city. London, and by extension England, is here emphatically part (again, the greatest part) of the European community.

In other instances, however, such conflating language is more ambiguous about the relationship of the unit identified as "England" to the unit identified as "Europe." For example, while Dekker clearly positioned London at the heart of Europe in his pageant for King James, in John Marston's 1603–5 *The Dutch Courtesan*, Mary Fough praises the apprentices of the city as "the best of any men in Europe, nay, which is more in *London*," a construction that, like Chrisipus's praise of Franciscus in *The Knave in Grain*, could be read as either emphasizing London's centrality to Europe or, conversely, extricating the English city from its European context and setting it apart from that community.[86] In a similar way, Robert Greene, in his ca. 1590 *Scottish History of James the Fourth*, describes Ida, daughter of the countess of Arran, by noting, "All Englands grounds yeelds not a blyther Lasse. / Nor *Europ* can art her for her gifts, / Of vertue, honour, beautie, and the rest."[87] Greene's syntax is vague, but the apparent meaning seems to be a contrast between England and "*Europ*," since Ida is praised as being exemplary within the bounds of both territories; if the assumption was that England was part of "*Europ*," specifying "*England*" at all would have been unnecessary. A similar distinction may be implied by Samuel Rowley, in his popular 1604 *When You See Me, You Know Me*, when the rogue Black Will asserts to the disguised King Henry VIII that "theres not a sword and Buckler man in *England* nor *Europe*, but has had a taste of my manhood."[88] While a reading of Black Will's line that takes the "nor" as expansive without exclusion ("England" and, *even more than that*, the rest of "Europe" as well), the grammatical function of the conjunction "nor" may also imply an expansion with a distinction between "*England*" on one hand and "*Europe*" on the other. That is, it would be possible for Black Will to be the greatest sword and buckler man in England but not Europe or, conversely, in Europe but not England. Richard Brome also implies a nuanced distinction between England and Europe in his 1636–38 *The Antipodes*, when Doctor Hughball offers to provide a fantastic narrative of foreign lands but begins by promising to skip over Europe: "Of *Europe* ile not speak, tis too neare home: / Who's not familiar with the Spanish garbe, / Th' Italian shrug, French fringe, and German hugge?"[89] Europe is proximal to "home" (England) but it is not "home"; rather, Europe is constituted of other lands (Italy, France, and Germany), which, though well known to the English, are distinct from England. Indeed, Hughball employs the same ambiguous measure of distance to characterize Europe—"too neare home"—as he also uses to describe Arabia, Paphlagonia, Mesopotamia, Mauritania, Syria, Thessalia, Persia, and India: "All still is too neare home."[90] Europe, in the doctor's hyperbolic estimation, is as distant, and distinct, from England as India.

Perhaps the play that most profoundly and fully articulates the idea of separating England from Europe, however, is, as Todd Andrew Borlik's chapter in this volume shows, Greene's 1586–90 *Friar Bacon and Friar Bongay*, in which Bacon plans to conjure a brass wall around the island so that "all the Legions Europe doth containe, / . . . should not touch a grasse of English ground."[91] As in his later *Scottish History of James the Fourth*, Greene, in *Friar Bacon and Friar Bongay*, implies that England is distinct from Europe when Clement informs Bacon that, should his work come to pass, "*England* and *Europe* shall admire thy fame," and King Henry makes the distinction even more evident when he welcomes the "Great men of *Europe*" to England by declaring that "*Albion* is another little world," divided and protected from the Continent by "the walls of old *Oceanus*" and the "promontory cleeves" of "*Englands* shore."[92]

English identity, then, has long been caught up in fraught relations with Europe and European identity. England was a part of Britain and, to many, a part of Europe—Francis Bacon (twice) in his *New Atlantis* wrote of "wee . . . here in Europe," and Thomas Hobbes, in *Leviathan*, referred to England as "these parts of Europe"—but the emergent nation also wanted to stand apart or above its archipelagic and continental identity.[93] This tension between English exceptionalism and broader identities within which Englishness might be subsumed is captured in the first part of this volume's subtitle, "England *and/in* Europe." Is England's relationship to Europe the prepositional "in," which highlights common ground with other European national identities, or is it the conjunctive "and," emphasizing England's sense of difference from a continental identity? Again, one may discern resonances between the nascent nation's attempts to define itself against a broader collective identity and the contemporary neonationalist response of globalization. The chapters that follow interrogate this and other uncanny connections between early modern and twenty-first century England as they play out on the stage.

About the Volume

The contributors to *None a Stranger There: England and/in Europe on the Early Modern Stage* draw upon a wide range of early modern texts—literary works, such as plays, poems, and masques, as well as legal treatises and laws, religious works, medical texts, ballads and broadsides, and even dueling treatises. Their work connects to and contributes to an extremely diverse and fruitful branch of scholarship on early modern culture, literature, and politics. And their methodologies incorporate literary criticism, theater history, performance studies, linguistics, book history and textual criticism, and a range of other disciplinary approaches.

For a volume that took form during the height of the COVID-19 pandemic, it is fitting we begin with Margaret Tudeau-Clayton's chapter on the parallels between what she describes as the "precarious contingency" of national identity provoked by our own moment of global crisis and how plays such as *Sir Thomas More* and *King Lear* negotiate similar tragic experiences centered around reversals of status. Juxtaposing the ways in which the pandemic has compelled affluent Western countries to live the kind of traumatic, marginalized experience that those countries historically assumed to be the lot of the "Other" countries of the world—the global South, the developing world—the chapter considers the linked dramatic and political function of tragic irony, whereby human subjects are placed in the position of those they have treated as objects of rejection or hate. In so doing, Tudeau-Clayton focuses on the idea of peripeteia as less a formal aesthetic principle and more a reality reflecting what Sir Philip Sidney terms "the uncertainty of this world." Linking modern and early modern rhetoric and ideas about disease, infection, and well-being with questions about national and ethnic identity, as well as England's—and Englishness's—relationship to non-English people and places, Tudeau-Clayton asks us to consider how the physiological might stand as a metaphor for the political and how the health and perils of the body politic were dramatized on a human scale on the early modern stage.

As the Reformation and Counter-Reformation swept Europe, national identity became inextricably linked to the question of confessional identity—the familiar contest between the transnational church of Rome and the sovereign churches of the Protestant sects, but also conflicts among

the Protestant sects themselves, not to mention the age-old exclusion of
the "stranger" within Europe—the Jews—and the "stranger" whose border
was thought to mark the very edge of Europe—the Turks. The impact of
Henry VIII's separation of England from the Catholic Church profoundly
altered the relationship between England and the rest of Europe in ways
similar to what has happened in the aftermath of Brexit, so much so that
Ian Morris parallels the two through the use of the (as he admits, unlovely)
term "Englexit": "both events are the only occasions when parts of the Isles
have walked away from a Continental empire of soft power . . . Each exit
was driven by—and deepened—arguments within the Isles over identity,
sovereignty and geostrategy. Each had major consequences for prosperity,
brought on a constitutional crisis and took longer to resolve than anyone expected."[94] England's split from Rome was not, of course, the only—
or even the most significant—national break from the Catholic Church
during the Reformation; as Delanty notes, this repeated fracturing of "the
unifying vision of Christendom" itself brought about "the emergence of
a secular notion of Europe."[95] Given the significant effects such breaks
had on national identity, it is not surprising that theatrical expressions of
England's connections to and separation from Europe in the wake of "Englexit" often centered around the staging of religious traditions, stereotypes, and theological beliefs. Our next two chapters explore two revealing
examples of the intersections between faith and national identity in the
context of English theatrical practice and performance culture.

Turning our attention to the English abroad, Kevin Chovanec highlights the critical role that religious belief and confessional identity played
in the transnational movement of English drama and players. Drawing on
both archival records and close readings of plays—particularly *Esther*, one
of the most popular biblical plays from the traveling players' repertoire—
Chovanec explores how English players abroad in Europe employed typological readings of shared biblical texts to suggest that religious identity could transcend national differences and emphasize the history and
cultural imaginary shared between Reformed players and Reformed audiences across national boundaries. The figurative significance of the Jewish
exiles in *Esther* allowed the players to explore their own role as strangers in
foreign lands while still claiming kinship with their audiences. This simul-
taneous otherness and sameness, Chovanec argues, is key to the players'
transnational strategy of insinuating themselves in various courts and cities
across the Holy Roman Empire. Capitalizing on the "exilic" resonances
in both the biblical text and Protestant culture, the players promoted the

value of foreigners within a multiconfessional and multiethnic empire and argued for an ecumenicism that would facilitate their travel, seen perhaps most clearly in their most significant revision to the biblical source narrative: excising the confessional violence at the end of the play—typically staged in most other Esther dramatizations—and thus implicitly arguing for a return to the irenic policies of past Hapsburg rulers as a way of mitigating the violence and destruction of the Thirty Years' War.

Early modern ideas about national identity developed alongside a complex and evolving understanding of the concepts of race and color, particularly as those categories intersected with other aspects of identity, such as socioeconomic status and religious belief. In his chapter, Jamie Paris begins with several pressing questions about these intersections: What would it have been like to be a Black Christian in early modern England? Would an early modern Black Christian, for example, have felt welcome worshipping at a church with mostly white parishioners? Lower-class Black people in England were allowed to (or forced to) convert to Christianity, but they were typically constrained to a marked form of Christian identity that denied them belonging within the early modern English (white) Christian community while ensuring they retained an intersectional identity as "Black Christians." Following on Chovanec's discussion of how English players drew upon shared religious identity to transcend national borders, Paris's chapter takes up these issues of hybridity and faith to engage with the question of Black belonging in early modern England through a discussion of Thomas Middleton's 1613 pageant *The Triumphs of Truth*—a text perhaps best known to history for being the first use of the phrase "white people" in English literature, when a Black Christian King who is visiting England tells the audience,

> I see amazement set upon the faces
> Of these white people, wond'ring and strange gazes;
> Is it at me? Does my complexion draw
> So many Christian eyes that never saw
> A king so black before?[96]

The Black king is unequivocally a Christian and is the first stage representation of a Black person who is unambiguously moral and upstanding: what is notable about Middleton's Black Christian King is not so much his appearance but that he is not eventually revealed to be evil. According to Ian Smith, the early modern audience was rarely asked to look beyond the "chromodermal signifier" of Blackness in judging the morality of characters. *The Triumphs of Truth*, then, is a pioneering work of anti-racist literature, but, importantly, it is not *colorblind*. Paris argues that we should not take the relative goodness of the Black King in Middleton's pageant as a sign that religion is more important than race in the early modern period. Doing so misses the radical nature of Middleton's play and serves the interests of white innocence by advancing a misleading narrative that argues that early modern English people valued religion above race and were therefore racially innocent.

One of the paradoxes in the rhetoric surrounding Brexit turns upon the citation of English imperialism (with its assimilative and necessarily transnational idea of what constitutes "English" identity) alongside insistence upon English isolationism (with its own ancient pedigree in the imagery of the island-nation, cut off from the rest of the Continent) in order to construct a notion of English identity that was simultaneously globalized and sequestered. Both attitudes of isolation and empire presume a degree of exceptionalism (though the two are not necessarily twinned: the Spanish ambassador to Elizabeth's court thought that the island's separation from the rest of the Continent made it "the sick man of Europe") and both attitudes hinge upon memorializing English history as a pattern precedent for English future.[97] Such a jointure was not a twenty-first century invention: as the next four chapters of the collection show, the double deployment of both modes of tying the past to the present to the future—both the imperial and isolationist—formed an essential part of how early modern drama itself staged, or attempted to stage, precisely what it meant to be English.

Taking their cue from the ways in which various commentators on Brexit have invoked as a nationalistic showpiece Gaunt's speech celebrating the isle of England in *Richard II*, John Garrison and Kyle Pivetti focus on how anxieties about shame and national humiliation operate in Shakespeare's history plays to construct a sense of exceptional (and potential) Englishness. Across all of Shakespeare's plays, the word "shame" appears most often in the histories because, Garrison and Pivetti argue, the memorial impetus of the genre requires that its nationalistic discourses remain fixated on embarrassment about the past and wariness of how the future will look back upon the present as past. Looking back and imagining forward, that is, demand shameful responses. Hotspur's fears that the "chronicles" will remember him and his coconspirators with shame are aligned in the chapter with Hal's deliberate cultivation of embarrassment. This is all the more crucial as the narrative arc of shame in both tetralogies stems from the humiliation of Richard II at his dethroning. The past, embarrassing and unjust, necessarily brings the English community into existence. In their analysis of the history plays, Garrison and Pivetti also draw upon the early modern memory arts. These memorization and memorialization techniques depend regularly on the exploitation of shame, for they discover that this powerful affect cannot be so easily forgotten. Shakespeare shows that he understood this sticking power; moreover, he showed that it could bind the national, and nationalistic, audience that looks to the past for its own origins.

Early modern nationalism also provides Todd Andrew Borlik with a framework for conceptualizing and characterizing ideas about English isolationism and exceptionalism in the period. Examining the border wall and the image of "fortress England" in Robert Greene's *Friar Bacon and Friar Bungay* (1586–90) in the context of early 1590s nationalist discourse, Borlik's chapter considers the Elizabethan understanding of, and anxieties about, the literal boundary between England and Continental Europe. While Greene recognizes the need for an international outlook in geopolitics, Bacon's wall speaks to contemporary interest in coastal fortifications and brass ordnance common in the wake of the Spanish Armada of 1588. Greene lampoons the wall as magical thinking, but his play nonetheless clings to metaphorical walls as more cost-effective symbols of national security and autonomy in an increasingly globalized world. As Borlik argues, the play's awkward combination of pan-European sentiment and strident nationalism offers a prophetic commentary on post-Brexit Britain.

Not all of England's borders, of course, face the Continent. In her chapter, Vimala Pasupathi turns our attention northward to the long history of Anglo-Scottish relations and connects English perceptions of that relationship from the seventeenth century to attitudes in the twenty-first. In her chapter, Pasupathi considers the representation of proto-British and post-Stuart union—and the prospect of its dissolution—in J. W.'s 1628–37 play *The Valiant Scot* and Netflix's 2018 film *The Outlaw King*. Dramatizing Scottish resistance to the rule of England's Edward I in the thirteenth century, the Stuart play builds on Scottish chronicles' depictions of the succession crisis that enabled Edward's intervention in Scotland and pushes against narratives that support his claims of sovereignty in Scotland. Pasupathi argues that the play exemplifies what Roger A. Mason has called "Scotching the Brut," a "historiographical activity" forged explicitly against an "English historiographical tradition which insisted that Scotland was and always had been a dependency of the crown of England."[98] Reading the play alongside other depictions of Anglo-Scottish conflict in early modern historiography, Pasupathi examines these moments as early modern predicaments that resonate with—and sometimes inform—coverage of recent movements for independence and alternate unions as well as how the history of such ideas is depicted in the 2018 film *The Outlaw King*. Pasupathi invites us to consider why, after many major shifts in the relationship between England and Scotland and their respective positions vis-à-vis one another and Europe, portrayals of these "auld alliances" and resistance movements from the thirteenth century persist as cultural touchstones of English identity.

Matt Carter also focuses on the formation of English national identity in relation to England's relationship with its British neighbors. Working with the anonymous play *Mucedorus* (ca. 1590), one of the most popular plays on the early modern English stage, Carter demonstrates how the play's identity narrative uses early modern English class structures to separate England's "native" Briton identity from its larger "European" one. The play does this in part by representing an unfair combat between two competing martial identities—that of Bremo, the yeomanly staff fighter whose weapon reflects British, working-class soldiery, and Mucedorus, the courtly swordsman whose weapon reflects English aristocratic connections to the continent. The chapter notes how this combat draws parallels between the wodewose figure and English imperial ventures in Wales, Ireland, and Scotland that go back to the medieval period; it also calls attention to the more subtle commentary the play makes on the intersections between class distinctions, weapon choices, and English identity. Carter argues that Mucedorus's interactions with Bremo mirror the relationship between the English aristocracy and the large underclass that propped it up. Importantly, these linked narratives of violence and identity formation were invested in English ethnicity more broadly and sought to draw lines between early modern Englishness and premedieval narratives of the Briton, Welsh, and Celtic people who had long occupied the British Isles. By drawing parallels between the "primitive" native peoples of the British Isles and the substantial body of nonaristocratic English people who comprised the bulk of the army, *Mucedorus* stages a justification of English imperialism that relies on the consumption of non-English culture and the destruction of its practitioners.

Contests over national identity inevitably impact upon specific institutions within the nation beyond broader categories such as ethnic identity, sovereignty, and political boundaries. As the final two chapters of *None a Stranger There* demonstrate, early modern England's project of defining itself in relation to its place in the European community informed also how communities *within* the nation—such as the village and the city— were understood to reflect upon, and help shape, that process of national definition.

Like Tudeau-Clayton, Heather Bailey is interested in the idea of the body politic and the literalization of that metaphor through the association of immigrants with the imagery of both physiological and sociopolitical disease. Those concerns were of importance not only in the context of the nation's body politic but also in towns and villages across the country, including, Bailey shows, in the Windsor represented in *The Merry Wives of Windsor*. In her chapter, Bailey examines how Shakespeare draws on early modern medical discourses concerning wine and sack, imported from abroad, as both a cause and cure for a variety of ailments of the physical body and the English commonwealth, both on a national but also local level. Because Shakespeare repeatedly implies that Falstaff's individual body represents the "English" body, Bailey argues that Falstaff's consumption of wine symbolizes the complex and often fraught relationship of immigrants in communities such as Windsor to the English body politic. Just as sack was associated with foreign influence, yet also perceived to be beneficial to the individual body, immigrants perceived as introducing contagion to the English body politic were, in fact, essential to the health and restoration of the locality and the country.

Concepts of belonging and inclusion can thus be defined along national lines, but also within local domains; indeed, the two—national identity and local belonging—often rely upon one another, particularly during periods of change and instability in one or both categories. William Casey Caldwell reminds us of this important point in his chapter on Shakespeare's *The Merchant of Venice* and its representation of urban citizenship. Brexit, Caldwell notes, raises fractious issues related not only to national sovereignty but also to citizenship and the city. During Brexit, cities tended to vote differently from rural areas, and the sense of political belonging many felt became split between a sense of urban identity and national disidentification. The referendum also destabilized the position of nonnaturalized and citizen immigrants living inside British cities, as well as that of British citizens living abroad. *The Merchant of Venice*, Caldwell observes, partakes of a history of citizenship grounded in the city over and against political status defined by nationality that resurfaces in Brexit with new force. In his chapter, Caldwell argues that recovering the meaning of urban citizenship so integral to early modern city life and its drama is crucial for an understanding of the central opportunities and violences in the play, including Shylock's bid for alternative civic inclusion via the flesh bond and the bond's recasting as enabling an alien's attempt on the life of a citizen. In addition, Shylock's reencoding from ambiguous internal "other" to alien "both" links directly with the meaning of urban citizenship in the period and evokes the city/nation split so central to Brexit and questions of EU citizenship.

In his 1977 classic *The Break-Up of Britain*, Tom Nairn declared, "neonationalism has become the gravedigger of the old state in Britain."[99] For Nairn, neonationalism as expressed primarily in Scottish separatism threatened "the vital mystique of Britishness." But Britishness has turned out to be more tenacious, and, paradoxically, perhaps also always more tenuous, than it had once seemed; indeed, in 2023 the roles have perhaps reversed—Scottish separatists seek a referendum that would lead to greater connection with Europe while UK prime minister Rishi Sunak lauds the way Brexit has drastically reduced immigration.[100] Given Nairn's metaphor, it is tempting to reflect on *Hamlet*'s gravediggers and their suspicion that whether Hamlet remains mad in England or not, "it's no great matter there." The decentering of England in *Hamlet* is just one of many examples of how the early modern stage asked its audiences to think in global terms—John of Gaunt might, in Boris Johnson style, describe England as "this sceptered isle . . . this little world" unto itself, but, as Carlo Ginzburg puts it, "just as no man is an island, no island is an island."[101] Tensions around Brexit and the spread of neonationalism provide an occasion to look anew at the drama of the early modern period, to think about what our inevitable interconnectedness means for national identity, theology, epidemiology, racial identity, and the writing, and rewriting, of history both then and now.

Notes

1. Peter Kirwan, "*The Merry Wives of Windsor* (RSC/Live from Stratford-upon-Avon) @Broadway, Nottingham," *Bardathon* (blog), (University of Nottingham), September 13, 2018.

2. Fiona Laird, "Political Responsibility in the Age of Brexit," CapX, July 16, 2016. Web.

3. Shafik Mandhai, "Protests in UK against Post-Brexit Racism," *Al Jazeera*, March 18, 2017.

4. Brodie Wadell, "The Evil May Day Riot of 1517 and the European Union Elections of 2014: Writing about the History of Anti-Immigrant Politics," *Many Headed Monster*

(blog), December 7, 2021; Joseph Campana, "Introduction: After Sovereignty," *Studies in English Literature, 1500–1900* 58, no. 1 (Winter 2018): 1.

5. L. Monique Pittman, *Shakespeare's Contested Nations: Race, Gender, and Multicultural Britain in Performances of the History Plays* (London: Routledge, 2022), 157–81; Marina Gerzic, "Broadcasting the Political Body: *Richard III*, #Brexit and #Libspill," *Shakespeare Bulletin* 38, no. 1 (Spring 2021): 109–29; Stephen O'Neill, "Finding Refuge in *King Lear*: From Brexit to Shakespeare's European Value," *Multicultural Shakespeare: Translation, Appropriation, and Performance* 19 (2019): 120; Bridget Escolme, "Brexit Dreams: Comedy, Nostalgia, and Critique in *Much Ado about Nothing* and *A Midsummer Night's Dream*," in *The Oxford Handbook of Shakespearean Comedy*, ed. Heather Hirschfield (Oxford: Oxford University Press, 2018), 455–69.

6. Kevin A. Quarmby, "Little Did We Know," *Scene* 3, no. 1 (2019): n. p.; Ben Haworth, "Play Review: *The Revenger's Tragedy*," *Cahiers Élisabéthains* 92, no. 1 (April 2017): 105–7. Web.

7. Anna Blackwell, *Shakespearean Celebrity in the Digital Age: Fan Cultures and Remediation* (New York: Palgrave, 2018), 167–70. See also Sally Barnden, "'Never Did or Never Shall': Shakespeare Quotation and the Nostalgic Politics in 2016," in *Early Modern Criticism in a Time of Crisis*, ed. David J. Baker and Patricia Palmer (Tome Press), accessed February 13, 2024, Web.

8. On early modern nationhood, see Liah Greenfeld, *Nationalism: Five Roads to Modernity* (Cambridge, MA: Harvard University Press, 1995); Anthony D. Smith, *The Antiquity of Nations* (Cambridge, UK: PolityPress, 2004); Richard Helgerson, *Forms of Nationhood: The Elizabethan Writing of England* (Chicago: University of Chicago Press, 1992); Philip Schwyzer, *Literature, Nationalism, and Memory in Early Modern England and Wales* (Cambridge, UK: Cambridge University Press, 2009); and Lotte Jensen, ed., *The Roots of Nationalism: National Identity Formation in Early Modern Europe, 1600–1815* (Amsterdam: University of Amsterdam Press, 2016).

9. On early modern Britain's founding myths, see Schwyzer, *Literature*; Herbert Grabes, "'Elect Nation': The Founding Myth of National Identity in Early Modern England," in *Writing the Early Modern English Nation*, ed. Herbert Grabes (Leiden: Brill, 2001), 173–89; Roger Mason, "Scotching the Brut: Politics, History and National Myth in Sixteenth-Century Britain," in *Scotland and England, 1286–1815*, ed. Roger Mason (Edinburgh: John Donald, 1987), 60–84. On Brexit and nostalgia, see Francesca Melhuish, "Euroscepticism, Anti-Nostalgic Nostalgia and the Past Perfect Post-Brexit Future," *Journal of Common Market Studies* 60, no. 6 (November 2022): 1758–76; Lisa Suckert, "Economic Nostalgia: The Salience of Economic Identity for the Brexit Campaign," *Socio-Economic Review* 21, no. 3 (July 2023): 1721–50; Anna Islentyeva, "National Myth in UK-EU Representations by British Conservative Prime Ministers from Churchill to Johnson," *Societies* 12, no. 1 (January 2022): 1–17.

10. On early modern Britain's centralized state, see Perry Anderson, *Lineages of the Absolutist State* (London: Verso, 1974), 113–42; Steve Hindle, *The State and Social Change in Early Modern England, c. 1550–1640* (New York: St. Martin's Press, 2000). On Brexit and authoritarianism, see Peter Dorey, "Explaining Brexit: The 5 A's-Anomi, Alienation,

Austerity, Authoritarianism and Atavism," *Revue Française de Civilisation Britannique: French Journal of British Studies* 27 (2022): 7–28; Ivor Crewe, "Authoritarian Populism and Brexit in the UK in Historical Perspective," in *Authoritarian Populism and Liberal Democracy*, ed. Ivor Crewe and David Sanders (New York: Palgrave, 2020), 15–31; Pippa Norris and Ronald Inglehart, *Cultural Backlash: Trump, Brexit, and Authoritarian Populism* (Cambridge, UK: Cambridge University Press, 2019).

11. See, for example, Ursula Lanvers, Hannah Doughty, and Amy S. Thompson, "Brexit as Linguistic Symptom of Britain Retreating into Its Shell? Brexit-Induced Politicization of Language Learning," *Modern Language Journal* 201, no. 4 (Winter 2018): 775–96; Andrea Musolff, "Hostility towards Immigrants' Languages in Britain: A Backlash against 'Super-Diversity'?" *Journal of Multilingual and Multicultural Development* 40, no. 3 (2019): 257–66.

12. Afua Hirsch, "We Have to Avoid 'Integration' Becoming Another Form of Racism," *Guardian*, September 13, 2019.

13. John Stow, *The Chronicles of England from Brute unto This Present Yeare of Christ* (London: Ralph Newberry, 1580), 482.

14. Transcribed in David George, ed., *Records of Early English Drama: Lancashire* (Toronto: University of Toronto Press, 1991), 255; the original manuscript is National Library of Wales, MS 5390D. On the Knowsley masque, see R. J. Broadbent, "A Masque at Knowsley," *Transactions of the Historic Society of Lancashire and Cheshire for the Year 1925* 77 (1925): 1–16; Julie Sanders, *The Cultural Geography of Early Modern Drama, 1620–1650* (Cambridge, UK: Cambridge University Press, 2011), 124–26.

15. George, *Lancashire*, 261.

16. George, *Lancashire*, 252.

17. National Archives, Kew, State Papers Domestic, SP 18 12/81, fol. 83; Simond D'Ewes, *A Compleat Journal of the Votes, Speeches, and Debates, Both of the House of Lords and House of Commons throughout the Whole Reign of Queen Elizabeth* (London: Jonathan Robinson, 1693), 506. For discussions of assimilation and integration in early modern England, see Lien Bich Luu, "Assimilation or Segregation: Colonies of Alien Craftsmen in Elizabethan London," in *The Strangers' Progress: Integration and Disintegration of the Huguenot and Walloon Refugee Community, 1567–1889, Essays in Memory of Irene Scouloudi*, ed. Randolph Vigne and G. Gibbs (London: Huguenot Society of Great Britain and Ireland, 1995), 160–72; Andrew Pettegree, "'Thirty Years On': Progress toward Integration amongst the Immigrant Population of Elizabethan London," in *English Rural Society, 1500–1800: Essays in Honour of Joan Thirsk*, ed. John Chartres and David Hey (Cambridge, UK: Cambridge University Press, 1990), 297–12.

18. On *Calvin's Case*, see Jacob Selwood, *Diversity and Difference in Early Modern England* (Farnham, UK: Ashgate, 2010), 87–128.

19. On the Windrush scandal and other instances of anti-Black racism amid Brexit, see Adrian Favell, "Crossing the Race Line: 'No Polish, No Blacks, No Dogs' in Brexit Britain? Or, the Great British Brexit Swindle," in *Europe's Malaise: The Long View*, ed. Francesco Duina and Frédéric Merand (Leeds: Emerald, 2020), 103–30; Nira Yuval-Davis, Georgie Wemyss, and Kathryn Cassidy, *Bordering* (Cambridge, UK: Polity, 2019), 97–129.

20. Favell, "Crossing," 104.

21. Margo Hendricks, "Race: A Renaissance Category?" in *A New Companion to English Renaissance Literature and Culture*, ed. Michael Hattaway (New York: Blackwell, 2003), 697.

22. Imtiaz Habib, *Black Lives in the English Archives, 1500–1677* (Farnham, UK: Ashgate, 2008), 56.

23. Kim F. Hall, *Things of Darkness: Economies of Race and Gender in Early Modern England* (Ithaca, NY: Cornell University Press, 1995), 125.

24. Ian Smith, *Race and Rhetoric in the Renaissance: Barbarian Errors* (New York: Palgrave, 2010), 7.

25. Dennis Austin Britton, *Becoming Christian: Race, Reformation, and Early Modern English Romance* (New York: Fordham University Press, 2014), 22.

26. See, for example, John Brannigan, *New Historicism and Cultural Materialism* (New York: Bloomsbury, 2016), 78.

27. David J. Baker, "Time to Leave: Brexit and Politics of Chronology," in Baker and Palmer, *Early Modern Criticism in a Time of Crisis*. Web, no pagination.

28. Paolo Freire, *Pedagogy of Freedom: Ethics, Democracy, and Civic Courage* (Lanham, MD: Rowman and Littlefield, 1998), 102.

29. On the politics of "original practices," see Ayanna Thompson, *Passing Strange: Shakespeare, Race, and Contemporary America* (Oxford: Oxford University Press, 2011), 97–118; Laury Magnus, "Michael Radford's *The Merchant of Venice* and the Vexed Questions of Performance," *Literature/Film Quarterly* 35, no. 2 (April 2007): 108–20.

30. Andrew Hiscock, *Shakespeare, Violence and Early Modern Europe* (Cambridge, UK: Cambridge University Press, 2022), 4.

31. See, for example, Florian Kläger and Gerd Bayer, "Introduction: Early Modern Constructions of Europe," in *Early Modern Constructions of Europe: Literature, Culture, History*, ed. Florian Kläger and Gerd Bayer (New York: Routledge, 2018), 1–23, 1; David Blanks, "Europeans before Europe: Modernity and the Myth of the Other," in Kläger and Bayer, *Early Modern Constructions of Europe*, 27; Roberto M. Dainotto, *Europe (in Theory)* (Durham, NC: Duke University Press, 2007), 14–47; Heikki Mikkeli, *Europe as an Idea and an Identity* (Basingstoke, UK: Macmillan, 1998), 18–19; Gerard Delanty, *Inventing Europe: Idea, Identity, Reality* (London: Palgrave Macmillan, 1995), 6 and 65; John Hale, *The Civilization of Europe in the Renaissance* (New York: Scribner, 1994), 3.

32. Delanty, *Inventing Europe*, 3.

33. Robert Bartlett, *The Making of Europe: Conquest, Colonization, and Cultural Change, 950–1350* (Princeton: Princeton University Press, 1993), 291; Norman Davies, *Europe: A History* (Oxford: Oxford University Press, 1996), 238; Hale, *Civilization*, 3.

34. Pietro Martire d'Anghiera, *The Decades of the Newe Worlde or West India*, trans. Richard Eden (London: William Powell, 1555), 4D3r. This was not, of course, the first use of the adjective "European": Denys Hay argues that the coinage of "European," derived from the rarely used classical terms *Europaeus* and *Europensis*, should be attributed to Pope Pius II in the mid-fifteenth century (Denys Hay, *Europe: The Emergence of an Idea* [Edinburgh: Edinburgh University Press, 1957], 86–87).

35. Giovanni Botero, *The Travellers Breviat*, trans. "I. R." (London: John Jaggard, 1601), R3v.

36. J. D., *The Knave in Graine, New Vampt* (London: John Nicholson, 1640), E3r.

37. Delanty, *Inventing Europe*, 41–42. Beyond the diversity of nations and cultures within the geographic area of Europe, Delanty also identifies two larger "notions of Europe" that took form at this time which he refers to as "Oceanic Europe" and "Continental Europe": the former took shape as "the idea of Europe as the West with its destiny beyond the seas" while the latter was "the old idea of Europe as a Christian bastion against the Muslim Orient" (47). As the examples given in this introduction suggest, many English writers in the period—including playwrights—aligned the western island country of England with "Oceanic Europe."

38. Blanks, "Europeans," 28.

39. Dainotto, *Europe*, 5.

40. Thomas Campion, *The Description of a Maske* (London: Laurence Lisle, 1614), A4v–B1r. Campion's decision to crown all of the different regions of the world differed from the typical European practice of only representing the iconographic figure of "Europe" as wearing a crown (see Pim den Boer, "Europe to 1914: The Making of an Idea," in *What Is Europe? The History of the Idea of Europe*, ed. Kevin Wilson and Jan van der Dussen [New York: Routledge, 1993], 13–82, 48–58). Dainotto provides a useful contextualization of other iconographic personifications of Europe, Asia, Africa, and America, noting how such devices served not only to distinguish the presumed "civilization" of Europe from the presumed "savagery" of the other continents but also to obscure or erase the plurality of communities within Europe itself under the tidy fiction of "identity/sameness" (39).

41. John Tatham, *Londons Triumphs* (London: s. n., 1657), B2r.

42. Anonymous, *The Treasurie of Auncient and Moderne Times* (London: William Jaggard, 1613), 2C1v.

43. Richard Flecknoe, *The Marriage of Oceanus and Brittania* (London: s. n., 1659), D1r.

44. Flecknoe, *Marriage*, C4v–D1r.

45. Flecknoe, *Marriage*, D1r–1v.

46. Kläger and Bayer, "Introduction," 4.

47. Thomas Brightman, *A Revelation of the Apocalyps* (Amsterdam: Judocus Hondius and Hendrick Laurenss, 1611), 4S1v–2r.

48. Kläger and Bayer, "Introduction," 3; Dainotto, *Europe*, 11 (Dainotto dates the rise of the secular idea of Europe to the institution of universities in the thirteenth century [30]). On the early modern equating of "Europe" with "Christendom," see also den Boer, "Europe," 32–38.

49. Richard Bernard, *Rhemes against Rome* (London: Edward Blackmore, 1626), I7v. Bernard clearly places England within the European community by identifying its Lutheran identity: "It [that is, Lutheranism] is in more Kingdomes in Europe, then the Pope hath full jurisdiction in, as in England, Scotland, with all adjacent Ilands belonging to both Kingdomes" (I7r).

50. Anonymous, *The Merry Devill of Edmonton* (London: Arthur Johnson, 1608), D4v.

51. Thomas Randolph, *A Pleasant Comedie, Entitled Hey for Honesty, Down with Knavery* (London: s. n., 1651), G3r.

52. Sir Thomas Roe, *A True and Faithfull Relation, Presented to His Majestie and the Prince, of What Hath Lately Happened in Constantinople* (London: Bartholomew Downes, 1622), C4r.

53. Samuel Purchas, *Purchas His Pilgrimes* (London: Henry Featherstone, 1625), 6P5v.

54. Dainotto, *Europe*, 33.

55. Thomas Dekker, *The Shomakers Holiday. Or, the Gentle Craft* (London: Valentine Sims, 1600), F2v and C3r. In the anonymous jests about Smug the Smith published in 1631, shoemaking is again identified as a pan-European trade when Smug raises a "full Cann of the best liquor . . . to all good fellow Shoo-makers in Europe" (T. B., *The Life and Death of the Merry Devill of Edmonton, with the Pleasant Prancks of Smug the Smith* [London: Francis Faulkner, 1631], C1v).

56. W. Mark Ormrod, "England's Immigrants, 1330–1550: Aliens in Later Medieval and Early Tudor England," *Journal of British Studies* 59 (2020): 245–46.

57. William Shakespeare, *The Tempest*, in *Comedies, Tragedies, Histories* (London: William Jaggard and Edward Blount, 1623), A4r.

58. Crystal Bartolovich, "'Baseless Fabric': London as a 'World City,'" in *"The Tempest" and Its Travels*, ed. Peter Hulme and William H. Sherman (Philadelphia: University of Pennsylvania Press, 2000), 13–26, 18. Bartolovich argues that Prospero's island can be read (also) metaphorically as the increasingly diverse and globally cosmopolitan London and as the island nation of England more broadly—an island "that Europe permeates" but that also was, by Shakespeare's time, "permeating Europe" in return (26).

59. William Slatyer, *The History of Great Britanie* (London: William Stansby, 1621), A4r.

60. *Cymbeline*, 1.6.57–59. Citations here to *Cymbeline* are from *The Arden Shakespeare Complete Works*, ed. Richard Proudfoot, Ann Thompson, David Scott Kastan, and H. R. Woudhuysen (London: Bloomsbury Publishing, 2021).

61. *Cymbeline*, 3.1.46–47.

62. *Cymbeline*, 3.1.54–55.

63. *Cymbeline*, 3.1.12–14.

64. *Cymbeline*, 3.4.135–39. "Livers" is a southern and southwest English dialect word for "living creatures or inhabitants" (*Oxford English Dictionary*, s.v. "liver, n.2," 1.a).

65. *Cymbeline*, 5.5.14–15.

66. *Cymbeline*, 5.5.84, 90–91, and 86–88.

67. *Cymbeline*, 5.5.459–61.

68. *Cymbeline*, 5.5.472–75.

69. *Cymbeline*, 5.5.478–80.

70. Tangentially, though appropriately enough, the word "remain" is used fourteen times in *Cymbeline*, more than in any other Shakespeare play but *Coriolanus* (with which it is tied).

71. Rachel Ellen Clark, "The Anti-Brexit *Cymbeline*," *Early Modern Culture* 12 (2017): 137.

72. Lisa Hopkins, "*Cymbeline*, Presented by the Royal Shakespeare Company at the Royal Shakespeare Theatre, Stratford-upon-Avon, 2016," *Early Modern Literary Studies* 19, no. 1 (2016). Web, no pagination.

73. On these productions and their political contexts, see Barbara Louise Eaton, "Journey's End: A Theater History of Shakespeare's *Cymbeline*" (PhD diss., University of Maryland at College Park, 1996), 179, 186, 207, 210, and 215.

74. William Shakespeare, *Hamlet*, in *Comedies, Tragedies, Histories*, 201v.

75. Ellen Welch, *A Theater of Diplomacy: International Relations and the Performing Arts in Early Modern France* (Philadelphia: University of Pennsylvania Press, 2017), 4.

76. Robert Wilson, *A Right Excellent and Famous Comedy Called The Three Ladies of London* (London: s. n., 1592), B1v.

77. Christopher Marlowe, *The Troublesome Raigne and Lamentable Death of Edward the Second* (London: William Jones, 1594), G4v.

78. Ben Jonson, *The Comical Satyre of Every Man Out of His Humor* (London: William Holme, 1600), M3r.

79. Thomas Heywood, *The Iron Age, Contayning the Rape of Hellen: The Siege of Troy* (London: s. n., 1632), A3v.

80. Heywood's imagery is, however, explicitly imperialist since the fall of Troy narrative is, as he acknowledges in the second part of *The Iron Age*, a contest between Europe (the Greeks) and Asia (the Trojans); in the opening speech of the second part, Agamemnon lauds his generals as the "Terrors of the *Asian* Monarchy, / And *Europes* glory" (*The Second Part of the Iron Age* [London: s. n., 1632], B1r). The reason the two phoenixes of London and Rome can rise in Europe from Troy's ashes is because the great Asian city was destroyed by European conquerors. Helen too, in the play's conclusion, acknowledges that it was her beauty that "set two parts of the World at warre," namely, "the *Asian* Monarchy" and "this of *Europe*" (K4r).

81. Anonymous, *The True Tragedie of Richard the Third* (London: William Barley, 1594), H2v.

82. George Chapman, *All Fools* (London: Thomas Thorpe, 1605), I4v.

83. Thomas Dekker, *The Pleasant Comedie of Old Fortunatus* (London: William Aspley, 1600), D1v.

84. Philip Massinger, *The Maid of Honour* (London: Robert Allot, 1632), C1r; John Ford, *The Chronicle Historie of Perkin Warbeck* (London: Hugh Beeston, 1634), H4r.

85. Thomas Dekker, *The Magnificent Entertainment Given to King James, Queene Anne His Wife, and Henry Frederick the Prince* (London: Thomas Man, 1604), B1v.

86. John Marston, *The Dutch Courtezan* (London: John Hodgets, 1605), C2v.

87. Robert Greene, *The Scottish Historie of James the Fourth* (London: s. n., 1598), C4r.

88. Samuel Rowley, *When You See Me, You Know Me* (London: Nathaniel Butter, 1605), D3r–v.

89. Richard Brome, *The Antipodes* (London: Francis Constable, 1640), C3v.

90. Brome, *Antipodes*, C3v.

91. Robert Greene, *The Honorable Historie of Frier Bacon, and Friar Bongay* (London: s. n., 1630), B1r.

92. Greene, *Frier Bacon*, A4v and B4r.

93. Francis Bacon, *Sylva Sylvarum* (London: William Lee, 1627), 2H4v and b4v; Thomas Hobbes, *Leviathan* (London: Andrew Crooke, 1651), 2A3v.

94. Ian Morris, *Geography Is Destiny: Britain and the World: A 10,000-Year History* (New York: Farrar, Straus and Giroux, 2022), 235. On Henry's break with Rome as a precursor to Brexit, see also Rosamund Oates, "Brexit to Bonfire Night: Why the Reformation Still

Matters," *Conversation*, October 31, 2017. For a contrary view, see Michelle L. Beer, "Brexit, the English Reformation, and Transnational Queenship," *Journal of the History of Ideas Blog*, February 20, 2019.

95. Delanty, *Inventing Europe*, 67.

96. Thomas Middleton and Anthony Munday, *The Triumphs of Truth*, in *Thomas Middleton: The Collected Works*, ed. David M. Bergeron, Gary Taylor, and John Lavagnino (Oxford: Clarendon Press, 2020), 411–18.

97. Quoted in Hale, *Civilization*, 6.

98. Roger A. Mason, *Scotland and England 1286–1815* (Edinburgh: John Donald Publishers, 1987), 60.

99. Tom Nairn, *The Break-Up of Britain: Crisis and Neo-Nationalism* (London: Verso, 1977), 89.

100. Alasdair Sandford, "'Brexit Is Delivering' Says Sunak as UK PM Rejects 'Any Alignment with EU Laws,'" *EuroNews*, November 22, 2022.

101. Carlo Ginzburg, *No Island Is an Island: Four Glances at English Literature in a World Perspective* (New York: Columbia University Press, 2000), 88.

1

"The Uncertainty of This World"

Shakespeare in "Unprecedented" Times

Margaret Tudeau-Clayton

On Friday, March 27, 2020, standing alone on the steps of St. Peter's Basilica in Rome, the pope addressed "the city and the world" on the global pandemic. In a meditation on the biblical narrative of Christ's calming of the storm he invited us all to see ourselves "in the same boat" at this time of worldwide disorienting turbulence. Meanwhile, on the other side of the Atlantic, a cruise liner—the third to date—was refused entry to ports because passengers and/or crew had COVID. Well-heeled Westerners were thus precipitated into "the same boat" as thousands of refugees refused entry into Mediterranean European ports during the ongoing migrant crisis. The irony would not have been lost on early modern dramatists, not least Shakespeare, who recurrently dramatizes the reversal that places human subjects in the position of those they have judged, rejected, or ignored. Of particular pertinence is his contribution to the multiauthored playtext *Sir Thomas More*, in which the eponymous protagonist asks his off- as well as on-stage audience of English citizens to imagine themselves as strangers in Europe treated with the violence with which they treat strangers in London. Inherited from classical drama, the reversal—*peripeteia*—is of course a key structural feature in early modern theory and practice of drama, especially tragedy. I propose that the global COVID-19 crisis allowed us to see this not only as a formal principle but also as a reflection of "the uncertainty of this world" as Philip Sidney puts it, a non-species-specific condition of precarious contingency, which has been the lived experience of most of humanity for most of history.

In a review essay on a first spate of books on the pandemic in the *London Review of Books*, in December 2021, John Lanchester evoked "generational obliviousness" as a factor in the mismanagement of the crisis by "leaders in the West."[1] This was not a new idea: in 1983, William McNeill observed that obliviousness characterized the population at large: "One of the things that separate us [i.e., 'us' in the rich world] from our ancestors and make contemporary experience profoundly different from that of other ages is the disappearance of epidemic disease as a serious factor in human life."[2] The sudden dissolving of this separation in 2020 triggered a scrabble to find cultural and intellectual responses to the lived experience of epidemic disease in the experience of ancestors near and far, including the early moderns. Shakespeare was, inevitably, singled out, although his works provide relatively little in the way of direct references to, or dramatic uses of the ever-present reality of the plague; indeed, in this respect Shakespeare has been contrasted with contemporaries such as Thomas Dekker and Ben Jonson.[3] This approach is valuable, but I want to look rather at how the lived experience of the COVID-19 crisis opened new ways of seeing early modern theory and Shakespearean practice. If the word "unprecedented" has been repeatedly used to describe the crisis in the West, justly in some respects, it might also be applied to the brief period since World War II that, in the rich world especially, saw levels of (admittedly uneven) development in medicine, science, technology, and material comfort and security for many, if not most, unknown to previous generations. This unprecedented development separated the spoiled children of the rich world from their ancestors, as much, if not more, than the experience of epidemic disease. The crisis of the pandemic afforded an opportunity to recognize that they/we are "in the same boat" of precarious contingency, which has been and remains the lived experience of most of humanity, although how extensively this opportunity will be seized remains to be seen.

This common condition is evoked by Philip Sidney in his theory of tragedy and dramatized by Shakespeare through sudden, unpredictable, and sometimes inexplicable turns, or reversals. This chapter examines, first, how the Shakespearean contribution to *Sir Thomas More* dramatizes ironic reversals, exposing the precarious position both of those who are victims of exclusionary violence and of those who exercise authority; second, how in *Romeo and Juliet* the plague figures as an agent of the contingency that defeats human projects; and finally, via Sidney's discussion of tragedy, how, in *King Lear*, the plague is a figure for the workings of contingency in arbitrary (in)human socioeconomic (in)justice. In a radical reversal, the eponymous figure of absolute power finds himself in the place of the dispossessed and destitute whom he had previously ignored.[4] Experiencing their lived reality, he calls for social justice and solidarity, a call reiterated by the Earl of Gloucester who, in a parallel reversal, finds himself likewise in the place of the dispossessed and destitute.

The lived experience of having "been there" is regularly given as a motive by those ordinary, but also extraordinary, people who have helped refugees in the ongoing migrant crisis in Europe. It is cited, for instance, by those who remember the massive displacement of peoples, especially in Germany, after World War II and those who lived through the recent war in former Yugoslavia and who are now trying to help migrants trapped at the borders of Europe.[5] More recently, on August 23, 2021, a London rabbi commented in *Metro* on the generous response to his appeal for newly arrived refugees from Afghanistan: "Among a group of people who have arrived in the UK as refugees themselves, there is a particular nerve that is hit when we hear about people who are coming here without (anything)."[6] On the other side of the Atlantic, Kevin Tuerff, one of over sixty-five hundred "strangers" "stranded in Gander," Newfoundland, after the 9/11 attacks, was inspired by his experience of generous welcome "to dedicate his life to kindness and openness to strangers."[7]

More prominent, if less immediately personal, have been the appeals made by figures of political and religious authority. In November 2014 Barack Obama reminded Americans that "we were strangers once too," as he lobbied for support of his proposed regulation of five million illegal immigrants, while on September 6, 2015, in an article in the *Guardian*, Jonathan Sacks, then the chief rabbi of London, recalled those who welcomed Jewish refugees in the late 1930s and drew attention to the biblical injunction "Love the stranger because you were once strangers" in an appeal for "a bold act of collective generosity."[8] Obama and Sacks were not the first thus to appeal to scripture and the memory of relatively recent persecution. In March 1593 MP Henry Finch made the same appeal during the most important of the sixteenth-century parliamentary debates around "aliens" or strangers, which took place on the occasion of a bill introduced on behalf of London citizens to limit strangers' trading practices. As I have examined, this parliamentary debate lies behind the multiauthored playtext of *Sir Thomas More* as, in the contribution generally assumed to be Shakespeare's, the intervention by Finch lies behind the eponymous protagonist's call to citizens that they imagine themselves in "the strangers' case" as exiles in continental Europe, treated with the "hideous violence" with which they treat strangers in London (6.155, 148).[9]

As Stephen O'Neill has documented, Shakespeare's contribution to this playtext, especially the powerful closing appeal by More, has been taken up and remediated on digital platforms to promote solidarity with migrants. Through such remediations, he observes, "Shakespeare is extended into new contexts and brought to new audiences" and becomes "a way to empathize with the oppressed, to face those peoples who find themselves disenfranchised by structural inequalities or war, and to exercise ethical responsibility."[10] Strikingly, these remediations (and O'Neill) ignore the complication that the exclusionary violence denounced by Shakespeare's More reflects intra-European white-on-white "racist resentment."[11] An opportunity has consequently been lost to mobilize the speech on behalf of migrants from Eastern Europe, who were singled out in the run-up to Brexit, during which "EU migrants, in particular those from Eastern Europe, were scapegoated and blamed for the country's ills."[12]

Ironically, these remediations also lose sight of the fact that More's closing appeal was itself a remediation of the parliamentary intervention by Finch, which was, moreover, remediated not only for the platform of the stage but also for the platform of the pulpit in the late summer/autumn of 1594 when, in a sermon (published in 1600) on the Hebrew Bible's book of Jonah, George Abbot (future archbishop of Canterbury) rehearsed the case made by Finch on behalf of strangers.[13] Like the remediations of More's speech in the twenty-first century, these remediations for stage and pulpit took the case for the welcoming of strangers "into new contexts." There are, however, telling differences between them, which highlight the rhetorical strategies and implied ethical position of Shakespeare's contribution, as pertinent now as then.

Abbot's remediation is inserted into a discussion of the mariners' treatment of the "straunger" Jonah (in Jonah 1) with "the humanitie which beseemeth all men of reason."[14] It is introduced by a reminder of "the unkindnesse of our nation," specifically "the comon sort," after the St. Bartholomew massacre (1572) and the influx of refugees from France when, "by a most unhospitall [*sic*] kinde of phrase," "our Englishmen use to terme them, no better than French dogs." This insult is echoed in the first scene of the *Sir Thomas More* playtext when Doll, a citizen's wife, addresses a stranger as "you dog's face" (1.9); it is picked up again in the citizen leader's call to "Burn down their kennels" (4.78). It is then pointedly referenced by Shakespeare's More, when he asks citizens to imagine hostile locals in continental Europe who would "spurn you like dogs" (6.151). In *The Merchant of Venice*, the Venetian Christian Antonio would similarly "foot" the Jew Shylock "as you spurn a stranger cur," an echo that strengthens the case for the pertinence of the question of "aliens" in this play too.[15] Abbot connects such "unhospitall" treatment to recent "conspiracies" by "some of the meaner people" in "One Citie of our land," a reference to London, which Finch singles out from the nation for its hostility toward strangers. Abbot doubtless has in mind the unrest and expressions of hostility that followed the rejection by the Lords of the bill against strangers' trading practices, after it had been passed in the Commons. These included a "Libell, Fixte upon the French Church Wall" in which strangers were vilified with Jews as the cause of socioeconomic ills: "like the Jewes you eate us up as bread."[16]

A contemporary equivalent to this libel appeared on the doors of housing for immigrants in Norwich on January 31, 2020—the date of the official departure of Britain from the European Union—as the *Guardian* reported.[17] Titled "Happy Brexit Day," the poster declared that the speaking of any language other than "the Queens English" would not be tolerated and that those who wished to speak another language should return to their country of origin, leaving their accommodation for "British people" so that "we can return to what was normality before you infected this once great island." An archaic and enduring commonplace (in the libel, for instance, strangers are likened to "Egipts plagues"), the stranger as vehicle of infection is reiterated in Shakespeare's contribution to *Sir Thomas More* in relation to food when London citizens complain, "They bring in strange roots" that "breed sore eyes" "enough to infect the City with palsy" (6.11–15). Expressed by "the meaner sort," this opinion is discredited implicitly as an instance of popular "conspiracies" (Abbot) directed against strangers, who are scapegoated, as Eastern Europeans were scapegoated by Brexiteers, although in "provincial England" rather than in London, which again proved an exception to the rest of the nation if in the opposite sense—voting massively to remain in Europe and welcoming strangers.[18]

Like food (and dress), language has always been privileged as a metonymy of national identity. Specifically, the trope of "the Queen's" or "the King's English" has consistently been used, as it is in the Norwich poster, as an instrument of exclusion.[19] From the earliest recorded instance (1553) it is, moreover, used to privilege citizen "plainness" over elite latinate word forms, "Frenche English," and "Englishe Italianated."[20] There is thus a charge of meaning to the seemingly casual assertion of "plain English" against "French Fleming" and "Fleming French" (4.71–3) by one of the citizens in an earlier scene by another of the contributors to the playtext who, unlike Shakespeare, evinced citizen hostility against strangers.[21] The racialization produced by this promotion of plain English language/culture is explicit in *The Pedlar's Prophecy*, an anonymous play contemporary with *The Merchant of Venice* (1596), in which the offspring of mixed intra-European marriages are described as "Aliaunt Sonnes" who have "altered the true English blood and seed / And therewithal English plain maners and good state," a claim which, as Andrew Pettegree observes, taps into a "seam of naked racial prejudice" and which we might compare with the reification today of an essentialized "normal" English/British "way of life" (as in the Norwich poster).[22] Indeed, a racially inflected discourse of biological reproduction is frequently transferred to language, as in William Haughton's citizen comedy *English-Men for My Money* (performed 1598), which voices fear of national/racial miscegenation through the projection of the "generation of Languages that our House will bring foorth" if the English daughters of a Portuguese Jewish father marry their European suitors.[23] Like the aforementioned 1593 libel, this xenophobic play combines hostility toward Jews with hostility toward strangers from Europe—the Dutch, Italians, and above all the French. Described as "a clipper of the Kings English: and . . . an eternall enemie to all good Language," the (generic) Frenchman and his language are denigrated throughout, notably when the same commentator observes, "Pigges and *French-men*, speake one Language, *awee awe*" (a mocking imitation of "ah oui, ah oui").[24] The French and their language/culture are thus dehumanized through assimilation with the lowest of the animals in an assumed hierarchy of species as well as nation-races, in another archaic and enduring racializing move that frequently precedes and justifies exclusionary violence.

Against the "conspiracies" of "the meaner sort" in London, Abbot sets the "disposition" of "the wise and godly" (which included the queen and her Privy Council), who treat strangers "as brethren, considering their distresses, with a lively fellow-feeling," evoking the kinship and attendant solidarity summoned by Finch and Shakespeare's More.[25] Appropriately for his platform, Abbot then fleshes out Finch's arguments from biblical precept, quoting a verse from Leviticus that makes explicit what Finch implies by a quotation from Exodus, namely that the injunction "to deale well with all straungers" is undergirded by the lived experience of the Israelites: "The time once was, when themselves were straungers in that cruell land of Egypt." Finally, he reiterates Finch's evocation of recent history when the English were given "refuge" in Europe from "bloudie persecution" in "Queene Maries days." However, he deflects the ethical import of Finch's closing evocation of future possibility by adding to "their case may be our case" the pious wish "which day the Lord long keep from us." Abbot thus prays for protection for "us" from the future possibility of experiencing the stranger's "case," while Finch, on the contrary, urges that "we" imagine ourselves in such a case and act accordingly, citing the "golden rule" derived from Christ's Sermon on the Mount (Matthew 7:12): "We may be strangers hereafter. So let us do as we would be done unto."

In marked contrast to Abbot, Shakespeare, for the platform of the stage, turns the ethical imperative of the golden rule into the response of the assembled on-stage audience of hostile citizens: "Faith, 'a says true. Let's do as we may be done by" (6.157). The expression of conviction "'a says true" underscores the persuasive force of the preceding speech, which reworks Finch's evocation of future possibility as a vivid scene that calls on citizens to imagine themselves as strangers in Europe, objects of "hideous violence" (6.148) like that which they seek to inflict on strangers in London. Appropriately then for this platform, the exercise of the imagination is privileged over the exercise of memory, whether of Hebrew-biblical precept or recent history, which Abbot privileges for the platform of the pulpit. Indeed, the success of Shakespeare's More—a stark contrast to Finch's failure to persuade his fellow parliamentarians—serves to advertise the importance of the imagination in bringing about changes in perception and behavior. Shakespeare's remediation thus bears out the point made by Richard Rorty that "solidarity . . . is to be achieved . . . by imagination, the imaginative ability to see strange people as fellow sufferers."[26]

In addition, Shakespeare's More invites his audience to imagine the strangers as being in the same situation as native internal immigrants, dispossessed of their means to live by the practice of enclosure.[27] This is done by means of a near quotation from a denunciation of the practice by Raphael Hythloday in the historical More's *Utopia*. Hythloday's depiction of the victims of enclosure as "wretched souls . . . woeful mothers with their young babes. . . . Away they trudge finding no place to rest in" is turned by Shakespeare's More into an explicit call to exercise the imagination: "Imagine that you see the wretched strangers, / Their babies at their backs, with their poor luggage / Plodding to th'ports and coasts for transportation" (6.85–7).[28] This move is important because, like Brexiteers who scapegoated East European immigrants, those hostile to the strangers argued that they were responsible for the increase in the numbers of native poor, though, tellingly, strangers were not included among the "causes of poverty" listed in an official "assessment of 1597."[29] In the parliamentary debate of 1593, for instance, "Mr *Dalton* . . . imputed the Beggery of the

City to Strangers."[30] Echoed in the 1593 libel—"Our pore artificers doe starve & dye"—the argument is reiterated in highly charged terms in the declaration of a "bill" of "wrongs" (1.99) earlier in the playtext: "Aliens and strangers eat the bread from fatherless children, and take the living from all the artificers, . . . whereby poverty is much increased. . . . for craftsmen be brought to beggary" (1.123–8).[31] The recurring prominence of such emotionally charged arguments highlights the stakes of Shakespeare's move, which directs attention away from strangers to the practices responsible for the swelling numbers of the poor in London, where resources were "strained" by internal immigrants who far outnumbered strangers.[32] A sharp contrast to representations of the strangers in the rest of the playtext, as others have remarked, this is a crucial strategy through which, instead of pitting native poor against strangers, Shakespeare urges citizens to imagine them as "fellow sufferers," with nowhere to go and without the means to live, victims of what Shakespeare's More calls "mountainish [i.e., barbarous] inhumanity" (6.156).

Indeed, this inhumanity is defined in the immediately preceding lines not only (more conventionally) as a denial of a common identity/origin as "made" by God but also as a denial of shared natural resources by those who, in their exclusionary violence, act as if "the elements / Were not all appropriate to your comforts / But chartered unto them" (6.152–54). Carrying as it does the sense of protected privilege, in particular with respect to land ownership, "chartered" evokes the privilege of private property, which, in Hythloday's ideal commonwealth, is rejected for the ideal of all things in common. For Church of England minister Francis Trigge, who quotes approvingly from Hythloday's denunciation in a tract against enclosure addressed to King James (1604), the doctrine of all things in common exemplifies the "charity" of the "Primitive Church," betrayed by the practice of enclosure, which More "affirmes" "makes beggars."[33] The "members of Jesus Christ" are, Trigge urges, called on to live, like Christ and Abraham before Him, "like poore pilgrims and travailers," using the goods of the earth "as wise travailers doe their Innes," unlike enclosers and merchants, who seek to "use the earth to the most advantage."[34] For Shakespeare's More then as for Trigge, a just relation to others entails a just relation to the common resources of the natural environment. This anticipates the eco-Marxist perception of the emergence of the unsustainable exploitation of natural resources concurrently with new forms of social injustice at the onset of market capitalism, which privileges economic self-interest and private property over shared ownership and solidarity.[35]

The reversal that citizens are called on to imagine by Shakespeare's More finds ironic echo in the playtext's structuring dramatic reversal, which sees More unable to do what he urges on the citizens, namely, to submit to the authority of the king. He is consequently excluded, "estranged from great men's looks" (13.131), and executed, like the leader of the citizen rebels. This leveling reversal is anticipated in a scene prior to the Shakespearean contribution by one of his coauthors who, if taking an opposed view of strangers (as I have indicated), shares a view of theater as a place where dramatized reversals expose the precarious contingency of subject positions, especially of those who exercise authority. In this scene the tellingly named Justice Suresby is set up by More, who stages a "merry jest" in order to "check the folly of the Justice / For blaming others in a desperate case / Wherein himself may fall as soon as any" (2.91–3), a purpose underscored by the closing observation of the Lord Mayor to the Justice that "this is strange / You being a man so settled in assurance / Will fall in that which you condemned in other" (192–94). More, too, will "fall in that which he condemns" in the citizens, an irony that places him, like Suresby, alongside those over whom he has exercised authority. Such reversals are repeatedly imagined as well as dramatized by Shakespeare. Of particular pertinence here is the call by Lear after he has suffered a radical reversal: "See how yon justice rails upon yon simple thief. Hark in thy ear: handy-dandy; which is the thief, which is the justice?"[36] Whether imagined or staged, such reversals highlight the precarious contingency both of those who administer (in)justice and of those who are their objects/victims. As Thomas Claviez observes, "contingency" is "the natural enemy" of "authority," intellectual as well as political.[37]

Claviez goes on to note that "we are now experiencing ever more intense feelings of contingency and precariousness" on account of the pandemic. Indeed, in the early stages, COVID was viewed as a social leveler, notably when it struck royalty (Prince Charles), cultural royalty (Tom Hanks), and figures of political authority (the prime minister of the UK and the presidents of Brazil, the United States, and France). Gradually, however, the statistics told another story—how COVID "feeds on inequality" and how "the virus did not discriminate, but society did."[38] In late March 2020, in one of the more substantial pieces on Shakespeare and the pandemic, Emma Smith (in the *New York Times*) took up Rene Girard's observation that the plague was repeatedly represented as a social leveler in the early modern period, as in a poem by Thomas Dekker published in 1604 with the grimly ironic title "News from Graves-End": "There friend, and foe, the yong and old, / . . . / Servant and Maister: Fowle and faire: / One livery weare, and fellowes are," and in Daniel Defoe's journal of the plague year of 1665 (published in 1722): "Here was no Difference made, but Poor and Rich went together."[39] Yet the historical evidence suggests again that the plague struck above all the poor, since "the wealthy purchased virtual immunity" by fleeing the city for the country and "few well known figures died of plague . . . which could be avoided by members of the less poverty-stricken classes."[40] Nevertheless, like the plague, the pandemic has afforded an opportunity to imagine a shared condition of precarious contingency, poor and rich together, an exercise of imagination like that which Shakespeare's More urges on citizens. This is to urge a "politics of identification" rather than a "politics of identity," a helpful distinction made by Tamil writer A. Sivanandan.[41]

A politics of identity was at stake in the arguments around Brexit, in which ideas of national identity intersected in complex ways with generational, educational, and socioeconomic fault lines.[42] A politics of identity was arguably at stake too in the conflict around "strangers" in early modern London, in which ideas of national identity intersected with social class to divide parliament and to set city against court. These divisions fed into the complex matrix of factors leading to a civil war that Michel Foucault described as the first "guerre des races," drawing on Christopher Hill's work on the "myth" (or, we might say, following Abbot, conspiracy) of the "Norman Yoke," which fueled hostility from the citizen class towards the (Norman-descended) noble elite as well as French refugees.[43]

As sociologist Gary Younge has observed, the rich West has been "taken over" by a politics of identity focused on essentialized differences, which has fractured societies along intersecting fault lines. To counter this trend, he calls for a renewal of a sense of "our universal humanity," commenting how "for the hundreds of thousands, if not millions, who roam the globe without papers, rights or citizenship the crucial issue is not to have their particular identity recognized, but to have their essential humanity acknowledged and respected."[44] This is the crucial issue too for the millions of poor within the rich world who are without proper shelter, food, and clothing, like the native poor whom Shakespeare's More associates with strangers. The current crisis invites then the recognition that, though some in the rich world may not (yet) be where the poor are, the precarious contingency of their lived experience is ours too, that "the uncertainty of this world" is a shared human condition.

That the pandemic has triggered such recognition is suggested by statements from prominent public figures who otherwise have almost nothing in common. On April 5, 2020, Dominique Strauss-Kahn, the morally compromised French economist and politician, wrote in *Politique Internationale*, "Aujourd'hui, nous reprenons conscience de la précarité de l'être" (today we are rediscovering the precarity of existence).[45] On April 30 of the same year, the American feminist philosopher Judith Butler gave an interview in *Truthout* in which they highlighted at once the "social inequality" and the "global vulnerability" exposed by the pandemic—"a shared condition of social life, of interdependency, exposure and porosity."[46] Among the many personal testimonies, American author Joyce Carol Oates wrote on May 15 in the *Times Literary Supplement*, "My life, normally so predictable, steadfast and (to a degree) enjoyable, has now become precarious as a runaway rollercoaster."[47] A week and a half earlier in the same journal, Australian author and critic Beejay Silcox told of the separation from her husband brought about by the pandemic, commenting, "The existential terror of Covid-19 isn't just its elevated mortality rate; it's the virus's blithe upending of certainty."[48]

The subtitle to Silcox's piece, "Star-Crossed by COVID-19," recalls the one play by Shakespeare in which the plague "features significantly," as Stephen Greenblatt observed, since what he calls the "ill-timed quarantine" "is an agent of the star-crossed lovers' tragic fate."[49] Romeo and Juliet do not, that is, die of the plague, but the immediate cause of their deaths is a confinement of suspected cases, "stayed," as Friar Lawrence later diplomatically reports, "by accident," thus representing the imposed confinement as a contingency that prevented him from bringing about the safe reunion he had planned.[50] At the close the lovers are recognized as "sacrifices of our enmity" (24.303) by their parents, figures of an entrenched tribal antagonism, but the immediate material cause of their deaths, as many have now observed, is a restriction on social circulation imposed by public health authorities: "The searchers of the town / Suspecting that we both were in a house / Where the infectious pestilence did reign / Sealed up the doors, and would not let us forth" (23.8–11). Iconic figures of a future generation are then sacrificed to a combination of a rigid tribal politics and a similarly rigid public health politics. The curse "A plague o' both your houses" (13.96) uttered earlier by Mercutio suddenly acquires a new resonance.

The disruption of long-term as well as more immediate plans has obliged the still relatively protected sociocultural elite in the rich world to confront—like Friar Lawrence—a precarious contingency from which they had previously been insulated, although they have not suffered (yet) from the economic disasters, even the food insecurity that others have suffered, many for the first time. In November 2020, Jacqueline Rose reflected in the *London Review of Books* how "disaster uncovers the material and racial faultlines of a society, but it also unforgivingly exposes the truth that no human subject is spared—in Freud's words, 'the perplexity and helplessness of the human race.'"[51] Moving sensitively between the impact of the pandemic and the writing of Freud during the deprivations of the first world war and the loss of his daughter Sophie to Spanish flu, Rose discovered new aspects to the work of an author she has spent a lifetime studying, including the pertinence of his definition of the human condition in terms of helplessness and perplexity. Similarly, the theory and practice of early modern tragedy look different in our new shared context, as do (as Austin Tichenor has observed) Shakespeare's plays.[52]

Take the recurrently wheeled out definition of tragedy by Philip Sidney in *An Apology for Poetry* (published in 1596): "The high and excellent Tragedy, that openeth the greatest wounds, and showeth forth the ulcers that are covered with tissue; that maketh kings fear to be tyrants, and tyrants manifest their tyrannical humours; that, with stirring the affects of admiration and commiseration, teacheth the uncertainty of this world, and upon how weak foundations gilden roofs are builded."[53] This definition has invariably been glossed as reproducing the inherited assumption of the "aristocratic nature of tragic action" addressed to those in power who are thereby warned against abuse of their position.[54] But if tragedy's political function of speaking truth to power is reasserted, it is enlarged to encompass the condition that is the bottom line of existence—"the uncertainty of this world" to which all are exposed. The rich and powerful may fall sick, as the figure of the ulcer indicates, which, if a metaphor for political corruption, is also a metonymy for the bodily disease of which it is the manifest symptom. They may as suddenly experience sexual desire as, in *Twelfth Night*, Shakespeare's noble lady Olivia discovers when a visit from Viola/ Cesario startles her from her self-imposed confinement: "How now?" she murmurs. "Even so quickly may one catch the plague?"[55] Similarly, Biron in *Love's Labor's Lost* declares to the princess and her ladies that his fellow lords, likewise startled out of a self-imposed confinement, "are infected; . . . / They have the plague, and caught it of your eyes."[56] Though a commonplace, the comparison of sexual desire to plague highlights the vulnerability to sudden life-changing events beyond human control that is precisely commonplace, every day and for everyone. While the upper and middle levels of society endured status or job insecurity as well as dire economic instability, the majority suffered, in addition, food and housing insecurity.

This generalized insecurity is advertised by one of Thomas Dekker's plague poems, in which personifications of war, famine, and "the Pestilence" compete for first place among the conditions that rendered life precariously contingent at every level.[57]

For Sidney, the recognition of the uncertainty of this world summoned by tragedy is attended by "admiration and commiseration," a reworking of the Aristotelian cathartic emotions of pity (*eleos*) and fear (*phobos*). If "commiseration" corresponds to the Aristotelian *eleos*, "admiration" does not correspond to *phobos*, as others have remarked. To Geoffrey Shepherd's proposed gloss, "a kind of emotional shock," I would be tempted to add a sense of awe, if "shock and awe" were not such an unfortunately loaded cliché.[58] A fuller, if indirect gloss is provided by one of Shakespeare's reliable commentators whose observation bears more generally on my argument: "They say miracles are past, and we have our philosophical persons to make modern and familiar things supernatural and causeless. Hence is it that we make trifles of terrors, ensconcing ourselves into seeming knowledge when we should submit ourselves to unknown fear."[59] This passage is cited by Greenblatt to support his view of Shakespearean accommodation of the plague: "Extreme suffering has become so familiar that it is banal—precisely the accommodation to the recurrent epidemics that we have noted through much of Shakespeare's work."[60] This is a startling misreading from a usually acute critic, since it is precisely accommodation (making "modern and familiar") that is critiqued here, together with the "seeming knowledge" with which "we" protect ourselves when "we should submit ourselves to unknown fear." "Unknown fear" is consistently glossed as fear of the unknown, but it might be taken too as a new form of fear experienced once the protective layer of seeming knowledge is dissolved by unexpected and inexplicable ("causeless") events—whether "miracles" or "terrors." As it happens the event that triggers this comment is not a terror but a miracle—a sudden curing of a king from a seemingly incurable sickness by a young female commoner. Like the comparison of plague and sexual desire, the joining of "terrors" and "miracles" here undoes an apparent opposition to expose the contingency manifest in unpredictable and inexplicable life-changing events. Dramatized on stage, such events call for the response of "admiration"—wonder tinged with fear—that attends tragedy's lesson in the shared condition of "the uncertainty of this world."

It is in *King Lear*, which may have been written during the theater lockdown of the summer of 1606, that the presence of the plague/the pandemic has been especially felt by several critics, including Paul Yachnin, who wrote in April 2020 that this "the darkest of the tragedies" "represents a sick world at the end of its days": "those few characters left alive . . . standing bereft in the midst of a shattered world seem not unlike how many of us feel in the face of the coronavirus pandemic."[61] The bereft state at the end of the play has, however, been brought about by human agents only—there has been no plague. The plague is evoked, but only in transferred senses, as when Lear in his rage describes his daughter Goneril as "a disease that lies within my flesh. . . . / . . . a boil, / A plague-sore, an embossed carbuncle / In my corrupted blood" (7.367–70). As the phrase "my corrupted blood" signals, the origins of the devastation lie in a patriarchal order that corrupts women by using them as objects of exchange to consolidate power of, and between, men. It also discriminates against those born out of wedlock, a practice the bastard son of the Earl of Gloucester, Edmund, denounces. In a powerful monologue Edmund represents this discrimination, in another telling transfer, as "the plague of custom" (2.3), weaving into his personal resentment a denunciation of the social stigmatization of the group—"Why brand they *us* with base, base, bastardy" (10, emphasis mine)—and a call for recognition—"Now gods stand up for bastards" (22)—a call we might gloss "bastards lives matter." But Edmund's will to take the place of his privileged older brother Edgar proves stronger than his will to change the discriminatory system: "Well, the legitimate Edgar I must have your land" (16).

As many have observed, the insulation of the powerful and wealthy from both their own corruption and the corruption of the system is expressed through the material language of clothing, which Sidney uses when, in the passage quoted earlier, he describes the "ulcers . . . covered with tissue" exposed by tragedy. In the play this uncovering reaches a climax in the encounter in the hovel during the storm between the king and the "uncovered body" (11.81) of the beggar Poor Tom. In this body Lear sees what he takes to be "the thing itself," "unaccommodated man" as "a bare forked animal," beside which the "three"—himself, the Fool, and Kent—are "sophisticated" (83–84). The word "sophisticated"—the only instance in the Shakespearean canon—is the most prominent trace of an intertextual link to an essay by Montaigne, as editors have noted. In this essay Montaigne laments how (in Florio's translation) "nature" has been "adulterated" and "sophisticated" by the "farre-fetcht discourses" of the educated elite and claims that the traces of "her image" are to be found rather among "unpollished men" from whom she "draws effects of constancie and patternes of patience" in the face of the devastations wrought by war and disease. "Testimonie" to "her proper, constant and universal visage" is to be found too among "beasts, not subject to favor or corruption, nor to diversitie of opinions."[62] It is to this state of universal nature that Lear aspires by throwing off his remaining clothes, which he addresses as "you lendings" (85) in what is another possible trace of Montaigne's reflections on the human and the animal, as I take up subsequently.

This discovery of "the thing itself" is, however, complicated for spectators by the dramatic irony that Poor Tom is not, as Lear assumes, one of the "poor naked wretches" (11.25) he has just addressed, but, as the quarto title page advertises, a "humor" "assumed" by the "unfortunate" "sonne and heire to the Earle of Gloucester." Invariably neglected by editors, who rarely reprint the full title page even in editions of the quarto text (as, for instance, the New Oxford), this announced prominence draws attention, as James Kearney observes, to "the centrality of Edgar's narrative, and particularly Edgar's stint as Poor Tom."[63] Indeed, the expectations raised by the title page are borne out by a substantial monologue in which Edgar dwells first on the material details of his disguise—"My face I'll grime with filth" (7.165) etc.,—and then on the material condition of the "Bedlam beggars" (170) he seeks to imitate. While the details of the disguise draw attention to the metatheatrical dimension and the artifice of social status it exposes, the details of the self-harm and "roaring voices" of the "Bedlam beggars" (170) invite spectators to imagine their suffering, rather as the vivid language of Shakespeare's More invites spectators to imagine the suffering of the victims of exclusionary violence. Edgar frames these descriptions by a generalized representation of his disguise as "the basest and poorest shape / That ever penury in contempt of man / Brought near to beast" (163–65). Far from "the thing itself," the poor beggar here exemplifies the contingency that afflicts both Edgar, "brought" by unforeseen circumstances to assume this disguise, and those he imitates, "brought" by circumstances beyond their control to a condition of extreme poverty close to the condition of "beast," a closeness formally expressed in the phonetic and orthographic overlap of "basest" and "beast."[64] In condemning this as "in contempt of man," Edgar attributes the beggar's poverty not to his own fault but to the ethical and political failure to recognize his humanity. Refuting the emergent view of poverty as "evidence of wickedness," which will harden into the insidious ideology of individual responsibility, Edgar's language here is comparable to the condemnation by Shakespeare's More of the "inhumanity" of excluding strangers and the native poor.[65] At the same time, the metatheatrical dimension highlights as artifice the difference between noble (Edgar) and base (Tom), who share the body of the (low-born) actor, as later expressions of the lived experience of cold underscore.[66] Indeed, (noble) Edgar as Poor Tom played by a low-born actor embodies the shared human condition of precarious contingency.

This thread is picked up in the plot of the life to which Edgar's story is the advertised parallel when Lear bursts out in response to his daughters' cruel progressive reduction of his number of knights to "What needs one?" (7.409):

> O reason not the need! Our basest beggars
> Are in the poorest thing superfluous.
> Allow not nature more than nature needs,
> Man's life's as cheap as beasts. (410–13)

In these psychologically compelling lines Lear pleads with his daughter not to do what he then struggles to do himself, namely rationalize the need he has for "more" than what "nature needs," which, in his case, is the hundred knights who serve as prostheses of the status to which he is viscerally attached. To support his case, he reaches for the figure of "our basest beggars," the royal possessive emphasizing not only his attachment to his status but also his instrumentalization of the beggars, who, like the knights, serve his "need." He needs beggars to need "more than nature needs," in order to affirm that the value of human "life" is a function of this "more." For Lear here as for Edgar, human life is "cheap" inasmuch as it approaches the condition of "beasts." This "more" will find echo when the sight of Poor Tom prompts Lear's reflection "Is man no more than this?" (11.71), and a very different response—that Tom is "the thing itself." This difference is a measure of the reversal that takes place and that undoes the hierarchy of species as well as the hierarchy between rich and poor. Indeed, there is already a turn here as Lear discovers "true need"—the need not for material signs of status but for the moral quality of "patience" (416–17), one of the qualities Montaigne, in the essay discussed earlier, finds among "unpollished men," who furnish examples of "patternes of patience" to those who have "sophisticated" nature. It is precisely to become "the pattern of all patience" (9.34) that Lear aspires as he battles mentally and physically in the storm.

In the quarto the ground is prepared for the reversal to come by a carefully placed description prior to Lear's entrance, furnished by a neutral "gentleman" (8.4–15; lines 7–15 in Q only). This depicts Lear in the storm as an emblematic figure of human "perplexity and helplessness" (to recall Freud), who "strives" "in his little world of man" in the face of indifferent "fretful elements" and who "runs" "unbonneted" in contrast to the "cub-drawn bear" that "would couch" and "the lion and the belly-pinched wolf" that "keep their fur dry." This advertises the instinctive knowledge animals possess, which the human figure is without, as he is without the natural protection enjoyed by these animals, in these respects privileged over the human. Tellingly, Shakespeare evokes particular lived realities—of a female bear drained by the birth of a cub and the hunger pangs of a wolf. This is to resist the violence of the "animot," Derrida's neologistic play on *animaux*, which highlights the violence of the lexical and semantic categories—"animal," "beast"—that erase diversity.[67] Indeed, both Lear and Edgar use the idea of the "animot"/"beast" to assert the difference and superior value of the human. This superior difference is here put into question—anticipating the radical reversal to come—even as the plural lived realities of particular animals are asserted.

As of the animals, so of the beggars. The word "unbonneted"—metonym for a state of deprivation—signals how in the storm Lear finds himself in the place of those he had instrumentalized, "our basest beggars." He begins to recognize this shortly after his entrance when he describes himself as "a poor, infirm, weak, and despised old man" (9.19). He begins too to see a generalized injustice, turning from nonhuman forces (nature/gods) to direct his anger at corrupt humans who conceal their crimes "under covert and convenient seeming" (9.52). Reluctant to take shelter, he is finally persuaded to enter the hovel where he will meet Poor Tom, but, at the entrance, suddenly turns—at least in the quarto version—to address the "poor naked wretches" whose condition he now shares.

> Poor naked wretches, wheresoe'er you are,
> That bide the pelting of this pitiless night,
> How shall your houseless heads and unfed sides,
> Your looped and windowed raggedness, defend you
> From seasons such as these? (10.25–30)

In the folio version this is preceded by an expressed intention to pray, which has led editors to construe the speech as a prayer, although when "confined" "to the subjunctive realm of prayer" the sharpness of its critical thrust is diminished.[68] The direct address in the quarto heightens the effect of vivid immediacy produced by the focused details of the description, which invite spectators—including the wealthy elite at court before whom the quarto version was performed in 1606—to imagine the lived experience of being without shelter, food or proper clothing, rather as Shakespeare's More invites off- and on-stage spectators to imagine the lived realities of the strangers/native poor. In her piece on Shakespeare and the pandemic, Emma Smith takes this speech as an illustration of the Shakespearean antidote to the indiscriminate destruction wrought by the plague/COVID, namely, the assertion of the value of individual lives. It is, however, an entire class of individuals that has been off Lear's radar, as he acknowledges: "O I have ta'en / Too little care of this" (29–30). That "this" refers to the structural injustice of an unequal distribution of resources is made clear by what follows when Lear addresses the wealthy and powerful (likewise conceived collectively), "Take physic, pomp," calling upon them to do as he has done: "Expose thyself to feel what wretches feel" (30–1) and to express the consequent solidarity, "That thou mayst shake the superflux to them, / And show the heavens more just" (31–2).

It has often been observed that Lear's call is reiterated in the parallel plot when the Earl of Gloucester encounters Poor Tom, although Kiernan Ryan has argued, like Chris Fitter before him, that Gloucester's speech "goes beyond" Lear's in its "clarifying and hardening of the attitude towards the rich and powerful," which, Fitter comments, "stabbed a nerve . . . throbbing . . . throughout the entire body politic."[69] Treating the plague as a synecdoche for everyday universal suffering (as Lear does in 11.53–54), Gloucester addresses Edgar/Tom as "thou whom the heavens' plagues / Have humbled to all strokes" (15.60–61), giving him his purse and moralizing the reversal he himself has suffered—"That I am wretched" (61)—as an illustration of a divine justice that he then calls down on the wealthy self-indulgent man who "will not see because he does not feel" (64–65). Thus, he summons the imperative to right the inequalities of an unjust system: "So distribution should undo excess and each man have enough" (66–67). This ethical and sociopolitical imperative is directly in line with an enduring radical strain in Christian thought, as Debora K. Shuger has argued, and Fitter has illustrated in reference to Tudor humanists as well as reformers.[70] It finds specific echo in a comment on the biblical story of Christ's feeding of the five thousand which is made by Erasmus in his *Paraphrases*, placed by royal injunction in parish churches across Elizabethan England.[71] Erasmus calls this an "evangelicall feaste," a feast, that is, which epitomizes the distinctive character of the Christian religion, including its implications for the just distribution of resources "that no man should lacke and no man have to muche."[72] In line with this, *King Lear* insists on the social injustice of an unequal distribution of resources, which it is the collective responsibility of the rich and powerful to correct, a contrast we might add to the aggressive bottom-up individualism of Edmund's pursuit of reparation for the discrimination from which, as bastard, he suffers.

For Margot Heinemann, one of the few remaining politically engaged Marxist critics at the end of the last century, the play's enduring political thrust lies in this condemnation of the (ever increasing) gap between poor and rich, although she recognizes a local political significance in the refusal of Cordelia and her ally the Earl of Kent "to collude with the corruption of absolute power," which, she argues, reflects the stand-off between parliament and king in the first decade of James's reign.[73] Her universalism, like that of the Marxist humanist criticism she practiced, was already under pressure when her piece came out in 1992 and has since been thoroughly critiqued as a vehicle of colonial oppression by many distinguished scholars who seek to replace it with the irreducible specificities of the intersecting lived experiences of victims of oppression.[74] The importance of this critique cannot be overstated, but, as David Schalkwyk has observed, other scholars (including some Shakespeareans) have taken up the challenge urged by Alain Badiou (among others) "to think the same" and "to grasp what is true for us all" in face of the evident manifold differences.[75] Indeed, Nivedita Majumdar has persuasively argued the case for a "radical universalism" such as was "recognized by Marx," which she sees exemplified in postcolonial writing, notably by the Indian author and activist Mahasweta Devi and the Tamil author and activist A. Sivanandan.[76] While Devi is "engaged . . . with the lived reality of marginalized populations" and calls not merely for "recognition" but "for equal access to resources and rights," Sivanandan takes a critical stand against "a narrow politics of identity" and calls for a "politics of identification" and a consequent "solidarity" "against capital's global assault."[77] Gary Younge, too, has called for a renewed sense of "our universal humanity," as I noted earlier, citing the case of the migrants failed by European governments that "refused to allow ships that had rescued people even to dock."[78] This is where I began suggesting that the refusal to allow cruise liners carrying tourists from the rich world to dock during the pandemic carried the potential to summon recognition—like the shared lived experience of insecurity—not so much of a common identity as of a common condition of precarious contingency. This has been and remains "what is true for us all," as tragedy teaches according to Sidney, and as

Shakespearean drama illustrates, mobilizing the imagination through sudden reversals to summon recognition of this shared condition and the attendant sense of kinship and solidarity.

I want to conclude, however, by returning to *King Lear*'s most radical reversal, which takes place when Lear encounters Poor Tom in the hovel. The sight of Tom's "uncovered body" prompts Lear to ask "is man no more but this?" and to respond "unaccommodated man is no more but such a poor, bare, forked animal as thou art" (11.81, 84–85). As I have indicated, this recalls his earlier assertion that "our basest beggars" need "more than nature needs" (7.412), a recollection that highlights the reversal that has taken place. For "unaccommodated man" is no longer considered "cheap" but is valued as "the thing itself," exemplary of an uncontaminated universal nature, just as the "seely-poore" and nonhuman animals are valued by Montaigne, who sets them against those who have "sophisticated" nature, as Lear sets the figure of "unaccomodated man" in exemplary contrast to his "sophisticated" (11.83) companions in the hovel.[79]

A Shakespearean formation that recalls earlier formations with the privative prefix "un"—"unbonneted" (8.14, used of Lear) and "unfed" (11.27, used of the naked poor)—"unaccommodated" represents a general category to which Lear now belongs. Indeed, he seeks now not to assert superior difference but to identify with the naked poor, throwing off his remaining clothes, which he describes as "you lendings" (11.85). This follows his recognition of a debt to nonhuman animals that the naked beggar no longer owes: "Thou owest the worm no silk, the beast no *hide*, the sheep no wool, the cat no perfume" (82–83, emphasis mine). The debt of humans to nonhuman animals is a recurring idea; editors, however, have noted that Shakespeare may owe something specifically to Montaigne who, in his celebration of animals in the essay entitled (in Florio's translation) "An Apologie of Raymond Sebond," evokes what he calls the "spoiles" humans take from animals "to hide and cover our nakedness," "under their spoiles of wooll, of haire, of fethers, and of silke to shroude us."[80] The word "spoils," which is used in other expressions of this idea, represents this relation as the invaders', or colonizers', predatory exploitation of resources over which they have no right. With the verb "owe," Shakespeare treats the relation rather in terms of human dependence, fragility rather than strength. Further, insofar as the naked poor are without this obligation to nonhuman animals, they are implied to have "more" than the rich and powerful, as they do for Montaigne. Similarly, the animals, which are particularized here, as in the description discussed earlier, owe nothing to humans—except the predatory exploitation of their bodies, which renders their existence only more precarious. Even then, as he discovers a likeness to animals, Lear discovers the ironic difference of the dependence of humans, especially the rich and powerful, on other animals for the material to "hide" this likeness and to mark the distinction at once between species and between rich and poor. As he later asserts, "Robes and *furred* gowns *hides* all" (20.150, emphasis mine). This picks up not only on the beast's "hide" that hides, but also on the "fur" that the lion and wolf instinctively know to "keep dry" in the storm, a natural protection which the rich and powerful appropriate—taking animals' lives as they do so—in order to hide their own corruption as well as their naked bodies. In the earlier passage the contrast with the "unbonneted" figure of the human points up how the bear, wolf, and lion are "favored more then us" by nature in this respect, as Montaigne puts it in the "Apologie."[81] The point is made still more forcefully by the prominent preacher and dean of Canterbury John Boys (1571–1625) in a commentary on Psalm 8, which may also lie at the back of Lear's reflections since it turns around the question "What is man?"[82] Boys contrasts "richly decked" flowers and "well armed" beasts with "unhappy base man" "borne to nothing but beggary."[83] The inversion of the hierarchy of species expressed through this idea is then a cultural commonplace, but it is an important discovery for the absolute patriarch habituated to a perception of the lives of beasts and beggars as "cheap" disposable extensions of himself.

Lear's discovery of the value of beggars and beasts is, however, as I discussed earlier, complicated for spectators by the dramatic irony that the "uncovered body" of Poor Tom is itself a cover assumed by one of the rich and powerful, the noble Edgar, who uses what he calls "presented nakedness" (7.167) to protect himself from a plot against his life. This irony inserts another difference into the perceived identity of "unaccommodated man" as a "bare forked animal," namely, the difference made to the state of nakedness by human consciousness, as "presented nakedness" indicates. As Derrida puts it, "L'homme ne serait plus nu parce qu'il a le sens de la nudité," while "l'animal ne se sens ni se voit nu."[84] ("Man could never be naked because he has the sense of nakedness," while "the animal neither sees nor feels itself naked."[85]) A difference—indeed an unbridgeable gap—is thus exposed even as likeness is asserted. Equally importantly, spectators are invited to hold alongside the view of the beggar's exemplary character the view expressed earlier by Edgar and taken up by Lear and Gloucester. Poor beggars, that is, may be exemplary, heroic even in their resilience to suffering, as they are for Montaigne, but they are also victims of social injustice, "brought" into "penury" "in contempt of man" as Edgar puts it—a denial of their humanity similar to the "inhumanity" toward strangers and the native poor dispossessed of the means to live that Shakespeare's More denounces.

King Lear's most radical reversal takes place then not at the level of the individual (the king turned beggar) or social class (the rich and powerful turned poor and helpless) but at the level of the species. Humankind is invited, that is, to recognize itself as at once animal and not animal, dependent on nonhuman animals, whose bodies humans exploit for food and clothing even as they represent them as inferior. In particular, the rich and powerful are exposed for their dependence on other animals to hide likeness and mark difference with respect to both nonhuman animals and the human poor. These hierarchical differences are marked not only through clothing—"le propre de homme"—but also through language, which, for Montaigne, is how men have "sophisticated" the universal visage of nature.[86] For humans discriminate through verbal representation of other humans as nonhuman animals, an archaic and recurring act of dehumanization illustrated, as we saw earlier, in the playtext of *Sir Thomas More*. For Derrida, famously, there is "pas de racisme sans une langue" ("no racism without a language") and "le racisme trahit toujours la perversion d'un homme 'animal parlant'" ("racism always betrays the perversion of a man, 'the talking animal'") while, for Claude Lévi-Strauss, race is "an outcome rather than a presupposition of cultural practices."[87] This was illustrated earlier not only by *Sir Thomas More* but still more prominently by other playtexts that mobilize linguistic and cultural differences to vehicle white-on-white intra-European racism, especially against the French. In a manner that is comparable, as I noted, to the racism expressed by Brexiteers against immigrants from Eastern Europe, this reminds us that the forms racism takes are as many and diverse in Europe/Britain today as then. For Montaigne, racism and speciesism both spring from fear of the other: though of "one same nature," "we blame and condemne" "whatsoever seemeth strange unto us, and we understand not" whether "men . . . from distant countries" whose "fashions, . . . countenance, and . . . clothes . . . altogether differ from ours"; or the "beasts" that are humankind's "fellow-brethren and compeeres."[88] Like Montaigne, Shakespeare summons a sense of kinship and solidarity, inviting humans to recognize their debt to nonhuman animals and the care consequently owed them, as he invites recognition of the care owed fellow humans who share the non-species-specific condition of precarious contingency. This is to recognize finally that we are indeed all "in the same boat"—like Noah and his family obliged to take refuge in a boat with the other animals of the earth, faced not with a global pandemic but with a global climatic catastrophe, which is, probably, where the world is headed next. Indeed, we are called to imagine this too by Shakespeare who, presciently, has his tragic hero call down not only on his daughters but also on the species of "ingrateful man" (9.9) extreme weather events—"a second flood," as R. A. Foakes comments, "and the destruction of the world."[89]

Notes

1. John Lanchester, "As the Lock Rattles," *London Review of Books*, December 16, 2021, 13.

2. William H. McNeill, "The Plague of Plagues," review of *The Black Death: Natural and Human Disaster in Medieval Europe* by Robert S. Gottfried, *New York Review of Books*, July 21, 1983.

3. Cheryl Lynn Ross, "The Plague of *The Alchemist*," *Renaissance Quarterly* 41, no. 3 (Autumn 1988): 439–58.

4. Unless otherwise mentioned, references to Shakespeare texts throughout are to William Shakespeare, *The New Oxford Shakespeare: The Complete Works: Modern Critical Edition*, ed. Gary Taylor, John Jowett, Terri Bourus, and Gabriel Egan (Oxford: Oxford University Press, 2016).

5. See the report by the TSR (Télévision Suisse Romande), June 22, 2021, "Notre reportage en Bosnie-Herzégovine ou des milliers de migrants tentent désespérément de rejoindre l'Europe" ["Our report from Bosnia-Herzegovina where thousands of migrants are desperately trying to enter Europe."]

6. Sam Petherick, "Synagogue Flooded with Thousands of Donations for Newly Arrived Afghan Refugees," *Metro UK*, August 23, 2021.

7. Kevin Tuerff, *Channel of Peace: Stranded in Gander on 9/11*. Austin, TX: River Grove Books, 2017.

8. Jonathan Sacks, "Refugee Crisis: 'Love the Stranger because You Were Once Strangers' Calls Us Now," *Observer*, September 6, 2015.

9. Margaret Tudeau-Clayton, "'This Is the Strangers' Case': The Utopic Dissonance of Shakespeare's Contribution to *Sir Thomas More*," *Shakespeare Survey* 65 (January 2013): 239–54. References to the playtext (scenes and lines in parentheses) are to John Jowett, ed., *Sir Thomas More* (London: Methuen, 2011).

10. Stephen O'Neill, "Shakespeare's 'Hand,' or 'the Strangers' Case': Remediating *Sir Thomas More* in the Context of the Refugee Crisis," *Borrowers and Lenders: The Journal of Shakespeare and Appropriation* 13, no. 1 (April 2020): n.p. Web.

11. Jowett, *More*, 135n10.

12. Christine Berberich, "BrexLit and the Marginalized Migrant," in *Brexit and Beyond: Nation and Identity*, ed. Daniela Keller and Ina Habermann (Tübingen: Narr Francke, 2021), 170.

13. Margaret Tudeau-Clayton, "Shakespeare and Immigration," in *English on the Move: Mobilities in Literature and Language*, ed. Annette Kern-Stahler and David Britain (Tübingen: Narr Verlag 2012), 88–90, 93.

14. George Abbot, *An Exposition upon the Prophet Jonah* (London: Richard Field, 1600), 87–88. In quotations from early modern texts, u/v and i/j are normalized.

15. *The Merchant of Venice*, 1.3.111. Andrew Tretiak, "*The Merchant of Venice* and the 'Alien' Question," *Review of English Studies* 5, no. 20 (October 1929): 402–9. See also James Shapiro, *Shakespeare and the Jews* (New York: Columbia University Press, 1996), 187–89.

16. Arthur Freeman, "Marlowe, Kyd, and the Dutch Church Libel," *English Literary Renaissance* 3, no. 1 (Winter 1973), 50. Shapiro, *Shakespeare and the Jews*, 184–85.

17. Matthew Weaver, "'Speak Only English' Posters Racially Aggravated Say Police," *Guardian*, February 2, 2020.

18. Richard J. Evans, "Breaking Up Is Hard to Do: Joining the European Union—and the Messy Business of Leaving It," *Times Literary Supplement*, November 27, 2020.

19. Margaret Tudeau-Clayton, "'The King's English' 'Our English'?: Shakespeare and Linguistic Ownership," in *Shakespeare and Authority*, ed. Katie Halsey and Angus Vine (London: Palgrave Macmillan, 2018), 113–33.

20. Thomas Wilson, *Arte of Rhetorique*, ed. T. J. Derrick (New York: Garland, 1982), 326.

21. Tudeau-Clayton, "This Is the Strangers' Case," 243–44.

22. Andrew Pettegree, *Foreign Protestant Communities in Sixteenth-Century London* (Oxford: Clarendon Press, 1986), 288–89 (playtext quotations from here).

23. William Haughton, *English-men for My Money: Or, a Pleasant Comedy, Called, A Woman Will Have Her Will* (London: W. White, 1616), sig. I3v.

24. Haughton, *English-men for My Money*, sig. B2v. The economic analogy carried in the recurrent collocation with "clip" is discussed at length in Margaret Tudeau-Clayton, *Shakespeare's Englishes: Against Englishness* (Cambridge, UK: Cambridge University Press, 2020), 34–36, 80–88.

25. Abbot, *Exposition*, 88.

26. Richard Rorty, *Contingency, Irony, and Solidarity* (Cambridge, UK: Cambridge University Press, 1989), xvi.

27. For the widespread resentment provoked by the practice, see Chris Fitter, "'So Distribution Should Undo Excess': Recovering the Political Pressure of Distributive and Egalitarian Discourses in Shakespeare's *King Lear* and Early Modern England," *English Literary History* 86, no. 4 (Winter 2019): 849–50.

28. Tudeau-Clayton, "This Is the Strangers' Case," 249.

29. Christopher Hill, *Society and Puritanism in Pre-Revolutionary England* (Harmondsworth, UK: Penguin, 1986), 254.

30. Simonds d'Ewes, "Journal of the House of Commons: March 1593," in *The Journals of All the Parliaments during the Reign of Queen Elizabeth* (Shannon, Ireland: Irish University Press, 1682), 479–513.

31. Freeman, "Marlowe, Kyd and the Dutch Church Libel," 50.

32. Shapiro, *Shakespeare*, 180–81. For enclosure as a cause of poverty see Hill, *Society and Puritanism*, 254

33. Francis Trigge, *To the Kings Most Excellent Maiestie. The Humble Petition of Two Sisters; the Church and Common wealth* (London: George Bishop,1604), sig. E2v, sig.G1r.

34. Trigge, *Humble Petition*, sig. D1r. Compare John Hale's pertinent observation in 1581: "The soil is not taken away, but the possession thereof is only transferred from one kind of person to another," quoted in Hill, *Society and Puritanism*, 254.

35. Benjamin Kunkel, "The Capitalocene," *London Review of Books*, March 2, 2017; L. A. Clarkson, *The Pre-Industrial Economy in England 1500–1750* (London: B. T. Batsford, 1971), 20–21.

36. *King Lear*, scene 20.137–38. Throughout I refer to the scene and line numbers of the Q text as reproduced in the New Oxford Shakespeare.

37. Thomas Claviez, "A Critique of Authenticity and Recognition," in *Critique of Authenticity*, ed. Thomas Claviez, Kornelia Imesch, and Britta Sweers (Wilmington, DE: Vernon Press, 2020), 54.

38. COVID "feeds on inequality": John Lanchester, "As the Lock Rattles," *London Review of Books*, December 16, 2021, 16; "the virus did not discriminate": Gary Younge, *Who Are We? How Identity Politics Took Over the World* (New York: Bold Type Books, 2021), 9.

39. Emma Smith, "What Shakespeare Teaches Us about Living with Pandemics," *New York Times*, March 29, 2020; Thomas Dekker, *The Plague Pamphlets of Thomas Dekker*, ed. F. P. Wilson (Oxford: Clarendon Press, 1971), 94; Jennifer Cooke, *Legacies of Plague in Literature, Theory and Film* (New York: Palgrave Macmillan, 2009), 185n7.

40. Ross, "Plague," 439; Leeds Barroll, *Politics, Plague, and Shakespeare's Theater* (Ithaca, NY: Cornell University Press, 1991), 14. For a striking illustration in the parishes of London, see Scott Oldenburg, *A Weaver-Poet and the Plague* (University Park: Pennsylvania State University Press, 2020), 5.

41. As pointed out by Nivedita Majumdar, in *The World in a Grain of Sand: Postcolonial Literature and Radical Universalism* (London: Verso, 2021), 212.

42. Evans, "Breaking Up Is Hard to Do," 5.

43. Tudeau Clayton, *Shakespeare's Englishes*, 25–26.

44. Younge, *Who Are We?*, 9.

45. Dominique Strauss-Kahn, "L'être, l'avoir et le pouvoir dans la crise," *Politique Internationale* 167 (Spring 2020): no pagination.

46. George Yancy, "Judith Butler: Mourning Is a Political Act Amid the Pandemic and Its Disparities," *Truthout*, April 30, 2020.

47. Joyce Carol Oates, "My Therapy Animal and Me: Identity and Companionship in Isolation," *Times Literary Supplement*, May 15, 2020.

48. Beejay Silcox, "Those Who Leave and Those Who Stay: Star-Crossed by COVID-19," *Times Literary Supplement*, May 1, 2020.

49. Stephen Greenblatt, "What Shakespeare Actually Wrote about the Plague," *New Yorker*, May 7, 2020.

50. *Romeo and Juliet*, 24.250. All quotations are from the 1599 quarto text in the New Oxford Shakespeare.

51. Jacqueline Rose, "To Die One's Own Death: Jacqueline Rose on Freud and His Daughter," *London Review of Books*, November 19, 2020, 40.

52. Austin Tichenor, "Speaking What We Feel: Shakespeare's Plague Plays," *Shakespeare and Beyond* (blog) (Folger Shakespeare Library), August 27, 2021.

53. Philip Sidney, *An Apology for Poetry*, ed. Geoffrey Shepherd (Manchester, UK: Manchester University Press, 1973), 117–18.

54. Sidney, *Apology*, 189n34.

55. *Twelfth Night*, 1.5.248–49. I am grateful to Scott Oldenburg for pointing out the self-imposed "confinement" of Olivia.

56. *Love's Labor's Lost*, 5.2.422–23.

57. Dekker, *Plague Pamphlets*, 105–12.

58. Sidney, *Apology*, 190.

59. *All's Well That Ends Well*, 2.3.1–4.

60. Greenblatt, "What Shakespeare Actually Wrote."

61. Paul Yachnin, "After the Plague, Shakespeare Imagined a World Saved from Poison, Slander and the Evil Eye," *Conversation*, April 5, 2020.

62. John Florio, *The Essayes or Morall, Politike and Millitarie Discourc of Lo: Michaell de* Montaigne, . . . Now Done into English (London: Val. Sims for Edward Blount, 1603), 625, 620.

63. James Kearney, "'This Is above All Strangeness': *King Lear*, Ethics and the Phenomenology of Recognition," *Criticism* 54, no. 3 (Summer 2012): 455.

64. Fitter, "So Distribution Should Undo Excess," 849–50.

65. Christopher Hill, *Puritanism and Revolution* (New York: Schocken Books, 1964), 218.

66. Kearney, "This Is above All Strangeness," 460.

67. Jacques Derrida, *L'animal que donc je suis* (Paris: Gallée, 2006), 10–11.

68. Kiernan Ryan, *Shakespearean Tragedy* (London: Bloomsbury, 2021), 201.

69. Ryan, *Shakespearean Tragedy*, 200, 201; Fitter, "So Distribution Should Undo Excess," 854.

70. Debora K. Shuger, "Subversive Fathers and Suffering Subjects: Shakespeare and Christianity," in *Religion, Literature, and Politics in Post-Reformation England, 1540–1688*, ed. Donna B. Hamilton and Richard Strier (Cambridge, UK: Cambridge University Press, 1996), 49–50; Fitter, "So Distribution Should Undo Excess," 836–58.

71. Erika Rummel, "The Theology of Erasmus," in *The Cambridge Companion to Reformation Theology*, ed. David Bagchi and David C. Steinmetz (Cambridge, UK: Cambridge University Press, 2004), 34.

72. Desiderius Erasmus, *The First Tome or Volume of the Paraphrase of Erasmus upon the Newe Testamente*, trans. N. Udall (London: Edwarde Whitchurche, 1548), fol. lxxxi^v.

73. Margot Heinemann, "Demystifying the Mystery of State," *Shakespeare Survey* 44 (1992): 75.

74. For a valuable overview of early modern race studies, which includes a critique of the assumed universality of Shakespeare, see Peter Erickson and Kim F. Hall, "'A New Scholarly Song': Rereading Early Modern Race," *Shakespeare Quarterly* 67, no. 1 (Spring 2016): 5.

75. David Schalkwyk, "Foreword," in *South African Essays on "Universal" Shakespeare*, ed. Chris Thurman (London: Routledge, 2016), xx.

76. Majumdar, *World in a Grain of Sand*, 11.

77. Majumdar, *World in a Grain of Sand*, 141, 156, 212.

78. Younge, *Who Are We?*, 9.

79. Montaigne, *Essayes*, 6, 20, 625.

80. R. W. Dent, *Shakespeare's Proverbial Language* (Berkeley: University of California Press, 1981), 165; Montaigne, *Essayes*, 280.

81. Montaigne, *Essayes*, 280.

82. Psalm 8:4 (Geneva).

83. John Boys, *An Exposition of the Proper Psalmes Used in Our English Lyturgie* (London: Edward Griffin for William Aspley, 1617), 20–2[1].

84. Derrida, *L'animal que donc je suis*, 20

85. Jacques Derrida, *The Animal That Therefore I Am*, ed. Marie Louise Mallet, trans. David Wills (New York: Fordham University Press, 2008), 5.

86. Derrida, *L'animal que donc je suis*, 19.

87. Jacques Derrida, "Racism's Last Word," trans. Peggy Kamuf, *Critical Inquiry* 12, no. 1 (Autumn 1985): 292; Staffan Müller-Wille, "Claude Lévi-Strauss on Race, History, and Genetics," *Biosocieties* 5, no. 3 (September 2010): 342.

88. Montaigne, *Essayes*, 269, 260.

89. William Shakespeare, *King Lear*, ed. R. A. Foakes (London: Thomas Nelson and Sons, 1997), 3.2.0.1n.

2

Profiting in Babylon

Transnationalism and Typology in the Biblical Drama of the English Traveling Theater

Kevin Chovanec

In the *Esther* play included in the *Engelische Comedien und Trage-dien* (1620), a collection of plays performed by English players traveling on the Continent, the subplot offers a moment of remarkable cultural fluidity. Interspersed with scenes from the scriptural story of Esther, a German-marked peasant, Hans, contests with his wife both verbally and physically for dominance of their household. Violence and slapstick comedy, both staples of the English travelers, characterize the subplot, which links into the central plot of the Babylonian court through a rather flimsy device: Hans is charged with building the gallows, a key prop for the play's climax. Yet when Hans's son appears unexpectedly near the end of the second act, we discover that he has been in France cultivating multilingual and multicultural performance:

> SOHN: In Franckreich bin ich gewesen.
>
> HANS: Ahah/ da hab ich einen versuchten praven Sohn. Mein lieber Sohn hastu den die Frantzose gelehret?
>
> SOHN: O Ja Vater die must ich ja haben.
>
> HANS: Potz schlapperment/ mein Frantzoösscher Sohn wird zu grossen Ehren kommen/ den er die Frantzosen gelehret. Aber mein Sohn hastu den gelehret?
>
> SOHN: Gelernet? Das shehet ihr an mein Wehr und Waffen wol/ mit diesen Bogen springen verdiene ich viel Geldt.

[SON: I've been in France.

HANS: Ahah, I have such a brave, ambitious son. My dear son, did you learn French?

SON: O yes, father: I had to.

HANS: Fanatstic! My French son will come to great honor, since he's learned French. But son, what have you learned?

SOHN: Learned? I'll show you, with full display. I earned a lot of money with these arching leaps.]

Though Hans is a comic character (and eventually made a fool by his own ambition), his pride in his son's multilingualism and theatrical skill perhaps reflects a moment of ironic self-reflection from the players on their own unstable status as migrants. By learning French, Hans claims, his son has become French ("mein Frantzössicher Sohn"), which implies a certain national, ethnic, and cultural fluidity and which Hans sees as an opportunity for social mobility. The son, however, conflates learning the language with learning a performance style and in fact prioritizes the latter when he demonstrates his art to his parents. His "springen" allowed the traveling English players to demonstrate a strength of the theater, famed for its acrobatics, and the son's performed leaping inspires Hans to try to replicate the acrobatics, imagining himself performing before rulers at court: "Wer weiss hie hie kan noch wol mein Glück stehen / alssden würde ich in grosses ansehen kommen bey grossen Herren" ["Who knows how my fortune might stand, and then I'll get a great reputation from great lords"].[1] While this may simply be a joke, a peasant's delusions of grandeur, Hans's desire to perform before his prince recalls the fact that the English players performed at both popular festivals and some of the most learned courts in the empire, a reminder that wealthy and cultured dukes enjoyed the same performances (or similar, at least) witnessed by popular audiences. The scene thus translates performance as a kind of language with a specific cultural provenance (French) that is both comprehensible, obtainable, and desirable to everyone.[2]

While the English traveling theater for centuries faced critical denigration, a recent interest in early modern transnationalism and cross-cultural exchange has led to a radical reevaluation of the players' art.[3] We have recognized the porousness of the borders of early modern nations, and, moreover, we have begun to understand in more complex ways the networks of theater stretching across early modern Europe and, indeed, the globe.[4] Scholarly investigation has now turned to focus on the players' successes, to try to understand how the English travelers navigated culturally, linguistically, and religiously diverse spaces while finding ways to connect with their foreign audiences.

As we consider the shape of early modern transnationalism, however, we might heed the warning of Frederick Cooper: "It is salutary to get away from whatever tendencies there may have been to analyze social, economic, political, and cultural processes as if they took place in national and continental containers; but to adopt a language that implies there is no container at all, except the planetary one, risks defining problems in misleading ways."[5] My intention in this chapter is to place the theater of these English travelers in a religious frame, investigating how international Protestant connections and assumptions might have shaped their performance. Protestantism offers a possible framework—though, of course, not the only one—and part of this chapter will attempt to show that the traveling players both assumed and consciously constructed the social "container" of shared religion. If Hans's "Frantzössicher" son implies that nationality is constructed or performed, the play invokes a typology that makes religious identity seem much more permanent, though perhaps also never entirely stable.

This strategic use of shared religious community in the play corroborates hints of the players' foregrounding of religious identity in the archival record. Ralf Haekel, for example, has shown that the travel routes of players were often dictated by religious connections.[6] We know, too, that the players performed several biblical stories, both histories and tragedies, engaging not only the long tradition of medieval drama but also the popularity of biblical drama in Lutheran lands, where biblical works had long been used to spread the message of the Reformation and increase biblical literacy.[7] Indeed, the prevalence of biblical drama in the players' repertoire, especially compared to the relative dearth of biblical drama on the London stage in the period, strongly suggests that players recognized religious performance as key to their success. As we will see, however, the popularity of the English travelers on the Continent corresponded directly to an increase in the popularity of biblical theater in London, hinting that migration and travel may have shaped the London stage, countering the traditional view that the relationship between London and the traveling theater was unidirectional. Yet despite the centrality of religion in much of the work of the English players on the Continent, the biblical works in their repertoires have been understudied. In part, perhaps, this stems from early interest in linking translations to major playwrights in London; it may also come from the players' earned reputation for bawdiness, which has distracted from the biblical elements of their work. However, we still have not adequately explored the ways in which religious identification facilitated the transnational cultural exchange caused by English players on the Continent.

In this chapter, I would like to suggest that the players consciously recognized the "cultural translation" involved in bringing their art to the Continent and in fact worked to efface national and ethnic identities in the face of a wider, shared religious culture. They reframed themselves in their travel not as vagrants—as players in the period were often considered—but as migrants, invoking a shared Protestant history through the typology of the biblical play. At the same time, their experience of travel reshaped their presentations of scriptural history, influencing their reading of Esther's exile, as we can see by placing the work in the context of the dozens of Esther plays produced during the period. Like the Book of Esther itself, this play offers a strategy for successfully navigating life as a migrant in a complex, multinational empire.

Typology and the Shape of Transnational Thought

Even a cursory investigation of the playtexts of the English players on the Continent reveals a marked reliance on biblical and, more generally, religious drama. In addition to *Esther*, the players performed *The Destruction of Sodom and Gomorrah, Abraham and Lot, The Prodigal Son, Susanna* (based on apocryphal material), *A Play of the Prophet Daniel, A Comedy of the Prophet Jonah, Of a Rich Man and Lazarus,* and *David and Bathsheba* (based on the play by George Peele), besides unnamed "geistlichen komodien." This obviously contrasts with the repertoire performed on the London stage, as I will return to shortly, where, leading into the 1590s, troupes had gone decades without premiering a single biblical play; but it mirrors theatrical practice on the Continent, particularly in the German lands, where biblical drama was popular.[8] While scriptural theater had a long history throughout Europe, the Reformation reworked both its subjects and purposes. Still aimed at inculcating ethics and proper belief into the populace, biblical drama was recognized by humanists and Protestants as an ideal medium for encouraging their reforms. In the preface to his 1534 Apocrypha, Luther noted that the Hebrew Bible and Apocrypha contained fit dramatic material, and, following his lead, these subjects were frequently mined by Protestant writers.[9] Although England, especially later in the sixteenth century, had a less robust tradition of staging biblical stories, more appeared on stage than is sometimes recognized, and the English, like their continental coreligionists, demonstrated a marked preference for the stories of the Hebrew Bible, shifting away from the Corpus Christi and Passion plays of the medieval period.[10]

When the traveling players performed a biblical work, they invoked a vast semantic field of meaning that was shared across Europe. Not only were biblical stories more familiar to early moderns than to us, they implied a way of understanding history and a complex tangle of political meaning that has since been lost. As Kevin Killeen has argued, biblical allusion and exegesis came laden with "a heavy political and ideological freight," a language to which we are now often deaf, and the same resonances were conveyed when the well-known stories were interpreted on stage.[11] Typology, especially in Protestant lands, became a primary tool for engaging with biblical material, the "basis of Reformed hermeneutics."[12]

The Book of Esther is set during the Babylonian captivity, when King Ahasuerus, drunk with wine, seeks to replace his disobedient wife. He surveys several potential future queens and chooses Esther, a Jewish exile and orphan being raised by her cousin, Mordecai. Throughout the work, Mordecai's foil is Haman, a powerful member of the court who, for early modern audiences, stands in as the quintessential wicked counselor, and indeed, Haman strives to turn the Babylonian king against both Mordecai and the Jewish community. Through Esther's diplomacy and Mordecai's faithfulness to the king, especially in uncovering an attempted regicide, the Jewish orphan and her cousin avert a threatened genocide of the Jewish exiles and instead secure influence in Persia.

In part because of its wide appeal, Esther's story was well-known both in England and on the Continent, appearing in plays, epic poems, occasional verse, pamphlets, and sermons. Not only did the work promise that God's people would, in the end, overcome their enemies, it did so in a work filled with suspense, dramatic reversals, and even comedy. Like so many of the plays performed by the traveling players, *Esther* courted the cultural overlap between the peoples of Northern Europe, their shared foundational texts and beliefs. In the period, at least twelve Esther plays were published in the German lands, and another ten in France.[13]

Through typology, the Esther story became not simply an account of Jewish history but one of the most important resources for understanding moments in which the church faced persecution. Protestants viewed history as repeating, layered, and providential; thus, the stories of the Hebrew Bible were often repeated in the Christian one and could equally be applied throughout church history up to the present. Personal lessons might be drawn from these histories, but at the same time, spectators might allegorically recognize the cosmic struggle between God's people and their enemies. Esther, like most biblical figures, was a multifaceted type, employed often in the early modern period in sometimes contradictory ways.[14] She was an exemplar to noble women, a virtuous queen and thus a frequent parallel to Elizabeth I (as well as noble women in other Protestant countries).[15] She was also, however, born an orphan in the precarious situation of the Jews in Babylon, and her exile therefore broadened her exemplarity to a variety of social classes. Scholars have been particularly interested in the ways Esther was employed by women writers as they worked with biblical characters to carve out autonomy and authority.[16] As a wise and capable ruler and an obedient wife, Esther managed to navigate these sometimes competing roles successfully and demonstrated that God raised heroic women to lead his people.

Beyond the eponymous character's exemplarity, a typological interpretation of the Book of Esther assured readers that God would protect his people, even in the most desperate times. Because of the dire threat of genocide faced by the Jewish exiles, the book became an important touchstone for moments in which Christians felt besieged in the early modern period, especially times in which Protestants felt threatened by the success of the Counter-Reformation. In English versions of the Esther narrative, for example, including a Tudor interlude titled *The Godly Queene Hester*, and in the paratextual apparatus to the Geneva Bible, links are drawn explicitly between Jews in the Esther story and English Protestants.[17]

Yet while some studies of the typological link between Esther and Queen Elizabeth have read the story in the context of elect nationalism, these English readings of Esther tend to emphasize an isolationist element in the texts, a feature of these early modern works that contrasts sharply with the biblical story. Indeed, as scholars have stressed, Esther in the Bible is best understood in the contexts of diaspora. In S. D. Goitein's oft-quoted formulation, "Esther is an Exilic Book, written in the Exile, for the Exile."[18] Even when this has been contested, scholarship continues to place diaspora at the center of Esther's meaning and significance.[19] In fact, as many scholars point out, Esther holds a unique position among Hebrew Bible texts in never mentioning Israel, Jerusalem, or the Temple; in part, this has been read as symptomatic of diasporic experience.[20]

Considering this central aspect of the biblical work, the play, especially removed from England, speaks less to national chauvinism and more to the experience of dislocation. While the traveling players were economic opportunists rather than religious exiles, they were able with this story to invoke a rich, shared Protestant heritage of displacement and migration, a unifying typology that connected them with their audiences in the empire, highlighted the primary importance of religious identity, and promoted kindness to "strangers." They were also able to imagine, through Mordecai and Esther, a successful and productive life as strangers in the empire.

These strains of Hebrew-Bible thought, moreover, were not unique to the players. Rather, as several scholars have argued, exile was central to early modern Protestant experience and belief. Geert Janssen, for example, has shown the ways in which Dutch families created social and cultural identities based on the experience and memory of exile in the sixteenth century, ways of understanding their family's place in the republic that lasted for centuries after the original displacement.[21] More diffusely, the idea of the church in exile, the church as a small remnant of the holy continually besieged by the wicked, structured the lives of pious Protestants and even, according to Heiko Obermann, informed Calvin's theology.[22] Protestant writers discussing Esther in the early modern period invariably read the Protestant experience into the Hebrew Bible's account; as Pierre Merlin notes during the French Wars of Religion, experience characterizes the true church: "the state and condition of the Church in this world, to wit, to be dispersed here and there under the power and dominion of infidel Kings: to be basely accounted of, and hated of ambitious Courtiers."[23] Even the setting of the Esther narrative, the Babylonian captivity, was a dominant metaphor for Protestants living under Roman Catholic rule, first adopted by Luther and popular throughout Protestant lands.

Especially during times of interconfessional conflict, when Protestants feared a resurgent Rome, the Esther narrative offered hope of a final victory. As typology always does, the Protestant reading of the play creates additional layers, and both Esther and the Babylonian Jews mirrored the current state of Protestants within a multinational and multicultural Holy Roman Empire. The players of the *Esther* play in the *Engelische Comedien und Tragedien* seem to have been especially eager to stress these connections, highlighting the ways in which their German spectators aligned with the Jews in the biblical story. For example, they invoked the context of multinational empire immediately. In his opening speech, King Ahasuerus notes proudly that he rules "von India, biss in Mohren / uber 123.

Laender."[24] Ferdinand II and the Hapsburgs might have made similar—or even grander—claims. Throughout the play, the players implicitly reference the context of the Holy Roman Empire during the Thirty Years' War, continually tying it to the Babylon portrayed in *Esther* and suggesting parallels.

To most early moderns, the lesson to be learned from Esther was that God would succor his church, even when conditions seemed most desperate, a message often repeated in the pulpits. During times of interconfessional warfare, Protestants in England often identified coreligionists on the Continent as part of the same religious community, members of the same church (despite obvious internal discord). Obadiah Sedgwick, in a sermon printed during the early years of the English Civil War (1643), exemplifies this reading and demonstrates the kind of transnational assumptions both spectators and performers might have held of the biblical tragedy. For Sedgwick, *Esther* teaches above all the lesson of God's protection of his church: "The Church of God may fall into such an eclipse, into such an hour of temptation, that not only in the insulting fancies of the enemies, but also in all the commentaries of humane Reason, it may not only seem, but really be in the very way, nay upon the very brink of destruction . . . God will step in and prevent that."[25] Sedgwick assumes that Israel stands in perfectly for the church, the same community projected backward in time. Indeed, when giving scriptural examples that prove his claim, he lists the siege of Leiden (during the Dutch Revolt) alongside events and people from both the Hebrew and Christian Bibles. Recent history offered Sedgwick perhaps the clearest example—at least, the most well-known example—of God's enemies subverting his church, as the Catholics had attempted to do for the last millennium: "What should I speak of the defeatings & boundings of the Antichristian plots and furies, which have been acting above these thousand years; and notwithstanding all their lyings, decrees, devices, attempts, burnings, murtherings, resolves, confederacies, assistances with the power of Emperours, Kings, Rulers, they hitherto cannot, nor ever shall be able to destroy the Church of Christ."[26] For Sedgwick, this patterned history collapses different regional struggles into the same divine type, the same conflict repeated again and again in each generation.

Religious warfare is central to the type for many commentators, a lens through which the story of Esther was read and adapted. Merlin, for example, directly relates the narrative to his experience of religious war in France, aligning Haman with the Duke of Guise: "Therefore Haman is not yet dead, but his cruell minde reviveth in an infant number of men who being bewitched with the blasphemous voyces of Antichrist, craftily coloure, perswade themselves, that there is none other zeale, no other godliness, but in sheading the bloud of all those who consent not to their impieties."[27] The story works repeatedly, able to exemplify Catholic violence in different regional contexts because "in Aman there is to bee seene a most perfect paterne of a malicious & subtile enimie unto the Church."[28] Because of this background of confessional conflict, Esther also became associated with an interventionist Protestant sentiment in England. John Stockwood dedicates his translation of Johannes Brenz's *Discourse upon the Booke of Esther* (1584), for example, to Sir Francis Walsingham and praises him for his investment in the Protestant cause abroad: "the painefull indevour and diligent travaile of your Honor, and sondry others of your place, for the welfare of Sion, and for the prosperitie of Ierusalem."[29] Esther offered a type, then, that highlighted transnational religious affiliations and encouraged the English—and their continental coreligionists—to conceptualize themselves as part of this transnational Protestant community.

The play's publication twice during the Thirty Years' War, in 1620 and 1624, is particularly salient because the play often adopts the same language of religious war found in commentaries and pamphlets about the war. Certainly Mardocheus, Esther's cousin and caretaker and a hero of the play, preaches a message that would have resonated with Protestants during their early defeats. When he discovers Haman's plan to murder the Jewish exiles, he calls to God for protection from his church in a way that foregrounds the common Protestant conception of the church as a poor and oppressed flock:

> O Gott lass doch nicht unsere Feinde so trotziglich uber uns triumphiren, O strafe du die Hoffart, so werden wir nicht umbs Leben kommen, du bist ja aller Hoffertigen Feind . . . Herr du bist der ewige Allmächtige König, und wann dein Zorn ergrimmet, so muss der gantze Erdboden und alles was drauff is, erzittern. Niemand kan doch wieder deinen Willen thun . . . O Herr verlass nicht Israel du wirst es nicht verlassen.[30]
>
> [Oh God, do not let our enemies triumph over us so proudly; punish the courtly pride, so that we don't lose our lives. You are the enemy of all the proud . . . Lord, you are the eternal and almighty king, and the ground and all the world shakes when you become angry. No man can do anything against your will. O Lord, do not forsake Israel; you will not forsake it.]

The prayer is very traditional, noting God's providential control of history and his faithfulness in ensuring the triumph of his people over their enemies and asking for his protection; the familiarity of this message alone invites both the sympathy and the identification of the audience.

Mardocheus offers nearly the same speech twice, two of the longest passages in the text, and each time reminds God and the spectators both of his power and his past protection of his people: "O Herr verachte dein Häufflein nicht / das du aus Egypten geführet hast / erhöre unser Gebet und sey uns gnädig."[31] Even if this is all common, the familiarity of the message—the same one spectators would have heard frequently from the pulpit—and especially the performance itself reinforce the typological reading. Indeed, during the Thirty Years' War, as historians have shown, days of repentance and prayer were common in German lands as a means for mitigating the war's devastation.[32] Though often inconsistent in form, mixing the recitation of prayers, hymns, and scriptural reading, the liturgies for these days of prayer often follow a similar pattern, derived from Hebrew Bible models, first calling for the people to recognize their own sins, then acknowledging the church's enemies, and finally offering a comforting reminder of God's power and protection.[33] In the play, Mardocheus's response to the threat of genocide mirrors the Protestant response to the war, though of course, since both have the shared source of the Bible, this does not necessarily imply a direct influence; but it does suggest that German spectators might have been especially primed to see their own suffering reflected in the experience of the Jewish exiles.

The traveling performances of this well-known providential narrative, therefore, offer a reading of history that unites performers and spectators, and, through the use of biblical typology, the players solidified and even re-created a shared culture, drawing on the ritual practices of theater. As in medieval biblical drama, the players in performance drew the audiences into a repeating and patterned history that encouraged them to identify with their English (as well as French and Dutch) coreligionists. The play, in fact, registers the concept of sacred time by uniting the subplot with the main story, when the clearly German-marked peasant Hans (with his French son) visits the court of their king, the Persian Ahasuerus, addressing him directly.[34] The Hebrew Bible story is brought into the early modern moment often in the play: Ahasuerus is a "könig" and characters eat a kind of milk porridge with sugar. Hans is excited, as we have seen, that his son has been raised in France, blurring the story's temporality. This narrative of Esther, in its very generalizability, becomes a pattern that fits all interconfessional conflict, the same story told in various regions; it becomes part of the collective memory of the Protestant church.

The function of this typological pattern corresponds with what a large body of scholarship has termed "cultural memory," the narratives and meanings handed down that provide a "connective structure" for a culture, particularly through repetition and "presentification" of the past. For Jan Assmann, for example, these kinds of shared, repeated foundational narratives offer "a common area of experience, expectation, and action whose connecting force provides them with trust and with orientation."[35] While scholars of cultural memory have generally examined cultures in which ethnic and religious groups fully overlapped, for these players regional and religious identities were clearly and markedly distinct. The act of remembering itself, placing the Esther narrative of exile and salvation before the German audiences, argues for the primary importance of the religious community, as in performing these shared histories the players attempted to solidify the connections between English players and German spectators. In a creative and adaptive act, the players' performances could serve to imagine a shared and bounded community that ignored ethnic and regional differences.

In the German lands, the history of theatrical versions of Esther similarly prepared German audiences for a Protestant typological reading of the play. Although the story was popular across confessions, with a version produced also by the Jesuits, several early Esther plays by Protestant writers, from Hans Sachs to Thomas Naeogeorgus, incorporated Protestant messaging. Naeogeorgus's work, while not polemic in itself, inspired a tradition that translated and reworked his play to specifically counter Rome. Naeogeorgus focused his *Hamanus* (1543), as the title implies, around Haman, and when this Latin play was translated into German by later writers, Haman was often linked explicitly to the Catholics. In his German translation, *Haman. Die schöne und seer tröstlich Histori Hester* (1543), for example, Johannes Chryseus adapted the story for Protestant polemic; Wolffgang Kuntzel's play, *Die Schöne und Seer Tröstlich Histori Esther* (1564), a piecemeal work that compiles parts of Chryesus's translation along with parts of Hans Sachs's play and another version by Andreas Pfeilschmidt, includes an introduction that implicitly compares Catholics to Haman and praises Luther.

Indeed, this compositive, collaborative character of early modern drama suggests another reason biblical tragedy may have been quite congenial to the traveling players, reflecting the shared tradition and borrowing that allowed players to adapt these stories. The piecemeal character of the traveling theater was recognized even by contemporaries, as Fynes Moryson described the "pieces and patches" they performed; but often the discussion of this theater neglects the fact that they were participating in various traditions—especially biblical drama—that similarly encouraged appropriation, reuse, and adaptation of other works.[36]

The story of Esther did not only connect Protestant audiences through this typological reading, however; it also seems to have catered especially to the migratory life of the players, who, like the Jews in the story, are distant from their homeland and hoping to successfully integrate into a foreign context. Of course, the Jewish exiles had been forced from Israel, while the English travelers were economic opportunists; yet both navigate a foreign context as "strangers" hoping to thrive in a multicultural empire. When Sedgwick expatiates upon the way the wicked Haman discusses the Jews, he uses the same terminology often applied to migratory players: "That they were an infamous people (There is, saith he, in chap. 3.8. a certaine scattered and dispersed people) as if they have been a company only of poore, wandring, shifting, and shuffling vagabonds."[37] Early modern players, of course, were often denigrated as "vagabonds," whether they were traveling throughout England or on the Continent.[38] Similar language is used in the travelers' play, when Haman tells the king that the Jews are "ein betriegliches Volck . . . sie leben nicht nach des Königes / sonder nach ihrer sonderlichen und eigenen Gestzen" ("a deceitful people who do not live according to the king, but rather their own special laws").[39] While the Jews in the play are condemned as migratory exiles, their position as outsiders allows them to uncover the court's corruption and even save the life of the king. In staging a play that celebrated "vagrants" and exiles, the players reflected on their own situation in the empire, aligning themselves with the powerful myth of Protestant exile. Through this experience of travel and migration, as we will see, the players not only engaged with but even reworked this key typological text of Protestantism, resulting in a much more irenic and open reading of the scriptural narrative.

Protean Nationality

The national fluidity comically celebrated in the play's subplot, then, drew on wider habits of typological reading: the Esther story invoked migrant experience, as well as the tension between national and religious identities. As we know from archival records, the troupe that performed *Esther*, led by Robert Browne and perhaps associated with Queen Anne's Men in London, crossed confessional lines frequently and performed their plays in both Protestant and Catholic contexts.[40] If they indeed figuratively aligned themselves with the exiled Jews in the story, as the play invites us to speculate, they might also have experienced the kind of cultural fluidity represented in the play at those times that called upon them to downplay or hide national or religious identities. Esther, far from Jerusalem, faced a similar dilemma, and the players' reading of Esther suggests the facility with which an identity might be concealed. In one much-discussed moment of the text, for example, Mordecai advises Esther to keep her Jewish identity secret. In the words of the players' version, "Sage nicht an deine Freundschafft / und dass du auss Jüden Geschlecht gebohren" ("Say nothing of your friends, or that you were born into a Jewish family").[41] The play draws out Esther's ability to disguise her Jewish identity, waiting until the final, climactic scene for her to reveal her connection to Mordecai and the Jewish community. Just as in the subplot, in which the nationality of Hans's son is both uncertain and easily malleable, Jewish identity in the story of Esther is hidden, something that must be revealed or else remains unknown. This, Elsie Stern has argued, stands in contrast to other biblical narratives, which insist upon a clear and recognizable cultural and even ontological distinction between Israelites and non-Israelites.[42] Moreover, we find in this example that both religious and national/ethnic identity are not easily discerned. Like the Book of Esther, the play neither stages Jewish ceremonies nor references Jewish belief. Jewishness seems based in little other than the familial relations that structure Esther's loyalties.

Paradoxically, this very fluidity is generally interpreted by critics as a central anxiety—even a critique of diasporic Jews—in the biblical text.[43] If one might so easily pass as Babylonian, how do the Jews in diaspora retain their cultural distinctiveness? Similarly, what happens to the players' identity as they pass through Catholic and Protestant lands? At what point does this cultural fluidity, the ability to so easily "become" French, become threatening or problematic? Even in their defense of Esther's silence, early modern religious writers recognized this inherent tension, the fine line between pragmatism and Nicodemism. In Pierre Merlin's opinion, "It is indeed a high point of wisedome, not rashly to bewray that which may breede us hatred, envie, and contempt: but againe to denie the truth, & to dissemble what religion we professe when we are demaunded, is a treacherie, which redoundeth to the dishonor of God."[44] Not only might this cultural fluidity be seen as a threat to those in power, causing rulers to fear the unstable borders of identity and belonging—exactly the threat Haman claims the Jews pose—it could also cause anxiety for those among the marginalized group hoping to preserve distinction. The scriptural account is sometimes read by modern scholars as a work of satire produced by religious writers in Jerusalem who feared that the diasporic Jews were losing their distinctiveness and even risked becoming Babylonian.[45] Navigating the diasporic identity is difficult, and the play, like the biblical story, must set out a strategy for acculturation, a plan for both thriving in exile and yet maintaining one's own religious integrity. If the movement through various regional contexts, the players' cultural facility, could be staged as a positive, then it also hinted at the dangers inherent in this protean identity of playing.

For the players, however, Esther and Mordecai remained exemplars, migrants able to successfully navigate sometimes conflicting identities to find success. The performers seem to have consciously exploited the diasporic reading of the text, and yet at the same time their own experience of travel in the Holy Roman Empire shaped their interpretation of the biblical story. The players' version minimizes the bloodiness of the original plot, and in so doing renders the Esther story a much less apocalyptic and anti-Catholic text than other Protestant versions in the period. An ecumenical strand characterizes the play, aiming at a more irenic and inclusive kind of performance while still courting the Protestant refugee imaginary. In part, this is accomplished simply through the play's comedy, alleviating the polemics of the type and perhaps releasing some of the tension of a fluid, composite identity, the perceived threat of porous cultural borders and unstable nationality. As scholars have noted, this comedy was certainly a feature of the original biblical narrative (though this is generally not recognized in the early modern commentaries on the narrative): caricature, absurd and improbable events, verbal play, and practical jokes, as well as the general structure of the genre, all mark the biblical text.[46] It has been considered both a farce and a satire.[47] Including the comic subplot, in which both ethnic fluidity and gender hierarchy are the subject of jokes, further undermines the seriousness of the main plot and draws out these comic elements.

Yet the players are more pointed in their reinterpretation of the Esther narrative. In addition to the exaggeration of the latent comic elements, their version of the story excises some of the more controversial and violent material. Perhaps the most significant change in the play radically reshapes the end of the narrative. According to the scriptural text, the Jews killed over seventy thousand of those who rose against them, including women and children.[48] If at times this vengeance troubled early modern writers (as it does modern critics), it also, especially during interconfessional conflict, could attract them. Francis Quarles, for example, expands on the violence at length:

> That with the purple stream the thirsty soyle
> O'rflow'd: & on the pavement (drown'd with blood)
> Where never was before, they rais'd a flood:
> There lies a headlesse body, there a limb
> Newly dis-joynted from the trunk of him
> That there lies groaning; here, a gasping head
> Cropt from his neighbours shoulders; there, half dead
> Full heaps of bodies.[49]

For Quarles, this explosion of fitting justice against the church's oppressors represents the climax of the story. His poem dwells at length on the physical results of this violence, the severed limbs and headless corpses, even the gratuitous image of the gasping head bereft of a body. In the German and neo-Latin plays that stage the full biblical story, this scene of violence is similarly often the climax in the action; Hans Sachs, for example, extends his play to a seventh act focused entirely on the battle.[50]

The English travelers' play excises this bloody ending, however, and subjects only Haman and his sons to the death on the gallows that he had prepared for Mordecai. In fact, Mordecai in the play even pleads for the lives of Haman's sons, unwilling to see them subjected to punishment for their father's crimes. (This contrasts sharply with, for example, Andreas Pfeilschmidt's *Ein hübsch und Christlich Spiel des gantzen Buchs Ester* (1555), in which Esther herself requests that Haman's sons be hanged.) The players do refer to Ahasuerus's command that the Jewish subjects living in Babylon might defend themselves.[51] Yet this version of the story lacks the retributive thrust of the biblical account, and the violence is never staged. Instead, the play quickly moves back into the comic subplot. Rather than portraying the confessional violence, the final scene stages a wise king reconciling Hans and his wife, once again foregrounding the slapstick and bawdiness of the extrabiblical subplot. Immediately after the king decrees a right of defense for the exiles, for example, we see Hans's wife's confusion over what a queen is ("Königin? Was ist das ein Mann oder ein Fraw?") and whether a king or Bürgermeister is more powerful.[52] Even the marital tension gets resolved at the end, as the king rules that Hans and his wife might be separated by day while remaining good friends at night, in some ways simply circumventing the question of domestic authority.

It is tempting to speculate that the players chose to dampen the violence of the conflict in the play—in which most contemporaries would have read the interconfessional strife between Catholics and Protestants—because of the context of the Thirty Years' War and the players' experience on the road. The players, by so clearly invoking the diasporic context of the Esther narrative and its typological connection to transnational Protestantism, appealed to Protestant solidarity while also manipulating the meaning of exile in Esther to fit a more ecumenical model that facilitated their travel. In fact, the players reimagine all attempts to foment religious division as external threats aimed surreptitiously at undermining the stability of the kingdom and, more directly, the ruler. Religious toleration and coexistence allow for peace and prosperity, while persecution of a minority inspires conflict that eventually threatens the throne. To stress this point, the play clarifies Haman's hidden intentions by drawing on material from the Esther Apocrypha: by attempting to set the king's Babylonian and Jewish subjects against each other, Haman (a Macedonian councilor) had aimed to subject the Persian empire to the Macedonians. ("Alssdenn meynte der Bösewicht das Reich allein zu uberkommen / und dann dieser Perser Reich an die Macedonier zu bingen" ["Then the villain intended to conquer the kingdom alone, and then bring the Persian empire under the control of the Macedonians"]).[53] This paralleled the Counter-Reformation forces that encouraged the extirpation of Protestantism from Europe, as Protestant early modern commentators often noted. In Merlin's account, Roman Catholics have, like Haman, "assembled themselves, and bound themselves by oath, to oppresse, spoyle and destroy the rest of the Church, not onely in France or England, but in all places of the world, where the name of Christ Iesus is purely called on, and his Gospell sincerely taught."[54] But then even this kind of division, the play hints, might aim to undermine the authority of the empire and subject the king's/emperor's people to foreign rule—Macedonia in the Esther narrative, or, in the case of the Holy Roman Empire, Rome. The players could thus use traditional, Protestant readings of the type to imagine a tolerant empire, peaceful in the face of differing confessions.

The politics of the play, like the politics of the biblical book more generally, are markedly conservative and adamantly supportive of the monarch. Throughout the play, the story offers a pointed critique of courtly ambition but never attacks the king himself; quite traditionally, the play exculpates the king and lays the blame for the plot to murder the Jewish exiles on the wicked counselor, Haman. For example, the play stresses Haman's hubris.[55] The wicked Haman often soliloquizes on his own pride and scheming in the manner of an early and simplistic vice figure. In the end, the king, in a fitting act of justice, sentences him to be executed on the very gallows he had prepared for Mordecai and soliloquizes on the moral: "Den dein Hoffart bringt dich umbs Leben/ nun siehestu das Gott im Himmel die Stolzen niedrigen und die Demuetigen erheben kan" ("Because your pride leads you to death, now you see that God in heaven can lower the proud and raise up the humble").[56] The German "Hoffart" here is a particular kind of pride, a courtly and Machiavellian scheming that characterizes a desire for power in an underling who has no just claim to the throne. This courtier ambition, the play suggests, was then (and is, implicitly, still in the early modern period) the root of much suffering, but it will eventually be repaid in kind. Compared to the biblical passage, which assigns Esther direct credit for overcoming Haman, however, the tone seems to purposefully obscure agency, shifting "Hoffart" to the subject of the sentence, implying that Esther herself remains reluctant to take credit for even Haman's fate.

In addition to shifting the blame onto Haman, the wicked counselor, the players offer a rehabilitation of King Ahasuerus. While most early modern commentators saw Ahasuerus as a foolish, drunken, and heathen king, the play raises him to the role of a good, almost Christian king, highlighting his wise policies toward the Jewish people and his ability to reconcile both divided nations and a commoner and his wife. His imperial policy focuses chiefly on peace, for he knows that his good subjects are peace-loving:

> Wiewol wir mächtig seyn und groß auff Erden / haben wir
> dennoch unser Gewalt nicht wollen uberheben / sondern meistes
> theils beflissen gnädiglich und sanfft zu regieren / un den lieben
> Friede / dessen sich jederman von Hertzen erfrewet / zu halten.[57]
> (Although we are great and mighty on earth, still we do not
> wish to overreach our power, but we strive for the most part to gov-
> ern graciously and gently, and to keep the peace, which everyone
> desires heartily.)

This tolerant and rather disinterested king would permit the travel of Protestants even in Catholic lands, and, more broadly, remind audiences of the more irenic Hapsburg rulers who consistently tried to downplay religious divisions.[58] Early performances, during the life of Rudolf II, could have been seen as celebrating the irenic leader, while performances during the Thirty Years' War might have encouraged Ferdinand to return to the more religiously tolerant policies of his forebears. Once again drawing connections between the Babylonian context and recent history, then, the play suggests a thoughtful irenicism that would allow not merely the Jews in Babylon but also the English players in the empire to flourish in foreign spaces.

Conclusion: Migration and the London Theater

As this chapter has argued, the materials of the Esther play provided opportunities for the players to elide nationality with a focus on shared religious community. We might even say that within this account of exile, the play offered a strategy for succeeding as migrants, a tolerant and irenic rewriting of the Book of Esther that still courted Protestant solidarity. Of course, the traveling theater's plays, as scholars have shown, were rarely if ever performed in whole; they were cut and edited for each new performance, making the typological reading exceedingly difficult to recover.[59] We know, also, that performances could change drastically between Catholic and Protestant lands, as could the political significance of the Esther story.[60] We can never fully overcome the erasure of performance in the archive, but from the hints that remain, as I have argued, we might begin to uncover how the English players ingratiated themselves in foreign lands and performed solidarity with their coreligionists.

For theater historians, this dynamic fluidity of the players' text is perhaps most interesting in its connection back to the London stage. Although no biblical drama premiered in the middle decades of Elizabeth's reign, stories drawn from the scriptures began reappearing in the late 1580s. There was, in fact, something of a flourishing of biblical drama late in Elizabeth's reign, with at least twelve biblical plays premiering between 1590 and 1602, including a version of Esther, *Hester and Ahasuerus* (1594), that is no longer extant.[61] This resurgence of biblical material on the London stage has presented a scholarly enigma, and while cultural factors inside England might explain in part the renewed interest, perhaps the success of biblical plays in performance by the English travelers also played a role. As Annaliese Connolly has noted, most of these biblical plays (including Esther) belonged to the Admiral's Men, which was also the troupe associated with early performance on the Continent.[62] In fact, *Hester and Ahasuerus* was performed on June 5, 1594, along with *The Jew of Malta* and *Titus Andronicus*, both of which were also in Robert Browne's repertoire—the player whom scholars have most often connected with the texts in *Engelische Comedien und Tragedien* (which also contains *Titus*). The dates of this return to the Bible for plots and plays, 1590 to 1602, correspond exactly to the early years of the traveling troupes. This investment in biblical drama certainly prepared players in the Admiral's Men well for performance on the Continent, where biblical drama was much more popular, though we might also wonder to what extent the travelers' experience with the continental Protestant drama led to this reemergence of biblical plays in England.

The biblical book of Esther has been described as a book of identity in crisis; in many ways, the English traveling players recognized and exploited the scriptural narrative's ambiguities around ethnic, national, and religious identities, using the cultural fluidity inherent in the biblical story to insinuate themselves in the courts and cities of the Holy Roman Empire.[63] By exploring how the early modern traveling players employed transnational identities, self-consciously constructing the frames through which their audiences might interpret them, we might better understand not only how the players so successfully navigated these international spaces but also the ways in which travel, more broadly, shaped the early modern theater, which, especially in the last decade of the sixteenth century, was not simply a collection of isolated, national theaters but rather part of a densely connected transnational network.

NOTES

1. "Esther," in *Engelische Comedien und Tragedien*, ed. Manfred Brauneck, vol. 1 (Berlin: Walter de Gruyter, 1970), 38–39.

2. Work over the recent decades, building on several centuries of theater history, has unpacked the style and characteristics of this theater. Anston Bosman, for example, has explored "intercultural" facets of the theater ("Renaissance Intertheater and the Staging of Nobody," *English Literary History* 71, no. 3 [Fall 2004]: 559–85); M. A. Katritzky has unpacked the prominence of the theater's clown ("'A Plague o' These Pickle Herring': From London Drinkers to European Stage Clown," *Renaissance Shakespeare/Shakespeare Renaissances: Proceedings of the Ninth World Shakespeare Congress* (Newark: University of Delaware Press, 2014), 159–68) as well as the role of women within the theater (M. A. Katritzky, *Women, Medicine and Theatre 1500–1750* [New York: Routledge, 2017], 271–82); and George Oppitz-Trotman, in the most recent book-length study, has centered circulation (economic,

religious, cultural) and the ambiguity of travel to reevaluate the theater's larger role in key issues of the period, from the secularization of drama to the changing economy (*Stages of Loss: The English Comedians and Their Reception* [Oxford: Oxford University Press, 2020]).

3. See, for example, Bosman, "Renaissance Intertheater," 559–85.

4. Robert Henke and Eric Nicholson, "Introduction," *Transnational Mobilities in Early Modern Theater*, ed. Robert Henke and Eric Nicholson (Burlington, VT: Ashgate, 2014), 6.

5. Frederick Cooper, *Colonialism in Question: Theory, Knowledge, History* (Berkeley: University of California Press, 2005), 91–92.

6. Ralf Haekel, *Die Englischen Komödianten in Deutschland: Eine Einführung in die Ursprünge des deutschen Berufsschauspiels* (Heidelberg: Universitätsverlag Winter, 2004), 11.

7. Mark Chinca, "Biblical Drama," in *Encyclopedia of German Literature*, ed. Matthias Konzett (Chicago: Fitzroy Dearborn, 2000).

8. Ruth Harriett Blackburn, *Biblical Drama under the Tudors* (The Hague: De Gruyter Mouton, 1971). On the other hand, outside of London, as Paul Whitfield White has shown, biblical plays with Hebrew Bible patriarchs, Passion narratives, and the mystery cycles continued long past the Reformation in provincial areas (*Drama and Religion in English Provincial Society, 1485–1660* [Cambridge, UK: Cambridge University Press, 2008]). "But it mirrors": Chinca, "Biblical Drama," 101.

9. Chinca, "Biblical Drama," 101.

10. Louise B. Wright, "The Scriptures and the Elizabethan Stage," *Modern Philology* 26, no. 1 (August 1928): 47–56.

11. Kevin Killeen, "Hanging up Kings: The Political Bible in Early Modern England," *Journal of the History of Ideas* 72 (October 2011): 549.

12. Adrian Streete, ed., *Early Modern Drama and the Bible: Contexts and Readings, 1570–1625* (New York: Palgrave, 2011), 13.

13. Frank Ardolino, "Hans and Hammon: Dekker's Use of Hans Sachs and 'Purim' in *The Shoemaker's Holiday*," *Medieval and Renaissance Drama in England* 14 (2001): 151.

14. Saralyn Ellen Summer, "'Like Another Esther': Literary Representations of Queen Esther in Early Modern England" (PhD diss., Georgia State University, 2005).

15. Birgit Frank, *Assuerus und Esther am Burgunderhof: Zur Rezeption des Buches Esther in den Niederlanden (1450 bis 1530)* (Berlin: Gebr. Mann Verlag, 1998).

16. See, for example, Alison Thorne, "The Politics of Female Supplication in the Book of Esther," in *Biblical Women in Early Modern Literary Culture 1550–1700*, ed. Victoria Brownlee and Laura Gallagher (Manchester, UK: Manchester University Press, 2016), 95–110; Michelle Ephraim, *Reading the Jewish Woman on the Elizabethan Stage* (Burlington, VT: Ashgate, 2008).

17. Chanita Goodblatt, *Jewish and Christian Voices in English Reformation Biblical Drama: Enacting Family and Monarchy* (New York: Routledge, 2018), 29.

18. S. D. Goitein, *Bible Studies* (Tel Aviv: Yavney, 1957), 62.

19. Elsie R. Stern, "Esther and the Politics of Diaspora," *Jewish Quarterly Review* 100, no.1 (Winter 2010): 25–53; Joshua J. Adler, "The Hidden Message of the Book of Esther: Assimilation Is Not the Way to Salvation," *Jewish Bible Quarterly* 43, no. 4 (October–December 2015): 246–49.

20. Stern, "Esther and the Politics of Diaspora," 26.

21. Geert H. Janssen, "The Republic of the Refugees: Early Modern Migrations and the Dutch Experience," *Historical Journal* 60, no. 1 (March 2017): 233–52; Johannes Müller, *Exile Memories and the Dutch Revolt: The Narrated Diaspora, 1550–1750* (Leiden: Brill, 2016), 203–5.

22. Heiko Oberman, *John Calvin and the Reformation of the Refugees* (Geneva: Librairie Droz, 2010).

23. Pierre Merlin, *A Most Plaine and Profitable Exposition of the Book of Ester: Deliuered in 26. Sermons* (London: Thomas Creed, 1599), b4r.

24. Brauneck, "Esther," 5.

25. Obadiah Sedgwick, *Haman's Vanity* (London, 1643), B4r.

26. Sedgwick, *Haman's Vanity*, C2v.

27. Merlin, *Most Plaine and Profitable Exposition*, O5r.

28. Johannes Brenz, *A Right Godly and Learned Discourse upon the booke of Ester* (London: John Harrison, 1584), a7r.

29. Brenz, *Right Godly and Learned Discourse*, a2r.

30. Brauneck, "Esther," 46–47.

31. Brauneck, "Esther," 53.

32. Maike Neumann, *Buß- und Bettage: Geschichtliche Entwicklung–aktuelle Situation—Bedingungen für eine erneuerte Praxis* (Göttingen: Neukirchen-Vluyn, 2011).

33. Thomas Marks, "Singing Repentance in Lutheran Germany during the Thirty Years War (1618–1648)," *Music and Letters* 103, no. 2 (May 2022): 228.

34. In Clifford Davidson's account of the York plays, for example, he notes audiences were meant to feel "living contemporaries" with the staged characters, creating a collective memory of salvation history ("Memory and Remembering: Sacred History and the York Plays," in *Staging Scripture* (Leiden: Brill, 2016), 337.

35. Jan Assmann, *Cultural Memory and Early Civilization: Writing, Remembrance, and Political Imagination* (Cambridge, UK: Cambridge University Press, 2011), 2.

36. Charles Hughes, ed., *Shakespeare's Europe: A Survey of the Condition of Europe at the End of the 16th Century. Being Unpublished Chapters of Fynes Moryson's Itinerary (1617)*, 2nd ed. (New York: Benjamin Blom, 1967), 304.

37. Sedgwick, B2r.

38. Jeffrey Knapp, *Shakespeare's Tribe* (Chicago: University of Chicago Press, 2002), 61–79.

39. Brauneck, "Esther," 44.

40. William Schrickx, *Foreign Envoys and Travelling Players in the Age of Shakespeare and Jonson* (Wetteren, Belgium: Universa, 1986), 231.

41. Brauneck, "Esther," 17.

42. Stern, "Esther and the Politics of Diaspora," 25–53.

43. Adler, "Hidden Message of the Book of Esther," 246–49; Timothy K. Beal, *The Book of Hiding: Gender, Ethnicity, Annihilation, and Esther* (New York: Routledge, 1997).

44. Merlin, *Most Plaine and Profitable Exposition*, 111.

45. Stern, "Esther and the Politics of Diaspora," 25–53.

46. See especially Adele Berlin, *Esther: The Traditional Hebrew Text with the New JPS Translation/Commentary* (Philadelphia: Jewish Publication Society, 2001), xix and xx.

47. Berlin considers the work a farce; Stern considers it instead a satire of diasporic Judaism, produced in the kingdom of Judah.

48. The violence of the book has been central to modern scholarly debate, with some seeing the work as "vengeful, bloodthirsty and chauvinistic in spirit," while others attempting a defense. See C. A. Moore, *Esther* (Garden City, NY: Doubleday, 1971), xxx and 80. Early modern commentators similarly questioned the apparent excesses, though almost all eventually explained them as God's just punishment upon his enemies and the enemies of his church: "Hereby we perceive what punishment the enemies of the Church doo deserve, and what shall be their successe at the last" (466). In this context, the excision in the play of the Jewish reprisals against their enemies is all the more remarkable.

49. Francis Quarles, *Hadassa: Or the History of Queene Ester with Meditations Thereupon, Divine and Morall* (London: Richard Moore, 1621), 158.

50. Rudolf Schwartz, *Esther im Deutschen und Neulateinischen Drama des Reformationszeitalters: Eine Litterarhistorische Untersuchung* (Oldenburg: A. Schwartz, 1898), 10.

51. Brauneck, "Esther," 70–71.

52. Brauneck, "Esther," 73.

53. Brauneck, "Esther," 72.

54. Merlin, *Most Plaine and Profitable Exposition*, 200.

55. Brauneck, "Esther," 56–57.

56. Brauneck, "Esther," 67.

57. Brauneck, "Esther," 6.

58. On the Habsburg court irenicism, see Howard Louthan, *The Quest for Compromise: Peacemakers in Counter-Reformation Vienna* (Cambridge, UK: Cambridge University Press, 1997) and Joachim Whaley, *Germany and the Holy Roman Empire*, vol. 1, *Maximilian I to the Peace of Westphalia, 1490–1648* (Oxford: Oxford University Press, 2012), esp. 418–74.

59. Even the theater's earliest critic, Fynes Moryson, noted the plays were performed in "peeces and patches" (Hughes, *Shakespeare's Europe*, 304). Later critics tied this episodic character to what they perceived as the aesthetic failings of the theater (see Albrecht Cohn, *Shakespeare in Germany in the Sixteenth and Seventeenth Centuries: An Account of English Actors in Germany and the Netherlands, and of the Plays Performed by Them during the Same Period* [London: Asher., 1865], cvi).

60. Simon Williams, *Shakespeare on the German Stage* (New York: Cambridge University Press, 2004), 31–32.

61. R. A. Foakes, ed., *Henslowe's Diary*, 2nd edition (Cambridge, UK: Cambridge University Press, 2002), 21.

62. Annaliese Connolly, "Peele's *David and Bethsabe*: Reconsidering Biblical Drama of the Long 1590s," *Early Modern Literary Studies* special issue, 16 (October 2007): 20.

63. "a book of identity in crisis": Johnny Miles, "Reading Esther as Heroine: Persian Banquets, Ethnic Cleansing, and Identity Crisis," *Biblical Theology Bulletin* 45, no. 3 (August 2015): 131–43.

3

Astonished and Amazed

Early Modern English Black Christianity and
Respectability Politics in Middleton and Munday's
The Triumphs of Truth

Jamie Paris

Before you can read me
You got to learn how to see me
   —En Vogue, "Free Your Mind"

In 2015, during his speech announcing his intention to seek the Republican presidential nomination, Donald J. Trump warned that the country was in "serious trouble" because "we don't have victories anymore." He noted that the United States does not, for example, "win" trade negotiations with China and that America was being beaten by Mexico at the border. For Trump, what mattered was not that America was losing but that it was being humiliated by nations filled with Brown people. On immigration, for example, Trump said that Mexico is "laughing at us, at our stupidity." What was stupid, Trump implied, was that Americans were allowing scandalous Mexicans and South and Central Americans to immigrate through the southern border. As he infamously put it, "When Mexico sends its people, they're not sending their best. They're not sending you. They're not sending you. They're sending people that have lots of problems, and they're bringing those problems with us. They're bringing drugs. They're bringing crime. They're rapists. And some, I assume, are good people."[1] In a 1981 interview with Alexander Lamis, Republican strategist Lee Atwater suggested that in order for Republicans to remain electable after the passage of the Civil Rights Act, racist dog whistles needed to become more abstract. It hurt the party to be perceived as racist, but it did not hurt the party to discuss abstract issues like busing and cutting taxes that would have outsized impacts on the Black community.[2] For those who say that they like Trump because he does not talk like a politician, part of their attraction to him is the rhetorical rejection of Atwater and the Southern Strategy of finding ways to promote and endorse policies that disproportionately harm people of color without facing a backlash for stating racist intentions. Critical race theorist Eduardo Bonilla-Silvia calls this "colorblind racism," which he defines as a system that allows for racist outcomes while also attributing those racist outcomes to nonracial dynamics.[3]

To use the language of this chapter's epigraph, Trump is attempting to teach his audience how to read and see Mexican immigrants from a nationalist and neoracist perspective. The implications of his speech were that Mexico, or perhaps the Mexican government, was nefariously plotting to flood America with problematic people, and in turn that America was foolish to allow "them" to get away with it. Trump allows that "some" Latin American immigrants are "good people," but the quote implies that the vast majority of those being sent across the border are problematic drug dealers, criminals, and rapists. The "some are good people" move is essential for neoracist discourse. If they want to say that the prejudice is about culture and not race, they need to focus on those who will not culturally fit in the nation. With anti-immigrant discourse permeating the speech of Boris Johnson and many other Brexit defenders, the French anti-Islamic discourse of Marine Le Pen and the National Front, and Donald Trump framing the idea of "Make America Great Again" with anti-Latinx discourse, we see a suspicion that those with Brown or Black complexions who want to come to the nation are not "good people." Often speakers employing such rhetoric imply that some sinister outsider is sending bad immigrants to their countries, perhaps as a way of replacing the "good" people who already live there. These people do not belong, these neoracist leaders argue, because they cannot or will not assimilate to white, Eurocentric culture. As Etienne Balibar argues, neoracists use cultural differences to justify "policies of exclusion" under the logic of preservation.[4] Not only is the Other dangerous for the neoracist, but their culture is fragile and could slide into uncontrollable criminality if those who do not share Western values invade the country in uncontrollable numbers. The task of a good leader, for Johnson, Le Pen, or Trump, is to protect the nation from those strangers who would destroy it culturally from within, and in turn to teach their audiences how to read and see strangers not as fellow human beings in need of assistance and care but as threatening others whose welcome would pose an existential risk to the (white) nation. Often, this is done through paradoxically holding up some members of a minority group as good people, who are respectable and deserving of assimilation. While it might seem like a compliment to be held up as one of the "some good people," this status is fragile and can be revoked upon a real or perceived mistake that confirms any previous racist assumptions.

In Thomas Middleton and Anthony Munday's *The Triumphs of Truth* (1613), the King of the Moors is held up as a singular member of a minority group who is a "good person" who is welcomed to visit England on a religious pilgrimage. This text has become one of the most frequently cited and controversial mayoral pageants from the early modern period; the show is a "sustained moral allegory" that "relies on theme and symbolism rather than plot" to show how "Truth can prevail over Error."[5] One of the "errors" that *The Triumphs of Truth* explores is assuming that someone is, or is likely to be, amoral because they are Black. This chapter will focus on the entrance of the King of the Moors to the pageant. It will explore what the visual representation of the King of the Moors reveals about the status of respectable Black Christians in the early modern period. The King of the Moors, his queen, and his attendants are seen by the audience through a white gaze. The King of the Moors may be the first unambiguously "good" Black character in early modern performance. The show, moreover, is essential to the historical study of whiteness because it contains the first use of the phrase "white people."[6] Whiteness was often an elite property in the early modern period and, as Arthur Little Jr. argues, when the King of the Moors speaks to the white people, it marks a moment in early modern theater where "whiteness" is successfully stolen . . . from the elite world of the court" and delivered to "'the people' in the streets" as a way of describing the "white-skinned mass[es]."[7] Interestingly, this use comes from the Black King of the Moors, who is in turn astonished and amazed by seeing a multitude of white faces watching him intently. I am interested in the emotional labor that the King of the Moors has to perform to be seen as a Christian by the white people who are looking at him. That labor reveals many of the social and emotional costs involved with being perceived as a respectable Black Christian by skeptical, and potentially racist, white people.

The Triumphs of Truth was Middleton's first mayoral pageant (he would go on to write seven more). The pageant was dedicated to the new mayor of London, Thomas Myddelton, who was not related to the author, although Middleton did comment on their common name in his preface. Thomas

Myddelton's election was a moment of celebration for the Worshipful Company of Grocers guild. While it is hard to get accurate records, we know that the Grocers were prepared to spend up to £900 on the show.[8] Thus, the pageant was arguably "the most expensive and most spectacular of Jacobean Lord Mayoral Shows."[9] These pageants were expensive propaganda for the guilds and the commercial interests of the London economic elite, and many modern critics are quick to dismiss them. However, they were critical to the ecology of early modern theater. These pageants rivaled the kinds of masques and performances produced at the royal courts, and significant figures like Munday, Dekker, Webster, and Heywood wrote pageants to honor the mayor.[10]

Middleton wrote this pageant for the Worshipful Company of Grocers, a livery company established in 1345 for merchants in the grocery trade. As Robert J. Blackman argues, "The livery companies, with their political and municipal power, are peculiar to London. No other city has permitted such a development of its ministries and trades, nowhere else in England have chartered associations of the kind attained such wealth and power."[11] The company was responsible for maintaining the purity of spices, a field that was growing increasingly profitable, and for the setting of weights and measures. When Middleton wrote the pageant, moreover, the Worshipful Company of Grocers was still charged with regulating and distributing medicinal spices and herbs, although this task would be taken over by the Worshipful Society of Apothecaries in 1617. The founders of the company were known as the Pepperers, who can be traced back to at least 1231; indeed, they established the first mercantile company in England.[12] Many early modern actors were men freed from service to livery companies, like the Worshipful Company of Grocers. Such freedom could come through "servitude, patrimony, redemption, and translation," although in the early modern period servitude "was by far the most common method." To be freed by servitude, a young man would be bound to a master for a set number of years while he learned the craft, and when he was done with the apprenticeship he could "pay a fee to become free of the company, after which they were entitled to bind their own apprentices."[13] Middleton seems to have built a strong connection with the Worshipful Company of Grocers, since they hired him to write for the company again in 1617.

The tradition of mayoral pageants goes back to the middle of the sixteenth century, although the use of "triumphs" in the title of Middleton's pageant is also intended to evoke a Roman triumphs tradition. Roman triumphs were the highest honor of Roman life. During these celebration parades, victorious generals would show off important prisoners, display looted treasures, and perform religious rituals and sacrifices. The opening scene of William Shakespeare's *Titus Andronicus* shows a Roman triumph. The Lord Mayor's Show occurred annually; the mayoral pageants were put on each October twenty-ninth, when a new mayor would leave the guildhall in London, travel to Westminster, and take an oath to carry out his duties faithfully. The mayor would then return to the guildhall.[14] Most spectators would stay in one place to watch the set pieces: each set would have a particular scene or tableau, not unlike a medieval morality play or pageant. While the mayor and his three hundred-to-five-hundred-person train would see the entire procession as they walked back to the hall, the highly symbolic and allegorical argument of the show would only become clear to most viewers when the mayoral pageant was published as a book. When discussing pageants, it is therefore vital to pay attention not just to what is said by the characters but also to where it is said on the route. Each scene would be performed in an economically, politically, or theologically essential location.

The scene of interest to this chapter happens at St. Paul's churchyard, a space where critical religious sermons and lectures were given in the early modern period. The show features a "King of the Moors," who enters the stage on "a strange ship . . . which may raise greater astonishment, it having neither sailor nor pilot" (*Triumphs*, 399–401). The ship, moreover, has a silk streamer, with "*Veritate governor*: I am steered by Truth" written on it (402–3). The entrance would have been spectacular. The king, his queen, and their attendants would likely have been performed in blackface, perhaps while also using a collection of textiles to make their presentation seem more convincing.[15] Moreover, as Middleton notes in his stage description, all four of the characters were "of their own colour" (405). In this way, the show associates a Black man with truth and goodness and then has him speak in a highly symbolically charged sacred space. The show encourages the spectators to "exercise vigilance as Christian citizens."[16] It also asks the spectators to notice the color of the king without prejudging him.

The King of the Moors is a Christian convert, and thus he represents the hopes and dreams of English trade with Africa. As Ania Loomba notes, "Visual entertainments and pageants . . . [have] repeatedly featured an enormous variety of racial outsiders [and] personifications of lands with which there was real or desired trade."[17] In addition to being critical economic drivers for the theatrical community, early modern mayoral pageants were primarily works of racist propaganda designed to spiritually justify "the economics of colonialism" and prop up support for "expanded trade with both the East and West Indies [that] was producing new wealth for noblemen and guildsmen alike."[18] As Virginia Mason Vaughan argues in *Performing Blackness*, Middleton's primary interest was using colonial enterprise to spread the Protestant faith to the so-called new world. Thus, for Vaughan, Middleton's pageant demonstrates how the "black-faced devils" of the homiletic tradition had become amalgamated with the figure of the Black Moor of Africa in a conventional symbol of the qualities—barbarism, ignorance, impudence, and falsehood—in opposition to white Englishness and true religion. The battle between the forces of good and evil no longer figured in the next world but in the here and now of exploration and trade.[19]

The audience is shown through these productions that trade can be a force for good, because the King of the Moors was converted by the "good example" of English merchants and traders. His "true Christian faith" represents the power of trade "to convert infidels" (441–42). According to Farah Karim-Cooper, this is an age when "the color black . . . would have been loaded with [a] diverse range of negative associations for audiences."[20] The pageant attempts to show its audience that through the good example of Christian traders, some Black people may become coreligionists and thus leave behind lives of barbarism and ignorance. The implication is that without this trade, Black men and women, kings and queens, will remain infidels.

There is also an undertone of what will become Kipling's "white man's burden" in this show, where English merchants act as if they are morally obligated to convert non-Europeans to Christianity. Here it is important to remember that Myddelton was an investor in the Virginia colony. In "A Brief Report on the New-Found Land of Virginia" (1588), English colonist Thomas Hariot (sometimes spelled Harriot) suggests that English settlers should seek out "friendship and love" with the Pamlico in the lands currently called Virginia, so that they can be "brought to civilization" and the "embrace of true religion."[21] The First Charter of Virginia (1606) says that one of its key goals is "propagating of Christian religion to such people, as yet live in darkness and miserable ignorance of the true knowledge and worship of God, and may in time bring the infidels and savages, living in those parts, to human civility."[22] The King of the Moors, his queen, and his train are thus best-case fictive representations of what could happen if "heathens" were converted to Protestantism.

While scholars within premodern critical race theory may like the show, we like it with a caution that white and settler scholars do not always share.[23] For example, in his influential reading of the show, Gary Taylor argues that Middleton separates faith from skin color in the pageant; according to Taylor, what matters to Middleton is not skin color but "the boundary that separates Christians from non-Christians."[24] Perhaps, but Middleton chose to stress the skin color of the king, the queen, and his attendants. This is a triumph, after all, and they are being paraded as a victory in the same way the Romans might have paraded exotic peoples and animals from lands they had conquered. Part of what the scene is highlighting, moreover, is a question of conversion: Are the bonds of "whiteness" stronger than the bonds of faith? The audience clearly sees the king's color and the king says he is "astonished at the many eyes" that look at him at Paul's Churchyard (408). To be astonished is to be shocked out of a sense of self-possession or confidence; it is the feeling one has when they are placed into a state of terror.[25] The king, in other words, is terrified by the "multitude" (409) of white people he sees, perhaps realizing that his presence at a holy place puts himself, his queen, and his servants in danger of mob violence. The King of the Moors needs to manage the fears of the audience and his own fears about the audience. He must also manage the fears the audience might have about Christian merchants converting Black people and turning them into coreligionists; at the same time he represents a Black man who has to restrain himself from showing fear in the face of the amazement of his coreligionists.

According to Ian Smith, the London lord mayor's shows were tools that livery companies used to manage the fears white people had about trade with people from different ethnic, racial, and religious communities.[26] Dennis Austin Britton observes that the King of the Moors seems to be aware of the power of the white gaze.[27] The king does not try to convince the white mob of the inherent dignity of Black people. He does not say that he is scared, nor does he call out the white people for their racism. Rather, he tries to convince them that he is a Christian king and thus deserving of dignity and respect. The king seems to be a Protestant, and thus a coreligionist with the people who are watching him in shock and amazement. Moreover, the king speaks to the audience without showing the audience the difficulty of the emotional labor involved in being a Black man speaking to a courtyard full of anxious white people. Perhaps this is because this is a play written by white men, to celebrate a white mayor, and a part performed by a white man in blackface. One wonders if any of them could have understood the emotional difficulty of being a Black man and speaking in an anxious white space.

RESPECTABILITY POLITICS

The king's emotional labor reminds me of teaching. As a mixed-race (Black, Scottish, and Métis) scholar and educator, I deeply identify with the king's experience of astonishment at this moment. The fear that the king feels is the same emotion that makes scholars like Reni Eddo-Lodge say that they no longer wish to talk about race with white people who emotionally disconnect or act with "bewilderment" and "defensiveness as they try to grapple with the fact that not everyone experiences the world in the way that they do."[28] The fear that the King of the Moors feels is one that many Black people experience when they cross "the color line" and enter into white spaces. It is the fear an anti-racist educator has when they are unsure how white people will act toward them. It is the feeling I have any time that I am compelled to speak about racism in primarily white spaces. It is the fear I have right now, as a scholar and a writer, talking openly about my fears while bracing for the eventual pushback that comes from discussing race openly and honestly in premodern studies.

To speak about racism in a way that white people are likely to be able to hear, one must engage in what Arlie Russell Hochschild calls emotional labor. Hochschild argues that in some career fields, like that of flight attendants, employers look for employees who can perform emotional management "without showing the effort involved." Flight attendants, Hochschild argued, have to learn how to "relax and smile" while dealing with turbulence, hostile customers, and even sexual harassment as a way of demonstrating empathy for strangers.[29] Likewise, Black people who discuss racism under the pressure of the white gaze must do emotional labor by controlling their reactions to white fragility and intentional displays of ignorance. For example, if I am in a faculty meeting and someone uses a racist term to describe a student, I am expected to say something about it, and I am expected to do so without anger and in a way that makes the white person feel supported and cared for as a human being. Likewise, if a BIPOC person is pulled over by a police officer, there is a need for them to control their emotional reactions to the situation to avoid the dangerous potential consequences that come with escalations. However, the big difference is that Black people are not compensated with money for performing emotional labor around issues of racism but simply provided with temporary safety. Performing respectability is a kind of emotional labor frequently expected of Black people within white spaces.

The white gaze makes Black people responsible for how our racialized body makes white people feel. In *Black Skin, White Masks*, Frantz Fanon notes that Black people are rarely allowed "to be a man among men" because they are forced to confront the white gaze's power. The white gaze is imposed by white people who weave an image of Blackness "out of a thousand details, anecdotes, and stories" that evoke fear and dread about the potential of the Black body to harm others.[30] As George Yancy argues, the Black body is "criminality itself. It is the monstrous" when seen through the white gaze. Through the white gaze, a Black person "undergoes processes of dehumanizing interpellation." In this way, the white gaze is not just a metaphor but "an important site of power and control, a site that is structured by white epistemic orders that perpetuates such orders in turn."[31] The white gaze denies the Black person a sense of inwardness, or a sense that there is something internal about them as a person that is inaccessible by simply looking at them.[32] If someone sees me not as a person—a unique being with hopes, fears, and desires who longs to love and be loved—but as a potential criminal or monster because they see me through the white gaze, am I responsible for what they see? While Middleton does not answer this question in the affirmative in his pageant, he does dramatize the idea that it is the responsibility of a Black man to soothe the fears of those who see him through the white gaze.

As Britton argues, the King of the Moors gives us the first known dramatic usage of "white people" as a collective noun phrase in English; at the same time, his speech to the audience "directly engages in a long-standing association between white skin and Christian identity and between black skin and non-Christian identity."[33] The king, after all, simply assumes that the white people in the audience are Christians, and while this may be true, it is an assumption based on the audience members being white and not one based on asking the audience members about their faith. This would be no different from seeing a collection of Arabic people and assuming that they are all Muslims because they "look like Muslims." The king says:

> I see amazement set upon the faces
> Of these white people, wond'rings and strange gazes;
> Is it at me? Does my complexion draw
> So many Christian eyes that never saw
> A king so black before? No, now I see
> Their entire object, they're all meant to thee
> Grave city-governor, my queen and I
> Well honoured with the glances that pass by. (411–18)

The king acknowledges the strangeness of the gazes of the white people, and, in doing so, acknowledges that he is an object of wonder for them. It can be deeply uncomfortable to look strange to a mob of people one does not know, especially if one is unsure of one's safety in the face of that mob. The king performs emotional labor through empathy by placing himself in the position of the white onlookers and wondering if he too would feel amazement at seeing a Black king. Rather than call out the audience for finding him strange, or pointing out how it makes him feel uncomfortable, the king notes that the "entire object" of the gazes must be for the new mayor. It is as if the king is actively teaching the audience how to see him as part of the spectacle rather than focusing on him as the spectacle. If he and his queen are merely part of the show, he suggests to the audience, then he is "well honoured" by the glances of the audience. Note the shift from gazes to glances. While the white gaze would define him and fix his meaning within the horizon of the audience's prejudices about Blackness, the white glance merely acknowledges him as one of the members of the show. This difference is subtle, but it matters. I am never offended by someone seeing my color or noticing my skin tone. Seeing my race is part of seeing me. As George Lipsitz argues, the issue with colorblindness as an ideology is that it "pretends that racial recognition rather than racist rule is the problem to be solved."[34] What I am offended by is the white gaze and the way that the white gaze can reduce me as a person and limit any understanding about me to my race.

This issue can have life or death consequences for young Black people who are seen through the white gaze. For example, the question of the personal responsibility of young Black men for how they are seen within the white gaze was at the center of the media reactions to the 2012 murder of Trayvon Martin by George Zimmerman. When then-president Barack Obama first found out about the shooting, he called it "a tragedy" and said that "when I think about this boy, I think about my own kids." As Obama noted, if he had a son, "he'd look like Trayvon."[35] In contrast, for former Fox News personality Geraldo Rivera, the problem was how Martin looked and what he called the "understandable" reaction it generated in his shooter. Rivera thought that Martin's "hoodie is as much responsible for [his] death as [the shooter] George Zimmerman." Rivera suggested that parents of "dark-skinned" Black and Latino teenagers should not allow their children to "walk down the street in a hoodie or with their pants around their ankles," because if these children dress like gangsters, "Then people are going to perceive [them] as a menace."[36] For Obama, Trayvon

Martin was a child deserving of love and protection. For Rivera, Martin's parents could have saved his life by simply making him dress in a way that would not evoke white fears of Black criminality.

For Candis Watts Smith and Tehama Lopez Bunyasi, respectability politics is an ideology that insists that minorities can keep themselves safe and eventually lessen the fears of the dominant group "by presenting oneself in the way that is pleasing to members of the dominant group."[37] The idea comes from the turn-of-the-twentieth-century Black middle-class notion that Black people who were having issues overcoming racism and entering the job market could "raise" themselves by dressing, acting, and speaking in ways that better conformed to white cultural norms.[38] This ideology encourages Black people to believe that "respectable people are held in high regard because they comport themselves as such" and the focus tends to be on what Black people ought not to do or say, and when and where they ought not to do it or say it. It is an ideology that implies that "Black culture is of little value and confers minimal benefits in the effort to acquire social capital in civilized white society."[39] As Leah Goodridge powerfully reminds us, one of the ways that respectability politics invades our daily lives is through the construct of professionalism; while the idea of professionalism, in theory, applies to everyone within a profession, she notes that "it is used to widely police and regulate people of color" within professional environments.[40] In this way, those Black people who speak out about racism in a professional setting without performing the emotional labor necessary to appease the dominant group risk being called unprofessional. The king is strikingly professional in terms of his emotional regulation in this scene. Even if he is afraid of what the masses might think of him, he directs their attention away from himself as a spectacle and onto the mayor, where it is ostensibly supposed to go. The strangeness of this moment is that he is a monarch and a visiting dignitary and thus should by rights hold more power than the mayor. It is as if the show is saying that a Black king may be above the assembled white people who are watching the show, but he is symbolically or dramatically below the mayor and the men of rank and title toward whom the show is drawing the spectator's attention. Professionalism for Black people has always involved deflecting attention away from oneself, one's accomplishments, and one's emotional concerns, and turning that attention toward white people, especially if they happen to be powerful white men.

Respectability politics and the need for Black people to manage the emotions of white people may seem modern. Nevertheless, one could argue that it goes back to at least the early modern period and the way the early modern stage turned a religious language of anti-Blackness into a visual language that hardened into a racial difference.[41] Kim F. Hall argues that whiteness and Blackness are part of a moral binary in early modern thought. Whiteness was associated with Christian virtues like "purity, virginity, and innocence," while Blackness was associated with "baseness, sin, and danger."[42] Furthermore, as Britton notes, Black skin became a figure on the early modern stage "used to stand in for concepts and ideas that were seen as oppositional to Christian whiteness and purity."[43] For example, in Shakespeare's *Othello, The Moor of Venice*, after the titular character has successfully defended himself against accusations of witchcraft, the Duke tries to reunite Othello with his new father-in-law. The Duke says to the still-upset Brabantio: "If virtue no delight in beauty lack, / Your son-in-law is far more fair than black" (1.3.330–31).[44] The Duke suggests that Othello is ugly and black, but he has an inward virtue and fairness that would typically be associated with Christian whiteness. As far as the Duke is concerned, Othello is a respectable husband for Desdemona. His attitude, of course, stands in stark contrast to that of characters like Iago, Roderigo, and Brabantio, who refuse to see Othello as respectable. Underlying these associations between Blackness and not being respectable, as Ian Smith argues, is the sense that an outward appearance of Blackness signifies internal spiritual darkness. According to Smith, for many Black characters on the early modern stage, "what you see is what you get. The black African on the stage is presumed to be immediately knowable; he is visibly fixed in an intractable series of negative 'devil' stereotypes that require no further knowledge beyond the skin, no decoding of the chromodermal signifier."[45] To be Black on the early modern stage was to be the inverse of white Christian respectability. It was to have an identity that is all surface, or, to paraphrase Hamlet, to have one that does not pass show. Black characters like Othello, who appear to be respectable in the first act of the play, can be demeaned and dispirited by racist characters like Iago. Black men are frequently put in positions where they have to do emotional labor for white people who doubt their moral goodness because of their complexion. Characters like the Prince of Morocco from Shakespeare's *Merchant of Venice* must ask to be seen with respect and can be dismissed by racists like Portia.[46] Likewise, Othello has to explain before the Senate that he does not practice witchcraft. The foundations of Black respectability, thus, are precarious and depend not on the actions of the Black character but on the white gaze and how deeply a character has internalized anti-Blackness. To quote Sir Philip Sidney, respectability shows us the "uncertainty of this world" for Black characters, "and upon how weak foundations gilded roofs are builded." I am not sure that the fate of those who try to pass as respectable stirs "admiration and commiseration" for every reader, but it does for me and, I suspect, it will for most BIPOC readers who understand just how weak the foundation of respectability really is.[47] After all, for many of us, our reputations, careers, or even lives can depend on those seeing us through the white gaze noticing the gilding of respectable dress, speech, and actions.

SEEING WHITE PEOPLE

The "triumph of truth" in this show is the victory of English Protestantism, or the Christian truth, over the king's former paganism, and the victory of potential Protestant economic integration over a world with national and religious barriers to trade. Indeed, this is what Samuel Purchas intended with his 1613 travel narrative *Purchas His Pilgrimage*, a follow-up to Richard Hakluyt's *Principal Navigations*. Purchas envisions replacing a world where "so many Nations as so many persons hold commerce and intercourse of amity withal" with one where the world is "joined in one band of humanity" that "would be Christian." In this vision, Jews, Muslims, and Christians would all be united in "one Lord, one Faith, one Baptism, one Body, one Spirit, one Inheritance, one God and Father, so there may be thus one Church truly Catholic, One Pastor and one Sheepfold."[48] As Hall notes, "English trade, rather than fostering a mixing of cultures, will eradicate religious differences, as well as cultural and gender differences, under one patriarchal God."[49] Such a vision "serves to efface the multivariant anxieties over cross-cultural interaction that permeate English fictions of international trade."[50] Purchas is reassuring his readers that these cultural and religious exchanges can be one-sided, whereby the English can bring Christianity to the world without fearing that trade will bring with it different religious worldviews or that merchants might marry women from the new world. In this way, it matters that the king comes to England with his queen. While she does not speak in the show, she is present on the set to reassure the audience that this Black Christian king will not try to enter into any romantic relationships with white Christian women while he is visiting England. The King of the Moors and his queen are "exotic fiction[s]" designed to help the viewer imagine commerce and trade as a means of producing respectable Black Christian kings who would, nevertheless, be subservient to English political, religious, and economic desires.[51]

Coming back to Smith's reading of the show, one could say that the King of the Moors is managing the fears of a white audience by repressing his own. The king must assuage the fears of the crowd, assuring them that he has been converted to Christianity through "English merchants, factors, travelers, / Whose truth did with our spirits hold commerce" (437–38).[52] The show manages the white audience's fear of a Black man by suggesting that they have nothing to fear from him because he has been converted. Likewise, the show suggests that the audience has nothing to fear from increased trade and interactions with Black people because Christian merchants will take up the burden of converting them while trading with them.

This should not be taken to mean that converting to Christianity in the early modern period erased blackness, or that all Black people who converted to Christianity were treated as equals. After all, a Black Christian is still a marked racial identity in the premodern period. According to Geraldine Heng, we can see the way Black modifies Christianity as a way of demarcating "human beings through differences among humans that are selectively essentialized as absolute and fundamental, in order to distribute positions and powers differentially to human groups."[53] The difference in skin color between the terrifying Christians in the audience and the Black king and his court is a selectively essentialized difference that creates a wall between the king and his fellow Christians. It matters that this is a "multitude" (409), in the derogatory sense of "the common people" or "the masses," because whiteness in the early modern period was a question of class as well as race.[54] As Arthur L. Little notes, whiteness was an "elite property" and "the signifier of one's elite status."[55] Indeed, one could go as far as to say that the King of the Moors is not just noticing a difference between himself and the white people in the audience but flattering the masses by implying that they are the same as the mayor and the elite who are hosting his pilgrimage.

Even if the white people accept the King of the Moors as a Christian, it is not clear that they would read him as having a "whiteness of the soul, a whiteness that could not be claimed by non-Christian others."[56] If the audience does not accept the whiteness of his soul, then it is not clear that they will give him the kinds of rights typically afforded to Christian rulers. As the king notes,

> I must confess many wild thoughts may rise,
> Opinions, common murmurs, and fixed eyes,
> At my so strange arrival in a land
> Where true religion and her temples stand.
> I being a moor, then, in opinion's lightness,
> As far from sanctity as my face from whiteness. (419–24)

The "wildness" of the thoughts of the mob matter. The king cannot know if the mob will see him as a curiosity, or if this wild mass will hunt him and his queen like a pair of animals. They have, after all, the kind of "fixed eyes" that one sees on a creature that is tracking prey. The king, moreover, understands that the uneducated audience will see his Blackness as a barrier to sanctity. This matters because it is not clear that a character without sanctity, or a sense of holiness or sacredness, could claim sanctuary, or safety within a consecrated ground. Rather than express anger at the idea that some in the audience would not see him as a person with a soul, he forgives them for having "the judgings of th' unwise, / Whose censures ever quicken in their eyes, / Only begot of outward form and show" (425–27). When I think about what the king is saying here, I think about how white liberals love conversations about race and racism when these discussions chastise the uneducated, but they are deeply uncomfortable with the idea that they may have internalized a racist way of seeing the world that causes them to also make unwise judgements that they may not be fully aware of making. The King of the Moors accepts that the audience may be prejudging him, and he gently and carefully encourages them to look past his outward "form and show" to see the person underneath.

This is a challenging ask for the white people in the audience because they would be so accustomed to making unwise judgements about people's faith based on prejudgments about their skin color. As Heng notes, religion was able to function "socioculturally and biopolitically." The discourse of religion could be used to subjugate entire communities in ways that "biologize, define, and essentialize an entire community as fundamentally and absolutely different."[57] As Olivette Otele argues in *African Europeans*, in the premodern period, the color black "represented inferiority and the ugliness of human experiences on earth" and was part of "Christian notions of good, evil and the redemptive opportunity for salvation through atonement for one's sins. Africans were black or of dark skin. They were the color of evil, but they could repent, be saved and even become patron saints."[58] Furthermore, as Britton argues in *Becoming Christian*, it was possible to convert from being an infidel and to become a Christian in line with the ideas presented in Paul's Galatians 3:28, but this does not mean "that race, ethnicity, and gender became inconsequential to matters of religion. Although the Church of England's theology would necessarily maintain that whoever believes and is baptized will be saved, salvation appears to be an even greater miracle when bestowed on an Ethiopian, Moor, Turk, or Jew who converts to Christianity."[59] At the same time, in the premodern period we see that English theologians moved away from saying that baptism was essential for being a Christian, arguing that the children of white Christians were born as Christians, and thus the only people who needed to convert to Christianity were those "not born into the baptized race; the need to convert thus marked the convert as racially different from Christians"[60] Indeed, as Imtiaz Habib and Duncan Salkeld show, it was typical in parish records to mark nonwhite Christians with a geographic or ethnic identifier, like Blackmore, even if they were land-owning converts.[61] Thus, Middleton reminds us that while conversion is possible for a Black king, and in theory for his people, theirs would be a marked Christianity.

According to Ayanna Thompson, racism is a fiction that is unstable and does not refer "solely to skin color, somatic aspects, or phenotypes." Race is a production of racism and racist ways of seeing the world, and the task of racism is "to ensure an uneven distribution of goods, wealth, power, rights, etc."[62] One of the ways that this works is by accepting some "respectable" Black people into a liminal status of being not quite white but also not at the bottom of the social well.[63] For sociologist Roger Bastide, a primary division in Christian thought "is that of white and black" where "White is used to express the pure, while black expresses the diabolical. The conflict between Christ and Satan, the spiritual and the carnal, good and evil came finally to be expressed by the conflict between white and black, which underlines and synthesizes all the others." Thus, Bastide notes, "In America, when a Negro is accepted, one often says, in order to separate him from the rest of his race, 'He is a Negro, of course, but his soul is white.'"[64] Underlying this backhanded compliment is the worst kind of anti-Black racism, which proclaims that the life of this respectable Christian Black person matters because they have a white soul, while implicitly suggesting that the lives of those Black people who have a Black soul do not matter and are not worthy of preserving.

In closing, then, respectability politics is a trap. It is a process that BIPOC people use to police our own members, calling upon them to demonstrate that they can fit in with white culture, and it is weaponized by the media who are quick to point out when a victim of a crime may not be "deserving" of sympathy and attention because they did not live a respectable life. To return to my epigraph, the issue is not that Black people need to be more respectable. The issue is that we must challenge the limiting and racist assumptions within the white gaze. We need to learn how to see Black people without thinking of them as a threat. BLM activist and Canadian abolition scholar Robyn Maynard argues that those of us who care about Black life need to challenge the idea that criminal or violent young Black people are more deserving of violence than those who read as more respectable through the white gaze.[65] While previous scholars have focused on Middleton's pageant as racially progressive, or, like Gary Taylor, have suggested that Middleton is depicting differences of faith rather than those of race, my point is that it is impossible to separate the question of race and faith in this pageant, or to separate the depiction of the King of the Moors from the anti-Black racist context in which it was written. For Middleton, the life of the King of the Moors matters because he is a wealthy Christian convert, whose conversion promises both new Christians and continued trade between England and his kingdom. To use a contemporary phrase, Middleton is not saying that all Black lives matter. He is not viewing all Black people as deserving of dignity and respect as people. After all, the Queen of the Moors does not get a line in the show; we have no idea if she has converted to Christianity, or what she thinks about being in England. The servants, likewise, do not speak in the show. Thus, Middleton's focus is not on the inherent dignity of all Black people. Rather, he is focused on the respectability of a Black Christian king who is nevertheless marked as a "moor" in the show, and he uses the respectability of that Black Christian king to assuage fears that white audiences may have about that particular Black person. While we can see this as a relatively racially progressive moment in early modern theater, we ought not to lose sight of the fact that this is a work of propaganda for the sake of continued trade and one that reinforces the trap of respectability politics while suggesting that Black people must perform emotional labor to assuage the amazement of white people.

NOTES

Epigraph: En Vogue (Terry Ellis, Dawn Robinson, Cindy Herron, and Maxine Jones), vocalists, "Free Your Mind," by Denzil Foster and Thomas McElroy, released March 24,

1992, track 4 on *Funky Divas*, Atlantic Records (East West division). This new jack swing anti-racist anthem was recorded in January 1992. The song is influenced by Funkadelic's "Free Your Mind and Your Ass Will Follow."

1. *Washington Post* Staff, "Full Text: Donald Trump Announces a Presidential Bid," *Washington Post*, June 16, 2015. Web.

2. Alexander Lamis, "Exclusive: Lee Atwater's Infamous 1981 Interview on the Southern Strategy," *Nation*, YouTube, November 13, 2012. Web.

3. Eduardo Bonilla-Silva, *Racism without Racists: Color-Blind Racism and the Persistence of Racial Inequality in America*, 4th ed. (Lanham, MD: Rowman and Littlefield, 2014), 2–3.4th ed. (Lanham, Md: Rowman & Littlefield, 2014

4. Etienne Balibar and Immanuel Wallerstein, *Race, Nation, Class: Ambiguous Identities*, trans. Chris Turner (New York: Verso, 2011), 17–18.

5. Thomas Middleton and Anthony Munday, *The Triumphs of Truth*, in *Thomas Middleton: The Collected Works*, ed. David M. Bergeron, Gary Taylor, and John Lavagnino (Oxford: Clarendon Press, 2020), 997–1026. Parenthetical citations will be given in-text to the line numbers from this edition. In text, I will refer to this as Middleton's show, since he was the one responsible for writing down the text. Doing so is potentially controversial. Most scholarly editions of the show, including David M. Bergeron's, attribute the authorship to Middleton. Middleton appears to have dismissed Munday as an "impudent common writer," but Munday seems to have worked on this production and several of Middleton's other mayoral pageants. Nevertheless, many critics view Munday more as a consultant than as an author of the pageant, and Middleton seems defensive about the question of attribution. In his dedication for the pageant, Middleton says he has "directed, written, and redeemed [the pageant] into form" (13). In attributing the show to Middleton and Munday, this chapter follows Tracey Hill's and Mark Kaethler's arguments that Munday produced the main ideas for the show and worked with staging and costuming issues; meanwhile, Middleton was responsible for the script and the pageant book. Middleton collaborated with most of the prominent dramatists of his age, including Jonson, Dekker, Rowley, and Shakespeare. Middleton's collaborative shows and plays tend not to have a dominant dramatic Middletonian vision so much as what David Nichol calls a "multiplicity of voices." While it seems unlikely that Munday contributed lines to the pageant, it seems likely that his "voice" came out in the choices of settings, particularly in the visual representation of the King of the Moors. David M. Bergeron, "Anthony Munday: Pageant Poet to the City of London," *Huntington Library Quarterly* 30, no. 4 (August 1967): 345; Mark Kaethler, "Walking with Vigilance: Middleton's Edge in *The Triumphs of Truth*," *Early Theatre* 24, no. 2 (2021): 76; Tracey Hill, *Pageantry and Power: A Cultural History of the Early Modern Lord Mayor's Show 1585–1639* (New York: Manchester University Press, 2010), 88; Mark Hutchings and A. A. Bromham, *Middleton and His Collaborators*, rev. ed. (Liverpool: Liverpool University Press, 2007), 37; David Nicol, *Middleton and Rowley: Forms of Collaboration in the Jacobean Playhouse* (Toronto: University of Toronto Press, 2018), 6–7. "The play is a "sustained moral allegory": Margot Heinemann, *Puritanism and Theatre: Thomas Middleton and Opposition Drama under the Early Stuarts* (Cambridge, UK: Cambridge University Press, 1980), 127.

6. This is based on an Early English Books Online search. Personally, I think we must

be careful with claims like this. So many early modern performance texts have been lost, so we cannot know if this claim was made for the first time in this play or if this is just the first instance we can easily find. Gary Taylor, *Buying Whiteness: Race, Culture, and Identity from Columbus to Hip Hop* (New York: Palgrave Macmillan, 2005), 130–31.

7. Arthur L. Little Jr., "Introduction: Assembling an Aristocracy of Skin," in *White People in Shakespeare: Essays on Race, Culture, and the Elite*, ed. Arthur L. Little Jr. (London: Arden Shakespeare, 2023), 5.

8. George Unwin, *The Guilds and Companies of London*, 4th edition (London: Frank Cass, 1963), 278.

9. David M. Bergeron, *English Civic Pageantry 1558–1642* (London: Edward Arnold, 1971), 179.

10. Bergeron, "Anthony Munday," 345–46.

11. Colonel Robert J. Blackham, *The Soul of the City: London's Livery Companies. Their Storied Past, Their Living Present* (London: Sampson Low, Marston, 1932), 43–44.

12. John Benjamin Heath, *Some Account of the Worshipful Company of Grocers of the City of London* (London: W. Marchant, Printer, 1829), 43.

13. David Kathman, "Grocers, Goldsmiths, and Drapers: Freemen and Apprentices in the Elizabethan Theater," *Shakespeare Quarterly* 55, no. 1 (2004): 3.

14. For a sense of the route used for *The Triumphs of Truth*, see the Map of Early Modern London, which outlines the thirteen different staging locations used during the pageant, in the introduction to *The Triumphs of Truth: The Map of Early Modern London*, 7th ed., ed. Janelle Jenstad (Victoria: University of Victoria, 2022).

15. Ian Smith, "The Textile Black Body: Race and 'Shadowed Livery' in The Merchant of Venice," in *The Oxford Handbook of Shakespeare and Embodiment: Gender, Sexuality, and Race*, ed. Valerie Traub (Oxford: Oxford University Press, 2016), 170–85.

16. Kaethler, "Walking," 74.

17. Ania Loomba, "Introduction to The Triumphs of Honour and Virtue," in *Thomas Middleton: The Collected Works*, ed. Gary Taylor and John Lavagnino (Oxford: Clarendon Press, 2000), 1714.

18. Anthony Gerard Barthelemy, *Black Face, Maligned Race: The Representation of Blacks in English Drama from Shakespeare to Southerne* (Baton Rouge: Louisiana State University Press, 1987).

19. Virginia Mason Vaughan, *Performing Blackness on English Stages, 1500–1800* (Cambridge, UK: Cambridge University Press, 2005), 70–71.

20. Farah Karim-Cooper, "The Materials of Race: Staging the Black and White Binary in the Early Modern Theatre," in *The Cambridge Companion to Shakespeare and Race*, ed. Ayanna Thompson (Cambridge, UK: Cambridge University Press, 2021).

21. Thomas Hariot, "A Brief and True Report of the New Found Land of Virginia," ed. Paul Royster, *Electronic Texts in American Studies* 20 (2007): 38.

22. Anonymous, "The First Charter of Virginia; April 10, 1606" (Yale Law School: Avalon Project, 2008).

23. The phrase "premodern critical race studies" (PCRS) was first used by Margo Hendricks. For Hendricks, PCRS is not a theory but a movement that comes out of a generation

of scholars who engaged with critical race theory and rejected anti-blackness, colonialism, and misogynoir in all its forms while, at the same time, being deeply engaged in the historical study of the intersections of race, gender, class, and religion in the premodern period (Margo Hendricks, "Coloring the Past, Considerations on Our Future: RaceB4Race," *New Literary History* 52, nos. 3 and 4 [Summer–Autumn 2021]: 378)..

24. Taylor, *Buying Whiteness*, 131.

25. *OED Online*, s.v. "Astonish, *v.3.*"

26. Ian Smith, "Managing Fear: The Commerce in Blackness and the London Lord's Mayor's Shows," in *Historical Affects and the Early Modern Theater*, ed. Ronda Arab, Michelle M. Dowd, and Adam Zucker (New York: Routledge, 2015), 211–19.

27. Dennis Austin Britton, "Race and Renaissance Literature," in *Oxford Research Encyclopedia of Literature* (Oxford: Oxford University Press, 2022), 1–20.

28. Reni Eddo-Lodge, *Why I'm No Longer Talking to White People about Race* (London: Bloomsbury, 2018), ix–x.

29. Arlie Russell Hochschild, "The Managed Heart: Commercialization of Human Feeling," in *The Production of Reality: Essays and Readings on Social Interaction*, ed. Jodi O'Brien (Thousand Oaks, CA: Pine Forge Press, 2010), 320–24.

30. Frantz Fanon, *Black Skin, White Masks* (New York: Grove Press, 2008), 91–92.

31. George Yancy, *Black Bodies, White Gazes: The Continuing Significance of Race*, 2nd edition (Lanham, MD: Rowman and Littlefield, 2017), xxx–xxxiii.

32. Katharine Eisaman Maus, *Inwardness and Theater in the English Renaissance* (Chicago: University of Chicago Press, 1995).

33. Britton, "Race and Renaissance Literature."

34. George Lipsiz, "The Sounds of Silence: How Race Neutrality Preserves White Supremacy," in *Seeing Race Again: Countering Colorblindness across the Disciplines*, ed. Kimberlé W. Crenshaw et al. (Oakland: University of California Press, 2019), 23–51.

35. Barack Obama, "Obama: If I Had a Son He'd Look Like Trayvon Martin," YouTube, March 23, 2012.

36. Katherine Fung, "Geraldo Rivera: Trayvon Martin's 'Hoodie Is as Much Responsible For [His] Death as George Zimmerman,'" HuffPost, March 23, 2012. Web.

37. Tehama Lopez Bunyasi and Candis Watts Smith, *Stay Woke: A People's Guide to Making All Black Lives Matter* (New York: NYU Press, 2019), 102.

38. Fedrick C. Harris, "The Rise of Respectability Politics," *Dissent*, 2014.

39. Erin M. Kerrison, Jennifer Cobbina, and Kimberly Bender, "'Your Pants Won't Save You': Why Black Youth Challenge Race-Based Police Surveillance and the Demands of Black Respectability Politics," *Race and Justice* 8, no. 1 (January 2018): 9.

40. Leah Goodridge, "Professionalism as a Racial Construct," *UCLA Law Review (Law Meets World)* 38 (2022): 40–54.

41. Virginia Mason Vaughan, *Performing Blackness on English Stages, 1500–1800* (Cambridge, UK: Cambridge University Press, 2005), 7–9.

42. Kim F. Hall, *Things of Darkness: Economies of Race and Gender in Early Modern England* (Ithaca, NY: Cornell University Press, 1995), 8–12.

43. Britton, "Race and Renaissance Literature."

44. William Shakespeare, *Othello*, ed. E. A. J. Honigmann (London: Arden Shakespeare, 2016).

45. Ian Smith, "White Skin, Black Masks: Racial Cross-Dressing on the Early Modern Stage," *Renaissance Drama* 32 (2003): 34–35.

46. Jamie Paris, "'Mislike Me Not for My Complexion': On Anti-Black Racism and Performative Whiteness in William Shakespeare's *The Merchant of Venice*," *Journal for Early Modern Cultural Studies* 20, no. 4 (Fall 2020): 40–50.

47. Sir Philip Sidney, *An Apology for Poetry (or The Defense of Poesy)*, ed. R. W. Maslen (Manchester: Manchester University Press, 2002), 98.

48. Samuel Purchas, *Purchas His Pilgrimage* (London: Henry Featherstone, 1613), 1:56.

49. Kim F. Hall, "Guess Who's Coming to Dinner? Colonization and Miscegenation in 'The Merchant of Venice,'" *Renaissance Drama* 23 (1992): 87–88.

50. Hall, "Guess Who's Coming to Dinner?" 87–88.

51. Imtiaz Habib, *Black Lives in the English Archives, 1500–1677* (New York: Routledge, 2017), 7.

52. For more on this, see Habib, *Black Lives*, 141–42; Roslyn Knutson, "A Caliban in St. Mildred Poultry," in *The Selected Proceedings of the International Shakespeare Association World Congress Tokyo 1991*, ed. Tetsuo Kishi et al. (Newark: University of Delaware Press, 1994), 110–26.

53. Geraldine Heng, *The Invention of Race in the European Middle Ages* (New York: Cambridge University Press, 2018), 3.

54. *OED Online*, s.v., "Multitude, *n.*, 3.b."

55. Arthur L. Little, "Is It Possible to Read Shakespeare through Critical White Studies," in Thompson, *Cambridge Companion to Shakespeare and Race*, 271–72.

56. Little, "Is It Possible," 271.

57. Heng, *Invention of Race*, 3.

58. Olivette Otele, *African Europeans: An Untold History* (New York: Basic Books, 2021), 25.

59. Dennis Austin Britton, *Becoming Christian: Race, Reformation, and Early Modern English Romance* (New York: Fordham University Press, 2014), 21.

60. Britton, *Becoming Christian*, 36–37.

61. Imtiaz Habib and Duncan Salkeld, "The Reasonables of Boroughside, Southwark: An Elizabethan Black Family near the Rose Theatre," *Shakespeare* 11, no. 2 (2015): 137.

62. Ayanna Thompson, "Did the Concept of Race Exist for Shakespeare and His Contemporaries? An Introduction," in Thompson, *Cambridge Companion to Shakespeare and Race*, 7–8.

63. My phrasing here is an homage to Derrick Bell, *Faces at the Bottom of the Well: The Permanence of Racism* (New York: Basic Books, 1992).

64. Roger Bastide, "Color, Racism, and Christianity," *Daedalus* 96, no. 2 (Spring 1967): 34–49.

65. Robyn Maynard, *Policing Black Lives: State Violence in Canada from Slavery to the Present* (Halifax: Fernwood, 2017), 13.

4

THE NATION EMBARRASSED

Shameful Memories in the Henriad

JOHN S. GARRISON AND KYLE PIVETTI

JOHN OF GAUNT BEGAN SPEAKING again in 2016, as he so often does in times of national distress. His famous lines in *Richard II* build through a series of rhythmic repetitions, each layering myths of the nation, from its martial prowess to its divinely sanctioned lineage. This is the sort of passage playgoers memorize without conscious effort, and when it is trotted out, it may elicit eyerolls from Shakespeareans who know the conservative dreams that often follow:

> This royal throne of kings, this sceptered isle,
> This earth of majesty, this seat of Mars,
> This other Eden, demi-paradise,
> This fortress built by nature for herself
> Against infection and the hand of war,
> This happy breed of men, this little world.[1]

But Gaunt's vision took on new meaning in 2016 with Brexit (the UK's vote to exit the European Union). Claims of exceptionalism—and natural segregation—suddenly seemed all the more pertinent, and the journalists and politicians who knew their Shakespearean jargon jumped at the opportunity. Member of Parliament Chris Bryant opened his April 2016 *Guardian* piece, "This Sceptic Isle Would Most Displease Pro-Europe Shakespeare," with the assertion, "I have not a shadow of a doubt that William Shakespeare would have voted to remain."[2] His title taunts readers with a play on the "sceptered isle," turning it to "this sceptic isle" as a sardonic gesture at the poison of the Brexit ideology. Shakespeare,

Bryant insists, never turned away from Europe, never lost sight of either the Continent or the larger world. For Bryant, John of Gaunt conforms to that welcoming worldview: "The speech is hardly the epitome of English patriotism as it is spoken by John of Gaunt, a Flanders-born claimant to the throne of Castile who ends with the words 'this England . . . is now leased out . . . like to a tenement or pelting farm.'"[3] And so John of Gaunt entered the Brexit debate, still waging war over English identity centuries after his death.

Daniel Hannan, a key proponent of the initial Brexit movement, retaliated via *CapX*, a website advocating for "popular capitalism."[4] Hannan dismissed Bryant's editorial as "click-bait," specifically on the matter of John of Gaunt. "Hmm. Let's recall the full version [of the speech]," wrote Hannan, "bearing in mind that our country's present subordination before the EU is the result of the inky blots of the Treaty of Rome."[5] He quoted from the speech—"This land of such dear souls, this dear dear land, / Dear for her reputation through the world, / Is now leased out"—before directing a withering bit of sarcasm at Bryant, "Eerily apposite, no?"[6] Emma Smith, in her own April 2019 op ed in the *Guardian*, summarized the Brexit debates as Shakespearean tragedy, replete with the "wounded, self-deluded, malign or unheroic characters worthy of a Shakespearean cast."[7] John of Gaunt once again emerged, in the figure of "nostalgically principled" Dominic Grieve, a member of Parliament whose support of Remain recalled Gaunt's troubling vision of a fraught future for a changed England.[8] The "sceptered isle" speech echoed throughout these exchanges and others like them, shifting positions as it was reappropriated again and again. But if Shakespeare's political positions might slip between Remain and Leave depending on a twist of emphasis, the emotional impact of the speech seemed to be the same, regardless of any allegiance to Remain or Leave.

Mark Mardell, an editor and presenter for the BBC, showed as much in his June 2016 Brexit commentary based on *Richard II*'s iconic lines, writing, "As so often, Shakespeare put it best," before delivering a potential early modern slogan for twenty-first-century isolationism: "This blessèd plot, this earth, this realm, this England."[9] Mardell offered a sober and thoughtful commentary on the proposed separation, all the while recognizing the inextricable ties between English history and that of the Continent. By the end of his commentary, he returned to Shakespeare's particular emotional impacts: "We see ourselves as separate, and so we shall soon be cut out of councils and commission that are still shaping a continent. Some in Brussels may reflect smugly on how John of Gaunt's speech in

Richard II concludes: 'That England that was wont to conquer others / Hath made a shameful conquest of itself.'"[10] John of Gaunt's panegyric, after its wistful insistence on the grandeur of England, resolves in shame, and Mardell exploited the irony. Patriotism culminates not with fireworks but with the blush of embarrassment.

Others went even further. Fintan O'Toole, in a 2018 book titled *Heroic Failure: Brexit and the Politics of Pain*, once again invoked John of Gaunt. "If one were to ask most Brexiters for a piece of poetry that summed up their patriotic feelings," he wrote, "it would probably be John of Gaunt's mesmerizing evocation of a sacred England in *Richard II*."[11] Like Mardell, O'Toole seized upon the false fantasies of the speech; he pointed out that England itself is not an island and that any vision of a virginal England deliberately ignores the other nations and people populating the land. O'Toole, though, also made the turn to affect: "In the Brexit negotiations, the idea of national humiliation moved from fiction to reality. There was a strange ecstasy of shame."[12] Humiliation, he suggested, is the point. In fact, the word "ecstasy" conjures up raucous, perhaps libidinal, celebrations of national embarrassment. Gaunt himself finishes by saying that England "hath made a shameful conquest of itself" and that the island "is now bound in with shame" (2.1.63–66). That blush works in concert with the nostalgic impulse of the speech, not in opposition to it, and the "ecstasy" of shame is what makes John of Gaunt patriotic.

In this chapter, we take up the shameful conclusions of nostalgia with attention to Shakespeare's best-known and celebrated versions of English history. Shame runs throughout the Henriad: in the irresolute young prince, the bashful bride, and the consequences of military defeat, moments that may seem counter to the triumphant nationalism of *Henry V*. However, a once innocent Eden, destroyed in an ecstasy of shame, may just be the most telling image of England in the tetralogy. Indeed, such a dynamic may seem familiar to readers, as politicians of the contemporary era call forth the vision of a prelapsarian past (e.g., "Make America Great Again") to explicitly throw into relief the shameful state of the nation in the present. Inevitably, this strategy renders visible the dichotomy as false. This is a longing for a fiction, given that the past is often more fraught than the present. While the revelation of a shameful past may undermine the convenient dichotomy, it nevertheless fuels the project of nation-building. In fact, the discursive strategies coursing through both the Brexit debates and the Henriad underscore that a nation creates itself in the shameful yet celebratory exposure of its long history of failures and crimes.

Shameful Shakespeare

As we place our emphasis in this chapter on the Henriad, we follow Ewan
Fernie's assertion that the "theatrical experience of shaming is ritually re-
deeming and ethically productive."[13] We focus on the history plays because
of their concerns for English pasts and constructions of collective memory.
In that backward gaze, we find, the "shameful conquest" reappears, motivating performance and political identity alike. *Richard II* is a fitting starting place, for the play constantly debates the nature of emotion and the
affective origins of nationhood. In Melissa Sanchez's phrasing, "*Richard II*
demonstrates the folly and futility of attempting to extricate affect from
politics."[14] That affective dimension, though, is simultaneously mnemonic.
Jonathan Baldo argues that over the course of the play, "Richard is transformed from a monarch who is defined largely by his studied neglect of the
past to an embodiment of painful historical awareness."[15] To look back to
history is to experience an affective politics, and in *Richard II*, this means
confronting pasts the audience might want to forget.

Shakespeare's play opens with a crisis of memory as Richard navigates
the fallout from the Duke of Gloucester's execution. In the effort to obscure
his own crimes, the king pleads with his subjects:

> Let's purge this choler without letting blood.
> This we prescribe, though no physician.
> Deep malice makes too deep incision.
> Forget, forgive; conclude and be agreed. (1.1.157–60)

His lines could be a mission statement for Shakespeare's entire history
cycle: in expunging the trauma of civil war, the nation as a whole can "conclude and be agreed." The metaphor of surgery links that memory to the
body. Though Richard insists no bloodletting is necessary, he soon learns
that oblivion will not come so easily. The king admits as much in the ironic
gestures so common to Shakespeare's histories. In the speech just cited,
playgoers find Richard opening the history play with a wish for immediate
conclusion and blanket forgetting. Yet the audience knows that they will
now witness five acts of drama that will reinscribe the nation's chronicled
past. At the play's end, Richard will deliver an inverse of the Saint Crispin's
day speech, as if Henry's future nostalgia were instead future trauma. He
imagines his queen speaking with "good old folks" by the fire (5.1.41–42)
and instructs her,

> Tell thou the lamentable tale of me,
> And send the hearers weeping to their beds,
> For why the senseless brands will sympathize
> The heavy accent of thy moving tongue,
> And in compassion weep the fire out (5.1.45–49).

The memory now extends beyond his lifespan. Richard may as well be speaking to the audience at the playhouse, who hear now the "lamentable tale" and experience the emotional consequences. In *Richard II*, to remember is to feel; to feel is to remember.

John of Gaunt's vision of England collapses in a "shameful conquest," a fate with distinctly gendered undercurrents. He first imagines the nation as a "teeming womb" (2.1.56) or a woman who is "Dear for reputation through the world" (2.1.64). By the end of his tribute, this figure is ruined in an echo of the original moment of human shame, Eve's corruption in the Garden of Eden. In fact, the Queen later confronts English subjects in her garden, making the allusion explicit. When the gardener predicts Richard's deposition, the Queen demands, "What Eve, what serpent, hath suggested thee / To make a second fall of cursed man?" (3.4.82–83). Richard's story, then, falls into familiar patterns. In Sally R. Munt's terms, the expulsion from Eden is "the foremost shame narrative of Western culture" and marks the beginnings of human self-consciousness.[16] That same narrative drives the political machinations of Shakespeare's play, from the degradation of the physical land to the degradation of the king. Shame has conquered Richard's subjects and one might assume the audience alike. And just as Eve's fall will echo through human experience, John of Gaunt insists that this condition will persist. He challenges Richard,

> Why, cousin wert thou regent of the world,
> It were a shame to let this land by lease;
> But, for thy world enjoying but this land,
> Is it not more than shame to shame it so? (2.1.115–18)

The initial charge is geographical; Richard literally rents out land in the act of conquest. The earlier implication of the "teeming womb," however, sexualizes the legal issue. Richard has prostituted his kingdom and himself.

John of Gaunt concludes his tirade with another bit of Shakespearean irony, knowing that actors will recite these curses far into the future. He declares to the king, "Live in thy shame, but die not shame with thee! /

These words hereafter thy tormenters be!" (2.1.142–43). Richard imagines his "lamentable tale" shared by the "good old folks" around the fireplace; John of Gaunt inserts his own damnations into that story. And when BBC commentators allude to the "sceptered isle" in discussions of Brexit, they prove that premonition at least partially correct: his words do act as "tormentors" that preserve and remember the experience of shame.

Eve Sedgwick, in her foundational work on affect, begins with the subject of shame, for it is the emotion that shapes community through its isolation of the individual. Shame, she asserts, "makes identity. In fact, shame and identity remains in very dynamic relation to one another, at once deconstituting and foundational, because shame is both peculiarly contagious and peculiarly individuating."[17] Her analysis leads to an almost inevitable conclusion: "Shame, it might finally be said, transformational shame, *is performance*. I mean theatrical performance."[18] An actor can be met with refusal or acceptance from the witnessing crowd, but there is no separating the inward shameful turn from the moment of display, nor the persecuted figure from the crowd that watches—the crowd that becomes in the shadow of the Globe playhouse a collective national body.

Indeed, the genre of the history play has particular purchase in the analysis of shame. Sara Ahmed argues that emotions do not simply occur within an individual's experience but are best regarded as social and cultural practices, exchanges that constitute the individual and the social in the first place. She directly tackles political valences of emotion, a project that leads her to an extended analysis of shame, intimately tied to the construction of nationalism. She evocatively posits that "shame" is central to how we "assert our identity as a nation," and though her discussion fixates on contemporary politics, we find that it speaks aptly to early modern political dynamics.[19] If the genre of the history play serves a crucial function in constructing the early modern nation, then of course the genre returns to shame, using it in questioning and reasserting just who belongs in the "our" of "our identity as a nation."[20] So shame is theatrical, and shame constructs nationhood. Ahmed also implies shame's centrality in the reconstruction of the past, underscoring that the feeling links closely to memory. Shakespeareans have noted the memory-inflected operations of affect in the history plays. As Isabel Karremann argues, for example, a play such as *1 Henry IV* depends upon "the memory politics of nostalgia as well as its policy of affect."[21] But shame specifically plays a crucial function in the politics of Shakespeare's histories, following from the attempt to revitalize the past.

1 HENRY IV AND THE NATIONALIZATION OF SHAME

The public stage of early modern London provided a venue for ritual embarrassment in which all could partake. Steven Mullaney has characterized the playhouse as "an inhabited affective technology . . . within which, and with which, they could think and feel things not always easy or comfortable to articulate."[22] The space of the Globe, and its rival playhouses, created a unique emotional interaction by its very construction, even when those emotions might prove disturbing or unwanted. The stage was well-suited for all to participate in the memories of embarrassment—even if everyone wanted to forget.

Shakespeare raises the paradox of shameful memory at the opening of *1 Henry IV* with an anxious report of the battlefield and what becomes a troubling feminine presence for the male soldiers. The distress is made all the more pronounced when we consider that the battle is not Henry's desired crusade to "strands afar remote" (1.1.4) but rather the violent conflict with Glyndwr's Welsh rebels. Westmoreland reports to King Henry that upon the thousands of slain English soldiers

> there was such misuse,
> Such beastly shameless transformation,
> By those Welshwomen done as may not be
> Without much shame retold or spoken of. (1.1.43–46)

The lines deploy *occupatio*, a rhetorical device through which a speaker alludes to but provides no details about a tantalizing subject. Westmoreland clearly suggests why he would rather not give the full account of the Welshwomen mutilating the sex organs of their enemies: to do so would reiterate the "shameless transformation" of the English subjects.

George Puttenham explains just such a rhetorical motivation in *The Art of English Poesy* (1589), a contemporaneous guide to figures of speech. He describes the device as "*Aposiopesis*, of the Figure of Silence," which occurs "when we begin to speak a thing and break off in the middle way, as if either it needed no further to be spoken of, or that we were ashamed or afraid to speak it out."[23] Puttenham offers the example of a lover speaking to his "sweetheart, whom he checked for secretly whispering with a suspected person."[24] In the midst of questioning her, this speaker breaks off his speech, knowing that to get into the details risks shame on all parties. The quote reads, "And did ye not come by his chamber door? And tell him that—go to, I say no more."[25] This imagined character skirts the sexual content, knowing that whatever was said at the "chamber door" could threaten his masculinity. Also noteworthy is the memory involved: this lover is recalling what happened in the past and would rather not return to that shameful moment. Puttenham goes on to note regarding *occupatio*, "This figure is fit for fantastical heads and such as be sudden or lack memory."[26] Those who cannot remember might use "the Figure of Silence." Westmoreland does just so in his report. He cannot say what happened to his direct audience—King Henry—for fear of repeating the shame; it is as if he lost the memory. Better to forget the event than it be "retold," which is a strange sentiment coming in a history play that otherwise glories in retelling the past. The moment reveals that the history play is co-constituted by what the actors overtly display on stage and what the performance conjures implicitly in the minds of spectators.

Regardless of the lapses, members of the early modern audience and today's audience might know (or might now be motivated to find out) this past, thus stirring collective memory of the battle even as that memory is ostensibly erased. This is the work of *occupatio*—to recall the shame without naming the shame, to let it persist while denying its legacy. Westmoreland's report reinforces the dynamics that Raphael Lyne has traced in early modern literature "where the memory in the mind and the memory in the text extend but also challenge each other."[27] Although asked not to think about the event, those familiar with Shakespeare's source text, Holinshed's *Chronicles*, might recall the "shameful villainy" of the Welshwomen that day, including how they "cut off [the dead soldiers'] privates and put one part thereof into the mouths of every dead man, in such a sort that the cullions hung down to their chins; and not so contented, they did cut off their noses and thrust them into their tails as they lay on the ground mangled and defaced."[28] If "desire is death," as Sonnet 147 announces, we see dramatized here the connection of that formulation to shamefulness. Joseph Roach has argued that the "necrophilic impulse [. . .] serves the ends of performance in a particular way," given that necrophilia "seeks to preserve a sense of the relationship with the past by making physical contact with the dead."[29] In the case of *1 Henry IV*, this peculiar sexual practice is part of the long story that gave birth to the English nation. On the one hand, framing the Welshwomen as possessing perverse desires reverberates with a long history of politicized discourses that Jasbir Puar has shown portray the enemy as "pathologically sexually deviant" and the queerness of their bodies as "antination or antinationalist."[30] On the other hand, Holinshed's depiction also underlines the ways in which political rebellions interrupt normative heterosexual reproduction. That is, this rebellion destroys English fathers, who cannot then produce English sons. The Welshwomen sexualize the corpses in their abuse and so dramatize the impotence of the soldiers' penises and the perverse manner in which they are used. These English bodies serve metonymically for the threatened demise of Englishness, and the shameful sexual engagement with them points to the patriarchy's inability to produce additional English bodies through conquest. As with Puttenham's wounded lover, their shame abounds. So what are they doing in the genre of the emergent national identity?

Shakespeare, of course, proves selective with the history plays; he edits events to best serve theatrical—and political—purposes. The playwright's conscious crafting of his plays in the context of mnemonic practices has led a number of scholars to treat these plays not so much as history plays but as memory plays.[31] That is, these dramas are less concerned with what actually happened and more concerned with how the events have been remembered by subsequent generations. As such, Shakespeare must also grapple with material that might have best not been remembered, those emotions and events which could frustrate the nation-building impetus of the genre as a whole. What is curious about the opening of *1 Henry IV* is Shakespeare's habit of calling attention to that which would be better left behind. Reflecting on the capriciousness of recollection, Montaigne posits in his *Essayes* (1603) that "memory represents unto us not what we choose but what pleases her."[32] In order to control memory and suppress shame, one should endeavor to control recall. But *occupatio* does the opposite: it recalls not what we choose but what memory cannot lose. Montaigne adds, "Nothing so deeply imprints anything in our remembrance as to the desire to forget the same."[33] That is, the more we try to forget something, the more it stays with us. The history plays shore up the nationalistic impulses to forget, training the polity's memory one audience at a time.

If *occupatio* is useful for those with poor memory, it might also be useful for the collective that experiences shame and would pretend to forget. In a foundational article on collective memory, Paul Connerton lists the "Seven Types of Forgetting," a self-conscious allusion to Daniel Schacter's *The Seven Sins of Memory*. In response to those who note memory's failings, Connerton hopes to discover the uses of forgetting, as in repressing historical material that does not satisfy an official narrative. In his final type of forgetting, Connerton strikes a tone Puttenham might find familiar: he identifies "Forgetting as Humiliated Silence," the deliberate refusal to speak to embarrassments of the past, where "occasions of humiliation are so difficult to forget [make it] often easier to forget physical pain than to forget humiliation."[34] This claim articulates the consistent pattern of Shakespeare's histories—to reiterate the "collective shame" and "a desire to forget." Even in Westmoreland's deliberate silence, the embarrassment finds its retelling. Shame, in other words, is memory. And the history plays are full of shame because it's the only way to remember where England began. The history plays invest in a communal nostalgia; they also invest in a communal humiliation.

This context—where recollection and forgetting intermingle with each other and with the operations of gender and sexuality—sets into relief the charges Hotspur advances in the opening scenes of *1 Henry IV*. Hotspur's rebellion stems from his refusal to hand over Scottish prisoners, a refusal initially sparked when the effeminate courtier speaks to Hotspur with "lady terms" (1.3.45). This interaction echoes the gendered anxieties of Westmoreland's report, for the one who talks "so like a waiting gentlewoman" implicitly castrates Hotspur by demanding his rewards. It is after Henry exits that Hotspur invokes shame once again. Chastising his own family, Hotspur cries,

> Shall it for shame be spoken in these days,
> Or fill up chronicles in time to come,
> That men of your nobility and power
> Did gage them both in an unjust behalf,
> As both of you, God pardon it, have done:
> To put down Richard, that sweet lovely rose,
> And plant this thorn, this canker, Bolingbroke? (1.3.168–74)

Hotspur here agonizes over the future retellings of his, and his family's, actions: their shame will "fill up chronicles in time to come" as, specifically, the shame of those who overthrew Richard. Although Hotspur often stands out for his rejection of the domestic sphere in favor of the battlefield, his focus on family lets us know that he is not disinterested in matters of the family and of reproduction. Like the soldiers maimed by the Welshwomen, Hotspur has been threatened by feminine presence, and now his pride is at stake. The moment also toys with the history genre in the same reflexive manner as *Richard II*. After all, their shame shall in fact "be spoken" by English actors on stage long after the real Hotspur is dead, just as the lines of *Richard II* echo through that early modern technology of affect. What these rebels "have done" before is reiterated and retold, even when *occupatio* would rather it be erased.

The affective dimension of shameful recall also permeates the distinctions between English and Welsh identity. Stephen Greenblatt and Catherine Gallagher describe Glyndwr's vow to "call spirits from the vasty deep" as emblematic of the scholar's efforts to recapture distant historical periods.[35] The Welshman pledges that he can invoke demons or devils; the historical scholar calls forth the ghosts of another time. Greenblatt and Gallagher do mention Hotspur's skeptical response—"But will they come when you do call for them?" (3.1.53)—yet they do not go as far as to consider how that response develops. Hotspur tells Glyndwr,

> If thou have power to raise [the devil], bring him hither,
> And I'll be sworn I have power to shame him hence.
> O, while you live, tell truth and shame the devil. (3.1.57–59)

If Glyndwr's invocation serves as a metaphor for reproducing the past, as Greenblatt and Gallagher treat it, then the immediate response is to treat that past as worthy of shame. The magical conjuration becomes humiliation because embarrassment follows from telling the truth of what happened. As Lee Edelman observes, sex and history represent two categories that both rely on what happens "after" to inform their legitimacy. That is, "the privileging of reproduction as the after-event of sex [. . .] imbues straight sex with its meaning as the agent of historical continuity" while the authority of "historical knowing [. . .] depends on the fetishistic prestige of origin, genealogy, [and] telos."[36] Edelman's broader claims about the nature of sex and history can be extended to the situation of the sonneteer, who knows that shame attends to lust and its hellish pursuit of nonprocreative sex, and Hotspur in this moment links that same fallen affect to the dramatic genre of the history play. Put simply, what is produced from "the vasty deep" will embarrass you.

Hal is also no stranger to the role of shame. The young prince, we all know, begins the play in a state of ill repute, and he will deliberately orchestrate his arc of redemption. In the central confrontation with his father, Hal makes clear that he knows the theatrical value of shame. He imagines the forthcoming battle with Percy:

> I will wear a garment all of blood,
> And stain my favours in a bloody mask,

> Which, washed away, shall scour my shame with it.
> (3.2.135–37)

Like his rebellious counterparts, Hal must manage his reputation for future chroniclers as well as for future playwrights. If he has accumulated shame in the earlier moments of the play, in the climactic battles that shame will be washed away in blood. Ahmed argues that shame serves national purpose by allowing the collective to announce, "I'm sorry," thus reaffirming their status as a collective. Hal has predicted Ahmed's argument on the field of Shrewsbury. His shameful reputation, recorded in the chronicles alongside the civil wars of English medieval history, is scoured away through performance. He indulges shame on the part of the English so that they may emerge as English. The play's initial *occupatio*, like Hotspur's link between the past and the devil, seeks to obscure what happened. Hal gives away the next steps: sexual disgrace and invoking the devil prove necessary to the collective. Painful pasts are inevitably recalled with dishonor—all in the effort to restore honor.

Hal thus indicates the uneasy dynamics between the collective and emotional memory. So often, the history plays are associated with the rise of the nation and the resolution of ancient fractures.[37] What Hal understands, though, merges with theories of memory from the period: that which is painful sticks most effectively in the memory. Writing in a mode dedicated to remembering, playwrights who use the genre of history share a point of view with those writing on the art of memory during the Renaissance. And, as we will see, this shared perspective will have some unsettling strategies with uneasy implications. Namely, what is painful will make the past, and so make the collective that follows.

Shaming Bodies, Building Nations in *Henry V*

When the king stands before the walls at Harfleur in *Henry V*, his rhetorical strategy is not quite *occupatio*. Harry speaks a litany of horrors that may come to pass unless the French succumb to English might. Beyond the immediate violence, though, Harry makes potent the shame that will descend upon the French. The English soldier, he says,

> In liberty of bloody hand, shall range
> With conscience wide as hell, mowing like grass
> Your fresh fair virgins and your flow'ring infants. (3.3.89–91)

Harry renders the female body the site of sexualized violence, and he places the blame not on the perpetrating soldiers but on the men of Harfleur:

> What is 't to me, when you yourselves are cause,
> If your pure maidens fall into the hand
> Of hot and forcing violation? (3.3.96–98).

In obverse relation to the unsaid humiliations of *occupatio*, Henry indulges in the description, giving us much more access to the crimes that his troops *would commit* in comparison to whatever crimes the Welshwomen *did commit*. He's constructing a future, but in a play so obsessed with constructions of memory, Henry also manufactures an alternative past for the English playgoer of the 1590s:

> in a moment look to see
> The blind and bloody soldier with foul hand
> Desire the locks of your shrill-shrieking daughters,
> Your fathers taken by the silver beards
> And their most reverend heads dashed to the walls,
> Your naked infants spitted upon pikes
> Whiles the mad mothers with their howls confused
> Do break the clouds. (3.3.110–17)

The lines thrill in depictions of perverse violation, the likes of which were politely avoided in *1 Henry IV*. In the process, the speech also underlines the connection between shame and collective memory. By repeatedly placing guilt upon the French—"What say you? Will you yield and this avoid / Or, guilty in defense, be thus destroyed?"—Henry suggests that the incident would be remembered not for the violence he would perpetrate but rather for the guilt of the townspeople who engendered the violent attack (3.3.119–20).[38] Garrett Sullivan has argued that "shame and honor [. . .] are the end end-result of a disciplining process that produces a certain type of (honorable, honest) subject and helps to shape the subject's interactions with the world."[39] To forget these qualities, Sullivan argues, is to lose track of one's public self. Henry makes clear that a surrender by Harfleur will prevent him from committing dishonorable acts as much as it will save the townspeople the embarrassment of being defeated. In both cases, shame manifests as the basis of political identity, and the women of Harfleur play the part of victim, whether the violence is literalized or not.

Later in *Henry V*, the play explicitly links the French defeat with collective shame. As the battle turns against the French forces, Bourbon proclaims, "Shame, and eternal shame, nothing but shame! / Let us die!" (4.5.11–12). The French, a force similar to the rebellious Welsh in their failure to resist English nationhood, bring shame upon themselves. Just as the English must reconcile themselves to the acts of the Welsh during the rebellion, the French must now internalize shameful feelings because winning and losing at war—with all of the attendant links of that process with gender and sexuality—are necessary vicissitudes in the project of sustaining a national body. Brian Massumi uses the helpful term "thinking-feeling" to describe how emotions are integral to the operations of recollection because an event "can only retrospectively be 'owned,' or owned up to, in memory and post-facto reception."[40] Even though Massumi here discusses how an individual understands events in retrospect, we extend this claim to encompass collective memory, both in terms of the French characters reflecting on their defeat and in terms of playgoers witnessing this theatrical performance of shame. In fact, Shakespeare's characters ironically invoke that very process. Earlier in the play, the King of France describes the historical defeat at the hands of the Black Prince Edward as a "too-much-memorable shame," underscoring both the role of shame in military matters and shame's ties to recalcitrant recollection (2.4.56). These hauntings persist in the world of the play as much as in the collective audience, which witnesses again the lasting power of humiliation. When Orleans announces the failure of the French military effort, "Le jour est perdu, tout est perdu!," the Dauphin responds, "Reproach and everlasting shame / Sits mocking in our plumes" (4.5.2–4). The use of "everlasting" points to how shame and history are intertwined while the use of the plural pronoun "our" points to how this shame rests collectively upon the surviving French. In an invocation of Shakespeare's tragic Romans—particularly Lucrece—the Dauphin goes as far as to suggest that self-annihilation might alleviate the embarrassment of loss: "O perdurable shame! Let's stab ourselves" (4.5.8). Yet acts of individual suicide on the part of these historical figures would prove futile: personal oblivion cannot supersede the operations of their shame-ridden collective memory. The defeat has already been inscribed in the chronicles of the national history, and an English playwright strategically reinscribes it through emotion-filled theatrical performance.

And while the French seek to self-annihilate, the English coalesce their body politic. When Henry identifies the battleground as the field of Agincourt, Fluellen invokes the history of English conquest, a history which is both national and familial:

> Your grandfather of famous memory, an't please your Majesty,
> and your great-uncle Edward the Plack Prince of Wales, as I have
> read in the chronicles, fought a most prave pattle here in France.
> (4.7.97–101)

On one level, Henry's success on the battlefield will further cement the glory of the English nation as it has been captured in the written record. On another level, his prowess will prove his place in the patriarchal line, reinforcing those heteronormative logics that justify sexual desire as long as it contributes to the production of children and the security of the nation. This becomes the very purpose of the final scene, in which Henry strives to secure his possession of France through marriage and the implicit production of his heir. Although Shakespeare's audience might have understood that Henry's conquest fails with the next generation, at the moment, collective identity follows from procreation—achieved through the woman's shame, too. Before the final negotiations begin with France, Burgundy foresees the restitution of heterosexual propagation. He describes peace as "Dear nurse of arts, plenties and joyful births" (5.2.34), and he continues with an extended metaphor on the agriculture of France. At the end of war, the country's "husbandry doth lie on heaps, / Corrupting in its own fertility" (5.2.39–40); the meadow "conceives by idleness" (5.2.51) and grows only weeds; the vineyards become "defective in their natures, grown to wilderness" (5.2.55). Nature has succumbed to destruction and neglect. The time has come for Henry to reconstitute order through marriage and through his sexual abilities. If he follows from the model of his uncle, he will also propel that lineage, drawing upon the devices of the memory artist in doing so.

During the negotiations, Henry reminds Katherine of her feminine shame, even if he does so under the pretense of comforting her. As he escalates his flattery of the French princess, he tells her,

> Put off your maiden blushes, avouch the thoughts of your
> heart with the looks of an empress, take me by the hand and say
> "Harry of England, I am thine"[.] (5.2.218–20)

By projecting emotions upon Katherine, he manufactures her subjectivity.

The French princess demurs, he imagines, because of her "maiden blushes," so Henry tells her to forget the propriety of custom—or the shame of sexual longing—and accept the marriage, the peace, the promise of his future lineage. The line "Put off your maiden blushes," however, stands in stark contrast to the French lament at the end of battle, when "everlasting shame" dominates the scene. Henry may ward off Katherine's blush, but he also knows shame does not vanish so easily. In fact, he might just wish those blushes remain, because they emphasize her status as a reluctant, conquerable object of affection. Katherine later turns away from Henry's kiss and cites French customs; Henry answers, "We are the makers of manners, Kate, and the liberty that follows our places stops the mouth of all find-faults, as I will do yours" (5.2.252–54). She blushes, and he persists. In a sense, he cultivates the embarrassment in not just imperial and sexual aggression, but in mnemonic aggression. Burgundy in the same scene describes the princess as "a maid yet rosed over with the virgin crimson of modesty" (5.2.273–74), a remark that only sparks bawdy wordplay between the men. The point, then, is that Henry exploits Katherine's modesty, and by attending to the operation of shame across the Henriad, we can recognize it as the trick of a memory artist. He tells of Katherine's shamefulness and so manipulates its lasting power for English nationhood.

Henry thus comes from a line of men whose sexual congress is made pure. Edelman frames such an ideology as "the collective fantasy that invests the social order with meaning by way of reproductive futurism."[41] Considered in light of this notion, Henry's virtue and the justification of the English nationalistic project are reified by the notion that he is a child of great men and will assumedly produce more great men. Indeed, the King of France recognizes just this threat when he connects Edward the Black Prince to Henry's militarism, for Henry is "bred out of that bloody strain / That haunted us in our familiar paths" (2.4.51–52). That is, an earlier defeat plagues the French, and Henry is himself the spirit emerging from the depths of their cultural memory, resuscitated to remind the French of their shame. It is no wonder, then, that in his next line the French king laments his country's "too-much-memorable shame." That shame is Henry. In fact, when Exeter delivers Henry's claim to the French throne, he names it as "this most memorable line" (2.4.88). Sanguilineal inheritance, only made possible through the shameful act of sexual coupling, secures Henry's royal position. That shame-inflected inheritance also secures the national project at work throughout *Henry V*. Throughout the play and especially here in

Exeter's speech, claim to a royal bloodline is made alongside the presence of shame, recreated in the ashamed woman and the French soldier simultaneously. Defeat of the enemy obviously establishes national pride. Yet there is no Henry—and no Henry's England—without the humiliation of defeat.

This powerful calculus that intertwines sexuality and nationhood works not only vertically to valorize the family line but also horizontally to expand the scope of the national corpus. Fluellen, for example, seizes upon the moment of King Henry's swelling pride to redeem the Welsh and reinforce their place in the English body politic:

> If your Majesties is remembered of it, the Welshmen did good service in a garden where leeks did grow, wearing leeks in their Monmouth caps, which, your Majesty know, to this hour is an honorable badge of the service. And I do believe your Majesty takes no scorn to wear the leek upon Saint Tavy's day. (4.7.103–9)

In *1 Henry IV*, the Welsh female body was the site of shame and engaged in shameful acts that stymied the production of English subjects. Here the Welsh male body is a point of pride—growing things from the ground rather than severing bodies on the ground—and contributes to producing more English subjects. The perversions of the Welshwomen, whatever they were, are incorporated into a renewed collective. Henry responds, "I wear it for a memorable honor, / For I am Welsh, you know, good countryman" (4.7.110–11). The symbol of the Welsh is transferred to the king's body, and by extension the national English body. The act leads Fluellen to declare, "By Jeshu, I am your Majesty's countryman, I care not who know it. I will confess it to all the 'orld. I need not to be ashamed of your Majesty" (4.7.117–19). Fluellen absolves himself of shame based on the king's symbolic incorporation of the Welsh both into his singular body and into his other body: that of the English nation.

In his famous speech at Agincourt at the climax of the play, Henry deploys shame as a motivator for national pride in the same breath that he enjoins his soldiers to remember. The speech at first reflects upon the primacy of personal memory over the failures of collective because "old men forget; yet all shall be forgot, / But he'll remember with advantages / What feats he did that day" (4.3.51–53). Henry then goes on to counterpoise familial bonds on the side of those who fight with the conditions of sexual shame on the side of those English who do not fight:

> We few, we happy few, we band of brothers;
> For he today that sheds his blood with me
> Shall be my brother; be he ne'er so vile,
> This day shall gentle his condition;
> And gentlemen in England now abed
> Shall think themselves accursed they were not here,
> And hold their manhoods cheap whiles any speaks
> That fought with us upon Saint Crispin's day. (4.2.63–69)

The king's pronouncement that the men will be remembered in future depictions of the battle—and implicitly in productions of Shakespeare's play—is an overt reminder that the theater, as Marvin Carlson puts it, "is the repository of cultural memory but, like the memory of each individual, it is also subject to continual adjustment and modification as the memory is recalled in new circumstances and contexts."[42] A play that may have served as a rallying cry for supporting the English troops in World War II here takes up a patriotic strain while also more complexly rendering visible the coextensive operations of nation-building and managing shame in the sixteenth century. Henry's speech deploys terms of "proximity, solidarity, collegiality, friendship," bonds which Lauren Berlant counterpoises to the more frequently cited affective attachments that drive political alliance, "the hatreds, aversions, and not caring," in the hope that the former might be seized upon to realize "the ambitions and capacities of love" for its capacity to "to (re)build a world."[43] However, Henry's speech reveals the darker implications of even such seemingly positive attachments. Englishmen who did not fight are shamed. And the speech cannot help but echo his threat to rape the women of Harfleur, as both discourses celebrate English militarized sexual stamina over male sexual desire not tied to nationalized conquest. The men of the audience, having themselves not been at the battle of Agincourt, may even briefly wonder if their own manhoods should be assessed as equally cheap, especially given how "bodily shame" can be experienced "as a structure of memory or as a momentary perception of bodiliness."[44] Like the sonnets' speaker, their sexual congress is a wasteful, shameful enterprise. Yet it also does productive work. When men not at Agincourt have sex, they should think of England and remember those men who were at the battle. The manhoods of these non-soldiers, though devalued, can still produce English subjects who can at least further the project of recalling exemplary, unembarrassing men of the past.

The repeated nature of performance shapes memory in its provocations and resolutions of embarrassment. The audience must experience, across time and place, a continual rejection and absorption of these painful memories. Just as the king hears of the desecrations done to English soldiers but is left to imagine or shut out the specifics, playgoers must confront the disgraces of the past that are depicted even in history plays that seemingly celebrate the nation's past triumphs. Heather K. Love observes, "Although the capacity of shame to isolate is well documented, its ability to bring together shamed individuals into meaningful community is more tenuous."[45] Here we see this curious capacity of shame dramatized first in the speech at Agincourt and then in the exchange between Henry and Exeter. Shakespeare's playgoers might find themselves cheering Henry's troops, all the while realizing that they might never experience the level of glory that earned those soldiers their valorized place in history. Further, the audience knows that not all of the soldiers had the opportunity to return home to celebrate the victory. Indeed, those who died would not even know that the English had been victorious. Shakespeare's audience must negotiate such difficult identarian terrain as it is related by citizenship to victorious soldiers—not only at Agincourt but in more recent battles with the Spanish Armada or at Cadiz—and part of a national body that has rebelled and committed deplorable acts. As Ewan Fernie argues, "We must take up the shame of our violent epoch. In spite of a desperate, delusive tendency to sustain the imprisoning idol of selfhood, we must let it explode from its own internal tensions and contradictions, and adventure beyond the self. The spiritual and political health of our species depends on it."[46] In the histories, to "take up" shame requires the continual unfolding of the painful memory, to "adventure beyond the self" by living the tears and disgraces of the past. Fernie treats shame as an ethical force guiding spectators to better behavior; in the Henriad, collective humiliation becomes a joint venture in English political identity.

When the pundits of Brexit exchange lines from Shakespeare, when they recite the speeches of John of Gaunt, they participate in these very rituals, in the recitations that the characters had anticipated with horror. John of Gaunt, Richard II, Hotspur, and Henry all imagine shame trickling down through generations, shame for the actions they accomplished and what they didn't, shame for what is remembered and what they have sworn to forget. The Henriad, in other words, instantiates the complex role of the stage in nation-building, even if that process involves a "strange ecstasy of shame" that arrived with such immediacy in the Brexit deliberations. Shakespeare's memorial work reveals that there is nothing "strange" about this ecstasy, that contests over European identity in 2016 involve humiliation, just as they did in the 1590s.

And it is not just in the writing of political pundits that the troubling stirring of emotions that marks John of Gaunt's exit from the stage emerges in the turmoil of Brexit. In a survey of Britons living abroad during the Brexit debates, researcher Katie W. Higgins unveiled the acutely emotional impact for those who watched. Coursing through the language of the respondents is the vision of a "bad Britain" that has abandoned its worldly open-mindedness for isolation and xenophobia.[47] John of Gaunt imagined a fall from the state of innocence; the fall continues in the twenty-first century, for what was once good has been corrupted. Higgins asks the question of affect for those Britons living abroad: "Has the referendum caused you to reflect on your national identity, and in what way?" Their answers repeatedly imagine "a shift of feeling of pride in being British to shame and embarrassment in the lead up to and following the referendum."[48] Higgins quotes one female respondent living in Germany as saying, "My feeling of love for—and pride in—my British origin gave way to a feeling of deep shame, and I decided I could identify better with the values of my German country of residence than with what was going on in the UK."[49] On the surface, the woman rejects the national identity of her "British origin" and chooses instead the values of the political expatriate. In the context of the history play, the noble British lord witnesses the present and dismisses the nation he sees. Britain has been lost. What Higgins indicates, though, is that this separation, this emotional rejection of today's "bad Britain," requires the embrace of that original condition. Indeed, those who watch the proceedings with shame become the crowd united in their political identity; in asserting they are British no longer, they reiterate the British identity that paradoxically binds them. Another survey response reads, "I'm embarrassed to be British! We've become the laughing stock of the E.U."[50] In the respondents' despair, the glance looks backward at what was apparently British once before. But even in the history plays that imagine national origins, humiliation is key. It is the ecstasy that pulls the crowd together, turning them to the political collective. Even to reject the nation—to assert it as an unrecognizable version of itself—paradoxically requires putting oneself in the nation. It requires that the spectator watch from the ground as Richard cries for his failure and remembers the origins forever gone.

As the Brexit debates become the stuff of memory, it is inevitable that affect will attend. To remember, after all, is also to feel emotional impacts once again, maybe even for political events that one never experienced.

Writing on Brexit, political scientists Jonathan Moss, Emily Robinson, and Jake Watts cite the "affective turn" in their field, or the conscious attention to the role emotion plays in political decisions, not simply as a disruption to rational thought processes but as an inherent aspect of those thought processes.[51] These researchers also observe the humiliation running throughout the Brexit moment, although it remains just as fraught a part of national identity as we witness in the Henriad. They describe one respondent who "felt at first ashamed of what 'we' had done,' before slipping into sadness that 'other people had taken' her previous unappreciated European cultural identity from her." Her resentment casts blame on those who perhaps should feel ashamed, but in the same breath the embarrassment is a collective "we," as Sarah Ahmed had predicted. What "'we' had done" sticks, a memorial cue binding all. Shakespeare's audience does not hold the literal soldiers of Harfleur or Agincourt, but it confers their shames, negotiated against Europe in each performance, each staging, each ecstatic gathering for remembrance.

In *The Passions of the Minde in Generall* (1601), Thomas Wright describes the particular nature of the English as he seeks out the reasons why his countrymen would be considered a "simple" people in contrast to those of the rest of Europe; appropriately, he begins with the blush. His analysis is laced with the racial politics of climate and skin color, in a clear resonance with the 2016 moment. He says of English honesty, "The very blushing also of our people, sheweth a better ground, wherevpon Vertue may build, than certaine brazen faces, who never change themselves, although they committe, yea, and be deprehended in enormious crimes."[52] The threat of group embarrassment was always there, surfacing in the "crimes" that one could threaten to commit. Any sin, fault, or vice would be revealed in the face. In 1601 it made the English English, not that they remained innocent, but that their "crimes" were always visible. In the twenty-first century, the humiliating turn to past crimes, and the blush, still plays its part. Welcome to nationhood, it says, and shame on you all for watching.

Notes

1. All references to Shakespeare's plays draw from William Shakespeare, *The Norton Shakespeare*, second edition, ed. Stephen Greenblatt (New York: W. W. Norton, 2008). This quotation is from *Richard II*, 2.1.40–45.

2. Chris Bryant, "This Sceptic Isle Would Most Displease Pro-Europe Shakespeare," *Guardian*, April 21, 2016, accessed September 26, 2023. Web.

3. Bryant, "This Sceptic Isle."

4. See Daniel Hannan, "How Like a God: Shakespeare and the Invention of the World," CapX, April 23, 2016. Web. For a description of the website's purpose, see "About," CapX, accessed August 27, 2021. Anna Blackwell analyzes these Shakespearean Brexit debates in *Shakespearean Celebrity in the Digital Age: Fan Cultures and Remediation* (London: Palgrave Macmillan, 2019), see especially "Conclusion," 168.

5. Hannan, "How Like a God."

6. Hannan, "How Like a God."

7. Emma Smith, "May as Polonius, Gove as Cassius: Is Brexit a Shakespearean Tragedy?" *Guardian*, April 12, 2019. Web.

8. Smith, "May as Polonius."

9. Mark Mardell, "Brexit: The Story of an Island Apart," *BBC Magazine*, June 25, 2016. Web.

10. Mardell, "Brexit."

11. Fintan O'Toole, *Heroic Failure: Brexit and the Politics of Pain* (London: Head of Zeus, 2018).

12. O'Toole, *Heroic Failure.*

13. Ewan Fernie, *Shame in Shakespeare* (New York: Routledge, 2002), 111.

14. Melissa Sanchez, "Bodies That Matter in *Richard II*," in *Richard II: New Critical Essays*, ed. Jeremy Lopez (New York: Routledge, 2015). See also Jennifer Vaught, *Masculinity and Emotion in Early Modern English Literature* (Aldershot: Ashgate, 2008), 83–113.

15. Jonathan Baldo, *Memory in Shakespeare's Histories: Stages of Forgetting in Early Modern England* (New York: Routledge, 2012).

16. Sally R. Munt, *Queer Attachments: The Cultural Politics of Shame* (Burlington, VT: Ashgate, 2007), 80.

17. Eve Kosofsky Sedgwick, *Touching Feeling: Affect, Pedagogy, Performativity* (Durham, NC: Duke University Press, 2003), 36.

18. Sedgwick, *Touching Feeling*, 38.

19. Sara Ahmed, *The Cultural Politics of Emotion*, 2nd ed. (New York: Routledge, 2015), 102.

20. Moreover, Ahmed's theory of shameful nationhood depends upon the recovery of the past, except in this case the national collective looks to a past that appears unjust, unsavory, and embarrassing. "What is striking," she observes, "is how shame becomes not only a mode of recognition of injustices committed against others, but also a form of nationbuilding. . . . Recognition works to restore the nation or reconcile the nation to itself by 'coming to terms with' its own past in the expression of 'bad feeling'" (*Cultural Politics of Emotion*, 102).

21. Isabel Karremann, *The Drama of Memory in Shakespeare's History Plays* (Cambridge, UK: Cambridge University Press, 2015), 155.

22. Steven Mullaney, "Affective Technologies: Toward an Emotional Logic of the Elizabethan Stage," in *Environment and Embodiment in Early Modern England*, ed. Mary Floyd-Wilson and Garrett A. Sullivan (London: Palgrave Macmillan, 2007), 74.

23. George Puttenham, *The Art of English Poesy: A Critical Edition*, ed. Frank Whigham and Wayne A. Rebhorn (Ithaca, NY: Cornell University Press, 2007), 250.

24. Puttenham, *Art of English Poesy.*

25. Puttenham, *Art of English Poesy.*

26. Puttenham, *Art of English Poesy*, 251.

27. Raphael Lyne, *Memory and Intertextuality in Renaissance Literature* (Cambridge, UK: Cambridge University Press, 2016), 11.

28. Quoted in Marisa R. Cull, *Shakespeare's Princes of Wales: English Identity and the Welsh Connection* (Oxford: Oxford University Press, 2014), 67. The passage appears in Raphael Holinshed, *The Third Volume of the Chronicles of England, Scotlande, and Irelande* (London: 1586), 528.

29. Joseph Roach, "History, Memory, Necrophilia," in *The Ends of Performance*, ed. Peggy Phelan and Jill Lane (New York: New York University Press, 1998), 29.

30. Jasbir K. Puar, *Terrorist Assemblages: Homonationalism in Queer Times* (Durham, NC: Duke University Press, 2007), 77 and 87.

31. See, for example, Baldo, *Memory in Shakespeare's Histories*; Philip Schwyzer, *Literature, Nationalism and Memory in Early Modern England and Wales* (Cambridge, UK: Cambridge University Press, 2004); and Lina Perkins Wilder, *Shakespeare's Memory Theater* (Cambridge, UK: Cambridge University Press, 2010).

32. Michel de Montaigne, *The Essayes or Morall, Politike and Militarie Discourses of Lord Michaell de Montaigne*, trans. John Florio (London: Edward Blount, 1603), 286.

33. Montaigne, *Essayes*, 296.

34. He goes on to add, "And in the collusive silence brought on by a particular kind of collective shame there is detectable both a desire to forget and sometimes the actual effect of forgetting." Paul Connerton, "Seven Types of Forgetting," *Memory Studies* 1, no. 1 (January 2008): 67.

35. Stephen Greenblatt and Catherine Gallagher, *Practicing New Historicism* (Chicago: University of Chicago Press, 2000), 29.

36. Lee Edelman, "Ever After: History, Negativity, and the Social," in *After Sex: On Writing Since Queer Theory*, ed. Janet Halley and Andrew Parker (Durham, NC: Duke University Press, 2011), 111.

37. For instance, Phyllis Rackin, in *Stages of History: Shakespeare's English Chronicles* (Ithaca, NY: Cornell University Press, 1990), writes, the "Wars of the Roses, which had occupied much of the preceding century, destroying families, devastating the land, and disrupting ancient allegiances, made the study of recent English history a pressing concern for a nation that wished to preserve the peace and political stability of the present and to avoid the mistakes that had led to the insecurity of the past" (3).

38. In discussing shame and guilt here in the same breath, we do not mean to unproblematically conflate the two. Guilt is often understood as an inward experience of self-punishment while shame as the fear of external punishment. The *OED* defines the "sense of shame" as "guilty feelings" as early as 1647. For a thoughtful discussion of how Shakespeare troubles this distinction across his work, see Patrick Gray, "Choosing between Shame and Guilt: *Macbeth, Othello, Hamlet,* and *King Lear*," in *Shakespeare and the Soliloquy in Early Modern English Drama*, ed. A. D. Cousins and Daniel Derrin (Cambridge, UK: Cambridge University Press, 2018), 105–18.

39. Garrett A. Sullivan Jr., *Memory and Forgetting in English Renaissance Drama: Shakespeare, Marlowe* (Cambridge, UK: Cambridge University Press, 2005), 1.

40. Brian Massumi, *Politics of Affect* (Cambridge, UK: Polity, 2015), 94.

41. Lee Edelman, *No Future: Queer Theory and the Death Drive* (Durham, NC: Duke University Press, 2004), 28.

42. Marvin Carlson, *The Haunted Stage: The Theater as Memory Machine* (Ann Arbor: University of Michigan Press, 2003), 2.

43. Lauren Berlant, "A Properly Political Concept of Love: Three Approaches in Ten Pages," *Cultural Anthropology* 26, no. 4 (2011): 687.

44. Gail Kern Paster, *The Body Embarrassed: Drama and Disciplines of Shame in Early Modern England* (Ithaca, NY: Cornell University Press, 1993), 124.

45. Heather K. Love, "Emotional Rescue," in *Gay Shame*, ed. David M. Halperin and Valerie Traub (Chicago: University of Chicago Press, 2009), 257.

46. Fernie, *Shame in Shakespeare*, 245–46.

47. Katie W. Higgins, "National Belonging Post-Referendum: Britons Living in Other EU Member States Respond to 'Brexit,'" *Area* 51, no. 2 (2019): 277.

48. Higgins, "National Belonging Post-Referendum," 280.

49. Higgins, "National Belonging Post-Referendum," 280.

50. Higgins, "National Belonging Post-Referendum," 281.

51. Jonathan Moss, Emily Robinson, and Jake Watts, "Brexit and the Everyday Politics of Emotion: Methodological Lessons from History," *Political Studies* 68, no. 4 (November 2020): 837–56.

52. Thomas Wright, *The Passions of the Minde in Generall*, 2nd ed. (London: Walter Burre, 1604), 14r.

5

Building a Wall around Tudor England

Coastal Forts and Fantasies of Border Control in *Friar Bacon and Friar Bungay*

Todd Andrew Borlik

In *The Wall*, a 2019 dystopian novel by John Lanchester, a perplexed recruit finds himself patrolling a colossal border wall encircling all of Britain.[1] Despite the novel's unmistakably topical intent, the conceit of a walled-off Britain is not without precedent in English literature. In the late Elizabethan comedy *Friar Bacon and Friar Bungay*, a medieval magician dreams of engirdling the shores of England with a defensive wall of brass. Since the English and Welsh coastline extends for 5,881 miles (8,982 km), this would be an engineering feat that would make Hadrian's Wall—a mere eighty-four miles—look like a catwalk and would in fact rival the Great Wall of China in scale. As a structure of such size and expensive material was well beyond the Tudor state's technological and fiscal means, it is no wonder Friar Bacon outsourced its construction to supernatural forces.

In the end, to Bacon's chagrin, his much-vaunted wall never materializes, and the playwright Robert Greene seems to parody the jingoistic fantasy as magical thinking or politically misguided braggadocio. Nevertheless, the proposed wall in *Friar Bacon* invites further scrutiny because in several respects Greene's comedy echoes the patriotic and religious propaganda hailing England as an "elect nation" in the wake of the Spanish Armada's retreat. In our current political climate, it is almost irresistible to reexamine the rhetoric of wall-building in Tudor England as reflecting ideological discourses of national insularity. Rather than inspect the wall from our own present moment, however, this chapter approaches it from a more historicist bent. Specifically, it takes the measure of Bacon's brass wall by viewing it alongside the campaigns to build and refortify a network of artillery castles along England's coastline and to equip the English navy with brass (now called bronze) cannonry—campaigns in which leading patrons of the acting companies that performed this play were involved. In Greene's comedy, the magus's plan to erect an actual material wall fails spectacularly, but this does not diminish its potency as an emblem of English nationalism, as the final scene of *Friar Bacon* reimagines the wall as a tree-like Tudor rose bestowing a figurative protection over England's borders.

FOUNDATIONS FOR THE WALL

Considering that humans first mastered the smelting of the copper alloy bronze (which premoderns termed brass) around five thousand years ago, it should come as no surprise that brazen walls have a storied history stretching back into antiquity. In Homer's *Odyssey*, set during the late Bronze Age collapse, brass walls encircle the island of the wind god Aeolus. The Roman poet Horace speaks of Troy as protected by *murus aeneus*, or brazen walls.[2] Brass gates and walls also occur in the Hebrew Bible, and these passages, as we shall see, had a profound influence on English Protestants following Henry VIII's split from the Roman Catholic Church. In the early modern era, poets, playwrights, and religious writers invoke brass fortifications with increasing frequency. Lisa Hopkins records several allusions to brass towers in plays such as *The Spanish Tragedy*, *Wily Beguiled*, and *The Love-sick King* and notes that this structure functioned in the early modern imagination as a "byword for invincibility" at a time of growing nationalist fervor.[3] The reference in *The Spanish Tragedy* is particularly noteworthy, as Thomas Kyd's tragedy is contemporaneous with both Greene's comedy and the Armada scare, when national defense was in the forefront of public consciousness. As this chapter will elaborate, brass walls were encrusted with classical, religious, and militaristic connotations when Greene made them a major plot-point in *Friar Bacon*.

The identity of the person who first dreamed of girdling England in brass remains a mystery; nor is it certain where Greene encountered the scheme, if indeed he did not invent it. Greene's comedy is partially based upon legends of a historical monk, Roger Bacon, who lived in Oxford in the thirteenth century. Although Bacon might be dubbed a techno-futurist—indeed, a letter attributed to him speaks of marvels like submarines and flying machines—the only evidence to support the claim that he ever proposed a national wall comes from a conspicuously fictionalized romance published centuries after his death.[4] In *The Famous Historie of Fryer Bacon*, the eponymous scholar explicitly conceives of the wall as a bulwark against the threat of invasion: "Fryer Bacon, reading one day of the many conquests of England, bethought himself how he might keep it from the like conquests, and so make himself famous hereafter to all posterities. This (after great study) hee found could be no way so well done as one: which was to make a head of Brass; and if he could make the head to speak (and hear it when it speaks) then might hee be able to wall England about with Brass."[5]

While the earliest extant version of *The Famous Historie* dates from 1627, literary historians presume that Greene knew an Elizabethan version of it that has not survived.[6] Curiously, however, a similar fantasy occurs in *Doctor Faustus*, when Marlowe's conjuror speaks of commanding his spirits to "wall all Germany with brass."[7] Since *Friar Bacon and Friar Bungay* is likely a *Faustus* knock-off (both plays date from ca. 1588–90), it seems feasible that Greene could have lifted the idea from Marlowe.[8] This would invite the inference that either Marlowe first proposed the wall or was acquainted with Greene's lost source-text. But given *Faustus*'s messy textual history, one cannot rule out the possibility that its brass wall may have been interpolated at a later date when Marlowe's play was revived in repertory together with *Friar Bacon*. Another conceivable scenario is that Greene, Marlowe, or the unknown author of *The Famous Historie* based the wall on an episode in book 3 of Spenser's *Faerie Queene* (1590). When Britomart approaches Merlin's cave, Spenser explains why it echoes with the "rombling" sound of "brasen Caudrons":

> The cause some say is this: A litle whyle
> Before that Merlin dyde he did intend,
> A brasen wall in compass to compile
> About Cairmardin, and did it commend
> Vnto these Sprights, to bring to perfect end.[9]

Michael Drayton repeats this legend in *Poly-Olbion*, claiming that Arthur's wizard not only transported Stonehenge from Ireland in a single night but planned to environ Carmarthen in a brass wall: "And for Carmardens sake, would have fain have brought to pass / About it to have built a wall of solid Brasse."[10] John Henry Jones speculates the brass wall "was not part of the traditional myth of Bacon, but injected from Spenser."[11] However, Spenser's prefacing of the tale with "some say" suggests, if taken literally, that he may have drawn on a preexisting oral tradition, and Greene or the author of *The Famous Historie* would still deserve credit for expanding the wall from the borders of one Welsh county to the entire English and Welsh coast.

What emerges from this muddle is that the dream of a walled-off England is not so much a medieval invention but one that truly begins to grip the English imagination in the late sixteenth century during the panic triggered by the Spanish Armada. Spenser's attributing a defensive wall to Merlin is particularly apt as it befits the *Faerie Queene*'s strident nationalism. It is no coincidence that Merlin is a figurehead for Britishness and prophesizes the coming of Arthegall, "Strongly to ayde his country to withstand / The powre of forreiene Paynims, which invade thy land" (3.3.27). Significantly, however, Merlin's wall proves to be a monumental failure. In both Spenser and Drayton, he is imprisoned in a cave by Nimue, the Lady of the Lake, and never completes it. A similar storyline unfolds in *Friar Bacon and Friar Bungay*, as the conjuror falls asleep at the critical moment when his oracular brass head utters its secrets that would have enabled Bacon to raise the walls. Nevertheless, abandonment of the plan of a physical wall does not diminish the ideological potency of what the wall represents; it still functions as a rhetorical tool for imagining a unified and impenetrable England without the state laying a single brick or forging a single brass sheet of it.

Bacon's Wall and Anglo-European Diplomacy

The formation of English identity and the early modern construction of English nationhood have received a great deal of attention in redoubtable works by Richard Helgerson, Jeffrey Knapp, Andrew Hadfield, Claire McEachern, Andrew Escobedo, and Philip Schwyzer.[12] Somewhat surprisingly, however, none of these studies examine *Friar Bacon and Friar Bungay* or the topic of a nation-engirdling wall. In a recent monograph on the fortified city, Adam McKeown demonstrates that it functions as "an ideal not only of design but also of social and political organization, which was developed extensively but also critiqued in utopian literature of the period."[13] A similar argument could be put forward about the fortified nation, which was not simply a fantastical castle-in-the-sky but a military strategy and figurative trope with real purchase in late Tudor England, as Greene's comedy shares much of the ambivalence of the utopian texts vetted by McKeown.[14] Although the nationalistic overtones of *Friar*

Bacon and Friar Bungay have been incisively analyzed by Barbara Traister, Deanne Williams, and Brian Walsh, Greene's play demands reassessment as the most significant commentary on a national wall-building project in early modern English literature.[15]

But is it in fact a nationwide wall? When Bacon unveils his plans for the wall in the second scene of the play, the first in which he appears, the text is somewhat ambiguous on this point. With the aid of a talking brazen head (a magical device with a long pedigree in medieval romance), Bacon professes he will devote his esoteric knowledge to the cause of national defense:

> And I will strengthen England by my skill,
> That if ten Caesars lived and reigned in Rome,
> With all the legions Europe doth contain,
> They should not touch a grass of English ground.
> The work that Ninus reared at Babylon,
> The brazen walls framed by Semiramis,
> Carved out like to the portal of the sun,
> Shall not be such as rings the English strand,
> From Dover to the marketplace of Rye.[16]

This passage supplies both a motive and a classical exemplum for the enterprise. The allusion to Caesar recalls the Roman invasions of Britannia, both the aborted campaigns ordered by Julius Caesar in 55 and 54 BCE and the successful conquest during the reign of Emperor Claudius in 43 CE. In this detail, Greene presumably was following his source, *The Famous Historie*, in which Bacon conceives of the wall after reading in ancient chronicles of the four invasions of Britain. When *The Famous Historie* and Greene's *Honorable Historie* are juxtaposed, however, some notable differences emerge. In the former, Bacon intends to wall the entire nation. Greene's play appears to envisage a similarly vast partition when the Oxford don Burden reports a rumor that Bacon intends "to compass England with a wall of brass" (204), and Bacon later confirms that he plans to "girt fair England with wall of brass" (1583). Crucially, however, in the previously cited passage, Bacon speaks of the wall stretching only from Dover in Kent to Rye in East Sussex—a relatively modest distance of around 45 miles (28 km) in comparison to the whopping figure of 5,881. In the mind of Bacon and the play's audience, then, walling England might mean simply fortifying the coastline most vulnerable to invasion directly across the

channel from Calais by building coastal defenses that function as a synecdoche for a national wall. But since Bacon in the same scene asserts he will
"circle England round with brass" (351), the play depicts the friar himself
as somewhat uncertain about the scale of the project. The inconsistency is
revealing; the exact dimensions and location of the wall are, in other words,
not as important as the idea of it as a metaphor to conjure with, as it were,
in the discourse of nationhood.

Bacon's allusion to Semiramis is not found in the *Famous Historie* and
thus also appears to be Greene's own addition. The reference is noteworthy
in that the late Tudor era witnessed the rehabilitation of Semiramis by
Protestant supporters of Elizabeth, who saw the Babylonian queen, despite her reputation as a sybarite, as a precedent for strong female rulers:
"In respect of worldly pollicie, power, and magnificence, shee wonderfullie
gouerned about fortie yeeres, that mightie, golden, and first monarchie of
the Assyrians and Chaldeans, and the most Hystoriographers that write
of her life, haue her actes in admiration."[17] Chief among her admirable
acts was the construction of an enormous wall around her capital. Herodotus (whose landmark history had been translated in 1584) reports that
the walls of Babylon were a staggering 56 miles long, 80 feet thick, and
320 feet tall. An Elizabethan history lists similarly impressive dimensions:
"Her walles wer of an incredible magnitude and strength, being fifty cubites in breadth, and 300 cubites in higth. The circute and compasse of it
is sayd to be 480 furlonges. . . . The walles were made of bricke, compacted
together wt lime & pitch, . . . [and] beutified wt *an hundred gates of bras*."[18]
Although only the gates were forged of brass, the Babylonian defenses
provide an important historical model for Bacon's wall-building. Like the
suggestion that the wall might only extend from Dover to Rye, the success of Semiramis makes Bacon's wall sound less far-fetched, offering a
reminder that a civilization might erect such monumental structures, and
with a female ruler on the throne.[19]

Greene's depiction of the wall, however, is by no means unequivocally
positive. Despite the evident appeal of a border wall in an era rife with fears
of foreign invasion, the comedy also represents it as a hubristic and perhaps
even demonic enterprise. Burden accuses Bacon of enlisting a construction
crew of "devils and ghastly fiends" (202), and the friar confirms that he
will employ "Nigromancy" (228)—that is, invoke black spirits—to build it.
Such passages code the wall as a diabolical undertaking. More pointedly,
Bacon never even begins the wall, much less completes it, since his feckless
assistant fails to wake him at the critical juncture when the brazen head

speaks. In hindsight, Bacon confesses that the wall was an arrogant scheme (as the pun on "brazen" subliminally implies), beyond the scope of what is permitted to mortals, and he appears to second the verdict of the divine power that smashed his oracular head (and hence his hopes for the wall) when he subsequently smashes his own enchanted glass.

In lieu of the wall, the comedy substitutes the far more practical strategy of securing England's peace through marriage alliances with the royal households of Europe. Just as Bacon abandons his dream of the wall, Prince Edward must relinquish Margaret, the "fair maid of Fressingfield," to his friend Lacy and instead marry Eleanor of Castile to promote peace with this Spanish kingdom. To be sure, national bragging rights are at stake in the wizards' duel between Bacon and the German conjuror Vandermast; however, the magic they wield is neither English nor German but derived from occult texts originating in Egypt and ancient Greece and recovered by Italian humanists. When Bacon prevails, King Henry declares he has "honoured England" (1284), yet the king's patriotic pride in the beauty of the English landscape, and in the elegant architecture and intellectual prowess of Oxford, is tempered by his willingness to cooperate and forge alliances with European powers.[20] The alliance is cemented in the conviviality of the marriage feast, featuring a cornucopia of exotic delicacies imported from around the world: Egypt, Persia, North Africa, Candy (Crete), Spain, Judea, and Rome. The menu for the feast that concludes the play celebrates England's participation in pan-European, even global commerce. It is worth recalling that Greene himself apparently had a fatal love of imported Rhenish wine and had in fact traveled widely on the Continent—visiting Italy, Spain, France, Germany, and Poland. The author of *Friar Bacon and Friar Bungay* does not seem to be, in other words, what we in modern parlance would call a "Little Englander."

Critical opinion for the most part supports the view that Greene's comedy looks askance at the nationalist rhetoric that undergirds the wall. Although she is more interested in how the play deconstructs the historical boundaries between the medieval and early modern rather than in national boundaries, Deanne Williams has remarked that the smashing of Bacon's plans for the wall "undoes the dream of national insularity."[21] Seizing on Bacon's allusion to Brutus (Aeneas's descendent who settled Britain), Williams argues that Greene, while aware of the inevitable demise of empires, rejects the wall by appealing to a shared European history and humanist culture that unifies England and the Continent. Barbara Traister similarly deciphers the moral of the play as a warning against isolationism: "England's glory can best be served not by shutting her off from the rest of the world with Bacon's wall but allowing her communication and interchange with other countries. . . . There is no need for, but rather danger in, England's withdrawal behind brass walls."[22] While I applaud the sentiments behind these interpretations, my reading of *Friar Bacon and Friar Bungay* sees Greene as somewhat more conflicted or uncertain. Throughout his brief writing career, Greene vacillated between a sense of himself as a cosmopolitan intellectual and a desire to be a popular and profitable author among more fervent Protestant readers and audiences in London at a time when patriotic sentiment ran high and anxieties of a second Armada invasion still simmered. Both these authorial personas (*homo academicus* and *poeta publicus*, in Bryan Reynolds and Henry Turner's formulation) are present in much of his work and the attempt to reconcile them in *Friar Bacon and Friar Bungay* is in large measure what gives the play its complexity.[23] Ultimately, however, the two may not be reconciled so much as held in an uneasy suspension. By the same token, nationalism and multilateralism need not be mutually exclusive, and Greene may not soundly reject the former in favor of the latter but simultaneously pursue both with an ambivalence that continues to vex Anglo-European politics to this day.

In his *Historie of the Raigne of King Henry the Seventh*, Francis Bacon writes that the king brokered marriages between his daughters and the rulers of Scotland and France and that these alliances were as pleasing to him "as if hee thought hee had built a Wall of Brasse about his Kingdome."[24] While this simile appears to be Francis Bacon's rather than Henry's, it does suggest that marriage alliances can promote international harmony and national insularity at the same time. Greene arguably portrays Edward's marriage to Eleanor of Castile as an aggrandizement of England rather than an absorption of the country into a pan-European partnership. Tellingly, the wedding scene and play both conclude with Bacon's vision of other European nations bowing before Queen Elizabeth, and its final line exhibits unabashed jingoism: "Thus triumphs England over all the west" (2155). Moreover, Edward I was hardly a model of amicable international diplomacy; rather, he would go on to subjugate Scotland and Wales, constructing a ring of castles at strategic points around the Welsh coast. Greene's prince was, in other words, the chief architect behind the colonizing scheme to make England congruent with the island of Britain, reinforcing insularity as a keystone of English identity. Furthermore, Greene's audiences would have known that these marriage alliances with France and

Spain were by no means a safeguard of European peace. Having conducted a successful invasion of Britain himself, Henry VII was acutely aware of its vulnerability, and he continued to invest in national defense while negotiating European alliances. After his divorce from a Spanish princess, Henry VIII spent lavish sums on constructing artillery fortifications along the English coast, and these building projects were continued by his daughter Elizabeth at times of heightened threat, such as the Armada scare of the late 1580s. Situating Bacon's brass wall within the history of Tudor military engineering projects will allow us to sketch a more nuanced picture of the play's politics and of the image of fortress England in discourses of English nationhood.

Bacon's Wall and *The Practise of Fortification*

In a work debunking superstitions and musty fables, Thomas Browne proposes that Bacon's brazen head was an alchemical experiment to transmute lead into gold, and the brass wall a cryptic allusion to the "most powerful defence, and strongest fortification which gold could have effected."[25] Browne's opinion is often cited in the scholarship on *Friar Bacon*, but his line of reasoning has not been pursued with the diligence it merits. While it would be reductive to push an allegorical reading of Greene's comedy, there are some striking parallels between the rhetoric that buttresses both Bacon's brass wall and the spree of fortress building by the Tudor state. After the suppression of the northern Catholic uprising known as the Pilgrimage of Grace, Henry VIII turned his attention to the threat of foreign invasion. He developed an ambitious defense strategy known as the "King's Device" to ring the English coast with artillery forts based on the latest in Italian and German engineering. Between 1539 and 1547, the English government erected twenty-two of these so-called "Device Forts," from Dale in Pembrokeshire to Harwich in Essex. The direction of this treasury-draining project was put into the capable hands of Thomas Cromwell, who funded the construction with wealth confiscated from the dissolved monasteries. In the 1540s England's dismantled abbeys were effectively transformed into artillery forts. The twenty-two that Henry managed to construct represent only a small proportion of what he envisaged: "The Henrician castles that exist today along the south coast of England are the surviving vestiges of a much broader scheme . . . to protect the coastline of Britain from Berwick on the Anglo-Scottish border down to Kent, along the south coast, and up to South Wales."[26] In other words, Henry VIII

dreamed of encompassing England in a ring of coastal fortresses, tanta-
mount to walling the nation in brass.

Even with the tremendous capital siphoned from the church, however, Henry could not fund all the castles he wished and chose to focus
on Dover and the vulnerable Cinque Ports of the south coast across the
channel from France. By the late sixteenth century, the Cinque Ports had
come to include Rye, which then featured a decaying tower (Ypres Tower)
constructed by Henry III, the very king who appears in Greene's comedy.
In 1539 Henry VIII ordered the construction of a massive artillery fort
at Camber right beside Rye and equipped it with twenty-eight brass and
iron cannons. In a curious coincidence, this extensive refurbishment and
expansion of England's coastal defenses was necessitated by the advent of
gunpowder, a substance invented by the Chinese but first described in the
West by none other than Roger Bacon.[27] It was gunpowder and improvements in naval artillery that made Tudor England, especially after the split
with Rome, feel more vulnerable to invasion. While only a small percent-
age of Greene's audience may have known of Friar Bacon's role in bringing gunpowder to the attention of Europe, Bacon's plan to build a wall
"from Dover to the marketplace at Rye" would strike a chord with Tudor
playgoers, as these harbors remained cornerstones of England's national
defense in the late Elizabethan period. In fact, the production of Greene's
play on London stage by the Queen's Men and Admiral's Men coincides
with an upsurge of interest in military fortifications, and prominent figures
connected to these two acting companies were key movers behind plans to
shore up England's southern coastal defenses.

In 1589, either shortly before or after the premiere of *Friar Bacon*, Paul
Ive published *The Practise of Fortification*, a landmark treatise on military
architecture in the post-gunpowder age. As a blacksmith's son turned soldier and spy, Ive (or Ivy) could boast of a knowledge that was not purely
theoretical, as he had infiltrated and studied some of the new citadels built
by the Spanish in the Low Countries. Respected as the "leading English
consultant on fortifications" in Elizabeth's reign, he was employed in engineering projects at Dover Harbor in the late 1580s and at the Channel
Islands in 1593.[28] Three years later, Ive was appointed to survey the Cinque
Ports (including Rye) to estimate the expenses for improving the southern
coastal forts, recommending major upgrades to Dover Castle.[29] In other
words, Ive was the brains behind the push to refortify the nation's border
defenses at the very two harbors mentioned by Friar Bacon as possible
endpoints for his brass wall.

Could Robert Greene have known of Ive's *Practise of Fortification*? The playwright Christopher Marlowe certainly did, as evident from this passage in *Tamburlaine the Great, Part II*:

> The ditches must be deep,
> . . . The walls made high and broad,
> The bulwarks and the rampiers large and strong
> With cavalieros and thick counterforts,
> And room within to lodge six thousand men.
> It must have privy ditches, countermines,
> And secret issuings to defend the ditch.
> It must have high argines and covered ways
> To keep the bulwark fronts from battery. (3.2.73–76)[30]

As Marlowe scholars have noted, this speech is copied almost verbatim from Ive's treatise. "[A fort needs] deep ditches, high walls, great bulwarks, large ramparts and cavalieros. Besides, it must be large to lodge fiue or six thousand men. . . . I must also have countermines, priuie ditches, secret issuings out to defend the ditch, casmats in the ditch, couered wayes round about it, and an argine or banke . . . and other things necessarie for the keeping of it."[31] Since the *Tamburlaine* sequel probably dates from 1588, it would seem Marlowe must have read Ive's work in manuscript, most likely, as Charles Nicholl has speculated, through their mutual contacts in the intelligence network of Sir Francis Walsingham.[32] It turns out that Ive, like Marlowe, worked as an agent for Walsingham. In fact, Ive dedicated *The Practise of Fortification* to Walsingham and William Brooke, the lord warden of the Cinque Ports, acknowledging the "manifold benefits" he had received from them over the years.[33] The dedication to Walsingham should catch the eye of theater historians as the queen's secretary and spymaster also helped establish the Queen's Men, the very playing company that first performed *Friar Bacon and Friar Bungay* sometime around 1589.[34] Bacon's dream of a nation-encircling brass wall would certainly have piqued the interest of a militant Protestant like Walsingham with a documented interest in artillery fortifications. Cutting-edge fortification technology was an even more topical subject in 1589 than the scholarship on *Friar Bacon* has appreciated. As Greene and Marlowe moved in similar circles, it is not implausible that Greene was at least aware of Ive's border defenses and that Bacon's brass wall, despite its supposedly medieval and magical origins, reflects contemporary obsession with military engineering technology during the Armada scare.[35]

Little has been said up to this point about the fact that Bacon intends to forge his wall of brass. For the sake of clarity, it should be noted
that in early modern usage the word "brass" encompassed what we now
call bronze, and the two were only differentiated in the mid-eighteenth
century.[36] Both are copper alloys, the distinction being that brass includes
zinc whereas bronze is mingled with tin. In the sixteenth century, Henry
VIII, Queen Elizabeth, and the Lord Admiral Howard invested heavily
in cannons made of both iron and bronze (then called brass), and the latter was increasingly preferred due in part to the havoc the iron industry
wrought on England's woodlands. In a speech delivered before Parliament
in 1593, John Fortescue praised the queen for outfitting the navy with
brazen ordnance: "She did find in her navy all iron pieces, but she hath furnished it with artillery of brass."[37] The extensive renovations to the castle at
Berwick-upon-Tweed in the Elizabethan period included the creation of a
"brass bastion," so-called because it housed brass (bronze) cannons. Bacon's
scheme of a brass or brazen wall resonates with England's acquisition of
brass artillery that was vital to the nation's defense strategy in the Tudor
period, and especially around the time of the Armada.

Whether Greene composed the play before or after 1588, fears of a
Spanish invasion still lingered when the play was likely revived in 1590s.
Philip Henslowe's so-called diary records no fewer than nine performance
of "fryer bacone" at the Rose between 1592–93.[38] Although it has been
suggested that some of these productions by Lord Strange's Men might
actually have been a spin-off now known as *John of Bordeaux*, it is clear that
memories of Bacon and his wall did not fade.[39] Greene's play was printed
in 1594, and when a group of the Queen's Men re-formed as the Lord Admiral's company later that year, they took *Friar Bacon* with them. Their new
patron, Charles Howard, was, like Walsingham, a vocal supporter of naval
defense, tasked with refortifying the castles along the seacoast. He, too,
apparently knew of Paul Ive. In 1595 Howard recommended Ive to oversee
the improvements to the harbor defenses at Portsmouth.[40] Howard's company, the Admiral's Men, was still staging *Friar Bacon* in December 1602,
when Henslowe paid Thomas Middleton five shillings to compose a new
prologue and epilogue for a court performance.[41] Although Middleton's
additions have not survived, it is a reasonable bet that his epilogue echoed
Bacon's original prophecy in paying fulsome tribute to the queen, further
confirming that her reign would be remembered as a time of peace and
national pride. In his reading of Bacon's prophecy, however, Brian Walsh
calls it a "backhanded compliment" and observes that its ode to the *Pax*

Eliza may have stirred anxieties that England would not be able to sustain the peace after her reign.[42] Such concerns may have been deeply felt during the play's 1602 revival. Bacon's mystical vision is not one of perpetual concord but only of a temporary respite, and Walsh goes on to say that the defeat of the Armada did not allay fears of a future invasion or "foreclose the possibility of future Spanish or indeed Catholic threats."[43] Given the provenance of *Friar Bacon* with the Queen's Men, and the company's links through Walsingham to military engineers (as attested by Marlowe), Greene's comedy could be taken as an endorsement, albeit an ambiguous one, of increased spending on coastal defenses by vehemently Protestant factions at court.

Allusions to Bacon's wall continue to crop up well into the Jacobean period, when the nationalist fervor cooled and the king was pursuing alliances with Europe. Wall-building features in an anonymous 1606 play, in which a character dreams of erecting a wall around London: "O this Citty, . . . be it spoken in secret, Ile haue fenst about with a wall of brasse."[44] Bacon's attempt is recalled in another 1606 play, John Marston's *The Fawn*: "They say in England that a far-fam'd Frier had guirt the Island round with a brasse wall, if that they could haue catched, Time is, but Time is past, left it still clipt with aged Neptunes arme."[45] As this passage from Marston suggests, abandoning the wall does not mean abandoning the idea of a fortified and isolationist England. In the final section of this chapter, I turn from literal walls to metaphorical walls to proffer a more nuanced assessment of the nationalism of *Friar Bacon* and the late Elizabethan era.

Fortress England and Metaphorical Walls

The passage from Marston just cited raises the prospect that some of Greene's contemporaries might have considered walling a sea-ringed island an exercise in lily-gilding. After all, early modern English literature resounds with tributes to the geographical blessings that make the nation a natural fortress. The locus classicus for this sentiment is, of course, John of Gaunt's oration in Shakespeare's *Richard II*, in which the sea performs "the office of a wall" (2.1.47).[46] Through the still-common "topographical slippage" between England and Britain, the speech presents insularity as the "defining feature" of English identity.[47] Shakespeare recycles the jingoistic metaphor in *Cymbeline* but places it in the mouth of the sinister queen, who urges Cymbeline to defy the Romans while reminding him of

> the natural bravery of your isle, which stands
> As Neptune's park, ribbed and paled in
> With oaks unscalable and roaring waters,
> With sands that will not bear your enemies' boats,
> But suck them up to th' topmast. (3.1.18–22)

A deer park surrounded with a wooden pale seems far less daunting than Gaunt's wall or moat, much less Bacon's brass wall. While oaks might signify England's wooden war ships that repelled the Spanish fleet, the queen's villainous behavior undercuts her isolationist policy. In the tonal differences between the speeches in *Richard II* and *Cymbeline*, Shakespeare registers the change from the zealous patriotism of the Armada years under Elizabeth to the more Euro-friendly outlook of the pacifist King James.[48]

While these excerpts from *Richard II* and *Cymbeline* are well known, it is sometimes forgotten that Robert Greene peddled the vision of fortress England long before it was articulated by Shakespeare, that "upstart crow, beautified with our feathers," as Greene notoriously smeared him. Indeed, *Richard II* dates from ca. 1594–96, right around the time that *Friar Bacon and Friar Bungay* was first printed, and Shakespeare's image of a "sea-walled" (3.4.44) England and his Richard's contrast between human flesh and a wall of "brass impregnable" (3.2.164) may owe something to Greene's comedy. In scene 4 of *Friar Bacon and Friar Bungay*, King Henry III greets the German emperor and the King of Castile with a geography lesson:

> Great men of Europe, monarchs of the west,
> Ringed with the walls of old Oceanus,
> Whose lofty surge is like the battlements
> That compassed high-built Babel in with towers,
> Welcome, my lords, welcome, brave western kings,
> To England's shores, whose promontory cleeves
> Shows Albion is another little world. (445–52)

This curious speech neatly encapsulates the ambiguities that dog the play. King Henry appears to be boasting of his realm's invulnerability and exceptionalism but also reveals that the fortress England metaphor slices both ways. While the drift of the speech seems to be that the "walls of old Oceanus" protect England from Europe, the syntax hints that these same watery walls fortify Europe against invasion by England. Henry's invocation of Albion's white "cleeves" or cliffs on the southern coast depicts them as another geographical bulwark. However, picking up on Henry's bluster, the King of Castile retorts in kind by explicitly likening his country's topography to natural fortifications when he hails the "Pyren mounts swelling above the clouds, / That ward the wealthy Castile in with walls" (460–61). Clearly, England is not unique in possessing boundaries aligned with topographical features that aid in national defense.

The wall motif recurs a few lines later in the same scene when Castile's daughter, Eleanor, admires the English prince for his feats "done at the holy land fore Damas walls" (472). This line suggests that the European powers are unified by a common Christian faith greater than any narrow tribal allegiances, and again the wall acts as both a literal and symbolic border for defining community. Although Greene speaks of Damas or Damascus, Edward actually fought to defend the besieged crusader stronghold of Acre, which ultimately fell in 1291. In other words, Edward's feats in the Ninth Crusade turned out to be futile, and the city's heavily fortified walls proved all too penetrable. Incidentally, so, too, were those of Damascus, which—as Greene's audience would have known, thanks to Marlowe—was sacked by Tamburlaine in 1401. If the reference to Damas's walls could suggest vulnerability rather than security, the same could be said of Henry's fraught comparison of England to the walled city of Babel, rather than Semiramis's Babylon (also sacked by Tamburlaine), although the two were often conflated at the time.[49] Since Babel's tower famously toppled, the allusion smacks of excessive pride and collapsing walls rather than unassailable ones. Lastly, the fact that the European monarchs have already crossed the channel to attend Henry's political summit further conspires to undermine the confidence the king places in oceanic walls and cliffs.

These ambiguities persist in the final scene of the play, when Henry again addresses the foreign leaders:

> Glorious commanders of Europa's love,
> That makes fair England like that wealthy isle
> Circled with Gihon and swift Euphrates. (2143–45)

Once again, the king's syntax reflects his desire to garner the benefits of international cooperation while retaining a distinct sense of English national identity. He acknowledges "Europa's love" makes England wealthy, while the image of England as a "circled" island underscores its separateness. Gihon and the Euphrates are two of four rivers mentioned in Genesis as issuing from Paradise (from the Persian for "walled garden"), and their evocation here would make an implicit comparison between England and Mesopotamia, the site of both Eden and Babylon, the walled city. However, the Bible also describes Gihon as encircling the land of Cush, believed to be Ethiopia. Whether Henry sees England as another Babylon, Damascus, Eden, or Ethiopia, none could properly be described as unconquerable isles or invincible bastions. *Friar Bacon* is haunted by the sense that walls and buffers, whether natural or artificial, are not inviolable, even though its author still yearns to cordon off England as a realm apart from Europe.

Despite the ingenious efforts of engineers like Ive, the latest designs in angular bastions to deflect cannon-fire could not forestall the sense that the age of castles was nearing an end. In 1629, two years after the republication of *Famous Historie*, the divine John Andrewes would remark that even a high-tech brass wall is no guarantee of invulnerability: "Wherefore, if all our Nauie were ready, all our Ports fortified; all our Coasts guarded; all our men strongly armed, and our Land inuironed with a wall of Brasse; yet it is to be feared, that wee haue a Traytor within vs, euen our long continued and vnrepented sinnes, that will draw Gods vengeance vppon us."[50] As Greene's comedy was reprinted in 1630 with a blurb advertising it as "lately played" by Prince Palatine's company, this could be yet another reference to Friar Bacon's wall. While Andrewes fears betrayal from within, such comments also reflect the dawning realization in the post-gunpowder age that walled forts were no longer infallible defenses.

The recognition of the impracticality of a national border wall for England did not, however, in any way tarnish its appeal as a metaphor. Rather than completely abandon the wall in the post-gunpowder era, some of Greene's contemporaries repurposed it as a symbol, contending that strong, capable government functioned as the best wall of all. Interestingly, Queen Elizabeth herself was likened to a brass wall in a work on religious politics published in a 1589, and hence contemporaneous with the premiere of *Friar Bacon and Friar Bungay*. In *The Reformed Politicke*, the Huguenot Jean de Frégeville contends that England has enjoyed peace under Elizabeth because it has embraced the true faith of the Protestant Reformation: "We see that England, who hath mainteined the puritie of Gods lawes these 30 yeares, hath enioyed an assured peace vnder the handes of a woman, and yet such Realmes as be gouerned by men haue bene troubled: for that kingdome hath God preserued from both secret & open enemies, & to that nation hath bene *a wall of brasse*."[51] For Bible-toting Protestants, who knew the Hebrew scriptures well, Elizabeth seemed to fulfil the words of Jeremiah 1:18, "Behold, I this day have made thee a defenced citie, and an yron piller & walles of brasse against the whole land." The same image resurfaces in Jeremiah 15:20: "And I will make thee vnto this people a strong brasen wall." Such passages provided a scriptural warrant that a godly monarch would be enough to deter or repel a foreign invasion and may have been a vital cue for Greene or the author of *The Famous Historie* in having Bacon devise a brass wall.

This tribute to Elizabeth in *The Reformed Politicke* has an intriguing resonance with Bacon's final prophecy of a future ruler who will "overshadow Albion with her leaves" (2127). While King Henry professes himself stumped by Bacon's mystical vision, Elizabethan audiences would have had no difficulty decoding "Diana's rose" as an allusion to their virgin queen. The rose had been a symbol of the Tudor dynasty since the reign of Elizabeth's grandfather Henry VII. The tree-like rose seems a far more benign image of the English nation than the brass wall. Its function, however, in both defining and shielding the nation is very much the same. An enlightening comparison can be made with a metaphorical wall in another early modern play, William Rowley's *The Birth of Merlin*. While Rowley apparently knew the same story of Merlin's brazen wall around Carmarthen as Spenser and Drayton, he instead transforms it into a symbol of England's greatness. Aided by Merlin's "Knowledge, Arts, Learning, Wisdom . . . and Prophecy," the nation will be unconquerable: "His Art shall stand / A wall of brass to guard the Brittain Land."[52] England's security, according to Rowley, derives from its intellectual and cultural attainments rather than an actual wall. "Art" does not necessarily exclude what Ive would call the practice of fortification, but the impact of the image is to shift attention from physical walls to figurative ones, from forts to fortitude. This is, essentially, the same maneuver that Bacon makes in the final scene of Greene's comedy. Bacon relinquishes his brass wall but not his vision of national autonomy and integrity. His prophecy is not an ode to multilateral harmony in European politics but to alliances that bolster English supremacy: Apollo's sunflower, Venus's hyacinth, Pallas's laurel, and Ceres's carnation (emblems of other dynasties) bow down in fealty to "Diana's rose," and Henry's gloss is not far off: "Thus glories England over all the west" (2155). It is fitting that one of the possible inspirations for Greene's magus, John Dee, was an ardent nationalist and one of the great visionaries of British imperialism.[53] If Greene's play implies that a vast border wall is a chimera, it still arouses and half satisfies a yearning for such a wall and for the security and national identity it would seem to bestow. Adam McKeown has recently remarked that the vision of the nation as an embattled island fortress "changed England spatially by projecting a consolidated country organized around military needs and confined by military infrastructure."[54] In deploying the wall to effect the same change, *Friar Bacon* can dispense with the cumbersome chore of building a literal wall.

With the recent resurgence of nationalism in the United States and England, border walls have once again become high-voltage metaphors in geopolitics. For the sake of historical fidelity, it must be said that Bacon envisions the wall as a bulwark against Roman/Catholic invasion rather than immigration, as many Elizabethan immigrants were in fact Dutch and French Protestants seeking refuge from religious violence. Nevertheless, it would be irresponsible to ignore that Tudor England was in many respects a "thoroughly and unapologetically xenophobic society."[55] In the days of the Armada scare, the Florentine diplomat Petruccio Ubaldini remarked, "It is easier to find flocks of white crows than one Englishman (and let him believe what he will about religion) that loves a foreigner."[56] An anonymous libel (signed Tamburlaine) threatened to massacre the entire Dutch community in London in 1593, and Queen Elizabeth herself licensed the expulsion of "negroes and blackamoors" from the realm in 1601. The shade of "Diana's rose" did not shelter everyone. In light of the arguments put forward in this chapter, it seems sadly apt that a xenophobic altercation was perpetrated in an early modern playhouse by an audience clamoring for a revival of *Friar Bacon and Friar Bungay*.[57] If the failure of Bacon's project speaks to declining confidence in walled forts in the age of gunpowder, the idea of it must have retained a certain appeal to many in early modern London, where an influx of immigrants incited resentment and uncertainty about what it meant to be English. Bacon's wish to build an impossibly large border wall and yet serve as the host and master of ceremonies for an alliance with Spain and Germany perfectly captures England's ambivalence about its niche in early modern Europe in an era of incipient globalization: that "Britain seems as of it but not in it," to cite Innogen's memorable quip (*Cymbeline*, 3.4.138). In Bacon's desire to reap the fruits of international cooperation and trade while maintaining a staunchly independent nationalist identity, *Friar Bacon and Friar Bungay* offers an uncanny parable for the predicament of post-Brexit Britain.

Notes

An early version of this chapter appeared in *Early Theatre* 22, no. 2 (2019): 79–100. The author is grateful to the journal's anonymous reviewers and to Matteo and Scott for supportive feedback that helped to buttress the arguments.

1. John Lanchester, *The Wall* (New York: W. W. Norton, 2019).

2. D. E. W. Wormell, "Walls of Brass in Literature," *Hermathena* 58 (November 1941): 116–20.

3. Lisa Hopkins, "Profit and Delight?: Magic and the Dreams of a Nation," in *Magical Transformations on the Early Modern English Stage*, ed. Lisa Hopkins and Helen Ostovich. (Aldershot: Ashgate, 2014), 144, For more on brass in early modern literature, see Katherine Hunt's forthcoming monograph *The Brazen World*.

4. Paolo Zombelli, *White Magic, Black Magic in the European Renaissance* (Leiden: Brill, 2007); Brian Clegg, *Roger Bacon: The First Scientist* (London: Constable, 2003). On Bacon as a pan-European Franciscan who wanted to empower the Latin West against the threats of Islam and Tartary, see Amanda Power, *Roger Bacon and the Defence of Christendom* (Cambridge, UK: Cambridge University Press, 2013).

5. Anonymous, *The Famous Historie of Fryer Bacon* (London: F. Grove, 1627), B4v.

6. Robert Greene, *Friar Bacon and Friar Bungay*, ed. Daniel Seltzer (Lincoln: University of Nebraska Press, 1963), and *Friar Bacon and Friar Bungay*, ed. J. A. Levin (London: Ernest Benn, 1969). John Henry Jones, meanwhile, proposes that an alternate version of the prose romance, *The Most Famous History of the Learned Fryer Bacon*, is closer to the version that Greene knew and that its original publication was inspired by the success of the prose *Faust Book* (John Henry Jones, ed., *The English Faust Book: A Critical Edition Based on the Text of 1592* [Cambridge, UK: Cambridge University Press, 1994]). The possibility that the prose romance was written to capitalize on the popularity of Greene's comedy deserves more serious consideration than it has yet received. If true, the wall scheme might be Greene's brainchild.

7. Christopher Marlowe, *Doctor Faustus*, ed. David Bevington and Eric Rasmussen (Manchester, UK: Manchester University Press, 1993), 1.1.190.

8. The fact that Greene's *Alphonsus of Aragon* imitates Marlowe's *Tamburlaine* increases the likelihood that *Friar Bacon* postdates *Faustus* (rather than vice versa). See Bevington and Rasmussen, *Doctor Faustus*, 1; Jones, *English Faust Book*, 55.

9. Edmund Spenser, *The Faerie Queene*, ed. A. C. Hamilton (Harlow, UK: Longman, 2007), 3.3.10.

10. Michael Drayton, *The Works of Michael Drayton*, ed. J. William Hebel (Oxford: Basil Blackwell, 1933), 4.331–32.

11. Jones, *English Faust Book*, 62. A brass wall also features in a prophecy, allegedly made in 1569 and attributed to a conjuror who also appears in Greene's play, Tarquatus Vandermast. See Giovanni Cipriano, *A Strange and Wonderful Prophecy*, trans. Anthony Hollaway (London, 1595), A3v.

12. Richard Helgerson, *Forms of Nationhood: The Elizabethan Writing of England* (Chicago: University of Chicago Press, 1992); Jeffrey Knapp, *An Empire Nowhere: England, America and Literature, from "Utopia" to "The Tempest"* (Berkeley: University of California Press, 1992); Andrew Hadfield, *Literature, Politics, and National Identity: Reformation to Renaissance* (Cambridge, UK: Cambridge University Press, 1994); Claire McEachern, *The Poetics of English Nationhood, 1590–1612* (Cambridge, UK: Cambridge University Press, 1996); Andrew Escobedo, *Nationalism and Historical Loss in Early Modern England* (Ithaca, NY:

Cornell University Press, 2004); and Philip Schwyzer, *Literature, Nationalism, and Memory in Early Modern England and Wales* (Cambridge, UK: Cambridge University Press, 2004).

13. Adam McKeown, *Fortification and Its Discontents: Shakespeare to Milton* (London: Routledge, 2019).

14. McKeown has extended his arguments to the nation and Henry VIII's coastal fortifications in "Walled Borders and the Geography of Power in Henrician Prose," *English Literary Renaissance* 48, no. 2 (Spring 2018): 121–35. McKeown discusses the pushback against the national wall by historians such as William Camden and John Speed rather than focusing on utopian narratives or plays.

15. Barbara Traister, *Heavenly Necromancers: The Magician in English Renaissance Drama* (New York: Columbia University Press, 1984); Deanne Williams, "*Friar Bacon and Friar Bungay* and the Rhetoric of Temporality," in *Reading the Medieval in Early Modern England*, ed. Gordon McMullan and David Matthews (Cambridge, UK: Cambridge University Press, 2007), 31–48; and Brian Walsh, "'Deep Prescience': Succession and the Politics of Prophecy in *Friar Bacon and Friar Bungay*," *Medieval and Renaissance Drama in England* 23 (2010): 63–85.

16. *Friar Bacon and Friar Bungay*, ed. Christopher Matusiak, Queen's Men Editions (University of Victoria, 2019), 232–40. All quotations from the play are given in line numbers from this edition and hereafter cited in text.

17. John Bridges, *A Defence of the Gouernment Established in the Church of England* (London: Thomas Chard, 1587), 738–39.

18. William Alley, *Ptochhomuseioin* (London, 1565), 47r–v; italics added.

19. There has in fact been a seawall, known as Dymchurch Wall, protecting this section of the English coast since Roman times. In Roger Bacon's lifetime, another wall, known as the Rhee Wall, was constructed in nearby Romney Marsh.

20. Frank Ardolino, "'Thus Glories England over All the West': Setting as National Encomium in *Friar Bacon and Friar Bungay*," *Journal of Evolutionary Psychology* 9, nos. 3 and 4 (1988): 218–29.

21. Williams, "*Friar Bacon*," 43–44.

22. Traister, *Heavenly*, 74.

23. Bryan Reynolds and Henry S. Turner, "From *Homo Academicus* to *Poeta Publicus*: Celebrity and Transversal Knowledge in Robert Greene's *Friar Bacon and Friar Bungay* (c. 1589)," in *Writing Robert Greene: Essays on England's First Notorious Professional Writer*, ed. Kirk Melnikoff and Edward Gieskes (Aldershot: Ashgate, 2008), 73–94. My reading is closer to that of A. J. Hoenselaars, who argues that "Greene catered for a mixed audience who could both delight in . . . mild and un-stereotyped xenophobia . . . and accept as legitimate the unusual celebration of international harmony and peace by the royal representatives in the final scene" in *Images of Englishmen and Foreigners in the Drama of Shakespeare and His Contemporaries* (London: Associated University Press, 1992), 31–32.

24. Francis Bacon, *The Historie of the Raigne of King Henry the Seventh* (London, 1622), 231.

25. Thomas Browne, *Pseudodoxia Epidemica* (London: E. Dod, 1646), 361.

26. Peter Harrington, *The Castles of Henry VIII* (Oxford: Osprey, 2007), 6.

27. Bacon listed some of the basic ingredients in his *Opus Majus*, ed. Robert Belle Burke (New York: Russell and Russell, 1962), 2:629–30, but refers to their use in pyrotechnics rather than artillery. Lynn Thorndike long ago demonstrated that another recipe for gunpowder in cipher is not accurate and its attribution to Bacon is possibly spurious ("Roger Bacon and Gunpowder," *Science* 42 [1915]: 799–800).

28. Charles Stephenson, *"Servant to the King for His Fortifications": Paul Ive and* The Practise of Fortifications (Doncaster: P & G Military Publishers, 2008), 24.

29. Stephenson, *"Servant"*, 10–11, 24. See *Oxford Dictionary of National Biography*, s.v., "Ive, Paul (fl 1602)," (2018).

30. Christopher Marlowe, *Tamburlaine*, ed. J. S. Cunningham (Manchester: Manchester University Press, 1999).

31. Paul Ive, *The Practise of Fortification* (London: T. Man and T. Cooke, 1589), Aa3v–4r.

32. Charles Nicholl, *The Reckoning: The Murder of Christopher Marlowe* (London: Harcourt Brace, 1994), 119–20. Also see Benjamin Bertram, *Bestial Oblivion: War, Humanism, and Ecology in Early Modern England* (New York: Routledge, 2018).

33. Ive, *Practise*, Aa2r. Ive dedicated his other military treatise, *Instructions for the Wars* (a translation of a work by Raimond de Beccarie de Pavie) to William Davison, Walsingham's chief assistant.

34. Scott McMillin and Sally-Beth MacLean, *The Queen's Men and Their Plays* (Cambridge, UK: Cambridge University Press, 1998); Helen Ostovich, Holger Syme, and Andrew Griffin, eds., *Locating the Queen's Men 1583–1603: Material Practice and Conditions of Playing* (Farnham, UK: Ashgate, 2009).

35. Vin Nardizzi likewise sees *Friar Bacon* as an Armada play and notes that the rumors that the Spanish invaders intended to burn down the Forest of Dean and thus cripple England's navy "adds a certain appeal to Bacon's plan to protect England with bronze walls." See Nardizzi, *Wooden Os: Shakespeare's Theatres and England's Trees* (Toronto: University of Toronto Press, 2013), 51. (As noted elsewhere, during this period and for several centuries afterward there was not the same differentiation between the words "bronze" and "brass" that we now employ.)

36. The word "bronze" was imported from the Italian and initially applied to ancient art works; the first recorded appearance of bronze in the *OED* dates from 1739.

37. Quoted in David Childs, *Tudor Sea Power: The Foundations of Greatness* (Barnsley, UK: Seaforth, 2009), 61.

38. *Henslowe's Diary*, ed. R. A. Foakes, 2nd ed. (Cambridge, UK: Cambridge University Press, 2002), 16–21.

39. Lawrence Manley and Sally-Beth MacLean, *Lord Strange's Men and Their Plays* (New Haven, CT: Yale University Press, 2014), 93–94.

40. Stephenson, *"Servant"*, 22.

41. Foakes, *Henslowe's Diary*, 207.

42. Walsh, "'Deep Prescience,'" 64.

43. Walsh, "'Deep Prescience,'" 77.

44. Anonymous, *No-body and Some-body* (London, 1606), D3r.

45. John Marston, *Parasitaster, or the Fawn* (London: William Cotton, 1606), B2r. The

second 1606 edition reads "hill clipt," reinforcing the notion of England's natural defenses.

46. All Shakespearean quotations are from *The New Oxford Shakespeare*, ed. Gary Taylor et al. (Oxford: Oxford University Press, 2016).

47. Schwyzer, *Literature*, 4–5.

48. In *A Midsummer Night's Dream*, Shakespeare ridicules a hapless band of players who presume to bring a wall on stage. As Bottom's bombastic impression of Hercules likely spoofs Edward Alleyn's performance of the role at the Rose, and as Bacon explicitly compares his wall to those of Ninus of Babylon, whose tomb serves as a rendezvous point for Pyramus and Thisbe, it is conceivable that Snout's ludicrous impersonation of a wall would remind playgoers of Bacon's failed wall. For more on *Friar Bacon*'s place in the repertory, see Tom Rutter, *Shakespeare and the Admiral's Men: Reading across Repertories on the London Stage* (Cambridge, UK: Cambridge University Press, 2017), 62–70.

49. Per Sivefors, "Conflating Babel and Babylon in *Tamburlaine 2*," *Studies in English Literature* 52, no. 2 (Spring 2012): 293–323.

50. John Andrewes, *The Converted Man's New Birth* (London, 1629), 3.

51. Jean de Frégeville, *The Reformed Politicke* (London, 1589), 62–63.

52. William Rowley, *A Critical Old-Spelling Edition of The Birth of Merlin (Q 1662)*, ed. Joanna Udall (London: MHRA, 1991), 3.3.26–29.

53. William H. Sherman, *John Dee: The Politics of Reading and Writing in the Renaissance* (Amherst: University of Massachusetts Press, 1995), 149. As the main advisor on England's decision to reject the Gregorian calendar, Dee could be credited with helping create a temporal buffer between England and Catholic Europe.

54. McKeown, "Walled Borders," 121.

55. Schwyzer, *Literature*, 1.

56. Quoted in Garrett Mattingly, *The Armada* (Boston: Houghton Mifflin, 1988), 344.

57. Sometime around 1613 or so, an audience at the Curtain playhouse called out for a revival of the "Friars," and when the Venetian ambassador joined in by shouting "*frati*," the audience mistook his Italian for Spanish and began to jeer at and jostle him. Pointing to this incident, Jenny Sager reexamines the play's feast scenes to demonstrate that "xenophobia and hostility are revealed beneath the veneer of mutual hospitality" ("'Exchange Is No Robbery': Hospitality and Hostility in Robert Greene's *Friar Bacon and Friar Bungay* and *John of Bordeaux*," *Early Modern Literary Studies* 22, no. 1 [January 2021]: 1–12).

6

The Brut, the Bruce, and Brexit

Scottish Independence in *The Valiant Scot* (1637), *The Outlaw King* (2018), and *Robert the Bruce* (2019)

Vimala C. Pasupathi

In June 2019 former first minister of Scotland Alex Salmond took to Twitter to urge Scottish users to "ask @Cineworld to please #Think-Again and #ScreenTheBruce!," turning the new film about the eponymous historical Scottish king, *Robert the Bruce* (2019), into a hashtag and a cause.[1] In the preceding week, users had posed queries on the same platform about the film's release date to the operators of the London-based Cineworld cinema chain's Twitter account; they were soon provided with disappointing news: executives at what was then "the world's second-largest cinema operators" had determined that the film would not be screened in any of its locations in Scotland.[2] Without any immediate explanation for this decision, and in the absence of a convincing one days later, prospective viewers were left to speculate as to whether the film was "banned" because of its potential to influence the Scottish public's attitudes about the territory's status within Great Britain. Was the company afraid to release a film with the potential to inspire nationalist sentiment in Scottish viewers?

In the statement accompanying his tweet, former minister Salmond implored Cineworld to recognize the film's special importance for Scottish audiences but notably shied away from drawing direct connections between the crusade for Scottish independence waged by *Robert the Bruce*'s titular hero and the hashtagable shorthand of contemporary debates, #IndyRef and #Brexit. Instead, he offered a broad appeal, insisting that "people understand who they are through the stories that represent them." Although he described *Robert the Bruce* as depicting "a formative time in our country's history," and its content as being "as applicable in the winter of

1306 as . . . in the summer of 2019," he followed these more pointed assertions with a bland, universalizing claim, namely, that its "subject matter
addresses fundamental truths about what it is to be human."[3]

Touting the film's treatment of the Bruce narrative as one ultimately
concerned with humanity rather than national pride was, no doubt, a deliberate strategy on Salmond's part. After all, the film's release would not
be the first occasion on which his colleagues in Westminster had cause to
worry that historical fiction might produce genuine and actionable patriotic sentiment in Scottish audiences. In 2014 the infamous WikiLeaks
hack had brought to light an email documenting plans for an upcoming
meeting between Sony Pictures executives and then–UK prime minister David Cameron, which included an agenda noting "the importance
of OUTLANDER (i.e., particularly vis-à-vis the political issues in the
U.K. as Scotland contemplates detachment this Fall)."[4] Fans of the popular
novels on which the *Outlander* television show was based were quick to see
a connection between this meeting and the series' delayed premier in the
United Kingdom. Whereas American and Australian viewers were able
to watch the first season in August 2014, British viewers would not have
access to it until March of the following year—only after votes had been
cast in the referendum on Scotland's independence and the campaign for
independence had failed.[5]

The anxieties over historical representation that the distribution of
Outlander and *Robert the Bruce* seem to have animated in governing elites
are hardly exclusive to the twenty-first century. Indeed, the apparent attempt to control audiences' access and engagement in these cases must be
understood as part of broader, transhistorical pattern of production and
consumption in creative media in which representations of historic Scottish identity find both invested audiences and political notoriety at times
when Scotland's status vis-à-vis England has shifted in some crucial way.
Scholars of early modern literature have made much of the seventeenth-
century composition and reception of Shakespeare's *Macbeth*, perhaps the
best-known, but far from only, example of a fictional representation of a
historical Scotland that shaped the political sensibilities of (primarily English) audiences grappling with the prospect of an Anglo-Scottish union
centuries after the events depicted within it. The films *Braveheart* and *Rob
Roy* are also well-known examples, premiering in 1995, the same year in
which the Scottish Constitutional Convention (SCC) published a report
advocating for an independent parliament.

Certainly, 2019's *Robert the Bruce* makes for an interesting comparison with those films as well as with Shakespeare's *Macbeth*, especially the film adaptation from 2015, which one reviewer described provocatively as "a massively significant piece of post-referendum British cinema."[6] But, as I will argue in this chapter, we gain more insight into the phenomenon I have just described in regards to IndyRef and Brexit by considering *Robert the Bruce* together with a film released one year prior to it, *The Outlaw King* (2018), and by reading both alongside an understudied seventeenth-century play of unknown authorship, *The Valiant Scot* (1637).[7] These works are part of a more narrow subset of works, including John Barbour's *Brus* (1375), Walter Scott's *The Lord of the Isles* (1814), and *Braveheart*'s lower-budget contemporary, *The Bruce* (1996), that focus specifically on the fourteenth-century warrior king. Collectively, they establish Bruce's status as a cross-historical vessel for ambivalent nationalism: he is a figure whose apparent self-serving complacency or reticence to act is somehow matched by a perceived capacity to inspire more fervent conviction in other Scots. Circulating in print on the eve of a massive movement to defend the independence of the Scottish kirk—otherwise known as the National Covenant—*The Valiant Scot* (1637) proves especially useful for thinking about the reception of the two films produced in the aftermath of the Indy and Brexit referenda, affirming our sense of Bruce's enduring appeal and affording a glimpse of how that appeal might be exploited by purveyors of his story centuries later. To what extent can fictions about medieval Scotland impact the political realities of a present in which Scottish (or British) independence is just (or always) on the horizon?

The Brut

The period of time portrayed in *The Valiant Scot*, *The Outlaw King*, and *Robert the Bruce* spans roughly two decades, during the first Scottish War of Independence (1301–1321). The wars between Scotland and England lasted much longer, beyond the respective deaths of Edward I and Robert I, punctuated by what turned out to be temporary resolutions, such as the 1327 Treaty of Edinburgh-Northampton and the 1357 Treaty at Berwick. As Robert Crawford has shown in *Bannockburns: Scottish Independence and Literary Imagination, 1314–2014*, this period is not only crucial in the development of mythologies of Scottishness and Scottish nationalism in the middle ages and early modern period but also highly influential in later representations in literature and other media.[8] In addition to battlefields from Falkirk to Bannockburn and Neville's Cross, these conflicts were fought in the pages of chronicles; they were a key part of an "English historiographical tradition which insisted that Scotland was and always had been a dependency of the crown of England" as well as an opposing tradition—what Roger A. Mason calls "Scotching the Brut"—that insisted otherwise.[9] Looking briefly at how these debates developed and continued to circulate over time allows us to see both the origins of a long-standing political fight and the stakes of representing it in subsequent centuries.

The story typically begins with a succession crisis in 1286, caused by the death of Scotland's King Alexander III. In English sources, Edward stepped in to assist in settling the crisis at the request of a group of Scottish barons, invited, he claimed, as an acknowledgment of the superior authority English kings had long held in the north. This last detail is a matter of debate in the historiographical accounts, but there is no question that Edward was deeply aware of the important role that historical records could play in charting a course for the future. In *The Chronicles of England, Scotlande, and Irelande* (1577), Raphael Holinshed highlighted Edward I's use thereof as evidence the king was "not onlie ualiant but also politike."[10] Edward's "labouring to bring this diuided Ile, into one entier monarchie," as Holinshed explained it, began not with military force but rather with the king's command that "all the histories, chronicles, and monuments that were to be found within England, Scotland and Wales, . . . be sought vp and perused, that it might be knowen what right he had in this behalfe."[11] In the 1587 edition of Holinshed's *Historie of Scotland*, the royal order is described in similar terms, but with a striking addition: the accusation of Scottish writers that Edward "burnt all the chronicles of the Scotish nation, with all manner of bookes, as well those conteining diuine seruice, as anie other treatises of profane matters, to the end that the memorie of the Scots should perish."[12]

In the introduction to his 1965 compilation of primary sources in Anglo-Scottish relations, E. L. G. Stones insisted that there was no clear evidence that Edward I attempted, let alone managed, any such feat. Yet Stone also admitted that the available archive of medieval Scottish documents was "woefully meager" and that "our main impression of events has to be derived from English materials, which naturally express the English point of view."[13] The latter can be neatly summarized by a single feature of Anglo-Scottish relations: the "fact" that England had always exercised feudal suzerainty over Scotland. Scottish kings, accordingly, had never ruled autonomously, having always been subject to their English counterparts. Specific instances of Scottish kings who had sworn oaths of fealty to English kings proved that Scottish kings were constrained to do so in perpetuity. This basic narrative, as Edward I recounted it in a 1301 letter to Pope Boniface, proved that he was the "lord superior of the realm of Scotland," a status that could be traced back to "a certain valiant and illustrious man of the Trojan race called Brutus."[14]

The history lesson in the letter to the pope stemmed from Edward's need to justify his military occupation of Scotland. In the letter, he recounted the aftermath of his arbitration of the succession crisis, noting that he had awarded the crown to John Balliol and duly received the new king's oath of fealty as expected. Intervention from the pope was suddenly necessary, he explained, because Balliol and his nobles had later renounced their loyalty and begun to act "contrary to the obligation of their homage and fealty, and wickedly embarking upon the crime of treason, entered into plots, confederations, conspiracies and alliances for the disinheritance of ourselves our heirs, and our realm."[15] Alluding to the Scottish "Auld Alliance" forged with France, an agreement of mutual military aid against England, Edward insisted that this and other breeches of faith could not go unchecked, since it was "perfectly clear and well-known that the realm of Scotland belongs to us of full right, by reason of property and of possession."[16] At the close of his letter, he "humbly beseech[ed]" Boniface to not only confirm his right but also to ignore any "adverse assertions which come to [him] on this subject from [Edward's] enemies."[17]

This last urging gestures at what one of Edward's clerks confirmed after the king had sent his letter: that those "enemies," the same barons whom the king of England claimed had begged for his assistance, were also writing to Boniface and accusing Edward of "ground[ing] [his] right on old chronicles, which contain various falsehoods and lies."[18] They insisted that "the same old chronicles are utterly made naught and of no avail by other subsequent documents of greater significance" and thus would have "no force or effect in escaping the jurisdiction of the pope."[19] Toward that end, they had "endeavored to demonstrate their assertion by Chronicles and narratives of a contrary purport," proving the existence of an ancient line of Scottish kings from Fergus MacFerchard to Robert the Bruce.[20]

Scottish efforts along these lines did not materialize solely as a response to Edward's letter, but the missive did give the matter an obvious urgency and ensured that claims about Fergus and his descendants would be "repeatedly invoked to demonstrate the antiquity and autonomy of the Scottish kingdom" by later writers.[21] Promulgated by Scottish writers from John of Fordun and Hector Boece in the fourteenth and fifteenth centuries

to John Mair (or Major), George Buchanan, and Thomas Craig in the sixteenth, the alternate foundational narrative did not replace the Brutus legend so much as provide a means for arguing Scotland's equal status with
England in spite of it. Although Holinshed and other English chroniclers
were never convinced of the Scottish narrative's legitimacy, we can see evidence of its impact in their fervent efforts to refute the claims of Scottish
historiographers.

The occasionally hostile remarks printed in the margins of Holinshed's
Scottish Chronicle provide ample evidence that the discursive battle over
the Brut continued well into the late sixteenth century. Its continuation
throughout the seventeenth is evident in the 1695 resurrection and translation of a text by the Scot Thomas Craig, who originally composed it in
Latin in 1602 with the expressed purpose of combating Holinshed's "Fool-
eries and Scurrilities."[22] The Scottish journalist George Ridpath touted its
timeliness in the preface of his translation: though it had "lain dormant
near 100 Years in Manuscript," it was essential reading "for the Honour
of *Scotland*, and the Information of Foreigners who are frequently misled
as to our Affairs, and particularly on this Head, by English Historians."[23]

Not long after this text appeared, Scottish historiographical practice
would shift, with "enlightenment" writers eventually abandoning the myth
of ancient lineage as the primary legal basis of Scotland's claims for independence.[24] But even as the mythical lines of ancient Scottish kings
disappeared from intellectual and historical debates, tales of their most
victorious beneficiary persisted in fictional accounts of Robert the Bruce.
Bearing the traces of those debates, but exceeding them in visibility and
function, the three examples that concern this chapter, *The Valiant Scot* and
its twenty-first-century counterparts, *The Outlaw King* (2018) and *Robert
the Bruce* (2019) are all examples of "Scotching the Brut" in some fashion.
Having established the historical stakes of privileging Bruce's link to those
lines in broad strokes, I will now look at these particular iterations' significance in detail.

The Bruce

Robert the Bruce was one of seven barons with a strong claim to the Scottish throne in the aforementioned succession crisis in which Edward I in-
tervened. According to early modern Scottish historiographer John Mair,
Edward's initial choice of John Balliol over Bruce and the others was part
of the English king's long-term plan to use the crisis "for his own special

advantage," for "in sowing amongst the Scots the seeds of civil war . . . to the end that when the opposing parties had worn out each of them the strength of the other, or perchance using for himself the support of one of them, he might obtain the kingdom."[25] Bruce is implicated in the last part of that statement, and Mair is clear in connecting his willingness to take up Edward's banner with the enemies he made in both kingdoms. Bruce's status reached its lowest point after his infamous encounter with John Comyn in Greyfriar's kirk, a meeting agreed to with both mutual hopes of a future alliance between Scottish elites and mutual fears of betrayal. It culminated in Comyn's murder, with Bruce living in infamy thereafter. His struggles to attain the crown and regain the faith of his countrymen supply the primary conflict for all fictional accounts of these events, including the three we will consider here.

The differences among the three works that concern this essay are as illuminating as the basic plot elements they share with the events relayed in chronicles like Mair's. They present especially interesting points of comparison in the way they construct Bruce as a man and leader, each using familial relations, female characters, and the figure of William Wallace to highlight the future Scottish king's strengths, flaws, and motivations. Of additional interest here is each work's engagement with the Scottish barons' "Auld Alliance" with France, a somewhat small facet of the story that nonetheless bears significantly on how the two films and the seventeenth-century play comment on the matter of Anglo-Scottish union. Despite their differences and the different moments in which these works circulated, all three understand Bruce as man who must prove to his people that he is neither compromised by his early ties to England nor a danger to them in his aspirations for power.

The 2019 movie *Robert the Bruce* begins with a Bruce who is alone and on the run, very much in line with Mair's musings on the period of Bruce's social isolation after his murder of Comyn: "A strange spectacle, surely, this—of a man with manifold kindred in England and in Scotland, the inheritor in both kingdoms of wide domains, destitute utterly of the comforts of existence."[26] The film circumscribes this status within a broad narrative of hubris castigated in Bruce's earnest admission to his supporters: "I truly believed that God had chosen me to be King," he says, before adding, "God didn't choose me, I did. And everything I did to honor him, and everything I've done, defiled him instead." Even as this Bruce is plagued with self-castigation and self-doubt, the film itself never wavers in its conviction that Bruce had honorable intentions as the rightful king of

Scotland. This characterization is reinforced by two sets of sentences that appear on screen at the beginning of the film, the first informing viewers that "mighty clans align with England and her fearsome King, but Robert the Bruce, having fought with William Wallace, still believes in Scottish Independence."[27] The second set reads, "Once again, Scotland finds herself on the brink of civil war. Yet the fire for freedom burns in the hearts of the people." These framing sentences set up Bruce as a man united with Wallace in opposition to the "mighty clans" that had "align[ed] with" Edward I; they also encourage viewers to see Bruce in alignment with common Scots.

In starting with a defeated, humbled Bruce, *Robert the Bruce* distinguishes itself from its near-contemporary, *The Outlaw King*, and from the seventeenth-century *The Valiant Scot*. The other two works also focus on the character's alienation and uncertainty, but in contrast to *Robert the Bruce*'s lonely wanderer, *The Outlaw King* and *The Valiant Scot* begin with a Bruce who lives among sneering nobles in the English court. *The Outlaw King*'s Bruce is the son of a still-living father, suffering derision and antagonism from the English primarily out of deference to Robert senior, who speaks fondly of Edward I and values him as a childhood friend. Sensing his son's discomfort, the elder Bruce encourages him to be patient. "The important thing is we are favored," he says, assuring him confidently that "Edward will offer us the crown." To the younger Bruce's protests—"You'd be a lackey!"—he insists that this status is an acceptable trade-off for the eventuality of "being king" and securing the line of succession.

In *The Valiant Scot*, Bruce is similarly able to ignore the English aristocrats and focus single-mindedly on "the crown of Scotland" (1.4.29). In his first speech, we find him addressing Edward to ask his "Soveraigne" to "confirm his grant touching" it, but the king impatiently cuts him off with a promise to discuss it "some other time" (1.4.29–30). When Edward shifts the conversation from his Scottish subordinate's concerns to his "French designs," Bruce again asks for some reassurance from his "Gracious Liege," eliciting an exasperated response from the English king: "Th' art no Musician, Bruce," he says; "thou keep'st false time; We strike a bloudy lachrymae to France, / And thou keep'st time to a Scotch jigge to armes" (1.4.103; 1.4.52; 1.4.53–55). In *The Valiant Scot*, Bruce has no living father to placate him; instead, his incentive to be patient in the meantime is an opportunity to lead Edward's French campaigns.

The Valiant Scot spends considerable time from this point forward setting up the factors that lead Bruce to renounce his loyalty to Edward. In this way, the play is similar to *The Outlaw King*, which devotes significant screen time to the moments big and small that culminate in Bruce's change of heart. These include a deathbed scene in which Robert senior admits to having "made a grave mistake in trusting Edward," an admission that initiates the younger Bruce's reckoning with the scale of broken promises—those made by Edward to Bruce's family, and by Bruce's family to the Scottish people— that grows in subsequent scenes. In one, he watches silently as agents of the crown arrive in a town to collect taxes and to press young boys for Edward's armies, taking stock of the indignation expressed by Scottish commoners, noblemen, and officers; they implicate him in their suffering, lamenting, "You promised our taxes would be reduced once the wars with Edward were over!" and "You assured us these obligations would be over." In response, they are told they now must pay more as "compensation for the rebellion."

In *The Valiant Scot*, Bruce takes on a similar role as an initially detached witness to the ordinary Scots whose lives have been affected by an oppressive English rule. The playwright primarily details the impact of the English presence on an extraordinary Scot, William Wallace, the rebel soldier twentieth-century audiences know from *Braveheart*. Although Wallace is described in superlative terms by his followers and rivals, the playwright positions him first as one of several victims of conquest; the English nobles Edward has "plac'd in commision" have stripped Wallace's father of his titles and the land he describes as "purchas'd with the sweat / Of [his] deer [*sic*] ancestors" (1.1.56–57). His betrothed, Peggy Graham, is abducted for a "forced marriage" to one of the commissioner's sons, described as "the highest favour conquest can afford, / For a slave to joyn alliance with his Lord" (1.1.87; 1.1.97–98).

At first, the playwright's Bruce repudiates the rebellion that Wallace launches in response to this treatment, assuring Edward that he "had no hand in't" (1.4.70). But Wallace is intent on "winn[ing] Bruce from the English" and begins to achieve this goal in a scene that dramatizes a tale we see in chronicles like Mair's and in the epic poem by Barbour (5.2.72).[28] During a break in a battle in act 4, Wallace has a private meeting with Bruce in the forest, at which he insists that Bruce's legitimacy as king derives from the Scottish people rather than Edward's authority. He accuses him of being "made a mastive 'mongst a heard of wolves, / To weary those [he] shouldst be sheperd of"; when Bruce denies the charge, Wallace encourages him to "with a sharpe eye note but with what scorne / The English pay thy merit" (4.3.51–52; 4.3.58–59). Affirmed by comments made by the soldiers in the English army, Wallace's exhortation productively frames Bruce's transition from complacent to committed.

In *The Outlaw King,* Wallace does not appear as a living character, but his influence on Bruce's conduct is nonetheless clear.[29] In a key scene, English soldiers in the garrison town of Berwick hoist parts of his dismembered body into the air on spits in order to discipline and demoralize the battle's survivors. The cries of dismay quickly turn into violent skirmishes; although Bruce and a few other Scottish nobles stand aside, it is clear that seeing Scots grieve and resist in Wallace's name affects the future king deeply. Soon after, he calls the other magnates together and insists, "We swore vows on Edward's Bible that we will need to break ... People are up in arms. There can be no peace."

The position Bruce stakes out earns him a small band of followers and provides the occasion for the film's depiction of the encounter with John Comyn. At Greyfriar's, he firmly refuses to join Bruce, saying, "We already tried it. For eight bloody years. We failed." Furthermore, Comyn insists that Bruce and his family were responsible for that failure because they sought only to consolidate power for themselves. Comyn also dismisses Bruce's contention that Wallace's death has changed the tide of Scottish sentiment. Wallace, he says, "wasn't a man; he was an idea," and as such, he inspires no more unity in his absence than in life. Comyn concludes his rejection of an alliance by affirming his intention to turn Bruce in for treason. Reacting decisively to this threat, Bruce draws his sword and commits the act for which he will be excommunicated (though later absolved).

The encounter with Comyn is also important in *Robert the Bruce* but serves a different function. It is not a decisive turning point so much as a traumatic flashback presented at the film's beginning. Viewers' sense of the encounter is shaped both by dialogue—Comyn's taunting of Bruce that he will never "be loved as" Wallace, nor "brave like him [or] free like him"—and by its framing narration as an often-requested bedtime story. Through the female storyteller's words and her young listener's interjections, audiences are led to conclude that only Bruce had come to Greyfriar's in good faith. The voiceover both softens the visual violence of Comyn's murder and explicitly informs viewers of the "truth": whereas "the Bruce would fight for freedom, Comyn was a puppet of the English crown."

This description of Comyn in *Robert the Bruce* is one of very few references to England or Edward in the entire film. In the other cases, England is invoked solely as the source of a bounty, and Edward's impact on Scottish life is relayed primarily through broad equivocations (e.g., "We have known Scotland, clutched in the grip of a mighty hand"). "England" surfaces directly only once, within a rhetorical question, "Are you with

England or the Bruce?," and "English" features only once as well, in an expository narration that brings the audience forward from the kirk scene into the present day: "For many years he fought," the female voice says, gravely, before continuing, "For many years he lost. Again and again. He fought until the rivers flowed red with Scottish blood. Until he was hunted like an animal, by English and Scot alike."

This reference acknowledges that English people exist, but its primary importance is establishing Bruce's broad estrangement and specifically his divisiveness on native soil. It also sets up the actions that follow, for in heavy cinematic irony, Bruce and those who hunt him are hiding just outside the home in which this bedtime story is told. Successive shots that show him alone, wounded and shivering, emphasize Bruce's vulnerability, juxtaposed with others that reveal the callous brutality of enemy Scotsmen. After the bedtime story concludes, these enemies are given quarter by Morag, the woman who has been telling it, a widow of one of Bruce's soldiers. Over the meager provisions she supplies, the hunters rehearse the various resentments and recriminations that have divided the kingdom. Morag struggles to prevent the men at the table from engaging her son Scott, her niece, Iver, and her nephew, Carney, all orphans of fathers who fought in Bruce's name. Whereas the hunters are embittered by their perceived abandonment, Morag and her charges cling to a worldview in which their continued loyalty to Bruce is justified.

Just after this scene, Iver and Carney discover Bruce in his hiding place, by this time incapacitated from hunger and wounds. With help from Morag and Scott, they transform Bruce from a limping, doubting, and complacent man back into a king. The early scene of Morag's hospitality foreshadows the film's climactic battle, a small-scale skirmish outside a single-room house that pits hardened, embittered warriors against their younger, untested kin. With its localized, familial scale, the fight symbolically heralds Bruce's return as defender of a nation, capable again of inspiring young men—and now women—against fellow Scots who seek short-term profit.

Whereas *Robert the Bruce* characterizes Bruce through references to and depictions of Comyn and other Scots, *The Valiant Scot* and *The Outlaw King* do so through depictions of English characters. The 1637 play is invested in establishing the incompetence and brutality with which Englishmen conduct themselves, though it locates the worst qualities in English commissioners rather than in Edward I. The 2018 film places these qualities instead in Edward's son and successor, at one minute boyishly competitive and at another full of violent rage. The English prince is emphasized as Bruce's foil in various ways, but most obviously in his violent treatment of Bruce's wife, Elizabeth de Burgh. Early in the film, King Edward presents the younger Bruce with the daughter of the Earl of Ulster as a token of his gratitude for his and his father's loyal service. Whereas Edward I explicitly describes the match at the time as "symboliz[ing] the harmonious union of [their] two countries," his son later grabs Elizabeth violently by the hair in front of her parents, demanding that she sign papers annulling the marriage once Bruce defies the English king's authority. This conduct contrasts with the gentle, even passive Bruce we are shown at and after the wedding, depicted as a Scottish warrior but also a secretly sensitive man still mourning the death of his first wife. Much like his approach to the Scottish crown, the film's Bruce maintains a polite distance and does not claim ownership until the film has sufficiently convinced the audiences of his rights.

The Outlaw King's depiction of Elizabeth de Burgh, like the ahistorical character of Peggy Graham in *The Valiant Scot* and Morag and Iver in *Robert the Bruce*, adds another facet to Bruce's characterization and invites viewers to understand the marriage as both an actual legal instrument of statehood and a metaphor for Anglo-Scottish union and Scottish sovereignty. Whereas in the other works women represent the injustices or victims of English conquest, the 2018 film's Elizabeth is portrayed as a worthy partner for a Scottish rebel and king. She impresses Bruce and audiences alike when she intervenes in the conflict between English captains and a Scottish mother, helping the latter to prevent her twelve-year-old son from being sent off to fight a foreign war. She also performs a role similar to the one Wallace plays for Bruce in *The Valiant Scot*, assuring the audience that he is justified in fighting back. She tells him, "Power is in making decisions. Power is not allowing yourself to be buffeted on the tides of history, choosing a boat, climbing aboard and hoisting the sail." It is a strained metaphor for what will obviously be a war fought on land, but the profession of loyalty that follows it, "I choose you and whatever course you are charting," makes clear that the Englishwoman will be loyal to her husband, a man with whom she is evenly matched.

Although the two films present domestic happiness in different registers, *Robert the Bruce* and *The Outlaw King* both project a vision of an ultimately victorious King Robert whose motives are pure and ultimately modest. Both imply that independence stems from a simple desire for familial unity, stability, and safety; it is this desire, rather than a lust for power, they insist, that fuels Bruce's military achievements and underpins their urgency. A similar rhetoric of family obligation is at work in *The Valiant Scot*, despite the fact that the playwright denies his Bruce a wife and children. Under the thumb of "England [his] stepdame" until the play's final act, Bruce is depicted as a man whose growth has been stunted and who cannot be a literal or figurative father as long as he remains a prodigal son (5.1.15). In the anguished speech that signals his shift in loyalty, he cries, "Oh my parent, / Dear Scotland, I will no more be a goad / Pricking thy sides" (5.1.19–23). Promising never again to harm his own people, he refuses to follow an ensuing command from Edward, declaring, "I will not. I'm not his Butcher; / 'Gainst the Scots I will not fight" (5.1.29–31).

Bruce's defiance here presents an important contrast to his compliance in previous scenes, recalling his abject positioning in the first scene in which he appears. At that point, the king's granting of a commission to lead troops against France is a carrot to keep him complacent and to delay his receipt of the promised Scottish crown. Notably, Edward's French campaign is ahistorical, used by the playwright to explain Edward's methods for manipulating Bruce.[30] Appointing him as a captain keeps Bruce occupied and out of Scotland and also places him in further opposition to his fellow Scots; though leading troops against Frenchmen is not quite the same as the "butchery" he enacts fighting against his "parent" Scotland, it defies the aims of its other barons, whose Treaty of Paris (1295) codified promises for mutual aid with France's Philip IV.

The twenty-first-century films also invoke the "Auld Alliance" in brief, but meaningful, ways. In *Robert the Bruce*, a single allusion to it features a scene in which Carney takes a sword to a smith to be repaired at the instruction of his uncle. Known by the audience, but unbeknownst to Carney, the sword had once belonged to Bruce, but he abandoned it in a moment of despair. The smith recognizes the sword's quality; during his initial appraisal, he remarks that it has been made "Far from here, France maybe." This single remark suggests the smith's knowledge of his trade and also rewards viewers who know of the alliance and of Bruce's French ancestry. After it is repaired, Carney defies his uncle's instructions, first returning the sword to Bruce and later wielding it against the uncle who seeks to profit from Bruce's capture.

In *The Outlaw King* (2018), the allusion to France is made in a scene that marks a crucial shift in Bruce's military tactics. In this particular moment, he walks along the exterior of his own castle, which his men have just sacked at his command. Rounding the perimeter of what will apparently be his last time at his former home, he finds a pair of his loyal lairds, who stand alongside two abject men. "These gentlemen of France were in the dungeon," they explain; "They wish to join us." Bruce greets them with a warm (and by this point characteristically gentle) smile before addressing them in careful, earnest French. He assures them, "The French are always welcome," and they respond in French, "Thank you very much, Your Majesty." Broadly, this scene showcases both the desperation and resolve of the Scots, whose nobles would sooner destroy their family homes rather than allow the English to settle in them. In contrast to the violent, destructive frenzy that precedes it, Bruce's exchange with the liberated French prisoners is quiet and mutually affirmative; what might otherwise seem like a bland exchange becomes a pointed gesture at Scotland's peaceful partnerships with other nations. If the conversation in French is brief and formulaic, it takes on some gravity alongside others in *The Outlaw King* in which characters speak or sing in Gaelic, temporarily displacing English as the dominant mode of communication. It transpires with an ease and amity that also contrasts with the exchanges between the Bruce and the Prince of Wales, which range from mild expressions of antagonism to declarations of open war.

Practically speaking, the references to Franco-Scottish partnerships in all three works unsettle England's ostensible position as a superior power to the south and reframe it instead as a vulnerable state situated between two enemies. Symbolically and politically, the allusions signal the Scottish barons' agency in forging relationships with other governments; by exercising it, they defy Edward's legitimacy and his claims of perpetual sovereignty. These works' respective nods to Scotland's *other* alliance underscore what is evident in their sympathetic portrayals of Bruce and his relationships more broadly: that Scotland is neither well-served by English rule nor in actual need of it. How this message from the medieval past could be brought to bear on later conflicts between the two is the question that I will turn to in this chapter's final section. There, I will contextualize these works' production, promotion, and circulation more fully in order to reflect on their potential to shape contemporary audiences' attitudes toward Anglo-Scottish relations.

Brexit (and Other Deferred Conclusions)

The impressions that these representations of medieval Scotland would have left on their respective early modern and post-Brexit audiences cannot be sufficiently analyzed without first attending to how each work concludes, beginning with the earliest of the three. In *The Valiant Scot*, the defiant Scottish son ascends the Scottish throne in the play's final scene. But he is crowned by Edward I, a detail with no basis in the historiographical records of either nationalist tradition. The playwright's "unhistorical settlement," as George Byers deems it, rather surprisingly allows Edward to set the terms of Bruce's sovereignty, thereby affirming the former's superior status and continued control over the Scottish throne.[31] In fact, the playwright makes Bruce's concession to his inferior status a condition of his coronation, with Edward's order to "give us thy oath of fealty, and weare / Both Crown and title of thine Ancestors" (5.4.133–38). Bruce complies, proclaiming, "England is full of honour, / Bruce doth bend to thy command" (5.4.139–40). Despite the play's apparent advocacy for Wallace's cause in much of its earlier action, its ending undermines the power of Bruce's rejection of English authority and ultimately validates the formative premise of the English tradition, namely that Scottish liberty remains within England's control. The play goes further to make Edward's case than English historiographers by imagining Bruce's coronation in these unconventional terms.

In still another departure from chronicle sources, the playwright uses the same occasion to depict Bruce's murder of John Comyn, presented here as simply a coconspirator of the Earl of Mentith in turning Wallace over to the crown for a reward. Bruce explains his controversial deed as "a sacrifice of honour and revenge," adding, "No traitors' hand / Shall help to lift a crown to my head" (5.4.150–51). Bruce's final actions, kneeling to Edward and killing his countryman, seem to swiftly resolve all conflicts between the two kingdoms; the earlier focus on Edward's power-hungry commissioners and his desire to conquer Scotland is replaced by a narrative that blames the bloody conflict only on freedom-seeking zealots and mercenary Scots. This contrived ending is a radical turn for a play that "contains no nationalistic glorifying of England" and is primarily told "from the point of view of the Scottish rebels."[32] The playwright attempts to reconcile this apparent dissonance in the play's final lines, delivered by the English soldier whom Byers describes as the play's only "consistently honorable character."[33] He declares, "Now shall the Ghost of Wallace sleepe in peace, / And perfect love shall twixt these Lands increase" (5.4.152–53). In contrast to what historians from all eras know of the remaining years of Edward I's reign, these lines imply that Anglo-Scottish relations after this moment will remain amiable and even improve over time.

It is not hard to imagine why a (presumably English) playwright might feel compelled to preempt the messier, but better documented conclusion that the play had seemed to be building toward up to this point. The need to validate his primary audiences' sense of an English benevolent superiority seems to have superseded any initial interest in promoting Bruce as the hero who decisively ended England's occupation. If we look more specifically at the time of the play's earliest circulation, however, it seems likely that such a conclusion would have prevented it from being licensed for print in the first place. In April 1637, when the playbook appears in the Stationers' Register, Scots had their sights on a different text, the new liturgy Charles had planned for Scotland in an effort to ensure conformity with the Anglican prayerbook.. Authored by Scottish bishops but perceived to be the work of the English Archbishop Laud, the prayerbook set in motion what Maurice Lee describes as "the most famous 'uproar for religion' in all of British history."[34] What began as a protest at St. Giles in July quickly morphed into a highly organized resistance movement, with its principles articulated formally in the Scottish National Covenant. This document provided an explicit, preemptive rejection of any imposition by the Crown, affirming the independence of the Scottish church and its rejection of Laudian episcopacy.

It is fascinating to contemplate the impact *The Valiant Scot* might have had on readers' attitudes in the spring of 1637, not just in light of the play's conclusion but also with attention to its curiously prescient dedicatory epistle. It is addressed to the Scottish nobleman James Arran, then marquis of Hamilton and Charles I's principal advisor on Scottish affairs, and signed by a soldier named William Bowyer. Like Ridpath's dedication of Thomas Craig's legal history, Bowyer's letter appeals to his prospective patron's power and status as well as his personal ties to Scotland, premised on his presumed appreciation for a play that "contains the Character which History hath left to Posterity of your own truly valiant Countriman."[35] Whether that "Character" is intended to be Bruce or Wallace is left to the reader to determine, but there is no mistaking either the letter's patriotic appeal or its hope that what "History hath left" would still be meaningful.

We don't know whether Hamilton read the play, let alone whether he saw its content as a guide or a warning. But it is certainly the case that he shared several basic traits with Bruce in his early years. He was both an ardent supporter of the English monarch and a nobleman in line of succession to the Scottish throne; he was hated by some of his fellow Scots for the capitulations he urged them to make on behalf of Charles; and he was accused by English courtiers of secretly planning to unseat the king. The most striking convergence, though, is that his allegiance to Charles eventually meant going to war against his native Scotland; as John Kerrigan notes, "after *The Valiant Scot* was published, Hamilton was obliged by his Anglo-Scottish entitlements to become more like Bruce by leading Charles's army against the Scots in the Bishops' Wars."[36]

To be sure, neither the stationer John Waterson nor the printer Thomas Harper could know what would transpire in 1638 when they chose to publish *The Valiant Scot*. Nor could they know that Charles would respond to Scottish resistance with the threat of military force—or that his attempts to bring the Scots into submission by invading by land and sea would fail and precipitate war in two additional kingdoms. But they must have known that its subject matter was timely. That Harper, a staunch royalist, saw fit to print the play seems to support my conjectures about the play's wholly imaginary ending. Even if much of the play can be read as supporting Scottish resistance to English rule, its final scene also insisted that Scottish autonomy must always be limited, constrained irrevocably by Bruce's oath of fealty.

The playwright's attempt at a "both/and" compromise resonates with the final message of *The Outlaw King*, whose filming began nearly four hundred years later. Like *Robert the Bruce*, it was released after the vote on the United Kingdom European Union membership referendum, during the same period in which MPs were negotiating the precise date of "Brexit" and other details of its implementation. While the details of the plan do not align neatly as a parallel for the introduction of the prayerbook in 1637, the results of the vote similarly launched Scotland into what Nicola McEwen described in a December 2017 article as "deeply uncertain times," positioning it awkwardly "between two unions."[37] The majority of Scottish voters' desire to stay in the EU exposed a widening rift between them and the Westminster parties in government.

Although the Scots' rejection of Brexit was politically and culturally significant, it was "legally inconsequential" because it occurred as part of "a UK-wide referendum with a UK-wide electorate."[38] In contrast to the independence referendum in 2014, the results of Brexit "highlight[ed] the anti-democratic nature of current political arrangements whereby Scotland must accept political developments for which it has not voted."[39] In doing so, it raised the specter of yet another referendum on Scottish independence. As the then-first minister of Scotland Nicola Sturgeon explained it, Brexit represented "a significant and a material change in the circumstances in which Scotland voted against independence in 2014." Because "the supposed guarantee of remaining in the EU was a driver in their decision to vote to stay within the UK," the party was justified in asking its constituents whether their positions on independence had changed.[40]

It is remarkable, though not surprising, that two films about Robert the Bruce were released at a time when Brexit had made Scottish support for independence "historically high."[41] But just as remarkably, only one of them appears to endorse that outcome. Not unlike the ending of *The Valiant Scot*, *The Outlaw King*'s conclusion seems aimed at mitigating rather than fomenting the desire for Scottish autonomy from England. The film offers a series of sentences on screen that explain what happens after Bruce's victories at Loudoun Hill (1307). The first two supply information about the various fates of other characters: Bruce's fervent supporter James Douglas is "granted back his family lands" and the Prince of Wales will eventually be "killed by his own nobles." Then the copy turns its attention to Elizabeth, who, in previous scenes, is separated from Bruce and subjected to torture. With the reassuring news that the two were "reunited and raised a family together," audiences are treated to frames in which the happy couple meet and embrace on the beach, the camera panning out to reveal the castle that safely holds their daughter. As the shot expands, the text changes again to supply the news that "300 years later Robert's descendant James VI inherited the English Crown to become king of both Scotland and England."

Imposed over the image of Bruce and Elizabeth holding one another on the Scottish coast, the allusion to James VI's succession as James I underscores the two lovers' status as the natural and genealogical forerunners for the Union of Crowns in 1603. *The Outlaw King* thus invites audiences to understand this moment in time as both a contrast to a later time when the two countries achieved a settlement through political processes rather than military action *and* as a necessary precondition for that settlement. In envisioning the thirteenth- and fourteenth- century fights for independence as essential for peace and future union with England rather than a full separation from it, *The Outlaw King* highlights Bruce's hard-won victories only to inscribe Scotland within a congenial partnership with the traditionally stronger power. Additionally, Stuart ascension is pitched as a victorious end rather than a middle point in the two countries' relationship, implying an uncomplicated path to its audience's own "Great Britain." As early modernists know, the reign of James I and VI saw increasingly fraught negotiations with his Scottish church and Parliament, institutions that remained separate from their English counterparts. Their separateness would continue to be a source of conflict between James's successors and Scottish elites and the cause of Scottish resistance to Charles I's policies in the late 1630s, when *The Valiant Scot* appeared in print. Betraying no sense of future conflicts between these points in time, *The Outlaw King*'s final words also contain no hints of the later Act of Union in 1707, when the separation of Scottish and English political and religious institutions finally came to an end. In this way, *The Outlaw King* leaves history *as* history, circumscribing the significance of its story within a narrow chronological frame.

To some extent, the same is true of *Robert the Bruce*, though unlike both *The Outlaw King* and *The Valiant Scot* its final scenes make no effort to reconcile its account of Bruce's reign with the English-appeasing narrative of the Brut. Using the same expository technique as *The Outlaw King*, but presenting a very different message, the film ends with on-screen sentences that retain a singular focus on the titular Scot. "As King," we are told, "Robert the Bruce never owned a castle. Instead he made his home with the soldiers. And with the families of those he fought alongside." This brief, final comment reinforces the vision of Robert I as a man of the people, one who looks to the past not as a way to assert his right to possess a crown but as a way to maintain his humility and connection to ordinary Scots. In keeping with the rest of the film, England is absent; the struggle for independence is pitched as an internal battle within each Scot, who, once united with others, will ensure Scotland controls its own destiny.

The implications of both films for post-Brexit audiences are placed in sharper relief by the promotional comments of those who made them. In his public interviews about *The Outlaw King*, the director, David Mackenzie, explicitly fended off the suggestion that the film invited "thinking about contemporary parallels" and added emphatically that he and his team had "tr[ied] to tell the story from an apolitical standpoint."[42] Professing to be motivated only by the desire to tell "a story that hasn't properly been told," he drew a more explicit contrast between his own film and *Braveheart*, describing the '90s hit as having "much more of a rabble-rousing, 'rah rah' kind of tone, and—in this day and age—I just don't feel it's appropriate to be making that type of movie, to be honest. The forces of nationalism are expanding across the world, and I think one has to be very careful about that."[43] That tone, he insisted, was inappropriate for the current moment: "Even though I'm telling a true story about a national hero," he added, "I don't want 'Outlaw King' to be taken too literally as a rallying call." The point of making the film was to be "honest about the material without inciting a certain segment of the population."[44]

Mackenzie's comments about nationalism and *Braveheart* are striking on their own, but especially so in light of what Angus Macfadyen, the star and writer of *Robert the Bruce*, said about the same film in the following year. Although Macfadyen had played Bruce in the 1995 film, he was keen to portray the older Bruce in a manner distinct from the Bruce of *Braveheart*. Like Mackenzie, Macfadyen intended to tell his story in a way that "does not glorify war."[45] But that distinction notwithstanding, Macfadyen viewed *Braveheart*'s influence in terms that were notably more positive than did Mackenzie. In contrast to the latter's discomfort, Macfadyen spoke approvingly of the apparent rise in Scottish nationalism subsequent to it, and he credited the film with reinvigorating the Scottish National Party (SNP), "a spent force" prior to the film's release.[46] Macfadyen's interest in writing *Robert the Bruce* was rooted in the hope that *Braveheart*'s "sequel" could play a similar role, "boost[ing] support" for independence.[47]

Though Mackenzie and Macfadyen expressed different desires about the political import of their films for a post-Brexit Scotland, their respective depictions of Bruce clearly owe as much to the late 1990s as the 1290s and early 1300s. Evident in both filmmakers' comments is a shared belief in what the unapologetically nationalist Macfadyen invoked as "the power of a movie," even as Mackenzie claimed to wield it somewhat warily.[48] A version of that belief and wariness might also be at work in the controversy with which this chapter began, the initial decision by Cineworld not to show *Robert the Bruce* in Scottish theaters, arguably honoring the custom in the breech. In many respects, the hope (or fear) that a movie could change minds and votes is not an unreasonable one. After all, Macfadyen's claims linking *Braveheart* and the SNP track closely with a narrative promulgated by Scotland's first minister and are backed by references to the film in party documents.[49] Within two years of *Braveheart*, the SNP had achieved what had failed in a 1979 referendum and had not been possible since 1707: the formation of a "devolved" Scottish parliament, a legislative body separate from England's. In fact, as Murray Stewart Leith explains, many years later the film was understood to be a key ingredient for that electoral success, such that the SNP would continue to allude to it in its 2001 manifesto, despite that year's shift away from celebrating Scottish*ness* as a distinct national identity in order to mount more inclusive campaigns.[50]

Still, the crucial role played by what Salmond dubbed "*Braveheart* mania" can also be overstated, and the narrative that it alone delivered the votes ignores another, well-documented one making the same case for a broad spectrum of Scottish writers and artists. According to Cairns Craig

and others, the development of a divergent, newly Scotland-centered voting public was not moved to support devolution by a single film; rather, it
was the result of decades of work by creatives and academics, producers
whose "cultural action, in effect, [became] an alternative to the stalled nature of Scotland's political life in the long hiatus between 1979 and 1997."[51]
While *Braveheart* and *Rob Roy* have their place in Craig's account, they do
not have pride of place; they are merely part of a spate of art forms and
scholarly publications that "revitalised the understanding of Scotland's past
from the middle ages to the end of the twentieth century."[52] In this broader
view, devolution as it manifested in the late '90s was both the product of
a particular moment and the culmination of disparate efforts that, even
without a unified vision or intent, supplied a foundation for nationalist
sentiment.[53]

While this narrative of the power of culture to shape political attitudes
is entrenched in academic and public commentary, it also isn't without
limitations as an explanatory framework. For many, the results of the 2014
IndyRef exposed its flaws, with the 55 percent majority votes cast against
it highlighting the gap between the electoral behavior of a larger public
and the elite group that had advocated for it. The problem is not so much
that the narrative has inflated the role of culture, but that the production
and consumption of art, literature, and film cannot be neatly correlated
with voting. As Scott Hames observes in his study of Scottish literature
and devolution, to limit one's focus on culture without attending to developments in electoral strategy is to miss a crucial part of the story; to
conflate cultural developments with political activism around devolution is
also to "over-determine the critical repertoire through which we view and
value Scottish writing."[54] Even in Craig's positivist assessment, culture is a
merely a necessary component for, and "predictor of," political infrastructure; it is not, on its own, sufficient for conjuring Scotland's independence
within it.[55] What has been, and may yet be missing, is a majority that
will vote for independence—and, as Hames's work reminds us, a British
government that will provide the opportunity for Scots to hold a new referendum in the first place.

With respect to the first of these two conditions, there is much about
Bruce in both films that could appeal to such a voter, whether they identify
as politically progressive and want an egalitarian Scotland over a hierarchical Britain or as a more traditional Scot who takes pleasure in seeing his
countryman as subjects with an ancient and noble heritage. But is it also
the case the two films exemplify what Andrew Higson claims of British

heritage films and cinema broadly: "All film texts are the site of ideological tensions, audiences may read a text against the grain, [and] other more critical films exist which serve to challenge the nationalizing myths found in the most resolutely patriotic films."[56] The same is true, of course, of early modern history plays, and in this respect, *The Valiant Scot* is instructive. As I have already noted of the play, the ultimately supplicant Bruce that we see in the final scene appears to appeal to the royalist sympathies of its printer and dedicatee, if not also those of readers. But references to the play in a 1642 pamphlet supply the impression that later readers may have understood the work in different terms.

These references appear in *A Second Discovery by the Northern Scout*, a dialogue in which two Scottish (or Scots-supporting) characters discuss a group of players from the Fortune playhouse who had been imprisoned for putting on "a new old Play, called the Cardinall's conspiracie."[57] When they "gat their liberty," one explains, they "fell to act the Valiant Scot, which they Played five dayes with great applause, which vext the Bishops worse than the other, in so much as they were forbidden Playing it any more; and some of them prohibited ever playing again."[58] The other responds with approval and defiance: "Let the Bishops be as angry as they will, we have acted the *Valiant Scot* bravely at *Berwicke*; and, if ever I live to come to *London* . . . it may be acted there too, and that with a new addition; for I can tell thee, here's matter enough."[59] The example confirms nothing about the reception of the play itself, at least nothing beyond the affordances of its title. But its invocation in anti-Laudian propaganda makes clear that the context in which Bruce's story circulates and recirculates will change that story's significance in a specific instance and over time.

When *Robert the Bruce* premiered in April 2019, Macfadyen described its timing as "immaculate" and "perfect," presuming that the new referendum was imminent.[60] Scottish leader Nicola Sturgeon had proposed that a vote be held before the end of the Scottish parliamentary session in the spring of 2021, but it ultimately was deferred, one of many casualties of the global pandemic. Apparently undaunted, Sturgeon cited SNP victories that year as a virtual mandate, informing Boris Johnson that the second referendum was only a matter of "when, not if." Sturgeon's successor at the time of this writing, Humza Yousaf, expressed the same degree of confidence, but the "when" remains, as ever, in the distant horizon.[61] Indeed, more challenging than determining how each film might influence viewers' votes at a specific moment is the thorny matter of whether a vote will take place at all. In this respect, the problem is not the potential ambiguities of cinematic medievalism so much as the intricacies of devolved electoral politics.

As Hames explains, devolution was both an acknowledgment of Scotland's right to self-determination and an effort to quell Scottish nationalism. What it allowed was merely "a managerial sort of twentieth-century nationalism, . . . intended to strengthen the social, emotional and political anchorage of the UK's established governing arrangements"; rather than a "pro-British folksong," it is a tale of "Whitehall officials plotting how to canalise 'national feeling' in Scotland and Wales, carrying it safely away from separatism."[62] Paradoxically, the same process that allowed for an independent parliament also enshrined the superiority of the UK government on constitutional matters, locking twenty-first century Scotland in a position akin to that of the fourteenth-century Bruce at the end of *The Valiant Scot*.

That Scotland must defer its vote until England permits it has nothing to do with Edward I's specious documentation; rather, it is a holdover from the 1707 Act of Union, solidified as a precedent in the very legislation that enabled the second #IndyRef. As McEwen explains, the 2013 Edinburgh Agreement "temporarily transferred constitutional authority to the Scottish Parliament to facilitate a legal referendum, and committed both governments to respect the outcome of the referendum, whatever it may be."[63] Because the Westminster parties must abide by the latter, they are unlikely to grant the former at this time. If Scotland is closer than ever to displaying a "settled will" on the matter, those that most fervently desire independence must also tackle new divisions. The progressive, egalitarian agenda of the SNP now faces a more hostile Tory leader as well as a new internal rival in a more stridently nationalist party. Led by the scandal-plagued Salmond, the Alba Party has leaned into medievalism with an ad campaign called "Unite the Clans," starring Macfadyen in chainmail.[64]

The campaign's effects are hard to predict, but it is possible that its circulation may yet bring *Robert the Bruce*—now receded along with *The Outlaw King* in public memory—back to the prominent place it once held in online discourse. After all, Salmond and Macfadyen's campaigns against the Cineworld "ban" briefly garnered both films additional media attention in the summer of 2019. Currently, both films remain available to Scottish audiences on streaming platforms, where they may continue to find new audiences. If the pamphlet afterlife of *The Valiant Scot* is any guide, it is certainly plausible that they would find renewed interest if a referendum were announced.

Whether enabled by this chapter, an algorithm, or a new text entirely, history teaches us that Valiant Bruce will return to take on the Brut again.

NOTES

1. "Alex Salmond Calls on Cineworld to Show Robert the Bruce Film," *National*, June 28, 2019.

2. The description is Martin Hannan's, in "Cineworld 'Offered Robert the Bruce Film' but Didn't Answer," *National*, June 29, 2019.

3. "Alex Salmon Calls on Cineworld."

4. "David Cameron 'Met Sony over Outlander UK Release,'" *Scotsman*, April 20, 2015. Based on a series of novels by American author Diana Gabaldon, *Outlander* was set partly in the Scottish highlands in 1743, its historical world characterized by time travel and punctuated by Gaelic.

5. Representatives from Sony and the British government, as well as even Gabaldon herself, insisted there was no evidence that the political circumstances of 2014 had any negative impact on the show's reception or that the show was delayed for UK audiences out of deference to the PM's concerns over its influence in Scotland.

6. Robbie Collin of the *Telegraph*, from a tweet quoted in Robert Munro, "Performing the National? Scottish Cinema in the Time of Indyref," *Journal of British Cinema and Television* 17 (2020): 426.

7. *The Valiant Scot by J. W.: A Critical Edition*, ed. George F. Byers (New York: Garland Press, 1980); *The Outlaw King*, directed by David Mackenzie, screenplay by Bathsheba Doran, David Mackenzie, and James MacInnes (Toronto: Sigma Films, 2018), Netflix; *Robert the Bruce*, directed by Richard Gray, screenplay by Eric Belgau and Angus Macfadyen (Edinburgh: Yellow Brick Films, 2019), Hulu. Quotations and lineation from the play derive from the aforementioned edition; quoted material from the front matter from the seventeenth-century edition will be cited separately. Quotations from the films are included in the remainder of this chapter without further citation.

8. Robert Crawford, *Bannockburns: Scottish Independence and the Literary Imagination, 1314–2014* (Edinburgh: Edinburgh University Press, 2014). Crawford's study focuses on the site of the battle between Robert I and Edward II rather than Edward I and the Brut tradition (the primary focus of the present chapter), but he similarly understands this moment as taking on new resonances at multiple moments in history, especially in contemporary literature, television, and film. Crawford claims that "Bannockburn was the most literary of battles" and makes that site plural in his title in order to convey the sense of it being rewritten to serve different narratives over time (23).

9. Roger A. Mason, "Scotching the Brut: Politics, History and National Myth in Sixteenth-Century Britain," in *Scotland and England 1286–1815*, ed. Roger A. Mason (Edinburgh: John Donald, 1987), 60.

10. Raphael Holinshed, *The Firste Volume of the Chronicles of England, Scotlande, and Irelande. Conteyning the Description and Chronicles of England* (London, 1577), 317.

11. Holinshed, *Firste Volume of the Chronicles*, 286.

12. Raphael Holinshed, *The Chronicles of England, Scotlande, and Irelande* (London, 1587), 212.

13. E. L. G. Stones, "Introduction," in *Anglo-Scottish Relations 1174–1328: Some Selected Documents* (Oxford: Clarendon Press, 1970), xiii.

14. "To the Most Holy Father Boniface," in *Anglo-Scottish Relations*, 195.

15. "To the Most Holy Father," 211.

16. "To the Most Holy Father," 217.

17. "To the Most Holy Father," 217.

18. "Report to Edward I," in *Anglo-Scottish Relations*, 225.

19. "Report to Edward I," 225.

20. "Report to Edward I," 229.

21. Mason, "Scotching the Bruce," 60.

22. George Ridpath, *Scotland's Soveraignty Asserted. Being a Dispute Concerning Homage, against Those Who Maintain That Scotland Is a Feu, or Fee-Liege of England, and That Therefore the King of Scots Ow[e]s Homage to the King of England* (London: Andrew Bell, 1695), 428.

23. Ridpath, *Scotland's Soveraignty*, av, a2.

24. On this shift, see Kelsey Jackson Williams, *The First Scottish Enlightenment: Rebels, Priests, and History* (Oxford: Oxford University Press, 2020), especially 183.

25. John Major, *A History of Greater Britain, as Well England as Scotland . . . 1521*, trans. Archibald Constable (Edinburgh: Edinburgh University Press, 1892), 223.

26. Major, *History of Greater Britain*, 221.

27. As Andrew Higson notes, this expository technique is common in British heritage films. See his *Film England: Culturally English Filmmaking since the 1990s* (New York: Palgrave, 2011), 235.

28. 5.2.72. The scene's place in *The Valiant Scot* probably owes not to Barbour's *Bruce* but to a later epic, the often-printed *Wallace* by the poet Blind Hary, the text upon which the playwright drew more heavily than any other source. On Blind Hary, see Crawford, *Bannockburns*, 36–42, and Byers, ed., *Valiant Scot*, 65–82. Crawford also discusses Barbour at some length, 30–36.

29. An early version of the film included a conversation between Wallace and Bruce; the scene's excising is detailed in David Ehrlich, "How David Mackenzie Salvaged 'Outlaw King' after the Netflix Oscar Hopeful Crashed and Burned," IndieWire, November 8, 2018. Web.

30. On the play's French campaigns, see Byers, ed. *Valiant Scot*, 7–60.

31. *Valiant Scot*, 82.

32. *Valiant Scot*, 91.

33. *Valiant Scot*, 91.

34. Maurice Lee, *The Road to Revolution: Scotland under Charles I, 1625–1637* (Urbana: University of Illinois Press, 1985), 3.

35. J. W., *The Valiant Scot* (London, 1637), A2r–v.

36. John Kerrigan, *Archipelagic English Literature, History, and Politics 1603–1707* (Oxford: Oxford University Press, 2008), 96.

37. Nicola McEwen, "Brexit and Scotland: Between Two Unions," *British Politics* 13 (2018): 76.

38. McEwen, "Brexit and Scotland," 66.

39. This description is Andrew O'Hagan's, paraphrased by Arianna Introna in "Na-tioned Silences, Interventions and (Dis)Engagements: Brexit and the Politics of Contextualism in Post-Indyref Scottish Literature," *Open Library of Humanities* 6 (2020): 15.

40. Quoted in McEwen, "Brexit and Scotland," 71.

41. McEwen, "Brexit and Scotland," 76.

42. Ehrlich, "How David Mackenzie Salvaged 'Outlaw King.'"

43. Susan Swarbrick, "Director David Mackenzie on the Making of Outlaw King," *Herald* November 3, 2018; Ehrlich, "How David Mackenzie Salvaged 'Outlaw King.'"

44. Ehrlich, "How David Mackenzie Salvaged 'Outlaw King.'"

45. Steven Brocklehurst, "Robert the Bruce Film Is the 'Birth of a Hero' Says Angus Macfadyen," BBC Scotland News, June 23, 2019, accessed October 18, 2023. Web.

46. Quoted in Christopher O'Keeffe, "Edinburgh 2019: Robert the Bruce Himself Angus MacFadyen and Director Richard Gray Discuss the Return of the Scottish King," *Screen Anarchy*, July 8, 2019.

47. The quoted phrasing derives from a headline, but it accurately captures the sense of Macfadyen's comments in the interview ("Robert the Bruce's Angus Macfadyen Hopes Film Will Boost Independence Support," in the *Daily Record*, June 23, 2019.

48. Quoted in O'Keeffe, "Edinburgh 2019."

49. In Salmond's words, the party intentionally "campaigned on the back of the film" (quoted in Alan Riech, "Duncan Petrie, *Screening Scotland*," *Metro Magazine* 137 [2003]: 171). See also Ellen-Raïssa Jackson, "Dislocating the Nation: Political Devolution and Cultural Identity on Stage and Screen," *Scotland in Theory: Reflections on Culture and Literature*, ed. Eleanor Bell and Gavin Miller (New York: Rodopi, 2004), 107–20.

50. See Murray Stewart Leith, "Scottish National Party Representations of Scottish-ness and Scotland," *Politics* 28 (2008): 83–92.

51. Cairns Craig, *The Wealth of the Nation: Scotland, Culture and Independence* (Edinburgh: Edinburgh University Press, 2017), 274.

52. Craig, *Wealth of the Nation*, 275.

53. Craig, *Wealth of the Nation*, 278–80.

54. Scott Hames, *The Literary Politics of Scottish Devolution: Voice, Class, Nation* (Edinburgh: Edinburgh University Press, 2019), 305.

55. Craig, *Wealth of the Nation*, 280.

56. Andrew Higson, *Waving the Flag: Constructing a National Cinema in Britain*, 2nd edition (Oxford: Oxford University Press, 1997), 7.

57. *A Second Discovery by the Northern Scout: Of the Chiefe Actions and Attempts of the Malignant Party of Prelates and Papists, Proctors and Doctors, and Cavaliers That Are Now Resident in the County of Yorke* (London: B. W., 1642), 8.

58. *Second Discovery*, 8.

59. *Second Discovery*, 8.

60. Lucinda Cameron, "Robert the Bruce's Angus Macfadyen hopes film will boost independence support," *Daily Record*, June 23, 2019.

61. Crawford refers to this phenomenon by the popular portmanteau "neverendum" (*Bannockburns*, 1).

62. Scott Hames, "Spitfire Britain and the Zombie Union," *Drouth*, November 16, 2020.

63. McEwen, "Brexit and Scotland," 71.

64. "Watch: Robert the Bruce Actor Angus Macfadyen Stars in Video Supporting Alba," *National*, April 12, 2021.

7

English Imperialism and Staff Fighting in *Mucedorus*

Matt Carter

The anonymous play *Mucedorus* appeared in print for the first time in 1598. Subsequently, it experienced a prodigious history of reprinting and an unusually positive reception at court.[1] Given the play's apparent popularity, one would think that scholarship on it would be equally widespread. Searching for "Mucedorus" in the MLA Bibliography, however, returns merely twenty-six results, not all of which consist of criticism about the play itself. Analyses of *Mucedorus* do not, generally speaking, seek to analyze the play for its own sake but usually focus on one of two topics: the presence of a bear onstage and the play's authorship. While these analyses do engage with *Mucedorus*, in the case of both of these critical conversations the actual focus of analysis is not *Mucedorus* but William Shakespeare. In short, ursine investigations almost always have an ulterior motive. Critics from Tom Rooney (who argues that the bear was played by an actor) to Barbara Ravelhofer (who argues that an actual bear may have represented the character/animal in performance) are invested in the question of what happened onstage during productions of *Mucedorus* not only because of the tantalizing possibility of a live bear onstage but because the same may have occurred in productions of Shakespeare's *The Winter's Tale*.[2] The authorship question, similarly, seeks to locate or decentralize *Mucedorus* within the canon of Shakespeare's plays, for fairly self-evident, bardolatrous reasons.

Notably, a few scholarly arguments *have* emerged regarding *Mucedorus* that take the play on its own terms, but these do not significantly engage with each other in conversation. Furthermore, these analyses are usually invested in a shared notion that the play is poorly written and that there is therefore something mysterious about the joy that Elizabethan and Jacobean audiences took in it. Peter Hyland infers that the handful of commentaries on the play (including those discussing the question of the bear-or-not-bear and the authorship debate) are almost always infused with the idea that the benighted Elizabethan and Jacobean audiences were naive for liking it. *Mucedorus*'s popularity seems to stem, for many scholars, from the apparent fact that the play is simple—and so were its early audiences.[3] Hyland, fortunately, pushes back against this sort of hedging, offering a different solution: "I would say the play was popular because it presented the kind of spectacle that understood the pleasure the audience at all levels took in plays that were unashamedly theatrical."[4] Of course, even this more measured commentary on the "unashamedly theatrical" praises the play's boldness for pushing the proverbial envelope more than its success as a theatrical effort. In order for us to recognize more fully how *Mucedorus* speaks to the theatrical landscape of early modern London, it must be allowed to break free, both from the notion that it is somehow a bad play (that benighted early modern audiences are "telling on themselves" by enjoying) and from the shadow of a certain "Swan of Avon."

What I would like to do here is offer an alternative mode through which we might view *Mucedorus*, one that suggests that the play's inconsistencies of tone and dramatic action hint not at a poorly constructed Shakespearean castoff with a bear problem but rather at a complex, problematic play that subversively walks a tightrope between the class and ethnic dynamics of early English imperialism. Here, I shall examine *Mucedorus* on its own terms, unearthing cultural evidence that textures our understanding of early modern English aristocratic exceptionalism while also offering a direction for the critical conversation about the play that does not employ discussions of early modern bearscapes or of William Shakespeare. As it turns out, the concerns of *Mucedorus* highlight something specific about early modern English culture: that English folk in the period understood their class positioning through complex, intersectional lenses. While it would be a dubious proposition to claim that early modern ideas about race and about class were interchangeable, *Mucedorus* shows evidence of slippage between these two hierarchical narratives. When representing Bremo, the wild man who nearly absconds with the eponymous hero's wife-to-be, the play draws both on traditional narratives about early modern class and narratives about ethnicity—specifically, Welsh and Irish stereotypes filtered through the older trope of the "green man"—to construct a foil for the monarchical figure of Mucedorus. In other words, the play attempts to reassert royal authority by characterizing commonfolk as Others, and in order to do so, estranges the lower-class Bremo by situating him within a longstanding prejudice against heathens (in this case, "people of the heath," notwith-standing religious affiliation). Bremo is thus simultaneously human and not, simultaneously powerful and not, and simultaneously native and not.

I would not be venturing far from the typical reflections on the play to point out that Mucedorus is one of the most, if not the very most, trou-bling figures in his eponymous play. Hyland, for instance, examines the fact that Mucedorus is responsible for all three of the deaths in the text, counting him as the most dangerous member of the dramatis personae.[5] Hyland sees in this evidence that *Mucedorus* slips in and out of the typ-ical conventions of Romance literature; the hero becomes a weapon of mass destruction when he enters into the wilds. Richard Finkelstein sees the play's resistance to the usual theatrical and literary conventions (par-ticularly those that imply psychological consistency in its characters) as an "ideological flexibility accounting for its popularity with various au-diences."[6] Indeed, the representation and deconstruction of the romantic hero present in *Mucedorus* may well have spoken to both aristocratic and nonaristocratic viewers simultaneously. I would argue, however, that while Mucedorus's value system might be versatile (or maybe murky, depending on the way one views it), his function in the play is more archetypical than psychologically consistent. Regardless of whether or not lower-class mem-bers of the audience might identify with Mucedorus because his name is in the title, the interactions between Mucedorus and the wild man named Bremo that take place in the forest juxtapose Mucedorus, the royal figure, against Bremo, who stands in for the lower classes.

Of course, the play invites such class-based comparisons between Mucedorus and Bremo—both are potential husbands for Amadine—and Mucedorus's disguise as a shepherd connects him to the pastoral world of early English love poetry. In fact, *Mucedorus* participates in a longer tradi-tion of pastoral writing that frequently ties into conversations about nation-building. Patrick Cheney evocatively links the convention of a pastoral shep-herd's wooing practices—in Marlowe's "The Passionate Shepherd to His Love"—to a larger conversation about counternationhood.[7] He argues that Marlowe references Ovid's description of Polyphemus and Galatea to make a powerful antinational point. As in Marlowe's poem, the Ovid's ingenue can be wooed with woodland foods, such as chestnuts. The difference, in Ovid, is that a monster has disguised himself as a shepherd in order to woo her (Polyphemus is the same cyclops Odysseus eventually murders), and when he learns that his love has been snuggling up to someone else, he crushes him with a mountain. Cheney explains that Ovid's purpose was antinational in nature: the emperor Augustus was "legislating chastity into marriage"— an act that would have led to ruin for someone like Ovid.[8] Cheney cites W. R. Johnson, who sees Ovid's work as counterclassical, on the basis that "he is not congratulating us on our distress, he is warning us of it."[9] Johnson interprets Ovid's *Metamorphoses* as a criticism of Augustus's attempts to reform Roman society, and rather than seeing the poet's conflation of Augustus with Jupiter as "the famous mindless cleverness," he contends that the text is actually "an attack on Augustus' efforts to reform society by means of an artificial religious revival and the imposition of stringent and inhuman moral codes."[10] For Cheney, this comparison sheds light on Marlowe's poem because it highlights a larger Marlovian project: parodying and criticizing the most nationalistic poet of the day, namely, Spenser.[11]

In the case of *Mucedorus*, the same allusive imagery plays a slightly different role. Here, the shepherd is actually royalty in disguise, and the uncultured, monstrous Bremo is the competitor. When Mucedorus defeats Bremo in combat, he is "taming" a "wild" man—a common trope in depictions of the wodewose.[12] Bremo is not simply uncivilized; he stands in for the heathen world, both in the sense of the wild, untamed heath itself, and in the context of native English syncretism, a religious state of being that thrived in the medieval world but had evolved into a movement to reconcile Protestants and Catholics by the time *Mucedorus* graced the stage.[13] In medieval literature, syncretic figures were not necessarily viewed in a negative light. As Larissa Tracy asserts, texts like "Gawain [and the Green Knight] offer . . . service and devotion, integrating the forms of female divinity from the pagan mythology, the Kabbalah, and Christian tradition and illustrating how, at their center, these traditions share the same 'mother.'"[14] The DNA of the green man seems to have maintained some of that syncretic tradition into the early modern period, despite the general refutation of such hybrid religious practices in the wake of the Protestant Reformation. However, it seems at least one reason English culture allowed its green men to retain their apostate status was to enable English knights to drive them out. English festival culture had not only preserved the green man but had enshrined him as a staple nemesis within the larger universe of the highly metaphorical performances at court by the time *Mucedorus* was written. Robert Hillis Goldsmith explains this as a gentrifying process: the "wodewose," as it was called, transformed from an ivy and moss-encased creature to a hairy wild man in silken green clothing.[15] By 1515 it was already a commonplace that the knightly duties of modern English warriors included driving such uncivilized creatures from the sanctified halls of English castles. The Twelfth Night revels at Greenwich in 1515 included a group of knights mugging and expelling a green man.[16]

As time went on, the same tropes that animated accounts of the green men of medieval lore were conflated with prejudicial depictions of foreigners—especially when those foreigners were from lands England had assimilated or was trying to assimilate. For instance, Carole Levin and John Watkins cite the example of Robert Greene's "Coney Catching Pamphlets" as illustrative of urban Londoners' coequal antipathy to non–English speakers and country folk (there was a stereotype of Irish and Welsh folks being from exclusively rural locales, as well). In one pamphlet, a Welsh gentleman comes to London, where he is cozened by a group of seedy city natives who take advantage of his limited English to corner him and steal his purse. As Levin and Watkins describe the event: "This passage captures the vulnerability of the new arrival lacking the linguistic, cultural, and legal resources to defend himself against the urban criminals determined to profit from his ignorance. The Welshman becomes the ideal coney. He is simultaneously wealthy and untutored in the urban codes that might enable him to 'smoak' out the cozeners' trap before he fell into it."[17]

In short, the pamphlets represent the visiting Welshman as culpable in his own cozening; he cannot identify a way out of danger because he has not fully assimilated into the dominant English culture. While we might be tempted to sympathize with such a plight, the text, as Levin and Watkins explain, does not support that reading—the onus is on the outsider to understand the potential pitfalls of being in England. We might read this as an extension of the "civilizing" narrative ascribed to green men, then, because the same idea of assimilation that applies to outsiders applies to the wodewose. Bremo is not only a bad person, he is bad at assimilating himself into the dominant culture, which leads to his downfall. Therefore, in *Mucedorus*, the playwright inverts the trope somewhat; instead of a bumpkin coming into the city and failing to assimilate, we see Mucedorus bringing the city to Bremo. These acts of "civilizing" wild men would later echo uncomfortably with England's colonial endeavors in Ireland and North America and, in the Jacobean-Caroline periods, the East Indies—a colonial project that was central to nationalistic poets like Spenser.

Unlike Marlowe and Virgil, the author of *Mucedorus* reveals a Spenserian sympathy to the royalist perspective. Mucedorus's exercise of political authority over Bremo requires him to go outside of his jurisdiction when he enters the forest, but that trespass is seen as a welcome imposition because of Bremo's consistently bad behavior. Bremo understands his own nature as inherently violent; when he finds himself speechless in the face of Amadine's beauty, he intones:

> I think her beauty hath bewitched my force
> Or else within me altered nature's course. (xi.52–53)[18]

Bremo's character is inherently violent; it is a cause for concern when he cannot kill Amadine with his staff. For this reason, Mucedorus's disguise is not only justified, in the sense that it gives him access to Bremo's encampment, it also inverts the antinationalist sentiment of the disguised shepherd trope for pronationalist ends. As Cheney points out, in early modern literature, shepherds, or in many cases characters disguised as shepherds, often use what he calls an "invitation motif" as part of the wooing process.[19] Figures such as Marlowe's passionate shepherd and Ovid's Polyphemus establish themselves as solitary figures who exist outside of more communitarian, or "national," identities, tempting their beloved to eschew "civilization" in favor of a simple, rural life. Like Polyphemus, Mucedorus is a hidden danger to those around him, but unlike his cycloptic predecessor, Bremo is an even worse alternative than the play's eponymous protagonist.

In short, Mucedorus does not kill Bremo; he establishes a contractarian rule of law within the forest. Richard Helgerson points out that "the common law was quintessentially English, a sign of unity snatched from the play of difference: *e duobus unum.*"[20] Bremo's rugged individualism may seem attractive to some audience members or readers, but for an early modern English audience, it flies in the face of government and, by extension, cohesion. Notably, the same kind of movement, that of a civilized, knightly figure entering the woods in hope of generating order from chaos, defines Redcrosse Knight's journey in *The Faerie Queene.* David Galbraith points out that Redcrosse's encounter with Errour in the Wandering Wood shows him traveling "quite literally, from the forest to the trees."[21] The author of *Mucedorus,* then, uses the same kinds of Spenserian allusions as Marlowe, but in *Mucedorus,* those allusions reinforce the royalist sentiments of the original. By dressing as a shepherd, Mucedorus aligns himself with a "more English" version of the lower classes and positions this wholesome standardized Englishness in opposition to a more pagan, less English Other. Driving Bremo out is an act of colonialism in the name of establishing "order" in the woods.

What, then, is *Mucedorus* trying to say by weaponizing lower-class

Englishness against lower-class Otherness? I believe the answer can be found in *how* Mucedorus kills Bremo. One of the important elements of the wodewose, aside from his verdant clothing, was the wild man's stick, which Goldsmith summarizes as "a club with fireworks in the head of it."[22] In *Mucedorus*, Bremo's stick has transformed from a thick, unfinished club into a polearm. While the play seems to waffle about what kind of stick it is, sometimes calling it a "cudgel," (vii.29), the maneuvers Bremo uses strongly mirror the training devised for polearm combat.

By contrast, Mucedorus employs techniques more commonly associated with the English quarterstaff. English quarterstaff training is primarily documented in two sources: George Silver's *Paradoxes of Defense* (1599) and Joseph Swetnam's *School of the Noble and Worthy Science of Defense* (1617). One noteworthy reality of staff fighting in the period is that, unlike in sword training, most staff fighting emphasized threats to the head over threats to the body. Silver calls almost exclusively for head-bashing. Most of his defensive maneuvers assume the enemy is repeatedly beating down on the defender: "If you find him too strong for you upon his blowes from a loft [here, he gives a complex series of techniques to evade this attack and reply with a thrust of one's own]."[23] Other guards are designed to set up a head strike: "Back again towards that side that he striketh in at you, and out of that ward, then Instantly, eyther strike from that ward, turning back your staff, and strike him on that side of the head that is next your staff."[24] Swetnam's method offers more variety in the targets, but still, the head is ever-present: "If your enemie doe but once offer to lift vp his hand to strike, then presently choppe in with a thrust at his breast, shoulder, or face."[25] Indeed, Swetnam suggests that the best guard against attack is that which keeps the hands high and the point low, to defend against head strikes while also being able to preserve the body if needed, "turning the heele of hinderhand vpward withal" in order to respond by "lifting them vp, vpon the out-side of their foote or else by gathering him vp on their left arme."[26] This emphasis on threatening the head is noteworthy for our purposes, as this is also Bremo's primary strategy:

Bre. And, when thou strikest, be sure to hit the head.

Mu. The head?

Bre.   The very head.

Mu. Then have at thine! (xvii.66–67)

How is it possible that Mucedorus is able to beat Bremo's guard and take him down so soon after learning the staff maneuvers in the first place? It is certainly possible that Mucedorus fires off an unsporting blow that takes Bremo by surprise and kills him. I would argue, however, that this is partially a function of the techniques used by the two warriors, one of which resembles polearm fighting, which was primarily practiced by lower-class fighters whose training would have varied by region along with their weapons, as opposed to Mucedorus's traditional English quarterstaff techniques. As I will show, this is the case because these differences in styles connect to the play's larger royalist themes.

All staff weapons, including the unbladed quarterstaff, are technically considered polearms. Early modern armies were particularly interested in polearm training, as the pike and weapons like it enabled the rise of firearms—pike lines could literally stave off the cavalry long enough for musketeers to reload.[27] Polearms quickly became associated with particular European regions, due to differences in their design and construction. Flemish armies employed the *goedendac*, a spike-bristled club, which led to the development of the popular halberd by the Swiss shortly thereafter.[28] From Bern to Zurich, halberds would go on to take on highly specific forms from region to region.[29] The Bardiche was the polearm of Eastern Europe and Russia, the *couseque* in France and Italy, in England, the bill and "holy water sprinkler"—a long-handled spiky club (one of which was owned by Henry VIII)—the Jedburgh in Scotland, and in Wales, the "Welsh hook" was so popular that even the notably xenophobic Swetnam called it by the region's name.[30]

That being said, war was changing by the time *Mucedorus* was written. Polearms were in overabundance in Ireland, in fact: Sir George Carew, the Irish master of ordinance, complained that he had received such an unnecessary stockpile of black bills that he had to sell them to local farmers instead of storing them.[31] For his part, Sir Roger Williams, a Welsh mercenary serving under Sir Robert Dudley, generally praised the pike in particular but found most other polearms to be "naughty stuff."[32] Early modern soldiers were often conflicted about how pikers and other polearm users were to be viewed; despite their incredible abundance and widespread deployment, classist attitudes persisted among those with enough power and privilege to record their thoughts on the subject, namely, that wielders of polearms were useless or worse. For example, as Matthew Sutcliffe, judge-advocate general in the Low Countries during Essex's campaigns, exasperatedly declaimed, pike formations were rarely responsible for the "slaughter" or bulk of killing on the battlefield.[33] Indeed, in the play itself, Bremo shows a certain ambivalence around polearms:

> Who fights with me and doth not die the death? Not one.
> What favor shows this sturdy stick to those
> That here within these woods are combatants with me?
> (viii.20–22)

While not an outright criticism of the polearm, Bremo's comment highlights the weapon's association with rural fighters and its questionable success rate, echoing real-world statements to the same effect.

Not only were polearms associated with particular regions, they unfairly evoked the idea that rural warriors, who made up a large body of the fighters using them, were unskilled. This matters to the larger concerns of *Mucedorus* for two reasons. First, the association of these weapons with particular regions meant a combination of local pride in the specific weapon; and second, the methods by which other types of polearms were used meant that quarterstaff users, as a result of their weapons lacking the heavy heads attached to others, had an unfair advantage in a fight. Swetnam explains that "if your enemy have a Hooke, Halbert, or Bill in defending the false, the head of his weapon will so over-carrie him by the reason of the weight, that hee cannot command him nimbly backe againe, whereby to defend the false . . . if hee charge you with a blow, then slippe his blow, either by plucking in of your Staffe, keeping of the point upright untill his blow be past, and then you may answere him againe, either with blow or thrust."[34] Here, the term "slip," refers to the act of taking a traversing step out of the way of the blow, which hints at the relative slowness of weapons like the Welsh hook.

It is here that we need to once more emphasize the connections between pike lines, ethnicity, and the lower classes. Because polearms were the weapon of choice for lower-class men, and because of the way polearms varied from region to region, the assumed limberness of aristocratic English quarterstaff fighters served to set English aristocrats apart in contrast to the relatively slow, but powerful lower classes. Quarterstaff movements take advantage of the lightness of a headless staff to allow the warrior to move like a fencer, in contrast to the cumbersome (if downright) blows of working-class warriors. In fact, by turning to early modern teachings about English quarterstaff combat, we can predict how things will go with

Bremo when he fights against Mucedorus, who is not only a trained warrior but disguised as a shepherd, meaning his shepherd's crook would function more like a quarterstaff than a polearm. If Bremo's training reflected
that of a quarterstaff fighter, his movements would likewise mirror the
dancerly skill of an aristocrat like Mucedorus. If, instead, he fought like a
working-class man, he would rely on force (since numerical superiority is
not an option) to win the day. The play bears this prediction out: Bremo
anticipates that he will use a "down-driving blow" (xi.44) against Amadine.
Had he been trained in quarterstaff fighting instead of more traditional
polearm maneuvers, Bremo would follow the instruction of someone like
Joseph Swetnam, who warns against this practice: "Never strike one blow
with your staff, for he that doth but lift up his staff to strike, may easily be
hit by the defender with a thrust, for in the same motion that the oppressor
doth lift up his staff to strike the defender may with a speedy thrust hit him
in the brest and hold him off upon the point of his staff."[35] For audiences
in the know, this threatened "down-driving blow" against Amadine would
have cued them to think of Bremo as a polearm-user. While the weapon
of the wodewose is a stick with a squib shooting fire, such a weapon would
qualify as a polearm, not a quarterstaff, due to the heavy head at the end.[36]
We may, therefore, treat it in the same context—a lower-class, ethnically
specific weapon—as other polearms.

Let us return, then, to the moment of Bremo's death and see what
interpretive possibilities this moment of combat might hold. Again, Bremo's dialogue with Mucedorus recreates the exact mistake Swetnam warns
against:

Bre. And, when thou strikest, be sure to hit the head.

Mu. The head?

Bre.   The very head.

Mu.   Then have at thine! (xvii.66–67)

We might view Bremo's initial instructions to aim at the head in two ways:
either he is demonstrating a suboptimal maneuver, or he is sneakily trying to take Mucedorus down. In either case, Mucedorus seems to use the
thrusting maneuver Swetnam describes to sneak below Bremo's staff and
crush his head in the process. The moment of combat emphasizes Mucedorus's superior training, but it also highlights his aristocratic upbringing.

He may be using a shepherd's crook to strike the blow, but he wields it exactly like a quarterstaff. The emphasis in quarterstaff battle is on agility, while polearm users focus on forceful strength and numbers. Because Bremo is not only unskilled with the staff but also alone, Mucedorus is able to simultaneously assert his class superiority and his martial superiority. At the same time, having entered into the woods to establish his own government and order, Mucedorus sets himself apart from Bremo ethnically—he is not only an aristocrat but an aristocratic colonizer "taming" the woods. Therefore, the death of Bremo stages a moment of racially inflected class warfare, in which the limber, aristocratic, English, male body is contrasted with Bremo's Othered, lower-class one. As Bremo fits the usual character type of a wodewose, which is subhuman, while employing the martial capabilities of a polearm user, *Mucedorus* weaponizes commonly held classist attitudes to lionize and celebrate imperialism and colonization.

The slippage between classism and racism in the play may come as no surprise. Certainly, the historical tensions between working-class grunts in the army and their aristocratic officers were keenly felt. While in the past most nonaristocratic soldiers had been levied on an as-needed basis, the early modern period saw the rise of permanent militia organizations whose sole purpose was to preserve the skills of potential fighters in case of need. This, in turn, led to various local ordinances across Europe that civilians keep weapons at the ready in their homes should the need to use them arise.[37] The traditional defense of the aristocratic system—that knights and their lords were empowered so that they might defend their vassals— was rapidly breaking down, and the power to enact violence became more and more the purview of the lower classes.[38] Instead of engaging in battle directly, aristocrats were pushed into administrative roles, like modern-day officers, and frequently fought more regularly in duels against other aristocrats rather than in pitched battle, or, as Roger B. Manning puts it, "not only French noblemen, but also aristocrats from the Three Kingdoms, continued to have difficulty distinguishing between *duellum* and *bellum*— that is, between private combat and public war declared by authority of a sovereign or a state."[39] The inexperience and lackadaisical attitudes of such courtiers became more and more apparent as the years passed.[40] These class tensions were further exacerbated by aristocrats' role in conscripting soldiers. Often, as we see in *2 Henry IV*, aristocrats would cook the proverbial books in order to profiteer off the war in a variety of illegal ways, such as falsifying the number of recruits they levied.[41] In that play, Falstaff leaves the "likeliest" (III.ii.250) men behind, sending them home with the goal of counting them—and thus getting paid for them—regardless. The class tensions within the army were even deeper than that, though; one particularly illustrative punishment for misbehaving officers highlights how well-accepted these divisions really were. By the end of the seventeenth century, aristocrats accused of cowardice might end up being forced to carry a musket (a slightly more complex iteration of the older harquebus and blunderbuss) beside their own lower-class subordinates. This practice was understood as a form of punishment, taking away one's officer status while also removing from him the possibility to distinguish himself from the group.[42] Perhaps surprisingly, aristocratic warriors' primary purpose on the battlefield was more akin to a combination of logistics and cheerleading than fighting. A large portion of officers' work in early modern European armies was not only to provide structure and marching orders but also to encourage large bodies of lower-class troops. J. R. Hale cites the example of Bartolomeo Alviano, who pep-talked a ragtag mass of troops to avenge the burning of Mestre, and the counterexample of the Earl of Surrey, who in 1545 was criticized by one of his men, Elis Gruffydd, for completely failing to use kind words to motivate the army.[43]

This is particularly illuminating in regard to *Mucedorus* because of the way the play inverts this trope. When Bremo first meets Mucedorus, his instinctual reaction is to attack him, but Mucedorus talks his way out of a duel by employing proto-Hobbesian logic:

> If men which lived tofore, as thou dost now,
> Wild in wood, addicted all to spoil,
> Returnéd were by worthy Orpheus' means,
> Let me like Orpheus cause thee to return
> From murther, bloodshed, and like cruelty. (xv.90–94)

Rather than cheering Bremo's fighterly instincts to a frenzy, Mucedorus tries to deprogram him. Mucedorus understands his role as that of a civilizer—he must take the man from the woods under his wing and teach him to turn from his undirected rage to a better path. The paternalistic nature of this proposition is meaningfully similar to the perceived relationship between the English nobility and the commoners. Notably, two likely outcomes of this civilizing process are not part of Mucedorus's plan. For one thing, if Bremo only represented the idea of a "foreigner," one might expect Mucedorus to convince Bremo to let him leave with Amadine, not propose an alliance. Perhaps the two could agree to "live and let live."

Conversely, if Bremo is more like the lower-class soldiers his fighting style mimics, one might suspect placating him would be preferable for social cohesion. That is not what happens. Mucedorus's goal is not so much an attempt at *defusing* Bremo's rage but rather a push to *direct* it and enable it: "No, let's live and love together faithfully. / I'll fight for thee" (xv.96–97).[44] How do we process the fact that Bremo, who, both from the perspectives of class and nationality, fits somewhat comfortably into a category of "otherness" by the time he dies, meets neither expectation in this moment?

Levin and Watkins describe a tension in English narratives about foreigners that might shed light on this disconnect. Discussing Shakespeare's Shylock, they note that "he forces us to balance what empathy we feel for him as an outsider against our fears of him as a threat to civic society."[45] Here, too, we might find Bremo irredeemable because of his behaviors, but Mucedorus sees—or, given that he murders him shortly thereafter, at least claims he sees—the opportunity to civilize him. The use of Orpheus as his metaphor is telling: Orpheus famously tries to lead Eurydice out of the Underworld but fails because he disobeys Hades's edict and looks back at her, overwhelmed by not hearing her footsteps behind him. Comparing the woods to the Underworld and Bremo to Eurydice allows us to see a common attitude among English imperialists; Bremo's condition is unacceptable, he is not fully realized as a person, and only by following Mucedorus's lead can he step back into the "light" of the living world. This metaphor may well be the connective tissue between English ethnocentrism and the aristocratic prejudice against the lower classes. In this context, the play's royalist sympathies become evident fairly quickly. The purpose of nobility is to enter the uncivilized parts of the world and to dominate them, in order to lead them back to civilization. Illustrative here is the moment when Mucedorus first decides to disguise himself as a shepherd and enter the woods. He accompanies the pastoral transition with the following declamation: "Now must I learn to bear a walking staff, / And exercise some gravity withal" (xiv.18). The use of "gravity" here presents a paradox: one might normally expect Mucedorus to *lose* some degree of respect by dressing like a working man, but he sees it as the opportunity to gain the kind of prestige associated with older men. Perhaps, too, the shepherd figure brings a certain gravitas—he is salt-of-the-earth and an easy metaphor for royalty leading the people/flock. If, however, we recall his goal of leading Bremo out of the wilderness and into civilization, this disguise is metaphorically rich. Further, we might again read this moment as foreshadowing: Orpheus *fails* to lead Eurydice out of the Underworld—generically, can the outcome be any better for the wild-man Bremo? The play certainly does not believe so. Bremo is too uncultivated to be brought out of the woods. Only his destruction will suffice, and Mucedorus is uniquely equipped to facilitate that transition.

John Pitcher offers an insight into why he thinks *Mucedorus* experienced the kind of popularity it did in the early modern professional theater: "We do know that the King's Men had acquired the play by 1610, when they performed it at court. This revival was intended to amuse and flatter the sophisticated court audience by showing them a popular play which looked so old-fashioned, and artless, and clichéd, that they would be charmed by its naivety, and prompted to laugh at it in generosity."[46] This argument highlights the general critical assumption that *Mucedorus* is much like Bremo: quaint, "artless," and so forth. The only reason Pitcher can provide for *Mucedorus* appearing at court is that the erudite courtiers might have enjoyed it in much the same way the Athenian nobles laugh at and harass the rude mechanicals in *A Midsummer Night's Dream*. Pitcher's theory requires that we assume the nobility was "sophisticated in its tastes and desires," but perhaps the court's tastes were as diverse and "low" as the paying public theatre audiences. I argue instead that *Mucedorus*'s appearance at court was not the only example of pro-imperial thinkers using drama to lionize the power of the crown and bring onto the stage a propagandistic work that serves as both entertainment and as an apologia for the ongoing colonialist projects of the English crown. I find it telling that the same year *Mucedorus* was brought to the court for the second time (this time, for James I, rather than Elizabeth), the stage saw Shakespeare's *Cymbeline*, a play that appears to compare James favorably to the emperor Augustus. While *Mucedorus*'s flatness may not appeal to our modern sensibilities as readers and critics, this characteristic may have proven a strength in appealing to a royal court happy to indulge apologist depictions of its colonial endeavors abroad.

Viewing *Mucedorus* as monarchist agitprop opens up several new avenues of analyzing what the anonymous playwright was really trying to accomplish as an artist. Jean E. Howard explains that "many of the most powerful social institutions of church and state were invested in maintaining an official ideology of stasis and fixed identity, if not for themselves, then for those whose mobility or theatrical self-fashioning they found troubling."[47] This fixed identity was a significant in the process of imperialism, both within England and in its colonies. For example, Alan

G. R. Smith explains that England's policy toward Ireland, which shifted to an even more imperialist stance after the death of Thomas Cromwell, "aimed at creating by friendship and conciliation a united national state for Ireland. The essential aspect of their policy was the idea of 'surrender and regrant.' The Gaelic chieftains were asked to become feudal vassals of the Crown and to introduce English law and customs into their territories."[48] Noteworthy here is the idea of not merely holding territory but assimilating the cultural practices of the two lands; the emphasis on fixed identity was all-important for imperialists, since the unification process generated stability. Unfortunately, those like Bremo who seem to resist reprogramming were eliminated from society, rather than incorporated. The events of *Mucedorus* do not show a willful attempt to enter the "wild lands" and tame them, as with England's repeated expeditions into Ireland; rather, they depict a casual, almost naturalistic enactment of the philosophy of imperial conquest. Mucedorus's initial delay in finding Amadine, the reason they both end up in the forest and eventually at Bremo's home at all, is the reason he decides to tarry—"Well, here I'll stay, and expect her coming" (xii.10)—and it is to keep Amadine safe that he decides to civilize the wilderness and slay Bremo: "What, hie me home, said I? That may not be; / In Amadine rests my felicity" (xiv.5–6). Mucedorus wanders almost aimlessly into the woods and tames them as if by accident; the sprezzatura of it all is part of the propaganda.

Mucedorus's royalist sympathies and fairy tale–like plot hardly help it shake the stigma that early modern scholarship has cast upon it. Our own modern sensibilities are at odds with the early modern audiences who seem to have loved the play, at least if sales and reprintings are to be believed. That being said, I hope to have shown how the play does participate in contemporary political discussions in more nuanced ways than it often receives credit for. Howard's work on the way that antitheatrical rhetoric was often less aesthetic than political is useful here. Howard reminds us that "politics and aesthetics are inevitably intertwined, especially as antitheatricalists move to appropriate various forms of social authority to underwrite their views and give them the stamp of the natural."[49] In other words, the problem many antitheatrical writers had with the professional theater was that it undermined the solidity of the social categories that underpinned Elizabethan society. I can therefore slightly agree with *Mucedorus*'s detractors, to the extent that, if, as antitheatrical writers complained, the usual effect of professional plays in the period was to subvert the power of the state and to upset the so-called Great Chain of Being's prescribed hierarchies,

Mucedorus is an extremely unusual play. On the other hand, if we understand *Mucedorus* as political agitprop intended to reinforce the standing of the English crown, we might understand it as a kind of antiplay, or at least, an antitheatrical play. Rather than assuming that the discerning members of the court enjoyed the play ironically, perhaps we can view *Mucedorus* in the same light we use to examine state propaganda. Doing so allows us to learn something from reading plays such as this one, about how English political theory in the period relied on xenophobia and class tensions to reassert English identity. To its discredit, *Mucedorus* relies on prejudicial attitudes against the people of Ireland and Wales, filtered through the wodewose trope, as a means of justifying heavy-handed monarchical rule. In this way, the playwright responds to a need on the part of the emerging British Empire to rationalize its expansionist behaviors. Bremo becomes anything—maybe everything—that is not English, and because of the way he is characterized, he invites the kind of imperialist "civilizing" behaviors that England was beginning to put into motion at home and abroad.

Notes

1. Richard Finkelstein, "Censorship and Forgiven Violence in *Mucedorus*," *Parergon* 17, no. 1 (July 1999): 89–90.

2. Tom Rooney, "Who 'Plaid' the Bear in *Mucedorus*," *Notes and Queries* 54, no. 3 (September 2007): 261; Barbara Ravelhofer, "Henslowe's White Bears," *English Literary Renaissance* 32, no. 2 (Spring 2002): 315, 317.

3. Peter Hyland, "Scare Bear: Playing with *Mucedorus*," in *Shaping Shakespeare for Performance: The Bear Stage*, ed. Catherine Loomis and Sid Ray (Madison, NJ: Fairleigh Dickinson University Press, 2016), 205.

4. Hyland, "Scare Bear," 205.

5. Hyland, "Scare Bear," 210.

6. Finkelstein, "Censorship in Forgiven Violence," 89.

7. Patrick Cheney, "Career Rivalry and the Writing of Counter-Nationhood: Ovid, Spenser, and Philomela in Marlowe's 'The Passionate Shepherd to His Love,'" *English Literary History* 65, no. 3 (Fall 1998): 524.

8. Cheney, "Career Rivalry," 525.

9. W. R. Johnson, "The Problem of the Counter-National Sensibility and Its Critics," *California Studies in Classical Antiquity* 3 (1970): 127.

10. Johnson, "Problem of the Counter-National Sensibility," 147.

11. Cheney, "Career Rivalry," 530.

12. Tina Negas points out the important connections between green men and the "unity of humanity with the natural world," in Tina Negas, "Medieval Foliate Heads: A Photographic Study of Green Men and Green Beasts in Britain," *Folklore* 114, no. 2 (August

2003): 247. Robert Jordan offers further elaboration that the green man figure came, in the early modern period, to symbolize "man as savage creature without culture giving free reign to his brute appetites," in Robert Jordan, "Myth and Psychology in 'The Changeling,'" *Renaissance Drama*, vol. 3 (1970): 162.

13. Christopher Baker explains that religious syncretism took a new form in the early modern period, due in large part to the efforts of Georg Calixtus and other reformers, who sought to broker peace between Protestants and Catholics through syncretic theological projects. In other words, early modern syncretism was less about hanging on to outlawed pagan traditions than about reconciling humanist philosophy with denominational differences. See Christopher Baker, "Sidney, Religious Syncretism, and *Henry VIII*," *Studia Neophilologica* 86, no. 1 (2014): 19. Similarly, Thomas D. Hill notes that the idea of Old English syncretism only takes on meaning if the practices in question, when viewed from a Christian perspective, "conflict with Christian dogma." For example, a harvest festival does not meet the standard of religious blending, as its practice does not "necessarily conflict with Christian ideas about the role of God in ordering events or his benevolence as the creator of nature and the natural cycles of the agricultural year." See Thomas D. Hill, "The Rod of Protection and the Witches' Ride: Christian and Germanic Syncretism in Two Old English Metrical Charms," *Journal of English and Germanic Philology* 111 no. 2 (April 2012): 146.

14. Larissa Tracy, "A Knight of God or the Goddess?: Rethinking Religious Syncretism in 'Sir Gawain and the Green Knight,'" *Arthuriana* 17, no. 3 (Fall 2007): 36.

15. Robert Hillis Goldsmith, "The Wild Man on the English Stage," *Modern Language Review* 53, no. 4 (October 1958): 482.

16. Goldsmith, "Wild Man," 482.

17. Carole Levin and John Watkins, *Shakespeare's Foreign Worlds: National and Transnational Identities in the Elizabethan Age* (Ithaca, NY: Cornell University Press, 2008), 80.

18. Anonymous, *Mucedorus*, in *Elizabethan Plays, Revised Edition*, ed., Arthur H. Nethercott et al. (New York: Holt, Rinehart and Winston, 1971).

19. Cheney, "Career Rivalry," 526.

20. Richard Helgerson, *Forms of Nationhood: The Elizabethan Writing of England* (Chicago: University of Chicago Press, 1994), 104.

21. David Galbraith, *Architectonics of Imitation in Spenser, Draniel, and Drayton* (Toronto: University of Toronto Press, 2000), 32.

22. Goldsmith, "Wild Man," 483.

23. George Silver, *Master of Defence: The Works of George Silver* (Boulder, CO: Paladin Press, 2003), 304.

24. Silver, *Master of Defence*, 305.

25. Joseph Swetnam, *The Schoole of the Noble and Worthy Science of Defence* (London, 1617), Y1r.

26. Swetnam, *Science of Defence*, Y3v, Y3r.

27. Ewart Oakeshott, *European Weapons and Armour from the Renaissance to the Industrial Revolution* (Woodbridge, UK: Boydell Press, 2012), 44.

28. Oakeshott, *European Weapons and Armour*, 45.

29. Oakeshott, *European Weapons and Armour*, 46–47.

30. Oakeshott, *European Weapons and Armour*, 48, 53–54, 56; Swetnam, *Science of Defence*, Y4v.

31. Henry J. Webb, *Elizabethan Military Science: The Books and the Practice* (Milwaukee: University of Wisconsin Press, 1965), 91.

32. Webb, *Elizabethan Military Science*, 92.

33. Webb, *Elizabethan Military Science*, 88.

34. Swetnam, *Science of Defence*, Y4v–Z1r.

35. Swetnam, *Science of Defence*, X4r–X4v.

36. Goldsmith, "Wild Man," 483.

37. J. R. Hale, *War and Society in Renaissance Europe, 1450–1620* (Baltimore: Johns Hopkins University Press, 1985), 205.

38. Roger B. Manning, *Swordsmen: The Martial Ethos in the Three Kingdoms* (Oxford: Oxford University Press, 2003), 85. Hale goes into detail regarding the degree to which the Third Estate bore the brunt of the financial and physical burdens of wars waged in the period, while also being responsible not at all for starting them. J. R. Hale, *War and Society in Renaissance Europe, 1450–1620* (Baltimore: Johns Hopkins University Press, 1986), 103–5. Webb further elaborates that even the generalship became less and less the domain of aristocrats, citing instead a general's experience in battle and paternalistic leadership qualities. See Webb, *Elizabethan Military Science*, 55–57.

39. Manning, *Swordsmen*, 7.

40. Manning, *Swordsmen*, 10.

41. Hale, *War and Society*, 113.

42. Manning, *Swordsmen*, 63.

43. Hale, *War and Society*, 175.

44. This moment might, to readers who remember Mucedorus's shepherd's disguise, be an intentional callback to Marlowe's "Passionate Shepherd."

45. Levin and Watkins, *Shakespeare's Foreign Worlds*, 83.

46. John Pitcher, "'Fronted with the Sight of a Bear': *Cox of Collumpton* and *The Winter's Tale*," *Notes and Queries* 41, no.1 (March 1994): 50.

47. Jean E. Howard, *The Stage and Social Struggle in Early Modern England* (London: Routledge, 1994), 10.

48. Alan G. R. Smith, *The Emergence of a Nation State: The Commonwealth of England, 1529–1660* (Essex, UK: Pearson Education, 1997), 248.

49. Howard, *Stage and Social Struggle*, 39.

8

"Let Burnt Sack Be the Issue"

Immigrants as Threat and Remedy in William Shakespeare's *The Merry Wives of Windsor*

Heather Bailey

In act 3 of William Shakespeare's *The Merry Wives of Windsor*, the Host of the Garter Inn tries to make peace between two men, one a French doctor and the other a Welsh parson. The Host says, "Give me thy hand, terrestrial, so; give me thy hand celestial, so . . . your skins are whole, and let burnt sack be the issue."[1] While the word "issue" means the result of a union between two things, it can also mean a problem or end of something.[2] Sack—the "issue" of this attempt at sociopolitical reconciliation—is referenced symbolically as both a solution and cause of the disunity between these two men, both of whom are not native Englishmen. The Host, an Englishman associated with the Garter Inn, restores peace and multicultural unity and brings about a "healthy" union. This moment, I suggest, serves as one of many examples of wine's symbolic connections to the play's concern with "Englishness." The Host's reference to sack is significant as the drink is central to the establishment of sociopolitical unity. Because of its sweetness, sack was believed to be a physically healthy drink; however, as an imported wine, it was also associated with the threat of foreign influences on the English body politic. As I will show, Shakespeare's engagement with both medical and political discourses concerning sack highlights the ways in which the play draws upon the nuances and complexities of England's relationship to its immigrant population.

The location of Windsor itself and the scenes at the Garter Inn establish the idea that Windsor represents England. As Leo Salingar argues, the Garter Inn shares an important historical connection to English identity. The Order of the Garter was the highest order of knighthood and chivalry that existed in England, thus forming an important part of English identity. The play, in fact, was more than likely performed for the Garter Feast in 1597, which would have been held in Windsor.[3] Further, the town of Windsor itself, as critics such as R. S. White note, is "solidly rooted in its specified town planning, its diurnal activities, its local customs."[4] As Allison Outland argues, the "tangible Englishness of Shakespeare's Windsor" reveals itself through the frequent references to "familiar place names, home practices, and glimpses of everyday rural life."[5] These regional references position the play within the discourse surrounding what Richard Helgerson terms an "emerging nationalist ideology of Englishness."[6]

The Merry Wives of Windsor is full of moments that reinforce this underlying anxiety about the negative effects of immigrants to England. The characters frequently make jokes about how foreigners butcher the English language. Mistress Quickly, who is the servant of Caius, the French doctor, says that he abuses "God's patience and the King's English."[7] The Host says that the Welsh priest Sir Hugh Evans and his cohorts should not be killed, but disarmed: "Let them keep their limbs whole, and hack our English."[8] The Host's quip alludes to a metaphorical dismembering of the body politic. Another passage reinforces this idea when Evans is accused of teaching young Will to "hick and hack" during his language lesson.[9] In act 5, after hearing Evans's accent, Falstaff cries, "Have I lived to stand at the taunt of one that makes fritters of English?"[10] The words "hick" and "hack" and "fritters" establish that Evans destroys the English language with his accent specifically by breaking up, or tearing apart, the language. This occurs, as Margaret Tudeau-Clayton argues, at a time when the English language was increasingly defined as "plaine," excluding as it did "(the) French and a court-centered male elite associated with the French."[11] The metaphorical resonances regarding the supposed disintegration of the English language come to bear on larger sixteenth-century anxieties about the political and cultural disintegration of "Englishness," anxieties that carried racist, xenophobic implications. As Tudeau-Clayton contends, discourse concerning the "King's English," a "racially inflected character of 'true English blood' is associated with 'plain manners.'"[12] This points to a moment, Tudeau-Clayton writes, in which linguistic policing was deeply connected to "an aspiration to control the circulation of 'strangers,' perceived vehicles of contamination of English 'blood,' coin and language, and—the material, economic reason behind the ideological—a perceived threat to the interests of English merchants."[13]

However, I suggest that *The Merry Wives of Windsor* alludes to this

problematic ideology ultimately to subvert it. Many of the foreign characters, such as Sir Hugh Evans and Doctor Caius, are central to the plot
and the community in Windsor, as they assist Mistress Page and Mistress
Ford in their revenge against Master Ford and Falstaff. In this way, the play
resists the temptation to simply reinforce an ethnocentric view of Englishness and instead, as Tudeau-Clayton argues, promotes a view of English
identity as "gallimaufry," a term that originally referred to several different
meats mixed together but etymologically changed into a figurative expression meaning a "mobile and inclusive mix of (human and linguistic)
'strangers' without defining 'proper' boundaries."[14] Tudeau-Clayton maintains that *The Merry Wives of Windsor* presents an "international, inclusive
and mixed community" in contrast to the fixed, xenophobic notion of the
"King's English," in an effort to "resist" an exclusionary and racist definition of Englishness.[15]

     Like Tudeau-Clayton, I am interested in the ways that *The Merry Wives
of Windsor* promotes a more multicultural vision of Englishness and con-
tend that Falstaff's relationship to wine represents one complex way that
the play does so. As I will show, Falstaff supposedly suffers from the disease
of erotic melancholy and drinks sack to "heal" himself even while the drink
is possibly contributing to his diseased state. Through an examination of
sack's function in *The Merry Wives of Windsor*, I argue that Shakespeare
draws on the medical discourse concerning wine, and sack in particular
because of its association with foreignness, to highlight the ambiguous relationship of immigrants to the English body politic. Just as sack was both
beneficial and harmful to the individual body, immigrants were supposedly
threatening to the formation of a uniquely English identity even as they
were essential to the country's stability and economic growth. Considering
Falstaff's position in relation to Windsor and his excessive consumption
of sack, I suggest that Shakespeare uses Falstaff to engage with the complex relationship between England and foreigners. While Falstaff is English, he is a foreigner to the town of Windsor, a stand-in for England and
English identity. The word "foreigner" meant both a person from another
country and someone from "another parish, town, county, or district."[16]
As Tudeau-Clayton notes, Falstaff represents the "stranger" figure because
he wanders into Windsor, in a context where anyone outside of a paro-
chial community was viewed with suspicion as a "straying" traveler (i.e.,
stranger).[17] Simultaneously, Falstaff counters the rigid, xenophobic definition of Englishness by participating in linguistic "gallimaufry" through
his "synonymia" ("variation of an English") and by drinking excessively,

which was also contrary to the emerging definition of "Englishness" as temperate, since plain-speaking was associated with sobriety.[18] All of these factors, and in particular Falstaff's status as a "stranger" to Windsor and his excessive consumption of sack, signal Falstaff's central position in the play as a subversive figure who counters ethnocentric notions of a fixed, rigid English identity.

Scholars have turned their attention to what the description of food consumption in historical and literary texts can tell us about the relationship between conceptions of the body and society. For example, Timothy Tomasik and Juliann Vitullo state that "food and feasting can be understood not simply as the consumption of material goods but also as the figurative and symbolic representations of culture."[19] They clarify that "the politics of food consumption is one of the most important elements in the constructing of cultural and political identities through the inclusion of certain gastronomical traditions and the exclusion of others." More specifically, there has been a renewed scholarly interest in exploring the symbolic and social functions of drinking in early modern England. Authors in the collection *A Pleasing Sinne: Drink and Conviviality in Seventeenth-Century England* have focused on wine's ability to evoke a wide range of complex and often contradictory meanings, both physiological and social, in the sixteenth and seventeenth centuries.[20] Wine was drunk by both the higher and lower social classes in early modern England. It was often expensive to import because it was semi-perishable. As a result, argues Hori Motoko, there was a trend of "conspicuous consumption" of wine in early modern England: privileged people bought wine the most often, and their account books show a focus on wine purchases because it was seen as a marker of status to own large amounts of wine.[21] Consequently, Michelle O'Callaghan argues, taverns that served wine as well as ale became very important because they fostered "new forms of sociability among the urban elite."[22] However, Louise Hill Curth and Tanya M. Cassidy note that wine was also consumed by the general population, functioning as part of an early modern English daily diet.[23]

In addition to its symbolic and social functions, wine was also considered a medicinal agent of fundamental importance to the humoral body. Because it contributed to the innate heat of the body, Everett Mendelsohn argues, wine bolstered brain function and thought, as well as the digestive system and reproductive system.[24] In his treatise "The Tree of Humane Life," the seventeenth-century physician Tobias Whitaker maintained that those who drink wine look "faire, fresh, plump and fat" because wine is

"more pure and better concocted than any other juyce."[25] Indeed, Curth
and Cassidy argue that wine was considered a type of "wonder drug."[26] It
was believed to be so potent that it formed the central part of many reci-
pes of medicinal potions, working as a "strong ally" against disease.[27] For
example, "aqua vitae" was a concoction made from wine and was believed
to be extremely potent in curing a variety of ailments.[28] Sixteenth-century
physician Andrew Boorde recommends in his manual, *The Breviary of
Health*, that moderate wine consumption maintains a healthy humoral balance.[29] Tobias Whitaker writes in his manual, *The Tree of Humane Life*, that
wine allowed a person to go from "infancy to extreme old age without any
sickness" and that it will therefore prolong life "beyond all expectation."[30]
Samuel Pepys, despite being told to stop drinking wine, decided that he
needed to continue drinking it "upon necessity, being ill for want of it."
Pepys feared that by not consuming wine, he suffered "many evils" upon
his body.[31] Wine was also important in preventative health, in that it was
believed to help the body fight off disease as long as it was consumed in
moderation.[32] It formed the central ingredient in several medicinal elixirs
and potions. White or rhenish wine, for example, formed the base in a
remedy for the plague in John S. Shirley's *The Accomplished Ladies Rich
Closet of Rarities*.[33]

In the Galenic medical tradition, sack was considered healthier than
other kinds of wine because of its sweetness: Galen argued that sweet
wines have stronger medicinal properties than harsh ones because they are
"hotter in power" and consequently they are better incorporated into the
body.[34] Sweet wines were thought to be healthier because they contained
sugar, an ingredient that supposedly had potent medicinal qualities. Sweetness, based on Aristotelian theory, was correlated with happiness and a
positive mood.[35] From its earliest introduction to European society in the
thirteenth century, sugar was associated with medicinal food and drink
because physicians modeled their medical theories and praxis on Galenic
texts. For example, powdered sugar was used in food for invalids, often
with almond milk. In the 1644 pamphlet *A Cup of Sack Prest Forth*, sweet
red wine, or sack, is supposed to be able to cure a man of any illness.[36]
For several early modern medicinal remedies, sweet wine was crucial. The
sixteenth-century physician "A. T.," for example, maintained in *A Rich
Store-House or Treasury for the Diseased* that sack mixed with other herbs is
a potent remedy for back pain or to generally restore "nature."[37] Physician
James Hart maintained in his *Klinike or the Diet of the Diseased* (1633) that
sweet wines are better on the stomach because they warm the body.[38] Two

particular early modern medicinal draughts, claret and hippocras, were mixed with cinnamon and sugar.[39] The physician William Vaughan, in his *Approved Directions for Health, Both Naturall and Artificiall* (1612), prescribed some remedies that included sweet wine, such as one that involved mixing wine with "an ounce and a halfe of Cinamon, one pound of Suger, three drams of Ginger, and two scruples of Nutmegs."[40] After letting the spices sit in the wine for three days, the concoction could be used for "the heating and comforting of a colde and a weake stomack."[41] Additionally, if one wanted a preventative draught, they could pour a pint of wine and "afterwards put a little Suger vnto it" and in three days it would be ready for consumption until the patient's illness was "sufficiently purged."[42] In *2 Henry IV*, Falstaff comically expounds on the medicinal benefits of sack in order to justify his drunkenness: "A good sherry-sack . . . ascends me into the brain, dries me there all the foolish and dull and crudy vapours which environ it, makes it apprehensive, quick."[43] These examples, a sampling of many others like them, indicate just how widespread the belief in wine's medicinal properties was and at least partially explain why sack and other sweet wines increasingly became a regular commodity among Englishmen and women of all social classes.

Despite its medicinal qualities, sack also held a fraught status in terms of its association with immigrants because in the second half of the seventeenth century it was imported from regions of Spain, Portugal, the Canaries, and Maderia. Therefore sack, as Curth and Cassidy argue, is linked to the "politics of importation," which carries with it several anxieties about foreignness. In *1 Henry IV*, for example, Falstaff's sack is specifically referred to as a "cup of madeira."[44] A later example is found in Thomas Heywood's *Philocothonista, or, the Drunkard Opened, Dissected, and Anatomized* (1641), in which Heywood comically connects what men drink with their nationality, specifically saying that if a man is Spanish, he drinks sack or canary.[45] Heywood then discusses the consequence of so many kinds of alcohol being imported into England, specifically mentioning "Burn'd Sacke" as one kind and, "from other Islands, sweet wines," before stating, "It is unquestionable, but that where other nations and Provinces are contented with such wines or other liquors as their owne Climats affoord; Yet we, as if doting upon insatiety, borrow from them all."[46] Because sack was one such wine affected by changes in the economic landscape, early modern writers often allude to this anxiety by emphasizing sack's association with foreignness.

In *The Merry Wives of Windsor*, Falstaff claims he suffers from erotic melancholy—not because this is true, but rather so that he can justify his excessive wine consumption. Erotic melancholy was a disease that began when a person viewed the beloved and the beloved emitted scorching rays that entered the eyes. The beloved's image would then be permanently pressed into the brain's memory (believed to be a waxy substance) and would cause the body's humors to become overheated. The result was a medical condition with side effects that included insomnia, irritability, lack of concentration, and loss of appetite.[47] Falstaff draws on the medical discourse surrounding love sickness to justify why he needs his "medicine," though it is apparent that the alcohol might itself be furthering Falstaff's diseased state. Falstaff laments that the "appetite" of Mistress Ford's eye "did seem to scorch me up like a burning glass!"[48] This understanding of lovesickness reflects the ideas of physicians such as Jacques Ferrand, who writes in his *Treatise on Lovesickness* (1610) that love is like a poison that enters through the eyes and then is "generated within the body itself" after the beloved's image heats the rest of the body.[49] When Ford questions how Falstaff loves his wife, Pistol tells him "with liver burning hot."[50] Robert Burton, in *The Anatomy of Melancholy* (1621), explains that when a man falls in love with a woman after seeing her beauty, the liver is the organ most affected.[51]

When he is supposedly overcome with lovesickness for the two women, Falstaff relies on sack to fortify his efforts, which builds on Shakespeare's and the audience's awareness of wine's medicinal properties. Shakespeare establishes wine's medicinal role in act 1, especially at the household of the French physician, Dr. Caius. At one point his servant, Mistress Quickly, assures her servant Rugby that he will receive a "posset" (i.e., a medicinal drink fortified with wine) while he is keeping watch all night.[52] After he has been carried away in the buck basket and dumped in the Thames, Falstaff begs Bardolph to fetch him a "quart of sack; put a toast in 't" and subsequently states, "Come, let me pour some sack to the Thames'/ water, for my belly's as cold as if I had swallowed snowballs for / pills to cool the reins [i.e., kidneys]."[53] Here Falstaff relies on the warming properties of sack as an antidote to the unpleasant "medicine" of the cold water, which he compares to a pill used to treat kidney issues. Falstaff treats the sack as a remedy that will fortify and restore him after his traumatic experience of being forced to hide in the basket, and more importantly, for his recovery after being rejected by Mistress Ford. Falstaff's reference to sack as medicine to cure his love sickness is similar to a moment in John Ford's *The Lover's Melancholy*, in which Corax, a physician, specifically mentions wine as a medicine to rid Rhetias of his erotic melancholy. When Rhetias asks, "Are thy bottles full?" Corax responds, "Of rich wine; let's all suck together."[54] Similarly, when Ferrand speaks of dietary ways to prevent lovesickness, he refers to wine as one such remedy.[55] Whether Falstaff actually believes that sack has healing properties is questionable; however, Shakespeare uses these moments to engage with the broader question of whether the wine is actually bolstering Falstaff's health by drawing on the contemporary discourse surrounding the understanding of (foreign) wine as a cure for (English) erotic melancholy.

At another level, sack also supposedly facilitates Falstaff's diseased state. When he is forced by Mistress Page and Mistress Ford to hide in the buck basket, Falstaff refers to his humoral state after being in the basket as "glowing hot" and "hissing hot." He compares himself to "being stewed in grease, like Dutch dish" and being "stopped in like a strong distillation."[56] In using the word "distillation," Falstaff compares his body, which is in a diseased state, to a container holding a distilled liquid, which reminds the audience that Falstaff is indeed holding sack within his body. The sack therefore seems not to be helping Falstaff overcome his supposed erotic melancholy. Mistress Page even quips that Falstaff's "dissolute disease will scarce obey this medicine."[57] Falstaff's and Mistress Page's language here evokes the opinion of some early modern physicians, such as William Vaughan, who discredited sack's medicinal properties. Vaughan argued that sack is not healthy but instead "doth make men fatte and foggy, and therefore not to be taken of young men."[58] Robert Burton specifically lists wine as one of the foods that incites erotic melancholy.[59] According to Burton, wine increases the body's heat, resulting in scorched humors, which produce the hot, moist, sanguine stage of passion.[60] In this way, Shakespeare reinforces the ambiguity of wine's status as a healing drink, engaging with the debate among physicians concerning its benefits.

This ambiguity as to whether wine is a healing drink or one that further scorches the humors within Falstaff's body seems to parallel, at another level, the relationship of foreigners to the English political "body." Lovesickness was often used to metaphorically represent problems with the political body, as scholars such as Adam Kitzes argue.[61] Kitzes contends that the condition of melancholy in its various forms (including erotic melancholy) could be used to "describe a symptom of or cause for discontent, be it social, economic or otherwise."[62] Moreover, melancholy in all of its variations was also related to the "renewed interest in the classical theory of the 'body politic,'" which "posited an analogy between the individual human body and the collective 'body' that political organizations consisted of."[63] This analogy implied that bodies, like political institutions, were "vulnerable" to attacks in the forms of "disease" so that the "analogy between a healthy body and healthy state" remained commonplace.[64] For Kitzes, growing concerns over "political health" corresponded to renewed interest in, and use of, this analogy.[65] Falstaff's body is a particularly apt metonym for the English body politic because of the emphasis on the condition of his supposed diseased, overheated, lovesick body. While other characters in the play drink, the language used to describe Falstaff and that he uses himself to explain his experience is unique in revealing the supposed physiological implications of Falstaff's drinking.

Just as wine perpetuates Falstaff's disease, the conflicts between the different groups of foreigners are perceived as a threat to the unity of the political body. The body politic depends on goodwill and friendliness between members, which is potentially jeopardized by the conflicts between the many different groups of foreigners in the play. The host of the Garter Inn, when trying to make amends between Welshman Sir Hugh Evans and Caius, the French doctor, highlights the way in which the individual body, which needs to be cured by a physician, is linked to the body in a symbolic, spiritual sense. He says to the two men, "Peace, I say, Gallia and Gaul, French and Welsh, soul-curer and body-curer."[66] He further indicates that a truly healthy state of political peace is desirable and necessary by posing a rhetorical question to the men that reinforces the connection between the physical body and the politic(al) body: "Am I politic? Am I subtle? Am I a Machiavel?"[67] Mistress Quickly also appeals to the desire for a stable and unified political state in act 5 when she desires that Windsor Castle "may stand till the perpetual doom / In state as wholesome as in state 'tis fit."[68] Each of these characters desires a unified English political body that is contractual, and their statements reveal anti-immigrant sentiments about disunity that is supposedly created by conflicts between different immigrant groups and threatens the social bonds that maintain the political contract, just as wine threatens the health of Falstaff's body.

However, Shakespeare simultaneously undermines these xenophobic beliefs, since the act of drinking sack could also positively boost the body politic as a social "remedy," just as sack could function as a medicine to cure Falstaff of his "disease." Among men, drinking together was a sign of goodwill and often used to foster relationships and deals between them. As Alexandra Shepard argues, the bonds formed through drinking laid a foundation for society.[69] Slender draws on this understanding that drinking could be a positive sociopolitical act when he says that he won't be drunk "but in honest, civil, godly company."[70] While this moment is meant to be funny, Slender's use of the words "civil" and "godly" indicates that he is alluding to the discourse surrounding the understanding that drinking fostered male bonding, which contributed to political unity. After Anne Page enters with the wine, Mistress Page invites the quarrelling gentlemen to dinner, saying, "I hope we shall drink down all unkindness."[71] Thus, wine consumption within a community can help boost the health of the body politic. In Thomas Nashe's *Summer's Last Will and Testament*, Bacchus comically says, "Either take your drink, or you are an infidell."[72] The character of Bacchus articulates the understanding that drinking demonstrates one's participation and inclusion in the body politic while characterizing one who does not drink as a religious outsider.

Sack not only functions as a medicine to the body politic in a social, symbolic sense but also boosts the body politic at the physiological level. Jacques Ferrand maintains, based on Platonic theory, that occasional drunkenness among men is useful in purging out the blood that has been infected by looks from the women they love.[73] Falstaff, in *2 Henry IV*, expounds specifically on the virtues of sack, synthesizing the way sack's physiological effects also have broader sociopolitical consequences:

> The second property of your excellent sherry is the warming
> of the blood, which before, cold and settled, left the liver white
> and pale, which is the badge of pusillanimity and cowardice; but
> the sherries warms it and makes it course from the inwards to the
> parts extremes . . . this valour comes of sherries. So the skill in the
> weapon is nothing without sack . . . Hereof comes it that Prince
> Hal is valiant, for the cold blood he did naturally inherit of his
> father he hath, like lean, sterile and bare land . . . with excellent
> endeavour of drinking good and good store of fertile sherry, that
> he is become very hot and valiant.[74]

Falstaff justifies Prince Hal's consumption of sack by stating that after sack warms his blood, it produces courage, which in turn makes Prince Hal a capable ruler, despite the fact that earlier he had experienced fear due to the cowardice supposedly inherited from his father. Sherry is also described as fertile, in contrast to Prince Hal's original barrenness, since warmer wines like sack were believed to increase fertility.[75] Falstaff articulates the idea that sack has a positive physical effect on the body in warming it; this physical effect also produces a sociopolitical effect in giving Prince Hal courage, which reflects the intricate early modern understanding that wine's medicinal effects at the physiological level produces broader positive sociopolitical effects.

Falstaff, then, as both a heavy consumer of sack and a foreigner to the town of Windsor, allows Shakespeare to explore the ambiguous relationship of immigrants to England. R. S. White, like other critics, argues that Falstaff is an outsider because he is dangerous to Windsor's values and must be expelled from society in order for social order to be reestablished.[76] Allison Outland further concludes that Falstaff is a real threat to Windsor because of his immoral behavior, unlike the "benevolent foreigners" who contribute to the community of Windsor in a positive way.[77] There is certainly evidence in the play that Falstaff's actions do not adhere to Windsor's morals, particularly when it comes to his drinking habits. Sir Hugh Evans says that, like Job's wife, Falstaff is "given to fornications, and to taverns, and sack, and wine, and metheglins, and to drinkings and swearings."[78] Sir Hugh's comment suggests that he sees Falstaff's drinking as problematic because it is not confined to positive social bonding.[79] However, while Falstaff's moral code does not align with the other inhabitants of Windsor, his lack of morality is couched in terms of a foreign threat. The language used to describe Falstaff is replete with references not just to immorality but also to non-Englishness. Mistress Page refers to Falstaff as a "Flemish drunkard."[80] He is also referred to as a "Phrygian Turk" by Pistol, and toward the end of the play, the host of the Garter Inn warns Simple that Falstaff will "speak like an Anthropophaginian" to him.[81] The host thus connects Falstaff to distant foreign lands so often associated with cannibalism. In the early modern period, "Anthropophaginian" was used in travel narratives to describe indigenous peoples who were believed to engage in cannibalistic behavior.[82]

At the linguistic level, it is striking to see how Falstaff's threatening foreignness is often highlighted through the metaphorical language of wine. Once Falstaff returns from his involuntary swim in the Thames, he complains that his experience turned his body into a liquidated distillation of the unwanted parts of a fine culinary dish. He frames his experience by also comparing his physical bodily state to a foreign body. He first compares himself to being cramped and curled around inside the buck basket like a Spanish sword, a "bilbao," and then complains that he was sealed in like a "distillation" with clothes that have become "fretted" (i.e., fermented) in grease so that he becomes a melting "man of continual dissolution and thaw."[83] His "glowing-hot" and "hissing-hot" state, reminiscent both of his "liver burning hot" lovesick state and his current liquidated state in the buck basket, is like that of a "Dutch dish" that must be expelled into the Thames.[84] This scene echoes Mistress Ford's reference to Falstaff as a whale. When Mistress Ford receives her letter from Falstaff, she questions, "What tempest, I trow, threw this whale, with so many tons of oil in his belly, ashore at Windsor?"[85] Mistress Ford directly associated Falstaff with a foreign beast that has been tossed into Windsor. She proposes that the Merry Wives should take revenge on the misbehaving knight by convincing him that they are in love with him until "the wicked fire of lust have melted him in his own grease."[86] Now Falstaff has literally become a beached body on the shore of the Thames, othered by the liquids within his body, including the sack, and the water itself. He laments about how utterly "transformed" he was.[87] We see evidence of this in two instances. First, he worries that his brains have been made "buttered" (i.e., he's been turned into a fool).[88] As John Sutton argues, sea travel was perceived as dangerous because the body and brain were considered "excessively porous" and therefore susceptible to easily absorbing foreign evils.[89] More specifically, when men or women were in the water or at sea, their brains were thought to roll around and become muddled like the water.[90] Second, Falstaff worries that he would have died had the Thames not been so shallow, and if so he would have turned into a belly full of swollen water (like a beached whale) and reduced to a mound of dead flesh: "What a thing should I have been when I had been swelled? By the Lord, a mountain of mummy!"[91] Mummy, or mumia, was used in this period for medicinal purposes. Men and women consumed parts of the body for medical purposes. In her book *Medicinal Cannibalism*, Louise Noble calls this early modern practice "corpse pharmacology."[92] Here Falstaff's worst fear is that he will literally turn into a distilled version of a medicinal potion.

Falstaff's association with medicinal liquids, both consumed and expelled, and foreignness, echoes the descriptions of Dr. Caius toward the beginning of the play. Caius's foreignness seems to be directly tied to his use of medicinal wine, as jokes are often made at his expense that fuse these two identities together. For example, the Host, in many ways the central mouthpiece for Englishness due to his affiliation with the Garter Inn, mocks Caius at one point by calling him both ethnically pejorative terms ("Ethiopian" and "Francisco") and medicinal terms: "Aesculapius," "Galen," and "stale," meaning a wine or urine used for medicinal consumption and diagnosis.[93] Only a few lines later, the Host once again fuses these identities, calling Dr. Caius a "Castilian King Urinal," specifically a "urine bottle," where the word "Castilian" is a pun on both "castaleian," a physician who examines urine to diagnose patients, and "Castilian" (Spaniard).[94] This metaphor parallels the references to Falstaff in the buck basket, in particular when Mistress Ford quips that he might urinate on himself and therefore be in need of the washing that he is going to receive in the river.[95]

However, while Falstaff was considered a threat due to his foreign habits and foreign humoral state, the knight initially aligns himself with England when he attempts to "colonize" the two women he is wooing, Mistress Page and Mistress Ford. Shakespeare establishes the connection between the physical and sociopolitical body at the beginning of the play when Falstaff sets out to woo the women, framing his sexual conquest of their individual bodies as an explicitly colonialist metaphor. After proclaiming that he plans to woo Mistress Ford, he boasts, "I can construe the action of her familiar style; and the hardest voice of her behavior, to be Englished rightly, is 'I am Sir John Falstaff's.'"[96] Pistol's follow-up quip continues this metaphor: "He hath studied her well, and translated her will: out of honesty, into English."[97] Here Falstaff figures himself as a colonial conqueror, in a metaphor where his sexual dominance also equates to a cultural and linguistic dominance. The marker of Mistress Ford's sexual acquiescence is that she will be discoverable and transformed into an English woman.

In the very next few lines, Falstaff expands this colonialist metaphor by moving from the individual bodies of himself and Mistress Ford to the sociopolitical body, characterizing himself now not as an individual Falstaff but as England itself, engaging in trade relations with colonies. He proclaims, "She is a region all in Guiana, all gold and bounty. I will be cheaters to them [Mistress Page and Mistress Ford] both, and they shall be exchequers to me. They shall be my East and West Indies, and I will trade to them both."[98] Sack becomes a crucial commodity linked to this economic relationship. In his letters to the two women, Falstaff writes, "You love sack, and so do I. Would you desire better sympathy?"[99] Mistress Quickly's speech in the next scene connects sack's relationship to sociopolitical conquest with individual, sexual domination. She tells Falstaff how Mistress Ford reacted to reading his letter: "You have brought her into such canaries as 'tis wonderful. The best courtier of them all, when the court lay at Windsor, could never have brought her to such a canary. Yet there has been knights, and lords, and gentlemen, with their coaches; I warrant you, coach after coach, letter after letter, gift after gift, smelling so sweetly, all musk; and so rustling, I warrant you, in silk and gold, and in such allignant terms, and in such wine and sugar of the best and the fairest, that would have won any woman's heart; and I warrant you, they could never get an eye-wink of her."[100] The word "canary" is significant here not only because it refers to sack that was imported from the Canary Islands but because it conflates the social association of sack's relationship to the importation market with its physiological effect, as Mistress Quickly describes the "canaries" as a physical state.[101] Mistress Quickly encourages Falstaff that these other suitors "could never get her so much as sip on a cup with the proudest of them all."[102] This use of drinking vessels to represent Mistress Ford's relationship with her suitors indicates that she did not completely engage in the social contract of courtship with them, as she merely "sipped," and encourages Falstaff that he can do more than that with her, alluding to the possibility of full sexual satisfaction, or in the political sense, a mutually satisfactory commodity exchange.

Although Falstaff is pranked by the wives for his seduction efforts and othered while he is in the buck basket, at the end of the play he is restored to the community, along with all the other foreign characters, through the act of restorative drinking. After he is publicly humiliated for his behaviors, he is invited to drink a "posset" at the Page household, along with all of the characters. Mistress Page says to the entire cast in her final speech, "Let us every one go home, / And laugh this sport o'er by a country fire, / Sir John and all."[103] Ironically, while Falstaff becomes a festering, fermented distillation of sack after his failed seductions, or trade negotiations, with the wives, wine becomes part of the final reconciliation. The final lines of the play echo the earlier moment of reconciliation that the Host facilitates between Evans and Caius, the French doctor and the Welsh parson. The Host cannot escape some ambiguity as he describes the roles of the foreign doctor and priest in the community. He questions, "Shall I lose my doctor? No, he gives me the potions and the motions. Shall I lose my parson, my priest, my Sir Hugh? No, he gives me the Proverbs and the no-verbs."[104] The Welsh parson provides religious guidance, "Proverbs," to bring healing and unity to the sociopolitical body, even as his butchering of the English language, his "no-verbs," presents a threat. Despite the anxieties their presence evokes, both men are crucial to this moment of reconciliation at the Garter Inn, and symbolically, to the unity of the English political body.

NOTES

1. William Shakespeare, *The Merry Wives of Windsor*, ed. Stephen Greenblatt (New York: Norton, 2008), 3.1.88–89.

2. *Oxford English Dictionary*, s.v. "Issue," n.10 and n.12a (Oxford: Oxford University Press, 2011).

3. Leo Salingar, "The Englishness of *The Merry Wives of Windsor*," *Cahiers Élisabéthains* 59 (2001): 9.

4. William Shakespeare, *The Merry Wives of Windsor*, ed. R. S. White (New York: Harvester Wheatsheaf, 1991), 2–3.

5. Allison Outland, "Ridden with a Welsh Goat: Parson Evans' Correction of Windsor's English Condition," *English Literary Renaissance* 41, no.2 (Spring 2011): 316.

6. Richard Helgerson, "The Buck Basket, the Witch, and the Queen of Fairies," *Renaissance Culture and the Everyday*, ed. Patrician Fumerton and Simon Hunt (Philadelphia: University of Pennsylvania Press, 1999), 178.

7. Shakespeare, *The Merry Wives of Windsor*, ed. Stephen Greenblatt, 1.4.4–5.

8. Shakespeare, *Merry Wives*, 3.1.66–67.

9. *Merry Wives*, 4.1.57.

10. *Merry Wives*, 5.5.135–36.

11. Margaret Tudeau-Clayton, *Shakespeare's Englishes: Against Englishness* (Cambridge, UK: Cambridge University Press, 2020), 40.

12. Tudeau-Clayton, *Shakespeare's Englishes*, 2.

13. Tudeau-Clayton, *Shakespeare's Englishes*, 35.

14. Tudeau-Clayton, *Shakespeare's Englishes*, 5.

15. Tudeau-Clayton, *Shakespeare's Englishes*, 40 and 7.

16. *Oxford English Dictionary*, s.v. "foreigner," *n.* 1.

17. Tudeau-Clayton, *Shakespeare's Englishes*, 152.

18. Tudeau-Clayton, *Shakespeare's Englishes*, 21 and 53.

19. Timothy J. Tomasik and Juliann M. Vitullo, *At the Table: Metaphorical and Material Cultures of Food in Medieval and Early Modern Europe* (Turnhout, Belgium: Brepols, 2007), xi–ii.

20. See Adam Smyth, "'It Were Far Better Be a Toad, or a Serpent, than a Drunkard': Writing about Drunkenness," in *A Pleasing Sinne: Drink and Conviviality in Seventeenth-Century England*, ed. Adam Smyth (Cambridge, UK: D. S. Brewer, 2004).

21. Hori Motoko, "The Price and Quality of Wine and Conspicuous Consumption in England 1646–1759," *English Historical Review* 123, no. 505 (December 2008): 2–4.

22. Michelle O'Callaghan "Tavern Societies, the Inns of Court, and the Culture of Conviviality in Early Seventeenth Century London," in Smyth, *Pleasing Sinne*, 37.

23. Louise Hill Curth and Tanya M. Cassidy, "Health, Strength, and Happiness: Medical Constructions of Wine and Beer in Early Modern England," in Smyth, *Pleasing Sinne*, 45–46.

24. Everett Mendelsohn, *Heat and Life: The Development of the Theory of Animal Heat* (Cambridge, MA: Harvard University Press, 1964), 8–9.

25. Tobias Whitaker, *The Tree of Humane Life, or, The Bloud of the Grape Proving the Possibilitie of Maintaining Humane Life from Infancy to Extreme Old Age without Any Sicknesse by the Use of Wine* (London: H. O., 1638), C8.

26. Curth and Cassidy, "Health, Strength, and Happiness," 150.

27. Curth and Cassidy, "Health, Strength, and Happiness," 151.

28. Curth and Cassidy, "Health, Strength, and Happiness," 154.

29. Andrew Boorde, *The Breviary of Health Wherein Doth Follow, Remedies for All Manner of Sickness and Diseases the Which May Be in Man or Woman* (London, 1598), A7.

30. Whitaker, *Tree of Humane Life*, A1r and D8.

31. Samuel Pepys, *The Diary of Samuel Pepys*, ed. Robert Latham and William Matthews (London: Bell, 1970), 3:31.

32. Curth and Cassidy, 150–52.

33. John S. Shirley, *The Accomplished Ladies Rich Closet of Rarities* (London: Nicholas Boddington and Joseph Blare, 1690), A6.

34. Mark Grant, *Galen on Food and Diet* (London: Routledge, 2000), 188–89.

35. Johanna Maria van Winter, *Spices and Comfits: Collected Papers on Medieval Food* (Devon, UK: Prospect Books, 2007), 382–85.

36. *A Cup of Sack Prest Forth the Best Grapes Gathered the Last Vintage* (London, 1644), A2r.

37. A. T., *A Rich Store-House or Treasury for the Diseased* (London: Thomas Purfoot and Ralph Blower, 1596, 1596), D3.

38. James Hart, *Klinike or the Diet of the Diseased* (London, 1633), K1.

39. van Winter, *Spices and Comfits*, 341.

40. William Vaughan, *Approved Directions for Health, Both Naturall and Artificiall* (London: Roger Jackson, 1612), C7–8.

41. Vaughan, *Approved Directions*, C7–8.

42. Vaughan, *Approved Directions*, C7–8.

43. William Shakespeare, *The Second Part of Henry IV*, ed. Stephen Greenblatt (New York: Norton, 2008), 4.2.86–89.

44. William Shakespeare, *The First Part of Henry IV*, ed. Stephen Greenblatt (New York: Norton, 2008), 1.2.94.

45. Thomas Heywood, *Philocothonista, or, the Drunkard Opened, Dissected, and Anatomized* (London: Robert Raworth, 1641), G3.

46. Heywood, *Philocothonista*, G1.

47. Mary Ann Lund, *Melancholy, Medicine and Religion in Early Modern England* (Cambridge, UK: Cambridge University Press, 2010).

48. Shakespeare, *Merry Wives*, 1.3.58.

49. Jaques Ferrand, *A Treatise on Lovesickness*, ed. Donald A. Beecher and Massimo Ciavollela (Syracuse, NY: Syracuse University Press, 1990), 230.

50. Shakespeare, *Merry Wives*, 2.1.104.

51. Robert Burton, *The Anatomy of Melancholy*, ed. Holbrook Jackson (New York: New York Review, 2001), 3.2.40.

52. Shakespeare, *Merry Wives*, 1.4.7.

53. Shakespeare, *Merry Wives*, 3.5.3 and 18–20. See note by editor Walter Cohen.

54. John Ford, *The Lover's Melancholy*, ed. R. F. Hill (Manchester, UK: Manchester University Press, 1985), 1.2.152–54.

55. Ferrand, *Treatise on Lovesickness*, 252.

56. Shakespeare, *Merry Wives*, 3.5.103, 104, 102–3, 97.

57. Shakespeare, *Merry Wives*, 3.3.161–62.

58. Vaughan, *Approved Directions*, C3.

59. Burton, *Anatomy of Melancholy*, 3.2.64.

60. Lesel Dawson, *Lovesickness and Gender in Early Modern English Literature* (Oxford: Oxford University Press, 2008), 20.

61. Adam H. Kitzes, *The Politics of Melancholy from Spenser to Milton* (London: Routledge, 2006), 3.

62. Kitzes, *Politics of Melancholy*, 3.

63. Kitzes, *Politics of Melancholy*, 4.

64. Kitzes, *Politics of Melancholy*, 5.

65. Kitzes, *Politics of Melancholy*, 5.

66. Shakespeare, *Merry Wives of Windsor*, 3.1.81–82.

67. Shakespeare, *Merry Wives*, 3.1.84–85.

68. Shakespeare, *Merry Wives*, 5.5.55–56.

69. Alexandra Shepard, "'Swil-Bols and Tos-pots:' Drink Culture and Male Bonding in England, c.1560–1640," in *Love, Friendship, and Faith in Europe, 1300–1800*, ed. Laura Gowing, Michael Hunter, and Miri Rubi (New York: Palgrave Macmillan, 2005), 112.

70. Shakespeare, *Merry Wives of Windsor*, 1.1.150.

71. Shakespeare, *Merry Wives*, 1.1.163–64.

72. Thomas Nashe, *A Pleasant Comedie, Called Summer's Last Will and Testament* (London: Walter Burre, 1600), D1.

73. Ferrand, *Treatise on Lovesickness*, 321.

74. Shakespeare, *Second Part of Henry IV*, ed. Greenblatt, 4.2.92–96, 101–2, 104–6, 107–8.

75. Walter F. Otto, *Dionysus: Myth and Cult*, trans. Robert B. Palmer (Dallas: Spring Publications, 1965), 145–51.

76. R. S. White, ed., *The Merry Wives of Windsor* (New York: Harvester Wheatsheaf, 1991), 2–3, 13.

77. Outland, "'Ridden with a Welsh Goat,'" 301; 315.

78. Shakespeare, *Merry Wives*, 5.5.148–49.

79. Jeanne Addison Roberts, "Falstaff in Windsor Forest: Villain or Victim?" *Shakespeare Quarterly* 26 (1975): 9.

80. Shakespeare, *Merry Wives*, 2.1.20–21.

81. Shakespeare, *Merry Wives*, 1.3.77 and 4.5.8.

82. *Oxford English Dictionary*, s.v. "Anthropophaginian," *n*.1.

83. Shakespeare, *Merry Wives*, 3.5.96, 97, 98, and 100.

84. Shakespeare, *Merry Wives*, 3.5.103 and 104, 2.1.104, and 3.5.102.

85. Shakespeare, *Merry Wives*, 2.1.55–57.

86. Shakespeare, *Merry Wives*, 2.1.59–60.

87. Shakespeare, *Merry Wives*, 4.5.78.

88. Shakespeare, *Merry Wives*, 3.5.6.

89. John Sutton, "Spongy Brains and Material Memories," in *Environment and Embodiment in Early Modern England*, ed. Mary Floyd-Wilson and Garrett A. Sullivan Jr. (London: Palgrave Macmillan, 2007), 14.

90. Sutton, "Spongy Brains," 15.

91. Shakespeare, *Merry Wives*, 3.5.13–15.

92. Louise Noble, *Medicinal Cannibalism in Early Modern English Literature and Culture* (New York: Palgrave Macmillan, 2011), 5.

93. Shakespeare, *Merry Wives*, 2.3.24 and 25; *Oxford English Dictionary*, s.v. "stale," *n.5*. Also see note by editor Walter Cohen.

94. Shakespeare, *Merry Wives*, 2.3.29, See editor Walter Cohen's notes, specifically numbers 6 and 7.

95. Shakespeare, *Merry Wives*, 3.3.153.

96. Shakespeare, *Merry Wives*, 1.3.31–41.

97. Shakespeare, *Merry Wives*, 1.3.42–43.

98. Shakespeare, *Merry Wives*, 1.3.59–62.

99. Shakespeare, *Merry Wives*, 2.1.8.

100. Shakespeare, *Merry Wives*, 2.2.57–67.

101. Curth and Cassidy, 144–46.

102. Shakespeare, *Merry Wives*, 2.2.69–70.

103. Shakespeare, *Merry Wives*, 5.5.218–20.

104. Shakespeare, *Merry Wives*, 3.1.85–88.

9

"Thou Hast Incurred the Danger"

Shylock, Brexit, and Urban Citizenship

William Casey Caldwell

In 2014, two years before the Brexit referendum in the United Kingdom, the city of Manchester devolved from Britain's central government. This might seem like an anticipation of Brexit—much as the United Kingdom voted (by a slim majority) to exit the European Union, the city of Manchester voted to "exit" to a certain degree from the nation-state, consolidating municipal powers hitherto held by Westminster. The differences between the two events are important, however, in light of the history of citizenship. The vote to exit the EU represented a desire not only to wrest economic and political "autonomy" back into the hands of the United Kingdom from the EU but also to eject non-UK citizens dwelling within its borders. Brexit enacts a double movement: it seeks to shore up the power of the nation-state against rival nations on the outside, while disempowering individuals on the inside who had not been granted citizenship by that nation-state. Manchester's devolution represents, by contrast, a step toward a new localism meant to bring urban actors into closer contact with power structures and global resources intersecting with their communities, a goal that has been harmed by Brexit. Prior to Brexit, urban centers like Manchester, Sheffield, Liverpool, and London had their own highly developed relationships with the European Union that are now imperiled. Yet the density of diversity and specialization in many cities still makes them potent sites of resistance to the national trends of populism, xenophobia, and racism undergirding Brexit; it also offers the possibility of seeking new ways to foster international relations with the EU at the urban level.[1] Indeed, Manchester has continued its process of devolution since Brexit, as it seeks to increase proximity between the city's local, urban dwellers, locally elected officials, and global, political, and economic resources and institutions. The step back that Manchester took from the UK and the increased sense of urban rather than national citizenship the city seeks to foster represents, moreover, a historical shift back toward early modern urban citizenship, when citizenship was defined at the city level by contrast with subjecthood at the level of the state, before the developments of the French Revolution conflated citizenship with nationality. In Shakespeare's time, one was a citizen of London or York, not England. Citizenship and subjecthood were split between city and nation.

In this chapter, I will consider how Shakespeare's *The Merchant of Venice* offers an important meditation on the relevance of urban citizenship and how it is defined in terms of commerce, contracts, and its own alterity. I focus on two aspects of the play: Shylock's revaluation of usury as a radical bid for civic inclusion and the play's use of Shylock as an immanent other to define an urban citizenship, cement his exclusion from it, and alleviate the tension this exclusion creates. I argue that the latter process represents a response to the former, marking the limits of the play's ability to imagine a form of citizenship that lives openly with its alterity. Ultimately, Shakespeare's play is marked by a tension between sovereign/statist and urban notions of citizenship that resurfaces in our contemporary moment when, for example, the devolution of a city such as Manchester offers a means to combat the xenophobia motivating something as misguided as Brexit.

In Shakespeare's London, citizenship was achieved primarily through a long apprenticeship in a city's guild, after which one became "free of" London. It was an urban rather than national category, wherein one became a citizen of London, not England, after a seven-year period of indentured labor. Citizens attained the right to open their own shops and could run for alderman and mayoral positions. Furthermore, the companies to which they belonged held their own courts and juries for many legal disputes. Cities and the guilds that composed many of them were incorporated communities, a status often achieved by the granting of a charter from the sovereign that guaranteed certain political, economic, and juridical liberties. According to Phil Withington, incorporated cities were defined by three primary traits that lent them a strong resemblance to Aristotle's vision of the polis: they possessed a set of "civic structures . . . through which and by which freemen were governed and represented"; they encompassed the areas in which citizens lived; and they were constituted by households, "those places in which the primary affective and economic relationships of a person were likely to be based."[2] Withington concludes that "in these respects, incorporated communities resembled nothing less than the Aristotelian *polis*: a resemblance that . . . was far from coincidental."[3] Withington may have in mind the republican nature of Aristotle's model of the polis in relation to early modern chartered cities.

In what follows, I read Aristotle's *Politics* for its relevance to the dynamics of citizenship in *Merchant*, with two important departures from Withington's connection between early modern incorporated cities and the Aristotelian polis. First, while historians tend to define early modern citizenship in terms of how a group of merchants and artisans elected to form an association that constituted their citizenship as such, *after which* these incorporated communities acted as gatekeeping and policing institutions for noncitizens such as immigrant strangers and women, *Merchant* replicates the dynamic that Engin Isin refers to when he speaks of "citizenship and its alterity always emerg[ing] simultaneously in a dialogical manner and constitut[ing] each other."[4] In *Merchant*, the city's charter is invoked and placed in danger, but the language of stranger and citizen emerges simultaneously, late in the play, at the moment of the play's ultimate civic crisis leading into and through the trial scene. Shylock and Antonio are plotted onto the stranger/citizen binary in such a manner that the play is able to highlight, more than other citizen plays in the period, the mutually constitutive nature of these terms. "The alterity of citizenship," Isin writes, "does not preexist, but is constituted by it."[5]

Second, although *Merchant*'s invocation of an English city's form of incorporation, in terms of charter, freedom, and citizenship, has been suggested by some to be a structural flaw in the play at odds with depictions of Venice's modes of governance elsewhere in the play, I argue that this invocation introduces a decisive break from the Aristotelian model of citizenship. While Aristotle excludes all merchants, stranger or "native," from his definition of ideal citizenship, the English charter was explicitly a contract that constituted an incorporated city as a sworn association of merchants. The central pivots of the play's trial scene happen around this conjunction of contract, citizen, and stranger within an urban context. The play moves naturally from the radical, generative monetary contract between Shylock and Antonio to Venice's ur-contract, which founds the city in terms of commerce and citizenship.

Usury and the Reproduction of Aristotle's Polis

Around the same time *The Merchant of Venice* is likely to have been staged, the first English translation of Aristotle's *Politics* was published, under the

title *Aristotles Politiques or Discourses of Government* (1598).[6] Accompanied
by a line-by-line commentary on the text, this translation of the *Politics*
contains the origin of one of the most potent and oft-repeated critiques
of usury in the period. Turning to the beginning of *Aristotles Politiques*, the
reader would have found Aristotle moving very early in his definition of
the ideal polis to an interrogation of a life oriented toward money. Aristotle
condemns usury, or the lending of money with interest, as the pinnacle of
the "chrematistic" or money-oriented attitude, because he claims it makes
money engender money: usury is "the most contrarie to Nature" because
interest is a form of "issue or engindring," such that "usurie is naught else
but money begotten of money."[7] The commentator to *Aristotles Politiques*
offers a clarification: as all living creatures bring forth offspring, "every one
in his kind, commonly like their Parents," also "in usurie, the engendrer,
and the thing, is mony," which seems "contrary to nature, that a dead thing,
as mony, should engender."[8] The commentator suggests that the reproduction of money is not "kind"—that is, not natural——because it makes an
inorganic "dead thing" reproduce like living things. In usury, money begins
to reproduce as though it were like "every one in his kind."

   The Merchant of Venice appropriates the logic of monetary reproduction
from the Aristotelian critique of usury to sketch out an alternative form
of civic belonging for Shylock in which men can engage in procreation
with men. More specifically, the play sketches out and then seeks to block
an all-male alternative household within which usury's reproduction can
replace cross-sexual reproduction.[9] While the prioritizing of male friendship bonds over cross-gendered marriage is nothing new to early modern
drama scholars, the household conjured by the bond between Shylock and
Antonio radically transcends the furthest political, religious, financial, and
sexual limits typically ascribed to their contract.[10]

   Aristotle's own attack on usury's breeding is elaborated within his
definition of the household and the role of money within it. Although
the significance of usury for the Aristotelian definition of the household
has not been acknowledged by early modern theater scholars, what we
find in a play like *Merchant* is an exploration of the most radical possible
consequences of rewriting the role of money in relation to the husbandry
of reproduction. *Merchant* reworks Aristotle's critique into a vision of a
household that incorporates the management of monetary reproduction as
a legitimate form of thriving. Ultimately, I suggest that the pound of flesh
comes to designate an impending, yet impossible, birth between Shylock
and Antonio, wherein the imaginary pound as monetary denomination

would be made flesh within their household procreation. Shylock and Antonio seek to use each other to thrive and through this relationship *Merchant* models an alternative monetary imaginary that offers Shylock an alternative form of urban citizenship that is not, however, enshrined in any municipal law or article of a charter. In the trial scene, the play then ironically grants Shylock the legal civic belonging he sought but at the cost of an imaginative alternative homoerotic social bond.

Aristotle's critique of usury was a powerful and prevalent one in the early modern period, compulsively repeated in the many, virulent anti-usury tracts in circulation in England—though with some important modifications. As we move toward the early modern period, money's sexual deviancy in usury led early modern writers to associate it with sodomy, as another form of sexual perversion that diverts the "natural" and "sacred" ends of procreative sex.[11] Stage representations of usurers frequently depicted them as sexually rapacious and seductive because of the general sense of sexual perversion Aristotle's critique imputed to them, and plays often lumped usurers together with bawds, pimps, and prostitutes.[12]

Anti-usury discourse developed a shared vocabulary out of Aristotle, from which plays would also draw. Thomas Wilson's *A Discourse upon Usurye* reminds his readers that the term for interest "in greek means birth, because that money bringeth money."[13] Rice Vaughan's treatise on coinage refers to the production of money in specie, as physical coins, in general as "breeding"—a term repeatedly used by Shakespeare and his contemporaries in the "sexual" critiques of usury.[14] Miles Mosse's *The Arraignment and Conviction of Usurie* cites Hugo Cardinalis's claim that usury is a "sodomy in nature": Mosse notes that Cardinalis claims it is "against nature, for money to begette money, (in which sense one saide that usurie was *Sodomie naturae*, a kind of Sodomie in nature)."[15] As a "Sodomie in nature," usury perverts the natural act of procreative sex and applies it to money. Francis Meres suggests a correlation between "Paederastice" and usury in markedly similar language to that used by Shylock and Antonio: "As Paederastice is unlawfull, because it is against kinde: so usurie and increase by gold and silver is unlawful, because against nature; nature hath made them sterile and barren, & usurie makes them procreative."[16] Connecting "kinde" and "nature" as analogous yet somehow also different, Meres seems to prefer the word "kinde" for an illicit sexual act between living things, whereas "nature" he reserves for nonliving, natural substances. Similarly, act 1, scene 3 of *Merchant* contains multiple references to "kind" that link what is (un)natural with usury and procreation, and at one point Antonio mockingly asks Shylock, "when did friendship take / a breed for barren metal of his friend."[17] These texts evidence a common vocabulary and a messy array of concepts linking money, reproduction, nature, and sexual practices that *Merchant* reappropriates to construct its alternative urban citizenship.

The political stakes for usury's sexuality within these critiques have been elaborated by scholars who trace the ways in which sodomy as a concept was used to police other illicit activities in anti-usury discourse. Noting that the term "queer" has etymological roots in "coining terminology," Will Fisher has demonstrated, for example, the ways in which usury and sodomy were interarticulated concepts in the early modern period, "long before the linguistic connection was established."[18] Jody Greene notes that early modern conceptualizations of usury were "closely connected to discourses of male friendship and sodomy," but she also notes that usury could act as a locus for a "fantasy of reproductive homosexual sex" or a "procreative sodomy."[19] Within usury's "sodomitical economy," the role of money as "'a pledge or right between man and man' [. . .] has suddenly become unnatural, monstrous, corrupt, and able to reproduce."[20] Greene traces the seeds of this dynamic back to Aristotle's critique of usury's breeding of "like from like" and the combination of eroticism and sameness this carries with it.

The monetary imaginary of the time thus made possible a relation between desire and fantasy that sodomy as a concept was mobilized to police. Within this context, scholars such as David Hawkes, Fisher, and Greene have noted the political charge sodomy brought with it in its association with usury's "sexuality"—with Greene noting that this monetary eroticism was linked in more or less clear terms with the "notion of the sodomite as a destroyer of that most basic unit of the social fabric, the procreative, married, heterosexual couple."[21] What has gone unremarked, however, is how this "tricky sexual-political nexus" was already encoded in Aristotle's critique of usury in the *Politics*.[22]

When tracing *Merchant*'s use of terms like "kind," "breed," and "generation" from the many anti-usury tracts in the period back to Aristotle's critique of usury in the *Politics*, scholars have tended to isolate Aristotle's critique from its broader place within his definition of the polis. If we turn back to the beginning of the *Politics*, we find that Aristotle founds his vision of the polis on the "natural" desire to reproduce between a man and woman, using much of the same language from his critique of usury's breeding. In the words of the 1598 English translation, Aristotle suggests that the first building block of the polis is the relation of "the man and the

woman for procrcation [*sic*]"—something that they do according to "a certaine naturall desire in all other living wights" to "leave a like of their owne
kinde behind them."[23] The English commentator provides a gloss on this
passage, suggesting that the "first assembly" of man and woman is necessary to sustain the "meane of generation" upon which families, households,
and cities are founded.[24] For Aristotle, as Marcel Hénaff points out, "the
city is the end (*telos*) of the family and logically encompasses it."[25]

Aristotle then elaborates his definition of the household within the
polis, before critiquing, as a perversion of life within it, profit-seeking as an
end in itself—and usury as profit-seeking's worst, ultimate form. Despite
this clear setup, the structure of the text surrounding the discussion of what
Aristotle calls at times the "art acquisitive" displays a locus of instability
around where and how to deal with this aspect of the household as a building block of city life. Aristotle starts by declaring that "the nature of every
thing is to bee considered in the best partes thereof," and the "first and best
partes" of a family or household are "the master and servant, the husband
and wife, the father and children."[26] He adds, moreover, that "there is yet
another part which some men thinke to be Oeconomie, and others take
to be the principall part of a family," (i.e., the "acquiring and getting of
goods and possessions both mooveable and imooveable").[27] Having stated
that he will treat of this added element too, without suggesting where and
how it will fit in relation to what he has said are the "first and best partes,"
he says that he will start with the master and servant so that he can get at
what belongs to "necessary use."[28] This word "use," so key to early modern
anti-usury discourse and the rhetorical play of meanings in *Merchant*, is
perhaps *the* governing verb of I. D.'s translation of the *Politics* in terms of
oeconomie and the house or city.

At times, however, Aristotle's text muddies the difference between
household and city precisely where it tries to settle the specificity of *oeconomie*. Having stated that he will start with the master and servant, Aristotle
then immediately interrupts himself again to bring up the uncertain place
of *oeconomie*, noting that some have suggested that the skill of being a
master, "Oeconomie, or ordering a family," and governing a city, commonwealth, or kingly state are all the same thing.[29] He then brings up another
opinion: that the relation of a "master and his bondman is against nature"
since it is only law and not the "nature" of the individuals that causes them
to "differ."[30] Seemingly inspired by the question of one human's ownership
of another, he adds to the "partes of a family" "goods and possessions" and
suggests that the "skill to get goods" is a "part of the Oeconomie."[31] He

then introduces a distinction between "instruments" that "have life" and those that are "without life": to "possess goods, is nothing else but to possess a multitude of instruments" wherein a "servant is a living possession."[32] While a master owns a bondsman but merely employs a servant, the text seems to imply an expansive sense of possession, and thus membership in a family, that is linked to *use*. The master can use living people—bondsmen or servants—as well as things as instruments, and thus they are all part of the household.

We now have a more expansive definition of the members of a household that includes goods and possessions, both living and lifeless as parts of the family. Instead of moving on to the second and third elements (husbands and wives, fathers and children), the text turns to elaborate fully the nature of "Oeconomy," the relation that the art acquisitive has to it, and usury as its perversion. There is a part of *oeconomie* that is a natural or good form of "getting," and this good form provides for "the societie both of a Citie or Common weale, and also of a family."[33] The bad, "artificial" form of getting is enacted by way of "the trade of exchaunging."[34] A governor of a household or polis's use of the "art aquisitive, or the skill of getting money" is only healthy, or natural, when it is treated as a means to an end for procuring goods necessary for sustenance. The bad form of the art acquisitive, by contrast, "ingendrith money."[35] It is here, at the end of his critique of profit-seeking—in a long digression situated within his discussion of the master/slave relation—that Aristotle then critiques the usurer as someone who raises this profit-seeking to its fever pitch by making money from money.

As noted earlier, for Aristotle, among all the pursuits of money, charging interest is the most unnatural because it makes money "ingender." His rhetoric is quite strong on this point: "Above all the rest, Usurie deserveth to bee hated, for that by it menne gaine and profite by money, not for that intent and purpose for which it was ordained, namely, for the exchaunging of commodities; but for the augmenting of it selfe: which hath procured it the name of tokos [birth], to witte, issue or engendering: because things engendered, are like the engenderers; and Usurie is naught else but money begotten of money: in so much, that amongst all the meanes of getting, this is the most contrarie to Nature."[36] Aristotle's abhorrence of usury is not stated in terms of the devastating effects it can have for borrowers or the greed it exhibits in lenders—aspects later writers in the medieval and early modern period would add to the critique—but rather solely in terms of an unnatural breeding.

Aristotle has returned, though he does not himself acknowledge it, to the same context in which he founded the polis—the cross-sexual house-hold—in order to articulate his critique of usury. Having grounded the polis in a "certaine naturall desire" for cross-sexual reproduction, he then critiques usury as an unnatural perversion of this reproduction. The structural oddity of the text at this point may have contributed to the failure of scholars to read it within its broader context. That is, we have no prior reading of usury's unstated status in the text as a variant of the procreation that defines the core of the household and thereby the city.

Two important consequences follow from this instability within the polis for a reading of *Merchant*. First, usury, in perverting procreation within the household, itself understood as a parcel of the city, strikes at the root of the polis. As such, the usurer is intervening in, or invading, the political dimension of reproductive sexuality.[37] Without stating it directly, the *Politics* represents usury as scrambling the proper connections between money and reproductive sex that are routed through the household and that underpin the foundations of the city. The presence of and desire for money in the household becomes, in other words, the condition of possibility for an alternative form of procreation in the polis.

There is a second, positive possibility suggested by Aristotle's critique that shadows this first reading and threatens to subvert it. Elsewhere in the *Politics*, Aristotle concedes that foreign merchants, as profit-driven "others," are a necessary evil who should be located at the physical margins of the polis—nearby but not within; at ports, for example, since cities may need to trade with each other across the seas for goods necessary for their sustenance.[38] Overseas trade is a problem for Aristotle, though, because it brings in both strangers and merchants, two categories he somewhat conflates in the following passage: "Touching trafficke by sea, whether it bee profitable or hurtfull to well governed Cities, there are many doubts: for some affirme that it is very pernicious to the good discipline of a City, that strangers trained up in other lawes, resort thether: and that to people it much by the trafficke of the sea, in sending forth and receiving into the City a multitude of Merchants, it is against the ordinance and institution of a good governement. But if these inconveniences bee avoided, there is no doubt that it is better both for safety and abundeance of all necessaries, that a City or Countrey bee neare the sea."[39] Trade by sea brings with it two inconveniences that hopefully can be avoided: strangers "trained up in other lawes" and a "multitude of Merchants," with the implication that many of the latter are the former.

While overseas trade helps provide necessities and offers naval military advantages, the text criticizes most cities as using ports for profit: "And they which keepe open marts for al the world to repaire to, doe it to gaine thereby. If such covetous desire beseeme not a City, neither also dooth the keeping of such marts beseeme it."[40] The anti-immigrant sentiment is strong here in the context of commerce and the keeping of "open marts for al the world to repaire to." The solution to this problem looks a lot like the ghetto of the historical Venice and its parallel in the structural positioning of Shylock in the sociopolitical world of *Merchant*'s city: "But sith we see at this present in many Countries, harbors and havens lying commodiously neare the City, in such sort, that they are not within it nor farre from it, yet inclosed with wals and other like fortifications; certainely, if there growe any good by their communion, the City that is so seituated shall have it; and if there bee any inconnvenience, it may be easily avoided by statutes, declaring and appointing who may converse and trafficke together, and who not."[41] Ports should be near but not inside the city; and better yet, they can be walled off from the city proper, much like Venice's ghetto, to prevent too much intercourse with the city's citizens. Immigrants, merchants, and immigrant merchants are to be sequestered yet connected through the flows of money through the city.

Merchant aligns the figure of the geographically marginalized alien merchant with that of the usurer. What thus emerges from Aristotle's critique for a play like *Merchant* is an alternative reading of usury as offering a possible route into the polis for sequestered "others" via the polis's deepest root or defining aspect—that is, by seeking to participate in procreation from within the confines of the flows of money. Aristotle's figure of the usurer therefore not only offers an attack on profit but also maps a possible strategy for integration with the polis initiated from its boundaries. Within this context, the usurer ends up representing an alternative to cross-gendered marriage—itself defined as that "kind" or "natural" reproductive category between men and women offering the deepest, "sanctioned" foundation for the city.

Merchant's invocation of the city's charter and freedom, however, introduces a decisive break with the Aristotelian notion of citizenship. For Aristotle, all merchants, stranger or not, should be excluded from citizenship. According to Aristotle, "Citizens ou[gh]t not to live by mechanicall arts, because such a kind of life is base and contrary to virtue."[42] The commentator clarifies that merchants are included in the discussion here, noting that "in a good Commonweale, Artificers, Merchants, and Husbandmen, cannot be true Citizens."[43] Accordingly, merchants in general are grouped with strangers in the context of citizenship in the *Politics*. Cary Nederman claims that merchants and artisans are "to be classified with resident aliens and slaves," such that "those who earn their living necessarily possess the status of outsiders within their own community."[44] In the *Politics*, merchants are excluded from citizenship in part because they do not have the free time necessary to cultivate virtue.

Whereas Antonio would be grouped with Shylock in the *Politics*, especially because of Antonio's overseas trade, many early modern cities were founded on charters that were, according to Isin, "a contract between the lawmaking authority and the citizens as a corporation" that founded the city as "an economic association of merchants, craftsman and artisans."[45] Merchants constituted themselves as the citizens of a city through this sworn association, reversing the civic exclusion of merchants prescribed in the *Politics*. In London, guilds used their charter to achieve exclusive control over the pathway to citizenship. According to Steve Rappaport, the charter "forged an unbreakable link between gild membership and citizenship," such that "by virtually monopolizing avenues to the freedom, gilds achieved effective control over legal entry into and consequently full participation in London's economy."[46] This founding contract brought not only economic control but also judicial powers, including the right of the city to convene its own courts and juries, often in cases related to debts.[47] Citizens, in short, constituted a privileged minority class in London and were hence often a target of satire in plays of the period in a manner that would be hard to correlate with artistic treatments of modern national citizenship. The mention of charter and citizen in *Merchant* thus allows the play to add a negative hue to what in Aristotle was only glossed as an ideal.

In direct contrast to Aristotle's model, citizenship was a labor, occupational category in early modern cities with charters. While some have seen the invocation of the charter and urban citizenship in *Merchant*, especially so late in the play, as a structural flaw at odds with the rest of the play's implied political structure, the charter was the ur-contract of a city in early modern England.[48] Shylock's focus on contracts as, in part, providing agency to otherwise politically and socially disadvantaged urban denizens leads him, therefore, directly from an individual debt contract linking outsider and citizen to the contract that underwrites all contracts and founds the city and its economic form of urban citizenship. Bringing in the London context of the charter and urban citizenship allows the play to suggest to its audience that Shylock's pursuit of his unnaturally procreative contract threatens to strike at the contract of all contracts, the legal bond that constitutes the city.

"The Deed of Kind": Shylock and the Excess of Political Kindness

In his first encounter with Antonio, Shylock refers to the biblical story of Jacob's and Laban's sheep to defend usury's "excess." Through Shylock's speech about Jacob and Laban, *Merchant* appropriates the unstable relations between usury and the household established in Aristotle's critique to offer an alternative vision of a household founded on monetary reproduction. Shylock's speech first reimagines the role of usury in the polis as the "meane of generation" within the city. As he is a marginalized other, this reimagining represents a strategy by which a figure like Shylock can carve out a larger place in the polis, in and through the narrow point of access that the Christian Venetians allow him: commerce, and usury, specifically. Once Shylock and Antonio draw up a bond that allows them to use each other, they form a household that grants them both access to a specific form of procreation via money. The pound of flesh bond therefore comes to represent an extension of usury's essential dynamics wherein the bond between Shylock and Antonio projects an impending yet impossible monstrous birth. In the broadest terms, the play harnesses the sense of usury's generativity to suggest a radical bond between men through which the imaginary, virtual pound as monetary denomination will be made flesh.

Antonio has come to Shylock to act as surety for a loan to his friend, Bassanio. The first words Antonio speaks to Shylock declare that, while Antonio neither lends nor borrows "by taking nor giving of excess," in order to "supply the ripe wants of my friend, I'll break a custom" (1.3.57–60). Shylock lingers on these words, teasing Antonio, asking him to repeat himself, to which Antonio responds tersely, "I do never use it" (1.3.67). This line provides the word, "use," upon which Shylock then builds his defense—or rather, restatement—of usury's procreation.

Taking his cue from Antonio's pun on "use" as a common term for usury, as well as a homonym for "Jews," Shylock responds by piling on a further pun via "ewes" and the story of Jacob's and Laban's sheep.[49] In the biblical story, as Shylock recounts it, Laban has promised Jacob all the striped and spotted lambs from his flock, and Jacob is able to manipulate their breeding by placing "peeled . . . wands" or striped sticks in front of the "fulsome ewes," so that more "parti-colored" lambs are born (1.3.80–84).[50]

While explaining Jacob's "thrift," Shylock refers to the "wooly breeders" engaged in the "work of generation," and it is while they are doing "the deed of kind" that Jacob intervenes (1.3.79–81). When Antonio asks whether Shylock's story was "inserted to make interest good? / Or is your gold and silver ewes and rams?" Shylock replies, "I cannot tell, I make it breed as fast" (1.3.90–92).

Notice the retooling of the Aristotelian anti-usury vocabulary here. Shylock's speech repurposes terms like "breeding" and "meane of generation," transposing them upon a positive religious context. Shylock has also introduced the first instance of the word "kind" in their exchange, used here to refer to natural copulation—a meaning presaged by Shylock's term "work of generation." The phrase "deed of kind" performs much of the rhetorical labor here dedicated to reencoding the ethical valuation of usury's engendering. By recasting it, through analogy and biblical allusion, as a natural deed, doing what comes naturally, an act performed between two of a kind, Shylock offers a positive ethical valuation of "use" that correlates the reproduction of money, humans, and animals.[51] Shylock's refusal to submit his narrative of Jacob and Laban to Antonio's interpretive framework, moreover, allows for the meanings introduced in a phrase like "deed of kind" to remain open to still further modification later in the scene.

After all this work, however, Shylock appears to forsake it with his "kind offer" that leads to the pound of flesh. Once the heated interchange between Antonio and Shylock over lending reaches its boiling point, Shylock pivots seemingly away from the logic of reproduction altogether. In a fit of anger, Antonio uses a biblical allusion to draw a line in the sand between himself and Shylock, in terms of both religious difference and friendship. Antonio quips that:

> If thou wilt lend this money, lend it not
> As to thy friends, for when did friendship take
> A breed of barren metal of his friend?
> But lend it rather to thine enemy,
> Who, if he break, thou mayst with better face
> Exact the penalty. (1.3.127–32)

Antonio's use of "breed" echoes the lexicon of anti-usury discourse drawing upon Aristotle, and scholars often note that Antonio is referring more broadly here to the Jewish custom by which it is only acceptable to lend to "strangers." In this account, Antonio would be embracing the antagonistic basis that makes a loan on interest possible between them in the first place, implying that the only way any money will be breeding here is if they are enemies.[52] In response to this, Shylock seems to choose friendship over interest, suggesting that he "would be friends with you and have your love" and "take no doit / Of usance for my moneys," concluding that "this is kind I offer" (1.3.134–38). Shylock appears to drop the procreative element of usury; the word "kind" is then feverishly taken up by the other men. In response to Shylock's "kind . . . offer," Bassanio remarks, "This were kindness"; Shylock replies, "This kindness will I show," and this is the moment that Shylock proposes the bond of the pound of flesh—at which Antonio leaps, responding, "Content, in faith: I'll seal to such a bond / And say there is much kindness in the Jew" (1.3.138–49). The erotic charge Shylock introduced with the phrase "deed of kind" has been buoyed along by speakers through the scene even after the traditional form of procreative interest Aristotle critiques appears to have been dropped.

The Arden editor of *Merchant*, John Drakakis, is one of the only scholars to suggest, albeit obliquely, that Shylock might stitch something from usury's procreation into this speech, precisely where it seems, on the contrary, to disappear. In a footnote to Shylock's claim that "this is kind I offer" (1.3.138), Drakakis notes, "This gesture of brotherly friendship to Antonio invokes a more sinister meaning in its inadvertent (and perhaps even perverse) allusion to the *deed of kind* . . . Any reading of this line must balance these competing meanings which are active in this context."[53] Drakakis gestures toward, without naming, an erotic meaning contained in Shylock's "kind . . . offer," constructed through its allusion to his earlier analogy of usury's breeding as being like the "deed of kind." Shylock's allusion thus works against the surface claim he is making. On the surface, Shylock claims that he will "take no doit of usance," that he cancels out the entire procreative monetary dynamic he has just sketched and defended. The allusion to "the deed of kind"—the phrase that was key to the ethical revaluation of usury—implies, however, that monetary reproduction will continue in some way. Rather than being inadvertent, Shylock's wording initiates a subtle reworking of the *form* of interest that might be produced between him and Antonio. Interest will now reproduce in the flesh.

While other scholars have discussed connections between "kind" in this scene and Shylock's offer of brotherly friendship, they have tended to focus on its relevance to Antonio and Bassanio's homoerotic male amity or to Antonio and Shylock's religious difference. Noting that the word "kind" is often used by Shakespeare to refer to "loving male friendship," Amy

Greenstadt has suggested, for example, that Antonio's "eagerness to risk his flesh bespeaks a desire for a form of *kindness* that exceeds the traditional friendship ideal" that, for Greenstadt, ultimately leads to a bond with Bassanio that "mimics and challenges marital union."[54] Scholarship that reads "kind" in relation to the bond between Shylock and Antonio stresses, on the other hand, the senses of "kind" as either "considerate" or "similar to." That is, by offering a loan with no interest, Shylock starts to act more like a good Christian, a reading reinforced by the puns on "gentle" as "gentile" in lines like Antonio's farewell to Shylock: "Hie thee gentle Jew. / The Hebrew will turn Christian, he grows kind" (1.3.173–74).

The focus on friendship discourse and religious difference has occluded, however, our view of how the semantic chain of kindnesses in the scene continue to shape an erotic relation between Shylock and Antonio. Shylock's allusion to the deed of kind suggests that the pound of flesh will, in some new way, sustain the role of monetary reproduction within the bond between the two, and thereby the alternative possibility for civic participation Shylock has constructed around it. This becomes clearer as Shylock shows us more of what he means by "kind":

> This kindness will I show.
> Go with me to a notary, seal me there
> Your single bond, and, in a merry sport,
> If you repay me not on such a day,
> In such a place, such sum, or sums, as are
> Expressed in the condition, let the forfeit
> Be nominated for an equal pound
> Of your fair flesh, to be cut off and taken
> In what part of your body pleaseth me. (1.3.138–46)

The "perverse" meaning alluded to in Shylock's kind offer has now been elaborated here as the formation of a powerful bond with Antonio that invokes the flesh. Within this context, the pound of flesh forfeiture is referred to as a "merry sport," whose wordplay evokes the "deed of kind": the pun on "marry" in "merry," combined with the sexual connotations that "sport" often carried with it for Shakespeare, already conjures a sense of the pound of flesh as a fantasy production of a married, sexual sporting.[55] Shylock's reference to Antonio's "fair" flesh and his body in terms of how it "pleaseth me" also sustains the erotic connotations traversing the word "kind" across this scene. The vector of eroticism now runs directly between

Shylock and Antonio, leaving the much commented upon romance between Antonio and Bassanio to the side. Laura Kolb notes how Shylock's "counter-proposal" is "unusual" because "the obligation belongs solely to the merchant, underwritten by or for no one else," a move that "cuts Bassanio out of the deal [as debtor] altogether."[56] The bond Antonio leaps at effects an exclusion, shouldering Bassanio out, such that Antonio's strategy here in relation to Bassanio may be seeking to create more jealousy, rather than further obligation as other commentators have suggested. The fact that Antonio enters into an exclusive new relationship as a response to Bassanio's pursuit of marriage with Portia has generally not received sufficient attention.

Shylock's final lines in the scene continue to express a comic eagerness for the consummation of this bond, while turning to the language of home and thrift:

> Then meet me forthwith at the notary's;
> Give him direction for this merry bond,
> And I will go and purse the ducats straight,
> See to my house, left in the fearful guard
> Of an unthrifty knave, and presently
> I'll be with you. (1.3.168–73)

When Antonio replies, "Hie thee, gentle Jew," he demonstrates that he shares Shylock's sense of haste (1.3.173). Once this deed of kind that mimics the marriage bond or "merry bond" is notarized, Shylock will "purse" the money for Antonio. Shylock repeats the word, "purse," which scholars often note Antonio suffuses with erotic meaning in the play's first scene—specifically, as Antonio's offer of his testicles and seed of generation to Bassanio.[57] Drakakis again detects something erotic here, claiming that "the Jew will now become Antonio's *purse*, suggesting a perverse (and sterile) repetition of the Antonio-Bassanio relationship."[58] Again, it is not clear why Drakakis concludes this relation is "perverse," though it is indeed a repetition of the sense of pursing going on between Antonio and Bassanio, such that Shylock would supplant Bassanio, however. Rather than sterile, furthermore, this purse is now full of fertile money. This monetization of male genitals (or fertilization of money) is repeated ironically in the taunts of the boys echoing the aggrieved Shylock later in the play after Jessica has snuck away from Shylock's house: "his stones, his daughter, his ducats!" (2.8.24). "Stones" was a common pun for testicles in the period in addition to a term for precious jewels and it is not insignificant that the children echo these words to Shylock.

The apparent antagonism between Shylock and Antonio is no obstacle, moreover, to their new bond representing, for the audience, a fecund alternative household. A household represented, beyond the physical building, a profitable set of relations managed by a husband and wife. In the Protestant husbandry discourse of the period, the husband's duties were defined as out-of-doors, whereas the wife's were inside the physical home. In this discourse, anything that a husband "used" well was part of a virtual household that extended beyond the physical space defined by the walls of the home. As we saw in the *Politics*, goods and possessions are already part of the family. Furthermore, the 1573 translation of Xenophon's highly influential dialogue on *oeconomie*, *Xenophons Treatise of House Holde*, expands the spatial scope of the household beyond our modern sense of the physical walls of a house to "all that profitable that a man can use and order."[59] Socrates and Critabolus, the interlocutors in Xenophon's dialogue, both agree, as Lorna Hutson points out, that "a man's 'house' means more than the physical enclosure of his possessions within one fixed space; 'a man's house' (*oikos*) they decide must extend to all 'that a man hath.'"[60] The profitable "use and order" that defines this virtual household even extends to one's enemies. Socrates asks whether there be "not some men that have enemies," and whether "we shall say, that their enemyes be their goods or substaunce?" The conclusion Socrates reaches is that "it is a point than of a good husband, and a good order of a house, to have a waye, to use his enemies too, that he may get some profit by them."[61] The household is thus a dynamic web of relations, objects, and people that transcends the sense of a house as a set of walls and roof. The "use" of "his enemies" makes them a part of a household's "goods and substances" too, so long as they are used to a householder's advantage.

Antonio's declaration "I do never use it" resonates as a claim about "use" in terms of how he orders his household as a mobile set of profitable relations. In the merry bond drawn up between Shylock and Antonio, so long as they are using each other, their status as enemies or friends does not prevent them from forming a household together. The fertility of their "single bond," in terms of flesh rather than the usual interest, was already previewed, moreover, in the language of the Jacob-Laban story. The term "deed" already carries with it a legal sense of a bond or contract, which would have been reinforced through its association in Shylock's speech with copulation as a consummation of the marriage contract. The new deed or contract that Shylock kindly offers mirrors this dynamic, but now what is projected or fantasized as being cut away is a pound of human flesh.

As with the flesh of Christ in the Eucharist, the broader question is, therefore, what kind of presence the pound of flesh in the play achieves for the audience. Part of the nature of this presence is illuminated through the pun on "pound" in its monetary sense: as a perfectly familiar virtual form of currency in the period. The pound was a unit of account used to state prices, keep written records, and declare the value of domestic and foreign coins. The pound had never existed "in the flesh" in England: Shakespeare's audience was familiar with the fact that it was never minted as a physical coin but only circulated in speech and writing. It was a unit of account only ever known through language but with real effects in the material world, existing as what Carlo Cipolla refers to as "ghost money" or Thomas Luckett describes as "that invisible presence that animated the coin much as the soul animates the body."[62] It was present in the everyday lives of Shakespeare's audience, but in a diffuse form in language rather than an object form. The monetary pun in Shylock's line creates the expectation that the pound will be made physically present at some point in the play. By grounding its materiality in the flesh, rather than gold or silver, the play intensifies Smith's sense of "monstrous birth" or procreation that was already latent in usury's logic of engendering. The pound has always already been present as a structural element in the monetary system of the period but now the play is pregnant with its immanent corporeality.

The pound of flesh is thus already imagined in the play, but not simply as a virtual presence: it is *impending*, an ephemeral presence on its way to being materialized. As the play progresses, the incantatory nature of Shylock's demand for the pound of flesh begins to conjure it into an increasingly immanent or *almost* physical presence. Its legal status as a forfeiture or physical object to be produced as a penalty is independent of the spectral presence it attains in and through the speech of various characters across the play. Andrew Sofer has called this kind of presence in a play "dark matter," which he defines as "whatever is materially unrepresented on stage but un-ignorable."[63] For Sofer, Macbeth's dagger of the mind, for example, is "conjured by language, but not reducible to language," such that the "dagger's presence can only be inferred from its effects."[64] The dagger is there, just not in the same way the physical dagger is.

By contrast with *Macbeth*, the situation in *Merchant* is more akin to the effects created by the priest's incantations in the Catholic version of the Eucharist. Through the ritual effects enacted by the celebrant's speech, the invisible presence of Christ's flesh was believed to be transubstantiated, literally into corporeal presence. Julia Lupton makes a similar claim about what Shylock is doing, though she argues that this literalization should be understood in terms of circumcision. She argues that in adding the detail, in the trial scene, that he will cut out the pound of flesh nearest to Antonio's heart, Shylock is seeking to reliteralize and make once again physical what Paul rendered figurative and spiritual. Shylock would seek to render physical the liminal or virtual foreskin of Pauline Christianity, enacting a resurgence of the Judaism at the core of Christianity that Paul was not able to fully reencode.[65]

Many influential readings of Shylock and Antonio's bond imply that it is productive of *something* virtual in the play. Scholars such as Greenstadt, Ian McAdam, and Eric Santner each share, in their own way, the tendency to think of the pound of flesh itself in terms of some category of "liminal object."[66] Like Lupton, Greenstadt imagines the pound of flesh in terms of the foreskin, which would be a liminal object "in religious ritual and the symbolism of Shakespeare's play" that, like Freud's concept of the fetish, "refuses a choice between presence and lack."[67] Ian McAdam's analysis of the bond as "isolating and in a sense pathologizing the Eucharistic gesture of self-sacrifice" is structured around a floating, virtual Eucharistic object.[68] Eric Santner defines the pound of flesh as an ectoplasmic materiality, the "spectral remains" of the king's two bodies—or rather, of his divine, virtual body—as it passes over from the sovereign of political theology to the "People" of an emergent political economy.[69] Acknowledged or not, for each of these thinkers, the foreskin, the Eucharistic offering, or the king's spectral flesh are liminal objects hovering at the periphery of monetary utterance in *Merchant*—never quite arriving but still figuring from a distance the meanings in circulation within the play. Overtly political and erotic readings, in other words, often suggest the bond is generative of *something*—some fleshly excrescence, offspring, or floating object that inhabits the space of the play and playhouse without fully materializing there.

Yet, because each of these accounts neglects *Merchant*'s appropriation of the interplay between citizenship, usury, and the imaginary pound, they miss the monetary nature of this virtual flesh. The pound of flesh is not merely a liminal object but rather an impending one, a threatening birth whose arrival is immanent yet impossible. Marriage and usurious procreation combine in this single bond between Shylock and Antonio to sketch out a radical alternative *oeconomic* imaginary through which a virtual excess threatens to emerge from the abstract flesh of the family into the physical world. So much of the dramatic tension in *Merchant* is grounded in the sense that we are moving towards the actual arrival of this heretofore spectral, structural element.

Having imagined it, however, the play then seeks to divorce Shylock and Antonio, breaking the too radical merry bond that offers an alien moneylender an alternative way into the polis by merging the flow of money and sexual reproduction. Shylock himself links the birth of the pound in the flesh with the contractual foundation of the city—the latter being understood in an English context—when the pressure he applies to the city's charter brings the language of citizenship and the polis as corporation to the surface. There is hardly any lexicon of citizenship at use in the play until Shylock begins pursuing his bond against Antonio. We first hear of this secondhand from Antonio's friend Salerio, who has brought the news of Antonio's situation to Bassanio at Belmont. According to Salerio:

> He plies the Duke at morning and at night;
> And doth impeach the freedom of the state
> If they deny him justice. (3.2.276–78)

The "freedom of the state" refers to Venice's charter status and the sense of citizenship as becoming "free of" one's city.

Lest the language of freedom in terms of urban citizenship be lost on the audience, Shylock repeats it at the beginning of the trail scene. Demanding his forfeiture from the Duke, Shylock proclaims, "If you deny it, let the danger light / Upon your charter and your city's freedom!" (4.1.37–38). Charters as founding contracts would have been familiar to Shakespeare's audience in a variety contexts, from the city of London's charter to those founding guilds and universities; therefore, Shylock's threat of a danger incurred to the city's charter and the freedom (i.e., citizenship) it defines and enables would have resonated clearly as a contractual, commercial, and civic threat, all in relation to citizenship.[70] The city's charter, and the urban citizenship it defines, is the ur-contract or contract of all contracts explicitly thematized in the trial scene of the play. In addition to the physical threat to Antonio, the citizen, the trial scene revolves around a threat to the ultimate contract that citizenship itself depends upon.

The Englishness of this context has struck some scholars as inconsistent and perhaps evidence of incomplete revision rather than thematic unity. Drakakis cites J. Dover Wilson as believing that "this anglicization of the political order of Venice [is] inconsistent with earlier descriptions [. . .]

and hence evidence of partial revision of a putative promptbook."[71] Archer
suggests that the reference betrays a limitation in Shakespeare's conceptual
framework: "Venice's freedom is somehow chartered, like that of an English town: despite the classical—or at any rate civic—republican setting
of Venice, Shakespeare has difficulty conceiving of citizenship apart from
sovereignty and subjecthood."[72] Lupton notes the reference to the charter
without seeming to find it at odds with the play but believes that circumcision represents the primary contested contractual symbol governing the
scene—specifically, Shylock's attempt to reliteralize the Pauline circumcision of the heart.[73] However, the introduction of the charter allows the
play to connect Shylock's obsession with contracts to a contract that founds
the city itself, as a polis composed of citizens in a manner that is perfectly
harmonious with the play's overarching themes. The final blow to Shylock
occurs within this context, where the danger he sought to bring upon the
charter, and the citizenship that contract enabled, is turned against him.

Antonio and Portia are the ones who introduce the language of strangers, aliens, and citizens into this context. In an attempt to reassure Antonio
on his way to jail, his friend, Salanio offers that "I am sure the Duke / Will
never grant this forfeiture to hold," to which Antonio responds:

> The Duke cannot deny the course of law;
> For the commodity that strangers have
> With us in Venice, if it be denied,
> Will much impeach the justice of the state,
> Since that the trade and profit of the city
> Consisteth of all nations. (3.3.24–36)

Antonio's noting that the "trade and profit of the city / Consisteth of all
nations" is reminiscent of Aristotle's handwaving regarding those cities that
"keepe open marts for al the world to repaire to." Portia herself reiterates
the importance of this situation for the polis, when Bassanio asks the Duke
to deny Shylock's claim, declaring that the Duke cannot because "there is
no power in Venice / Can alter a decree established. / 'Twill be recorded for
a precedent, / And many an error by the same example / Will rush into the
state. It cannot be" (4.1.214–18). Shylock's invocation of the city's charter
would underscore for the audience that the Duke's jurisdiction did not
apply in this case, as a city's freedom was explicitly not an aristocratic but
a civic and economic affair.

Portia introduces the term "citizen" as she delivers her coup de grâce

against Shylock. After she turns the law against Shylock in the trial scene
with her biased strategies, creating an impossible scenario for him to exact
his pound of flesh by requiring that he draw no blood, Portia pushes a final
codicil that

> It is enacted in the laws of Venice,
> If it be proved against an alien
> That by direct, or indirect attempts
> He seek the life of any citizen,
> The party 'gainst the which he doth contrive
> Shall seize one-half his goods. (4.1.344–49)

This is the final pronouncement from Portia, the last move in her legal
strategy against Shylock before the Duke spares his life and Antonio
states his conditions regarding the use of Shylock's money for Jessica and
Lorenzo and his conversion to Christianity. Portia acknowledges she has
abruptly shifted the sense of Shylock's situation when she adds that Shylock has "incurred the danger," using the same term, "danger," with which
he himself threatened the city's charter (4.1.353, 357–58). Wrapping up
her attack with the concept of urban citizenship that was introduced by reference to the city's charter, Portia underscores its central role in the scene.
The climax of the trial scene is articulated in terms of the citizen-stranger
binary, though Antonio and Portia supplied the vocabulary that categorizes people in terms of how the charter apportions urban citizenship.

Antonio is not referred to as a citizen until the founding contract
of citizenship is invoked and the alterity of citizenship is explicitly constructed and labeled in proximity to the only use of the term "citizen" in
the play. The play thereby marks how strangers and aliens are constructs
just as much as citizens are: citizens did not first define themselves through
the sworn association constituting the charter and then define strangers or
aliens as those falling outside this association, rather the play represents
them as mutually dependent terms dialogically constructed simultaneously.
Merchant emphasizes, through Shylock, the centrality of what Isin calls
immanent others for the construction of the Venetian socius, not others
that dwell fully exterior to the community in other cities or countries. Shylock's and Antonio's marking as stranger and citizen does not predate the
action of the play; we do not enter in medias res into a conversation that
uses terms like strangers and citizens. Rather the play abruptly deploys
these terms when the action is nearly done and the contract of contracts

is in explicit danger. Scholars such as James Shapiro and Alan Stewart have discussed the common belief that Jews could never become grafted to any nation in which they dwelled, rendering them essentially permanent strangers or aliens to any soil.[74] While *Merchant* never suggests Shylock is an immigrant, the belief would apply to the descendants of immigrant Jews as well. *Merchant* does not place the level emphasis on the alienness of Jewishness that these scholars' insights might lead one to expect, however. Though Shylock certainly occupies a mostly separate social circle from the Christian Venetians, his identity in relation to the nation or city-state is not raised at the start of the play, while Portia's stranger suitors are immediately thematized in terms of nationality. Shylock is already established as a Jew, father, moneylender, and householder before the play labels him in a secondary, and somewhat indirect way, as a stranger—similarly for Antonio as citizen—as though Shylock's threat to the charter as contract is what marks him as alien, not necessarily his Jewishness per se. Perhaps, by rebound, this is also what marks Antonio as citizen.

Antonio's condition that Shylock convert to Christianity—"that for this favour / He presently become a Christian"—comes in response to their dispute being framed as a citizen/alien conflict by Portia and projects the final step in Shylock's movement across modes of civic belonging (4.1.382–83). Lupton notes that Shylock's religious conversion would naturalize him, presumably conferring many of the commercial liberties attending on the "natural" urban citizens of Venice.[75] This also allows the city both to efface the alterity it constructed to define citizenship and to protect the charter by allowing Shylock more access to the freedoms it underwrites. *Merchant* invokes citizenship to at least gesture toward absorbing Shylock within its traditional limits, rather than continuing to allow a symbolic, alternative "sworn association" between alien and citizen that would reproduce outside the normative bounds of the polis. The play marks him as an alien to the city, then seeks to defuse his threat to its founding contract by offering him a stake in its continued existence. It is almost as though the play needed to tip the matter over toward religious difference and conversion because Shylock did not fit comfortably in the stranger category that others sought to place him in. He is left with just enough wealth to perhaps act upon his new citizenship options, while the rest is left in trust with Antonio to be used on behalf of Jessica and Lorenzo. Oddly enough, Antonio's conditions also help circumvent a common problem for strangers in England regarding inheritance—the children of nonnaturalized immigrants were often barred from inheriting different types of wealth from their parents.

By serving as custodian for a portion of Shylock's wealth on behalf of Jessica and Lorenzo, Antonio acts as a double surety for an otherwise precarious inheritance (double because in principle Shylock's Christian status may have also added more assurance). While Antonio's conditions regarding Jessica and Lorenzo at first blush are geared toward Shylock's likely reluctance to leave them any money after he dies—hence the additional requirement that Shylock will them all he owns upon his death—they also index this legal obstacle for strangers.

Ultimately, *Merchant* has highlighted how much proximity citizens and noncitizens can have to the center of power when citizenship itself is an urban affair that is at the same time an international and commercial one—much as the devolution of the city of Manchester sought to bring civic actors into closer contact with the political and economic forces shaping their lives. Because early modern citizenship is codified through the sworn association or bonds of merchants, a single debt bond between a citizen and noncitizen can have profound implications that strike at the very core of a polis so defined. The kernel of issues that *Merchant* works through related to a city defined by a charter and international commerce, as well as the lack of fixity of immanent others within this context, indexes the historical promise of a perhaps paradoxically more local approach to international issues. The play offers an important opportunity to think more directly about the power of a stronger urban citizenry, about what was lost historically when citizenship and nationality were conflated, and about the urgency of more empowered and diverse local, civic responses to the xenophobia underlying a national referendum like Brexit.

Notes

1. For more on devolution and the UK, see for example, Bruce Katz and Jeremy Nowak, *The New Localism: How Cities Can Thrive in the Age of Populism* (Washington, DC: Brookings Institution Press, 2018); Bruce Katz and Alex C. Jones, "Where Does Brexit Leave UK Cities?" *Brookings* (blog), June 24, 2016; Bruce Katz and Alex C. Jones, "How 'New Localism' Is Democratizing Urban Growth," *Brookings* (blog), June 14, 2016; Bruce Katz, "Manchester, England: Devolution U.K. Style," *Brookings* (blog), November 6, 2014; David Beel, Martin Jones, and Ian Rees Jones, eds., *City Regions and Devolution in the UK: The Politics of Representation* (Bristol: Bristol University Press, 2021); David Beel, Martin Jones, and Ian Rees Jones, "Introduction: Onward Devolution and City Regions," in *City Regions and Devolution in the UK*, 1–22.

2. Phil Withington, *The Politics of Commonwealth: Citizens and Freemen in Early Modern England* (Cambridge, UK: Cambridge University Press, 2005), 10.

3. Withington, *Politics of Commonwealth*, 10.

4. Engin Isin, *Being Political: Genealogies of Citizenship* (Minneapolis: University of Minnesota Press, 2002), 3.

5. Isin, *Being Political*, 3.

6. Aristotle, *Aristotles Politiques, or Discourses of Government*, trans. I. D. (London, 1598). This text is a palimpsest of translations. The English translation and commentary are attributed to the otherwise anonymous "I. D."—the initials with which the writer signs off at the end of the dedicatory epistle (A3v). The anonymous English writer's text is a translation of the French original. The title page of *Aristotles Politiques* advertises itself, moreover, as a translation "out of Greeke into French" by "Loys Le Roy" (A1). Either the English translator or the publisher appended a bit of text below the French writer's name that states, "Translated out of French into Englisse" (A1).

7. Aristotle, *Politiques*, G4r.

8. Aristotle, *Politiques*, H1v.

9. I adapt the term "cross-sexual," rather than "heterosexual," from Valerie Traub's concept of cross-gender identification. See Valerie Traub, *Thinking Sex with the Early Moderns* (Philadelphia: University of Pennsylvania Press, 2016). The concept works at many levels for Traub but generally signifies a "process . . . of transiting across gender boundaries" (24). Rather than seeking to break down the male/female binary, or imply a change in one's gender, Traub's concept of cross-gender identification focuses on sites where knowledge is generated precisely through the contemplation of the specificity of another gender identification. When I speak of cross-sexual reproduction in this chapter, the phrase is meant to both invoke Traub's concept and adapt it to my emphasis on two valances of reproduction constructed around the male/female binary. For more on this concept, see Traub, *Thinking Sex*, 24–25 and 54.

10. The prioritizing of bonds between men over those between men and women, or women and women, in early modern England did not, in some contexts and modes, produce a radical or alternative politics. Sedgwick's critique of the prioritizing of male bonds above all others is foundational for critics looking at the positioning of women within homosocial and homoerotic ties; the whole tradition of erotic male friendship scholarship, from Alan Bray and Jonathan Goldberg to Mario DiGangi and Jeffrey Masten, examines this theme; and Valerie Traub's magisterial work on "lesbianism" in the period offers a counterbalance to the male friendship-centric work that has dominated the field. The work of scholars like Greenstadt has at times attempted to push back on the male-centric work of history of sexuality scholars in relation to *Merchant*, specifically. Hutson has also focused on male-to-male bonds in relation to the household and the housewife. For representative examples, see Eve Kosofsky Sedgwick, *Between Men: English Literature and Male Homosocial Desire* (New York: Columbia University Press, 2015); Alan Bray, *Homosexuality in Renaissance England* (New York: Columbia University Press, 1995); Jonathan Goldberg, *Sodometries: Renaissance Texts, Modern Sexualities* (Stanford: Stanford University Press, 1992); Mario DiGangi, *Homoerotics of Early Modern Drama* (Cambridge, UK: Cambridge University Press, 1997); Jeffrey Masten, *Queer Philologies: Sex, Language, and Affect in Shakespeare's Time* (Philadelphia: University of Pennsylvania Press, 2016); Laurie Shannon, "Nature's Bias: Renaissance Homonormativity

and Elizabethan Comic Likeness," *Modern Philology* 98, no. 2 (November 2000): 183–210; Valerie Traub, *The Renaissance of Lesbianism in Early Modern England* (Cambridge, UK: Cambridge University Press, 2002); Eliza Greenstadt, "Strange Insertions in *The Merchant of Venice*," *Queer Shakespeare: Desire and Sexuality*, ed. Goran Stanivukovic (London: Bloomsbury Publishing, 2017), 197–226; and Lorna Hutson, *The Usurer's Daughter: Male Friendship and Fictions of Women in Sixteenth-Century England* (London: Routledge, 1994).

11. For the foundational analyses of this dynamic, see Will Fisher, "Queer Money," *English Literary History* 66, no. 1 (Spring 1999): 1–23; Jody Greene, "You Must Eat Men: The Sodomitic Economy of Renaissance Patronage," *GLQ* 2, no. 1 (1994): 163–97. I return to their contributions later in this chapter.

12. See David Hawkes, *The Culture of Usury in Renaissance England* (New York: Palgrave Macmillan, 2010), 164–65.

13. Thomas Wilson, *A Discourse upon Usury* (London: s. n., 1572), 85.

14. Rice Vaughan, *A Discourse of Coin and Coinage* (London: Thomas Basset, 1675), 61.

15. Wilson, *Discourse*, 110.

16. Wilson, *Discourse*, 322r.

17. *Merchant of Venice*, act 1, scene 3, lines 128–29. All quotations, unless otherwise noted, are from *The Merchant of Venice*, Arden Third Series, ed. John Drakakis (London: Bloomsbury, 2010).

18. Fisher, "Queer Money," 1.

19. Greene, "You Must Eat Men," 170 and 171.

20. Greene, "You Must Eat Men," 173.

21. Greene, "You Must Eat Men," 166.

22. Greene, "You Must Eat Men," 166.

23. Aristotle, *Politiques*, D1r.

24. Aristotle, *Politiques*, D1r.

25. Marcel Hénaff, *The Price of Truth: Gift, Money, and Philosophy*, trans. Jean-Louis Morhange and Anne-Marie Feenberg-Dibon (Stanford: Stanford University Press, 2010), 81–82.

26. Aristotle, *Politiques*, E3r.

27. Aristotle, *Politiques*, E3r.

28. Aristotle, *Politiques*, E3r.

29. Aristotle, *Politiques*, E3r.

30. Aristotle, *Politiques*, E3r.

31. Aristotle, *Politiques*, E3r.

32. Aristotle, *Politiques*, E4v.

33. Aristotle, *Politiques*, F5r. He repeats the connection between a household and city "oeconomie" often, though frequently also softening the identification of the two through a language of simile and analogy. Later, in book 3, he suggests that "for as the Oeconomie is a kind of household government, so is the government of a citie, and the Oeconomie of one or more Nations" (S1v). Similarly, he stops short of saying they are exactly the same when he states that "every Nation and every citie has power over common things, and follows the example of the Oeconomie" (S1v).

34. Aristotle, *Politiques*, F5v.

35. Aristotle, *Politiques*, F5r.

36. Aristotle, *Politiques*, G5r.

37. This can help further explain why Aristotle turns so quickly to attack the usurer—and why he does so in reproductive terms—within his discussion of the proper function of the city or polis, and why he finds this figure so threatening. Given that no other negative aspects of charging interest on a loan are considered, the intensity of his vitriol against usury *as a perversion of procreation* is otherwise difficult to square with his broader analysis.

38. On Aristotle and Plato's sequestration of the merchant to the margins of the city, see Hénaff, *Price*, 74–75.

39. Aristotle, *Politiques*, 2K4r.

40. Aristotle, *Politiques*, 2K4r.

41. Aristotle, *Politiques*, 2K4r.

42. Aristotle, *Politiques*, 2K6r.

43. Aristotle, *Politiques*, 2K7v.

44. Cary J. Nederman, "Mechanics and Citizens: The Reception of the Aristotelian Idea of Citizenship in Late Medieval Europe," *Vivarium* 40, no. 1 (2002): 77–78.

45. Engin Isin, *Cities without Citizens* (Montreal: Black Rose Books, 1992), 17.

46. Steve Rappaport, *Worlds within Worlds: Structures of Life in Sixteenth-Century London* (Cambridge, UK: Cambridge University Press, 2002), 32.

47. See Withington, *Politics*, 8.

48. See Shakespeare, *Merchant*, 4.1.n38; John Michael Archer, *Citizen Shakespeare: Freemen and Aliens in the Language of the Plays* (New York: Palgrave Macmillan, 2005), 42.

49. This is an example of what Marc Shell has called Shylock's "verbal usury." See Marc Shell, *Money, Language, and Thought: Literary and Philosophical Economies from the Medieval to the Modern Era* (Berkeley: University of California Press, 1982), esp. 49.

50. See Genesis 30:37–43. The Bible seems to contain an implicit theory of perception here, namely, that parents' offspring will resemble what they are looking at while they copulate.

51. For more on this passage in relation to delineating the genealogy of the Jews versus others, see Shell, *Money, Language, and Thought*, 51–52. On the role of "use" and usury in this scene, see also Lars Engle, "'Thrift Is Blessing': Exchange and Explanation in *The Merchant of Venice*," *Shakespeare Quarterly* 37, no. 1 (Spring 1986): 20–37.

52. Scholars typically cite Deuteronomy 23:19–20 for this injunction. For a discussion of its relevance for these lines, see Shakespeare, *Merchant*, 1.3.n127–28; Shell, *Money*, 51; Hawkes, *Culture of Usury*, 62–64.

53. See Shakespeare, *Merchant*, 1.3.n138.

54. Amy Greenstadt, "The Kindest Cut: Circumcision and Queer Kinship in *The Merchant of Venice*," *English Literary History* 80, no. 4 (Winter 2013): 945 and 952; emphasis in the original.

55. See *Oxford English Dictionary*, s.v. "sport," *v.*6: "To engage in amorous behaviour or sexual activity."

56. Laura Kolb, *Fictions of Credit in the Age of Shakespeare* (Oxford: Oxford University Press, 2021), 101.

57. Antonio declares that "my purse, my person, my extremest means / Lie all unlocked to your occasions" (1.1.138–39).

58. See Shakespeare, *Merchant*, 1.3.n170 (emphasis in the original).

59. *Xenophons Treatise of House Hold* (London, 1573), C3r.

60. Hutson, *Usurer's Daughter*, 32.

61. *Xenophons Treatise*, A4r–v.

62. Carlo Cipolla, *Money, Prices, and Civilization in the Mediterranean World: Fifth to Seventeenth Century* (Princeton: Princeton University Press, 1956), esp. 38–51; Thomas M. Luckett, "Imaginary Currency and Real Guillotines: The Intellectual Origins of the Financial Terror in France," *Historical Reflections / Réflexions Historiques* 31, no. 1 (Spring 2005): 118.

63. Andrew Sofer, *Dark Matter: Invisibility in Drama, Theater, and Performance* (Ann Arbor: University of Michigan Press, 2013), 4.

64. Sofer, *Dark Matter*, 8.

65. See Julia Reinhard Lupton, *Citizen-Saints: Shakespeare and Political Theology* (Chicago: University of Chicago Press, 2014), 91–92.

66. Greenstadt, "Kindest Cut," 968.

67. Greenstadt, "Kindest Cut," 968–69.

68. Ian McAdam, "Eucharistic Love in *The Merchant of Venice*," *Renaissance and Reformation / Renaissance et Réforme* 38, no. 1 (Winter 2015): 114.

69. Eric Santner, *The Weight of All Flesh: On the Subject-Matter of Political Economy* (New York: Oxford University Press, 2016), 46–47.

70. While I don't have the scope to explore this here, it is important that Shylock's threat to the city's charter would not have direct relevance for Bassanio and Portia, as aristocrats, per se. The danger to the charter is an existential threat to citizens, a category to which Antonio belongs, as Portia is certain to make clear. This has important implications, in turn, for the rivalry between Portia and Antonio. I will develop this line of thought further in a future piece.

71. Shakespeare, *Merchant*, 4.1.n38.

72. Archer, *Citizen Shakespeare*, 42.

73. See, for example, Lupton, *Citizen-Saints*, 314–16.

74. See James Shapiro, *Shakespeare and the Jews* (New York: Columbia University Press, 2016); Alan Stewart, "'Euery Soyle to Mee Is Naturall': Figuring Denization in William Haughton's *Englishmen for My Money*," *Renaissance Drama* 35 (2006): 55–81; Edmund Valentine Campos, "Jews, Spaniards, and Portingales: Ambiguous Identities of Portuguese Marranos in Elizabethan England," *English Literary History* 69, no. 3 (September 2002): 599–616.

75. Lupton, *Citizen-Saints*, 338–39.

BIBLIOGRAPHY

PRIMARY SOURCES

Abbot, George. *An Exposition upon the Prophet Jonah*. London: Richard Field, 1600.

Alley, William. *Ptochhomuseioin*. London: s. n., 1565.

Andrewes, John. *The Converted Mans New Birth*. London: s. n., 1629.

Anonymous. *A Cup of Sack Prest Forth the Best Grapes Gathered the Last Vintage*. London: s. n., 1644.

Anonymous. *The Famous Historie of Fryer Bacon*. London: F. Grove, 1627.

Anonymous. *The Merry Devill of Edmonton*. London: Arthur Johnson, 1608.

Anonymous. *The Most Famous History of the Learned Fryer Bacon*. London: Thomas Norris, 1700.

Anonymous. *No-body and Some-body*. London: John Trundle, 1606.

Anonymous. *A Second Discovery by the Northern Scout: Of the Chiefe Actions and Attempts of the Malignant Party of Prelates and Papists, Proctors and Doctors, and Cavaliers That Are Now Resident in the County of Yorke*. London: B. W., 1642.

Anonymous. *The Treasurie of Auncient and Moderne Times*. London: William Jaggard, 1613.

Anonymous. *The True Tragedie of Richard the Third*. London: William Barley, 1594.

Anonymous. *Xenophons Treatise of House Holde*. London: s. n., 1573.

Aristotle. *Aristotles Politiques, or Discourses of Government*. Translated by I. D. London: s. n., 1598.

B., T. *The Life and Death of the Merry Devill of Edmonton, with the Pleasant Prancks of Smug the Smith*. London: Francis Faulkner, 1631.

Bacon, Francis. *The Historie of the Raigne of King Henry the Seventh*. London: Matthew Lownes and William Barret, 1622.

———. *Sylva Sylvarum*. London: William Lee, 1627.

Bernard, Richard. *Rhemes against Rome*. London: Edward Blackmore, 1626.

Boorde, Andrew. *The Breviarie of Health wherin Doth Folow, Remedies, for All Maner of Sicknesses & Diseases the which May Be in Man or Woman*. London: s. n., 1598.

Botero, Giovanni. *The Travellers Breviat*. Translated by "I. R." London: John Jaggard, 1601.

Boys, John. *An Exposition of the Proper Psalmes Used in Our English Lyturgie*. London: Edward Griffin for William Aspley, 1617.

Brenz, Johannes. *A Right Godly and Learned Discourse upon the Booke of Ester*. London: John Harrison, 1584.

Bridges, John. *A Defence of the Gouernment Established in the Church of England*. London: Thomas Chard, 1587.

Brightman, Thomas. *A Revelation of the Apocalyps*. Amsterdam: Judocus Hondius and Hendrick Laurenss, 1611.

Brome, Richard. *The Antipodes*. London: Francis Constable, 1640.

Browne, Thomas. *Pseudodoxia Epidemica*. London: E. Dod, 1646.

Campion, Thomas. *The Description of a Maske*. London: Laurence Lisle, 1614.

Chapman, George. *All Fools*. London: Thomas Thorpe, 1605.

Cipriano, Giovanni. *A Most Strange and Wonderfull Prophesie upon this Troublesome World*. Translated by Anthony Hollaway. London: s. n., 1595.

D., J. *The Knave in Graine, New Vampt*. London: John Nicholson, 1640.

d'Anghiera, Pietro Martire. *The Decades of the Newe Worlde or West India*. Translated by Richard Eden. London: William Powell, 1555.

D'Ewes, Simond. *A Compleat Journal of the Votes, Speeches, and Debates, Both of the House of Lords and House of Commons throughout the Whole Reign of Queen Elizabeth*. London: Jonathan Robinson, 1693.

———. "Journal of the House of Commons: March 1593." In *The Journals of All the Parliaments during the Reign of Queen Elizabeth*, 479–513. Shannon, Ireland: Irish University Press, 1682.

Dekker, Thomas. *The Magnificent Entertainment Given to King James, Queene Anne His Wife, and Henry Frederick the Prince*. London: Thomas Man, 1604.

———. *The Pleasant Comedie of Old Fortunatus*. London: William Aspley, 1600.

———. *The Shomakers Holiday. Or, the Gentle Craft*. London: Valentine Sims, 1600.

Erasmus, Desiderius. *The First Tome or Volume of the Paraphrase of Erasmus upon the Newe Testamente*. Translated by N. Udall. London: Edward Whitchurch, 1548.

Flecknoe, Richard. *The Marriage of Oceanus and Brittania*. London: s. n., 1659.

Ford, John. *The Chronicle Historie of Perkin Warbeck*. London: Hugh Beeston, 1634.

Frégeville, Jean de. *The Reformed Politicke*. London: s. n., 1589.

Greene, Robert. *The Honorable Historie of Frier Bacon, and Friar Bongay*. London: s. n., 1630.

———. *The Scottish Historie of James the Fourth*. London: s. n., 1598.

Hart, James. *Klinike, or the Diet of the Diseased*. London: Robert Allot, 1633.

Haughton, William. *English-men for my Money: Or, a Pleasant Comedy, Called, A Woman Will Have Her Will*. London: W. White, 1616.

Heywood, Thomas. *The Iron Age, Contayning the Rape of Hellen: The Siege of Troy*. London: s. n., 1632.

———. *Philocothonista, or the Drunkard Opened, Dissected, and Anatomized*. London: Robert Raworth, 1635.

———. *The Second Part of the Iron Age*. London: s. n., 1632.

Hobbes, Thomas. *Leviathan*. London: Andrew Crooke, 1651.

Holinshed, Raphael. *The Chronicles of England, Scotlande, and Irelande*. London: s. n., 1587.

———. *The Firste Volume of the Chronicles of England, Scotlande, and Irelande. Conteyning the Description and Chronicles of England*. London: s. n., 1577.

———. *The Third Volume of the Chronicles of England, Scotlande, and Irelande*. London: s. n., 1586.

Ive, Paul. *The Practise of Fortification*. London: T. Man and T. Cooke, 1589.

Jonson, Ben. *The Comical Satyre of Every Man Out of His Humor*. London: William Holme, 1600.

Lanchester, John. *The Wall*. New York: W. W. Norton, 2019.

Marlowe, Christopher. *The Troublesome Raigne and Lamentable Death of Edward the Second*. London: William Jones, 1594.

Marston, John. *The Dutch Courtezan*. London: John Hodgets, 1605.

———. *Parasitaster, or the Fawn*. London: William Cotton, 1606.

Massinger, Philip. *The Maid of Honour*. London: Robert Allot, 1632.

Merlin, Pierre. *A Most Plaine and Profitable Exposition of the Book of Ester: Deliuered in 26. Sermons*. London: Thomas Creed, 1599.

Montaigne, Michel de. *The Essayes or Morall, Politike and Militarie Discourses of Lord Michaell de Montaigne*. Translated by John Florio. London: Edward Blount, 1603.

Nashe, Thomas. *A Pleasant Comedie, Called Summer's Last Will and Testament*. London: Walter Burre, 1600.

Purchas, Samuel. *Purchas His Pilgrimage*. London: Henry Featherstone, 1613.

———. *Purchas His Pilgrimes*. London: Henry Featherstone, 1625.

Quarles, Francis. *Hadassa: Or the History of Queene Ester with Meditations Thereupon, Divine and Morall*. London: Richard Moore, 1621.

Randolph, Thomas. *A Pleasant Comedie, Entitled Hey for Honesty, Down with Knavery*. London: s. n., 1651.

Ridpath, George. *Scotland's Soveraignty Asserted. Being a Dispute concerning Homage, against Those Who Maintain That Scotland Is a Feu, or Fee-Liege of England, and That Therefore the King of Scots ow[e]s Homage to the King of England*. London: Andrew Bell, 1695.

Roe, Sir Thomas. *A True and Faithfull Relation, Presented to His Majestie and the Prince, of What Hath Lately Happened in Constantinople*. London: Bartholomew Downes, 1622.

Rowley, Samuel. *When You See Me, You Know Me*. London: Nathaniel Butter, 1605.

Sedgwick, Obadiah. *Haman's Vanity*. London: Samuel Gellibrand, 1643.

Shakespeare, William. *The Tempest*, in *Comedies, Tragedies, Histories*. London: William Jaggard and Edward Blount, 1623.

Shirley, John. *The Accomplished Ladies Rich Closet of Rarities*. London: Nicholas Boddington and Joseph Blare, 1690.

Slatyer, William. *The History of Great Britanie*. London: William Stansby, 1621.

Stow, John. *The Chronicles of England from Brute vnto This Present Yeare of Christ*. London: Ralph Newberry, 1580.

Swetnam, Joseph *The Schoole of the Noble and Worthy Science of Defence*. London: s. n., 1617.

T., A. *A Rich Store-House or Treasury for the Diseased*. London: Thomas Purfoot and Ralph Blower, 1596.

Tatham, John. *Londons Triumphs*. London: s. n., 1657.

Trigge, Francis. *To the Kings Most Excellent Maiestie. The Humble Petition of Two Sisters; the Church and Common Wealth*. London: George Bishop, 1604.

Vaughan, William. *Approved Directions for Health, both Naturall and Artificiall*. London: Roger Jackson, 1612.

Whitaker, Tobias. *The Tree of Humane Life, or, The Bloud of the Grape Proving the Possibilitie of Maintaining Humane Life from Infancy to Extreme Old Age without Any Sicknesse by the Use of Wine*. London: H. O., 1638.

Wilson, Robert. *A Right Excellent and Famous Comedy Called The Three Ladies of London*. London: s. n., 1592.

Wilson, Thomas. *A Discourse upon Usury*. London: s. n., 1572.

W., J. *The Valiant Scot*. London: John Waterson, 1637.

Wright, Thomas. *The Passions of the Minde in Generall*. 2nd ed. London: Walter Burre, 1604.

Secondary Sources and Editions

Adler, Joshua J. "The Hidden Message of the Book of Esther: Assimilation Is Not the Way to Salvation." *Jewish Bible Quarterly* 43, no. 4 (October–December 2015): 246–49.

Ahmed, Sara. *The Cultural Politics of Emotion.* 2nd ed. New York: Routledge, 2015.

Anderson, Perry. *Lineages of the Absolutist State.* London: Verso, 1974.

Anonymous. "Alex Salmond Calls on Cineworld to Show *Robert the Bruce* film." *National,* June 28, 2019.

Anonymous. "David Cameron 'Met Sony over *Outlander* UK Release.'" *Scotsman,* April 20, 2015.

Anonymous. "Esther." In *Engelische Comedien und Tragedien.* Vol. 1, edited by Manfred Brauneck, 3–77. Berlin: Walter de Gruyter, 1970.

Anonymous. "The First Charter of Virginia" (1606). Yale Law School: The Avalon Project, 2008.

Anonymous. *Mucedorus,* in *Elizabethan Plays, Revised Edition,* edited by Arthur H. Nethercott . Charles R. Baskervill, and Virgil B. Heltzel, 579–604. New York: Holt, Rinehart and Winston, 1971.

Anonymous. "Report to Edward I." In Stones, *Anglo-Scottish Relations 1174–1328,* 220–35.

Anonymous. "*Robert the Bruce*'s Angus Macfadyen Hopes Film Will Boost Independence Support." *Daily Record,* June 23, 2019.

Anonymous. "To the Most Holy Father Boniface." In Stones, *Anglo-Scottish Relations 1174–1328,* 192–219.

Anonymous. "Watch: *Robert the Bruce* Actor Angus Macfadyen Stars in Video Supporting Alba." *National,* April 12, 2021.

Archer, John Michael. *Citizen Shakespeare: Freemen and Aliens in the Language of the Plays.* New York: Palgrave Macmillan, 2005.

Ardolino, Frank. "Hans and Hammon: Dekker's Use of Hans Sachs and 'Purim' in *The Shoemaker's Holiday.*" *Medieval and Renaissance Drama in England* 14 (2001): 144–67.

———. "'Thus Glories England over All the West': Setting as National Encomium in *Friar Bacon and Friar Bungay.*" *Journal of Evolutionary Psychology* 9, nos. 3–4 (1988): 218–29.

Assmann, Jan. *Cultural Memory and Early Civilization: Writing, Remembrance, and Political Imagination.* Cambridge, UK: Cambridge University Press, 2011.

Bacon, Roger. *Opus Majus.* Edited by Robert Belle Burke. 2 vols. New York: Russell and Russell, 1962.

Baker, Christopher. "Sidney, Religious Syncretism, and *Henry VIII.*" *Studia Neophilologica* 86, no. 1 (2014): 17–36.

Baker, David J. "Time to Leave: Brexit and Politics of Chronology." In Baker and Palmer, *Early Modern Criticism in a Time of Crisis.* Web.

Baker, David J., and Patricia Palmer, eds. *Early Modern Criticism in a Time of Crisis.* Tome Pres, accessed February 13, 2024. Web.

Baldo, Jonathan. *Memory in Shakespeare's Histories: Stages of Forgetting in Early Modern England.* New York: Routledge, 2012.

Balibar, Etienne, and Immanuel Wallerstein. *Race, Nation, Class: Ambiguous Identities.* Translated by Chris Turner. New York: Verso, 2011.

Barnden, Sally. "'Never Did nor Never Shall': Shakespeare Quotation and the Nostalgic Politics in 2016." In Baker and Palmer, *Early Modern Criticism in a Time of Crisis.* Web.

Barroll, Leeds. *Politics, Plague, and Shakespeare's Theater*. Ithaca, NY: Cornell University Press, 1991.

Barthelemy, Anthony Gerard. *Black Face, Maligned Race: The Representation of Blacks in English Drama from Shakespeare to Southerne*. Baton Rouge: Louisiana State University Press, 1987.

Bartlett, Robert. *The Making of Europe: Conquest, Colonization, and Cultural Change, 950–1350*. Princeton: Princeton University Press, 1993.

Bartolovich, Crystal. "'Baseless Fabric': London as a 'World City.'" In *"The Tempest" and Its Travels*, edited by Peter Hulme and William H. Sherman, 13–26. Philadelphia: University of Pennsylvania Press, 2000.

Bastide, Roger. "Color, Racism, and Christianity." *Daedalus* 96, no. 2 (Spring 1967): 34–49.

Beal, Timothy K. *The Book of Hiding: Gender, Ethnicity, Annihilation, and Esther*. New York: Routledge, 1997.

Beel, David, Martin Jones, and Ian Rees Jones. "Introduction: Onward Devolution and City Regions." In *City Regions and Devolution in the UK*, 1–22.

Beel, David, Martin Jones, and Ian Rees Jones, eds. *City Regions and Devolution in the UK: The Politics of Representation*. Bristol: Bristol University Press, 2021.

Beer, Michelle L. "Brexit, the English Reformation, and Transnational Queenship." *Journal of the History of Ideas Blog*, February 20, 2019.

Bell, Derrick. *Faces at the Bottom of the Well: The Permanence of Racism*. New York: Basic Books, 1992.

Berberich, Christine. "BrexLit and the Marginalized Migrant." In *Brexit and Beyond: Nation and Identity*, edited by Daniela Keller and Ina Habermann, 167–82. Tübingen: Narr Francke, 2021.

Bergeron, David M. "Anthony Munday: Pageant Poet to the City of London." *Huntington Library Quarterly* 30, no. 4 (August 1967): 345–68.

———. *English Civic Pageantry 1558–1642*. London: Edward Arnold, 1971.

Bergeron, David M., Gary Taylor, and John Lavagnino, eds. *Thomas Middleton: The Collected Works*. Oxford: Clarendon Press, 2020.

Berlant, Lauren. "A Properly Political Concept of Love: Three Approaches in Ten Pages." *Cultural Anthropology* 26, no. 4 (2011): 683–91.

Berlin, Adele. *Esther: The Traditional Hebrew Text with the New JPS Translation/Commentary*. Philadelphia: Jewish Publication Society, 2001.

Bertram, Benjamin. *Bestial Oblivion: War, Humanism, and Ecology in Early Modern England*. New York: Routledge, 2018.

Blackburn, Ruth Harriett. *Biblical Drama under the Tudors*. The Hague: De Gruyter Mouton, 1971.

Blackham, Colonel Robert J. *The Soul of the City: London's Livery Companies. Their Storied Past, Their Living Present*. London: Sampson Low, Marston, 1932.

Blackwell, Anna. *Shakespearean Celebrity in the Digital Age: Fan Cultures and Remediation*. New York: Palgrave, 2018.

Blanks, David. "Europeans before Europe: Modernity and the Myth of the Other." In Kläger and Bayer, *Early Modern Constructions of Europe*, 27–40.

Bonilla-Silva, Eduardo. *Racism without Racists: Color-Blind Racism and the Persistence of Racial Inequality in America*. 4th ed. Lanham, MD: Rowman and Littlefield, 2014.

Borlik, Todd Andrew. "Building a Wall around Tudor England: Coastal Forts and Fantasies of Border Control in *Friar Bacon and Friar Bungay*." *Early Theatre* 22, no. 2 (2019): 79–100.

Bosman, Anston. "Renaissance Intertheater and the Staging of Nobody." *English Literary History* 71, no. 3 (Fall 2004): 559–85.

Brannigan, John. *New Historicism and Cultural Materialism*. New York: Bloomsbury, 2016.

Bray, Alan. *Homosexuality in Renaissance England*. New York: Columbia University Press, 1995.

Britton, Dennis Austin. *Becoming Christian: Race, Reformation, and Early Modern English Romance*. New York: Fordham University Press, 2014.

———. "Race and Renaissance Literature." In *Oxford Research Encyclopedia of Literature*, 1–20. Oxford: Oxford University Press, 2022.

Broadbent, R. J. "A Masque at Knowsley." *Transactions of the Historic Society of Lancashire and Cheshire for the Year 1925* 77 (1925): 1–16.

Brocklehurst, Steven. "Robert the Bruce Film Is the 'Birth of a Hero' Says Angus Macfadyen." BBC Scotland News, June 23, 2019. Web.

Bryant, Chris. "This Sceptic Isle Would Most Displease pro-Europe Shakespeare." *Guardian*, April 21, 2016.

Bunyasi, Tehama Lopez, and Candis Watts Smith. *Stay Woke: A People's Guide to Making All Black Lives Matter*. New York: NYU Press, 2019.

Burton, Robert. *The Anatomy of Melancholy*. Edited by Holbrook Jackson. New York: New York Review, 2001.

Cameron, Lucinda. "Robert the Bruce's Angus Macfadyen Hopes Film Will Boost Independence Support." *Daily Record*, June 23, 2019.

Campana, Joseph. "Introduction: After Sovereignty." *Studies in English Literature, 1500–1900* 58, no. 1 (Winter 2018): 1–21.

Campos, Edmund Valentine. "Jews, Spaniards, and Portingales: Ambiguous Identities of Portuguese Marranos in Elizabethan England." *English Literary History* 69, no. 3 (September 2002): 599–616.

CapX. "About." Web.

Carlson, Marvin. *The Haunted Stage: The Theater as Memory Machine*. Ann Arbor: University of Michigan Press, 2003.

Cheney, Patrick. "Career Rivalry and the Writing of Counter-Nationhood: Ovid, Spenser, and Philomela in Marlowe's 'The Passionate Shepherd to His Love." *English Literary History* 65, no. 3 (1998): 523–55.

Childs, David. *Tudor Sea Power: The Foundations of Greatness*. Barnsley, UK: Seaforth, 2009.

Chinca, Mark. "Biblical Drama." In *Encyclopedia of German Literature*, edited by Matthias Konzett, 100–3. Chicago: Fitzroy Dearborn, 2000.

Cipolla, Carlo. *Money, Prices, and Civilization in the Mediterranean World: Fifth to Seventeenth Century*. Princeton: Princeton University Press, 1956.

Clark, Rachel Ellen. "The Anti-Brexit *Cymbeline*." *Early Modern Culture* 12 (2017): 137–39.

Clarkson, L. A. *The Pre-Industrial Economy in England 1500–1750*. London: B. T. Batsford, 1971.

Claviez, Thomas. "A Critique of Authenticity and Recognition." In *Critique of Authenticity*, edited by Thomas Claviez, Kornelia Imesch, and Britta Sweers, 43–57. Wilmington, DE: Vernon Press, 2020.

Clegg, Brian. *Roger Bacon: The First Scientist*. London: Constable, 2003.

Cohn, Albrecht. *Shakespeare in Germany in the Sixteenth and Seventeenth Centuries*. London: Asher, 1865.

Connerton, Paul. "Seven Types of Forgetting." *Memory Studies* 1, no. 1 (January 2008): 59–71.

Connolly, Annaliese. "Peele's *David and Bethsabe*: Reconsidering Biblical Drama of the Long 1590s." *Early Modern Literary Studies* 16 (October 2007): 9.1–20.

Cooke, Jennifer. *Legacies of Plague in Literature, Theory and Film*. New York: Palgrave Macmillan, 2009.

Cooper, Frederick. *Colonialism in Question: Theory, Knowledge, History*. Berkeley: University of California Press, 2005.

Craig, Cairns. *The Wealth of the Nation: Scotland, Culture and Independence*. Edinburgh: Edinburgh University Press, 2017.

Crawford, Robert. *Bannockburns: Scottish Independence and the Literary Imagination, 1314–2014*. Edinburgh: Edinburgh University Press, 2014.

Crewe, Ivor. "Authoritarian Populism and Brexit in the UK in Historical Perspective." In *Authoritarian Populism and Liberal Democracy*, edited by Ivor Crewe and David Sanders, 15–31. New York: Palgrave, 2020.

Cull, Marisa R. *Shakespeare's Princes of Wales: English Identity and the Welsh Connection*. Oxford: Oxford University Press, 2014.

Curth, Louise Hill, and Tanya M. Cassidy. "'Health, Strength, and Happiness:' Medical Constructions of Wine and Beer in Early Modern England." In Smyth, *Pleasing Sinne*, 143–60.

Dainotto, Roberto M. *Europe (in Theory)*. Durham, NC: Duke University Press, 2007.

Davidson, Clifford. "Memory and Remembering: Sacred History and the York Plays." In *Staging Scripture*, edited by Peter Happé and Wim Hüsken, 334–59. Leiden: Brill, 2016.

Davies, Norman. *Europe: A History*. Oxford: Oxford University Press, 1996.

Dawson, Lesel. *Lovesickness and Gender in Early Modern English Literature*. Oxford: Oxford University Press, 2008.

Dekker, Thomas. *The Plague Pamphlets of Thomas Dekker*. Edited by F. P. Wilson. Reprint, Oxford: Clarendon Press, 1971.

Delanty, Gerard. *Inventing Europe: Idea, Identity, Reality*. London: Palgrave Macmillan, 1995.

den Boer, Pim. "Europe to 1914: The Making of an Idea." In *What Is Europe? The History of the Idea of Europe*, edited by Kevin Wilson and Jan van der Dussen, 13–82. New York: Routledge, 1993.

Dent, R. W. *Shakespeare's Proverbial Language*. Berkeley: University of California Press, 1981.

Derrida, Jacques. *L'animal que donc je suis*. Paris: Gallée, 2006.

———. *The Animal That Therefore I Am*. Edited by Marie Louise Mallet. Translated by David Wills. New York: Fordham University Press, 2008.

———. "Racism's Last Word." Translated by Peggy Kamuf. *Critical Inquiry*, 12, no. 1 (Autumn 1985): 290–99.

DiGangi, Mario. *Homoerotics of Early Modern Drama*. Cambridge, UK: Cambridge University Press, 1997.

Dorey, Peter. "Explaining Brexit: The 5 A's-Anomi, Alienation, Austerity, Authoritarianism and Atavism." *Revue Française de Civilisation Britannique: French Journal of British Studies* 27 (2022): 7–28.

Drayton, Michael. *The Works of Michael Drayton*. Edited by J. William Hebel. 5 vols. Oxford: Basil Blackwell, 1933.

Eaton, Barbara Louise. "Journey's End: A Theater History of Shakespeare's *Cymbeline*." PhD diss., University of Maryland at College Park, 1996.

Edelman, Lee. "Ever After: History, Negativity, and the Social." In *After Sex: On Writing Since Queer Theory*, edited by Janet Halley and Andrew Parker, 110–18. Durham, NC: Duke University Press, 2011.

———. *No Future: Queer Theory and the Death Drive*. Durham, NC: Duke University Press, 2004.

Eddo-Lodge, Reni. *Why I'm No Longer Talking to White People about Race*. London: Bloomsbury, 2018.

Ehrlich, David. "How David Mackenzie Salvaged *Outlaw King* after the Netflix Oscar Hopeful Crashed and Burned." IndieWire, November 8, 2018. Web.

Engle, Lars. "'Thrift Is Blessing': Exchange and Explanation in *The Merchant of Venice*." *Shakespeare Quarterly* 37, no. 1 (1986): 20–37.

En Vogue (Terry Ellis, Dawn Robinson, Cindy Herron, and Maxine Jones), vocalists. "Free Your Mind," by Denzil Foster and Thomas McElroy. Released March 24, 1992, track 4 on *Funky Divas* (Atlantic Records [East West division]).

Ephraim, Michelle. *Reading the Jewish Woman on the Elizabethan Stage*. Burlington, VT: Ashgate, 2008.

Erickson, Peter, and Kim F. Hall. "'A New Scholarly Song': Rereading Early Modern Race." *Shakespeare Quarterly* 67, no. 1 (Spring 2016): 1–13.

Escobedo, Andrew. *Nationalism and Historical Loss in Early Modern England*. Ithaca, NY: Cornell University Press, 2004.

Escolme, Bridget. "Brexit Dreams: Comedy, Nostalgia, and Critique in *Much Ado About Nothing* and *A Midsummer Night's Dream*." In *The Oxford Handbook of Shakespearean Comedy*, edited by Heather Hirschfield, 455–69. Oxford: Oxford University Press, 2018.

Evans, Richard J. "Breaking Up Is Hard to Do: Joining the European Union—and the Messy Business of Leaving It." *Times Literary Supplement*, November 27, 2020.

Fanon, Frantz. *Black Skin, White Masks*. New York: Grove Press, 2008.

Favell, Adrian. "Crossing the Race Line: 'No Polish, No Blacks, No Dogs' in Brexit Britain? Or, the Great British Brexit Swindle." In *Europe's Malaise: The Long View*, edited by Francesco Duina and Frédéric Merand, 103–30. Leeds: Emerald, 2020.

Fernie, Ewan. *Shame in Shakespeare*. New York: Routledge, 2002.

Ferrand, Jacques. *A Treatise on Lovesickness*, edited by Donald A. Beecher and Massimo Ciavollela. Syracuse, NY: Syracuse University Press, 1990.

Finkelstein, Richard. "Censorship and Forgiven Violence in *Mucedorus*." *Parergon* 17, no. 1 (July 1999): 89–108.

Fisher, Will. "Queer Money." *English Literary History* 66, no. 1 (Spring 1999): 1–23.

Fitter, Chris. "'So Distribution Should Undo Excess': Recovering the Political Pressure of Distributive and Egalitarian Discourses in Shakespeare's *King Lear* and Early Modern England." *English Literary History* 86, no. 4 (Winter 2019): 835–63.

Floyd-Wilson, Mary, and Garrett A. Sullivan, eds. *Environment and Embodiment in Early Modern England*. London: Palgrave Macmillan, 2007.

Foakes, R. A., ed. *Henslowe's Diary*. 2nd ed. Cambridge, UK: Cambridge University Press, 2002.

Ford, John. *The Lover's Melancholy*. Edited by R. F. Hill. Manchester, UK: Manchester University Press, 1985.

Frank, Birgit. *Assuerus und Esther am Burgunderhof: Zur Rezeption des Buches Esther in den Niederlanden (1450 bis 1530)*. Berlin: Gebr. Mann Verlag, 1998.

Freeman, Arthur. "Marlowe, Kyd and the Dutch Church Libel." *English Literary Renaissance* 3, no. 1 (Winter 1973): 44–52.

Freire, Paolo. *Pedagogy of Freedom: Ethics, Democracy, and Civic Courage*. Lanham, MD: Rowman and Littlefield, 1998.

Fung, Katherine. "Geraldo Rivera: Trayvon Martin's 'Hoodie Is as Much Responsible for [His] Death as George Zimmerman.'" HuffPost, March 23, 2012. Web.

Galbraith, David. *Architectonics of Imitation in Spenser, Daniel, and Drayton*. Toronto: University of Toronto Press, 2000.

George, David, ed. *Records of Early English Drama: Lancashire*. Toronto: University of Toronto Press, 1991.

Gerzic, Marina. "Broadcasting the Political Body: *Richard III*, #Brexit and #Libspill." *Shakespeare Bulletin* 38, no. 1 (Spring 2021): 109–29.

Ginzburg, Carlo. *No Island Is an Island: Four Glances at English Literature in a World Perspective*. New York: Columbia University Press, 2000.

Goitein, S. D. *Bible Studies*. Tel Aviv: Yavney, 1957.

Goldberg, Jonathan. *Sodometries: Renaissance Texts, Modern Sexualities*. Stanford: Stanford University Press, 1992.

Goldsmith, Robert Hillis. "The Wild Man on the English Stage." *Modern Language Review* 53, no. 4 (October 1958): 481–91.

Goodblatt, Chanita. *Jewish and Christian Voices in English Reformation Biblical Drama: Enacting Family and Monarchy*. New York: Routledge, 2018.

Goodridge, Leah. "Professionalism as a Racial Construct." *UCLA Law Review (Law Meets World)* 38 (2022): 40–54.

Grabes, Herbert. "'Elect Nation': The Founding Myth of National Identity in Early Modern England." In *Writing the Early Modern English Nation*, edited by Herbert Grabes, 173–89. Leiden: Brill, 2001.

Grant, Mark. *Galen on Food and Diet*. London: Routledge, 2000.

Gray, Patrick. "Choosing between Shame and Guilt: *Macbeth*, *Othello*, *Hamlet*, and *King Lear*." In *Shakespeare and the Soliloquy in Early Modern English Drama*, edited by A. D. Cousins and Daniel Derrin, 105–18. Cambridge, UK: Cambridge University Press, 2018.

Gray, Richard, dir. *Robert the Bruce*. 2019; Edinburgh: Yellow Brick Films. Hulu.

Greenblatt, Stephen. "What Shakespeare Actually Wrote about the Plague." *New Yorker*, May 7, 2020.

Greenblatt, Stephen, and Catherine Gallagher. *Practicing New Historicism*. Chicago: University of Chicago Press, 2000.

Greene, Jody. "You Must Eat Men: The Sodomitic Economy of Renaissance Patronage." *GLQ* 2, no. 1 (1994): 163–97.

Greene, Robert. *Friar Bacon and Friar Bungay*. Edited by J. A. Levin. London: Ernest Benn, 1969.

———. *Friar Bacon and Friar Bungay*. Edited by Christopher Matusiak. Queen's Men Editions, University of Victoria, 2019. Web.

———. *Friar Bacon and Friar Bungay*. Edited by Daniel Seltzer. Lincoln: University of Nebraska Press, 1963.

Greenfeld, Liah. *Nationalism: Five Roads to Modernity*. Cambridge, MA: Harvard University Press, 1995.

Greenstadt, Amy. "The Kindest Cut: Circumcision and Queer Kinship in *The Merchant of Venice*." *English Literary History* 80, no. 4 (Winter 2013): 946–80.

————. "Strange Insertions in *The Merchant of Venice.*" In *Queer Shakespeare: Desire and Sexuality*, edited by Goran Stanivukovic, 197–226. London: Bloomsbury, 2017.

Habib, Imtiaz. *Black Lives in the English Archives, 1500–1677.* Farnham, UK: Ashgate, 2008.

Habib, Imtiaz, and Duncan Salkeld. "The Reasonables of Boroughside, Southwark: An Elizabethan Black Family near the Rose Theatre." *Shakespeare* 11, no. 2 (2015): 1–22.

Hadfield, Andrew. *Literature, Politics, and National Identity: Reformation to Renaissance.* Cambridge, UK: Cambridge University Press, 1994.

Haekel, Ralf. *Die Englischen Komödianten in Deutschland: Eine Einführung in die Ursprünge des deutschen Berufsschauspiels.* Heidelberg: Universitätsverlag Winter, 2004.

Hale, John [Rigby]. *The Civilization of Europe in the Renaissance.* New York: Scribner, 1994.

————. *War and Society in Renaissance Europe, 1450–1620.* Baltimore: Johns Hopkins University Press, 1985.

Hall, Kim F. "Guess Who's Coming to Dinner? Colonization and Miscegenation in *The Merchant of Venice.*" *Renaissance Drama* 23 (1992): 87–111.

————. *Things of Darkness: Economies of Race and Gender in Early Modern England.* Ithaca, NY: Cornell University Press, 1995.

Hames, Scott. *The Literary Politics of Scottish Devolution: Voice, Class, Nation.* Edinburgh: Edinburgh University Press, 2019.

————. "Spitfire Britain and the Zombie Union." *Drouth.* November 16, 2020.

Hannan, Daniel. "How Like a God: Shakespeare and the Invention of the World." CapX. April 23, 2016. Web.

Hannan, Martin. "Cineworld 'Offered Robert the Bruce Film' but Didn't Answer." *National,* June 29, 2019.

Hariot, Thomas. "A Brief and True Report of the New Found Land of Virginia." Edited by Paul Royster. *Electronic Texts in American Studies* 20 (2007): 1–57.

Harrington, Peter. *The Castles of Henry VIII.* Oxford: Osprey, 2007.

Harris, Fredrick C. "The Rise of Respectability Politics." *Dissent* (Winter 2014): no pagination. Web.

Hawkes, David. *The Culture of Usury in Renaissance England.* New York: Palgrave Macmillan, 2010.

Haworth, Ben. "Play Review: *The Revenger's Tragedy.*" *Cahiers Élisabéthains* 92, no. 1 (April 2017): 105–7.

Hay, Denys. *Europe: The Emergence of an Idea.* Edinburgh: Edinburgh University Press, 1957.

Heath, John Benjamin. *Some Account of the Worshipful Company of Grocers of the City of London.* London: W. Marchant, 1829.

Hénaff, Marcel. *The Price of Truth: Gift, Money, and Philosophy.* Translated by Jean-Louis Morhange and Anne-Marie Feenberg-Dibon. Stanford: Stanford University Press, 2010.

Heng, Geraldine. *The Invention of Race in the European Middle Ages.* New York: Cambridge University Press, 2018.

Heinemann, Margot. "Demystifying the Mystery of State." *Shakespeare Survey* 44 (1992): 75–83.

————. *Puritanism and Theatre: Thomas Middleton and Opposition Drama under the Early Stuarts.* Cambridge, UK: Cambridge University Press, 1980.

Helgerson, Richard. "The Buck Basket, the Witch, and the Queen of Fairies: The Women's World of Shakespeare's Windsor." In *Renaissance Culture and the Everyday*, edited by

Patricia Fumerton and Simon Hunt, 162–82. Philadelphia: University of Pennsylvania Press, 1999.

———. *Forms of Nationhood: The Elizabethan Writing of England.* Chicago: University of Chicago Press, 1992.

Hendricks, Margo. "Coloring the Past, Considerations on Our Future: RaceB4Race." *New Literary History* 52, nos. 2 and 3 (Summer–Autumn 2021): 365–84.

———. "Race: A Renaissance Category?" In *A New Companion to English Renaissance Literature,* edited by Michael Hattaway, 690–98. New York: Blackwell, 2003.

Henke, Robert, and Eric Nicholson, "Introduction." In *Transnational Mobilities in Early Modern Theater,* edited by Robert Henke and Eric Nicholson, 1–20. Burlington, VT: Ashgate, 2014.

Higgins, Katie W. "National Belonging Post-Referendum: Britons Living in Other EU Member States Respond to 'Brexit.'" *Area* 51, no. 2 (2019): 277–84.

Higson, Andrew. *Film England: Culturally English Filmmaking since the 1990s.* New York: Palgrave, 2011.

———. *Waving the Flag: Constructing a National Cinema in Britain.* 2nd ed. Oxford: Oxford University Press, 1997.

Hindle, Steve. *The State and Social Change in Early Modern England, c. 1550–1640.* New York: St. Martin's Press, 2000.

Hill, Christopher. *Puritanism and Revolution.* New York: Schocken Books, 1964.

———. *Society and Puritanism in Pre-Revolutionary England.* Harmondsworth: Penguin, 1986.

Hill, Thomas D. "The Rod of Protection and the Witches' Ride: Christian and Germanic Syncretism in Two Old English Metrical Charms." *Journal of English and Germanic Philology* 111, no. 2 (April 2012): 145–68.

Hill, Tracey. *Pageantry and Power: A Cultural History of the Early Modern Lord Mayor's Show 1585–1639.* New York: Manchester University Press, 2010.

Hirsch, Afua. "We Have to Avoid 'Integration' Becoming Another Form of Racism." *Guardian,* September 13, 2019.

Hiscock, Andrew. *Shakespeare, Violence and Early Modern Europe.* Cambridge, UK: Cambridge University Press, 2022.

Hochschild, Arlie Russell. "The Managed Heart: Commercialization of Human Feeling." In *The Production of Reality: Essays and Readings on Social Interaction,* edited by Jodi O'Brien, 320–24. Thousand Oaks, CA: Pine Forge Press, 2010.

Hoenselaars, A. J. *Images of Englishmen and Foreigners in the Drama of Shakespeare and His Contemporaries.* London: Associated University Press, 1992.

Hopkins, Lisa. "*Cymbeline,* Presented by the Royal Shakespeare Company at the Royal Shakespeare Theatre, Stratford-upon-Avon, 2016." *Early Modern Literary Studies* 19, no. 1 (2016): no pagination. Web.

———. "Profit and Delight?: Magic and the Dreams of a Nation." In *Magical Transformations on the Early Modern English Stage,* edited by Lisa Hopkins and Helen Ostovich, 139–54. Aldershot: Ashgate, 2014.

Howard, Jean E. *The Stage and Social Struggle in Early Modern England.* London: Routledge, 1994.

Hughes, Charles, ed. *Shakespeare's Europe: A Survey of the Condition of Europe at the End of the 16th Century. Being Unpublished Chapters of Fynes Moryson's Itinerary (1617).* New York: Benjamin Blom, 1967.

Hutchings, Mark, and A. A. Bromham. *Middleton and His Collaborators*. Liverpool: Liverpool University Press, 2007.

Hutson, Lorna. *The Usurer's Daughter: Male Friendship and Fictions of Women in Sixteenth-Century England*. London: Routledge, 1994.

Hyland, Peter. "Scare Bear: Playing with *Mucedorus*." In *Shaping Shakespeare for Performance: The Bear Stage*, edited by Catherine Loomis and Sid Ray, 203–12. Madison, NJ: Fairleigh Dickinson University Press, 2016.

Jenstad, Janelle, ed. *The Triumphs of Truth: The Map of Early Modern London*, 7th edition. Victoria: University of Victoria, 2022.

Introna, Arianna. "Nationed Silences, Interventions and (Dis)Engagements: Brexit and the Politics of Contextualism in Post-Indyref Scottish Literature." *Open Library of Humanities* 6 (2020): 1–31.

Isin, Engin. *Being Political: Genealogies of Citizenship*. Minneapolis: University of Minnesota Press, 2002.

———. *Cities without Citizens*. Montreal: Black Rose Books, 1992.

Islentyeva, Anna. "National Myth in UK-EU Representations by British Conservative Prime Ministers from Churchill to Johnson." *Societies* 12, no. 1 (January 2022): 1–17.

Jackson, Ellen-Raïssa. "Dislocating the Nation: Political Devolution and Cultural Identity on Stage and Screen." In *Reflections on Culture and Literature*, edited by Eleanor Bell and Gavin Miller, 107–20. New York: Rodopi, 2004.

Janssen, Geert H. "The Republic of the Refugees: Early Modern Migrations and the Dutch Experience." *Historical Journal* 60, no. 1 (March 2017): 233–52.

Jensen, Lotte Jensen, ed. *The Roots of Nationalism: National Identity Formation in Early Modern Europe, 1600–1815*. Amsterdam: University of Amsterdam Press, 2016.

Johnson, H. R. "The Problem of the Counter-National Sensibility and Its Critics." *California Studies in Classical Antiquity* 3 (1970): 123–51.

Jones, John Henry, ed. *The English Faust Book: A Critical Edition Based on the Text of 1592*. Cambridge, UK: Cambridge University Press, 1994.

Jordan, Robert. "Myth and Psychology in *The Changeling*." *Renaissance Drama* 3 (1970): 157–65.

Jowett, John, ed. *Sir Thomas More*. London: Methuen, 2011.

Karim-Cooper, Farah. "The Materials of Race: Staging the Black and White Binary in the Early Modern Theatre." In Thompson, *Cambridge Companion to Shakespeare and Race*, 17–29.

Karremann, Isabel. *The Drama of Memory in Shakespeare's History Plays*. Cambridge, UK: Cambridge University Press, 2015.

Kaethler, Mark. "Walking with Vigilance: Middleton's Edge in *The Triumphs of Truth*." *Early Theatre* 24, no. 2 (2021): 73–98.

Kathman, David. "Grocers, Goldsmiths, and Drapers: Freemen and Apprentices in the Elizabethan Theater." *Shakespeare Quarterly* 55, no. 1 (2004): 1–49.

Katritzky, M. A. "'A Plague o' These Pickle Herring': From London Drinkers to European Stage Clown." In *Renaissance Shakespeare/Shakespeare Renaissances: Proceedings of the Ninth World Shakespeare Congress*, 159–68. Newark: University of Delaware Press, 2014.

———. *Women, Medicine and Theatre 1500–1750*. New York: Routledge, 2017.

Katz, Bruce. "Manchester, England: Devolution U.K. Style." *Brookings* (blog), November 6, 2014.

Katz, Bruce, and Alex C. Jones. "How 'New Localism' Is Democratizing Urban Growth." *Brookings* (blog), June 14, 2016.

———. "Where Does Brexit Leave UK Cities?" *Brookings* (blog), June 24, 2016.

Katz, Bruce, and Jeremy Nowak. *The New Localism: How Cities Can Thrive in the Age of Populism*. Washington, DC: Brookings Institution Press, 2018.

Kearney, James. "'This Is above All Strangeness': *King Lear*, Ethics and the Phenomenology of Recognition." *Criticism* 54, no. 3 (Summer 2012): 455–67.

Kerrigan, John. *Archipelagic English Literature, History, and Politics 1603–1707*. Oxford: Oxford University Press, 2008.

Kerrison, Erin M., Jennifer Cobbina, and Kimberly Bender. "'Your Pants Won't Save You': Why Black Youth Challenge Race-Based Police Surveillance and the Demands of Black Respectability Politics." *Race and Justice* 8, no. 1 (2017), 7–26.

Killeen, Kevin. "Hanging up Kings: The Political Bible in Early Modern England." *Journal of the History of Ideas* 72 (October 2011): 549–70.

Kirwan, Peter. "*The Merry Wives of Windsor* (RSC/Live from Stratford-upon-Avon) @ Broadway, Nottingham." *Bardathon* (blog), University of Nottingham, September 13, 2018).

Kitzes, Adam H. *The Politics of Melancholy from Spenser to Milton*. London: Routledge, 2006.

Kläger, Florian, and Gerd Bayer. "Introduction: Early Modern Constructions of Europe." In *Early Modern Constructions of Europe*, 1–23.

Kläger, Florian, and Gerd Bayer, eds. *Early Modern Constructions of Europe: Literature, Culture, History*. New York: Routledge, 2018

Knapp, Jeffrey. *An Empire Nowhere: England, America and Literature, from "Utopia" to "The Tempest."* Berkeley: University of California Press, 1992.

———. *Shakespeare's Tribe*. Chicago: University of Chicago Press, 2002.

Knutson, Roslyn. "A Caliban in St. Mildred Poultry." In *The Selected Proceedings of the International Shakespeare Association World Congress Tokyo 1991*, edited by Tetsuo Kishi et al., 110–26. Newark: University of Delaware Press, 1994.

Kolb, Laura. *Fictions of Credit in the Age of Shakespeare*. Oxford: Oxford University Press, 2021.

Kunkel, Benjamin. "The Capitalocene." *London Review of Books*, March 2, 2017.

Laird, Fiona. "Political Responsibility in the Age of Brexit." CapX, July 16, 2016. Web.

Lamis, Alexander. "Exclusive: Lee Atwater's Infamous 1981 Interview on the Southern Strategy." *Nation*. YouTube, November 13, 2012.

Lanchester, John. "As the Lock Rattles," *London Review of Books*, December 16, 2021.

Lanvers, Ursula, Hannah Doughty, and Amy S. Thompson. "Brexit as Linguistic Symptom of Britain Retreating into Its Shell? Brexit-Induced Politicization of Language Learning." *Modern Language Journal* 201, no. 4 (Winter 2018): 775–96.

Lee, Maurice. *The Road to Revolution: Scotland under Charles I, 1625–1637*. Urbana: University of Illinois Press, 1985.

Leith, Murray Stewart. "Scottish National Party Representations of Scottishness and Scotland." *Politics* 28 (2008): 83–92.

Levin, Carole, and John Watkins. *Shakespeare's Foreign Worlds: National and Transnational Identities in the Elizabethan Age*. Ithaca, NY: Cornell University Press, 2008.

Lipsiz, George. "The Sounds of Silence: How Race Neutrality Preserves White Supremacy." In *Seeing Race Again: Countering Colorblindness across the Disciplines*, edited by Kimberlé W. Crenshaw et al. Oakland: University of California Press, 2019. 23–51.

Little, Arthur L., Jr. "Introduction: Assembling an Aristocracy of Skin." In *White People in Shakespeare: Essays on Race, Culture, and the Elite*, edited by Arthur L. Little Jr., 1–28. London: Bloomsbury, 2023.

———. "Is It Possible to Read Shakespeare through Critical White Studies." In Thompson, *Cambridge Companion to Shakespeare and Race*, 268–80.

Loomba, Ania. "Introduction to *The Triumphs of Honour and Virtue*." In *Thomas Middleton: The Collected Works*, edited by Gary Taylor and John Lavagnino, 1714–18. Oxford: Clarendon Press, 2000.

Louthan, Howard. *The Quest for Compromise: Peacemakers in Counter-Reformation Vienna*. Cambridge, UK: Cambridge University Press, 1997.

Love, Heather K. "Emotional Rescue." In *Gay Shame*, edited by David M. Halperin and Valerie Traub, 31–52. Chicago: University of Chicago Press, 2009.

Luckett, Thomas M. "Imaginary Currency and Real Guillotines: The Intellectual Origins of the Financial Terror in France." *Historical Reflections / Réflexions Historiques* 31, no. 1 (Spring 2005): 117–39.

Lund, Mary Ann. *Melancholy, Medicine and Religion in Early Modern England*. Cambridge, UK: Cambridge University Press, 2010.

Lupton, Julia Reinhard. *Citizen-Saints: Shakespeare and Political Theology*. Chicago: University of Chicago Press, 2005.

Luu, Lien Bich. "Assimilation or Segregation: Colonies of Alien Craftsmen in Elizabethan London." In *The Strangers' Progress: Integration and Disintegration of the Huguenot and Walloon Refugee Community, 1567–1889, Essays in Memory of Irene Scouloudi*, edited by Randolph Vigne and G. Gibbs, 160–72. London: Huguenot Society of Great Britain and Ireland, 1995.

Lyne, Raphael. *Memory and Intertextuality in Renaissance Literature*. Cambridge, UK: Cambridge University Press, 2016.

Mackenzie, David, dir.. *The Outlaw King*. 2018; Toronto: Sigma Film. Netflix.

Magnus, Laury. "Michael Radford's *The Merchant of Venice* and the Vexed Questions of Performance." *Literature/Film Quarterly* 35, no. 2 (April 2007): 108–20.

Major, John. *A History of Greater Britain, as Well England as Scotland . . . 1521*. Translated by Archibald Constable. Edinburgh: Edinburgh University Press, 1892.

Majumdar, Nivedita. *The World in a Grain of Sand. Postcolonial Literature and Radical Universalism*. London: Verso, 2021.

Mandhai, Shafik. "Protests in UK against Post-Brexit Racism." *Al Jazeera*, March 18, 2017.

Manley, Lawrence, and Sally-Beth MacLean. *Lord Strange's Men and Their Plays*. New Haven, CT: Yale University Press, 2014.

Manning, Roger B. *Swordsmen: The Martial Ethos in the Three Kingdoms*. Oxford: Oxford University Press, 2003.

Mardell, Mark. "Brexit: The Story of an Island Apart." *BBC Magazine*, June 25, 2016.

Marks, Thomas. "Singing Repentance in Lutheran Germany during the Thirty Years War (1618–1648)." *Music and Letters* 103, no. 2 (May 2022): 226–63.

Marlowe, Christopher. *Doctor Faustus*. Edited by David Bevington and Eric Rasmussen. Manchester, UK: Manchester University Press, 1993.

———. *Tamburlaine*. Edited by J. S. Cunningham. Manchester, UK: Manchester University Press, 1999.

Mason, Roger. "Scotching the Brut: Politics, History and National Myth in Sixteenth-Century

Britain." In *Scotland and England, 1286–1815*, edited by Roger Mason, 60–84. Edinburgh: John Donald, 1987.

Massumi, Brian. *Politics of Affect*. Cambridge, UK: Polity, 2015.

Masten, Jeffrey. *Queer Philologies: Sex, Language, and Affect in Shakespeare's Time*. Philadelphia: University of Pennsylvania Press, 2016.

Mattingly, Garrett. *The Armada*. Boston: Houghton Mifflin, 1988.

Maus, Katharine Eisaman. *Inwardness and Theater in the English Renaissance*. Chicago: University of Chicago Press, 1995.

Maynard, Robyn. *Policing Black Lives: State Violence in Canada from Slavery to the Present*. Halifax: Fernwood, 2017.

McAdam, Ian. "Eucharistic Love in *The Merchant of Venice*." *Renaissance and Reformation / Renaissance et Réforme* 38, no. 1 (Winter 2015): 83–116.

McEachern, Claire. *The Poetics of English Nationhood, 1590–1612*. Cambridge, UK: Cambridge University Press, 1996.

McEwen, Nicola. "Brexit and Scotland: Between Two Unions." *British Politics* 13 (2018): 65–78.

McKeown, Adam. *Fortification and Its Discontents: Shakespeare to Milton*. London: Routledge, 2019.

———. "Walled Borders and the Geography of Power in Henrician Prose." *English Literary Renaissance* 48, no. 2 (Spring 2018): 121–35.

McMillin, Scott, and Sally-Beth MacLean. *The Queen's Men and Their Plays*. Cambridge, UK: Cambridge University Press, 1998.

McNeill, William H. "The Plague of Plagues." Review of *The Black Death: Natural and Human Disaster in Medieval Europe* by Robert S. Gottfried. *New York Review of Books*, July 21, 1983.

Melhuish, Francesca. "Euroscepticism, Anti-Nostalgic Nostalgia and the Past Perfect Post-Brexit Future." *Journal of Common Market Studies* 60, no. 6 (November 2022): 1758–76.

Mendelsohn, Everett. *Heat and Life: The Development of the Theory of Animal Heat*. Cambridge, MA: Harvard University Press, 1964.

Middleton, Thomas, and Anthony Munday. *The Triumphs of Truth*. In *Thomas Middleton: The Collected Works*, edited by David M. Bergeron, Gary Taylor, and John Lavagnino, 411–18. Oxford: Clarendon Press, 2020.

Mikkeli, Heikki. *Europe as an Idea and an Identity*. Basingstoke, UK: Macmillan, 1998.

Miles, Johnny. "Reading Esther as Heroine: Persian Banquets, Ethnic Cleansing, and Identity Crisis." *Biblical Theology Bulletin* 45, no. 3 (August 2015): 131–43.

Moore, C. A. *Esther*. Garden City, NY: Doubleday, 1971.

Morris, Ian. *Geography Is Destiny: Britain and the World: A 10,000-Year History*. New York: Farrar, Straus and Giroux, 2022.

Moss, Jonathan, Emily Robinson, and Jake Watts. "Brexit and the Everyday Politics of Emotion: Methodological Lessons from History." *Political Studies* 68, no. 4 (November 2020): 837–56.

Motoko, Hori. "The Price and Quality of Wine and Conspicuous Consumption in England 1646–1759." *English Historical Review* 123, no. 505 (December 2008): 1457–69.

Mullaney, Steven. "Affective Technologies: Toward and Emotional Logic of the Elizabethan Stage." In Floyd-Wilson and Sullivan, *Environment and Embodiment*, 71–89.

Müller, Johannes. *Exile Memories and the Dutch Revolt: The Narrated Diaspora, 1550–1750.* Leiden: Brill, 2016.

Müller-Wille, Staffan. "Claude Lévi-Strauss on Race, History, and Genetics." *Biosocieties* 5, no. 3 (September 2010): 330–47.

Munro, Robert. "Performing the National? Scottish Cinema in the Time of Indyref." *Journal of British Cinema and Television* 17 (2020): 425–48.

Munt, Sally R. *Queer Attachments: The Cultural Politics of Shame.* Burlington, VT: Ashgate, 2007.

Musolff, Andrea. "Hostility towards Immigrants' Languages in Britain: A Backlash against 'Super-Diversity'?" *Journal of Multilingual and Multicultural Development* 40, no. 3 (2019): 257–66.

Nairn, Tom. *The Break-Up of Britain: Crisis and Neo-Nationalism.* London: Verso, 1977.

Nardizzi, Vin. *Wooden Os: Shakespeare's Theatres and England's Trees.* Toronto: University of Toronto Press, 2013.

Nederman, Cary J. "Mechanics and Citizens: The Reception of the Aristotelian Idea of Citizenship in Late Medieval Europe." *Vivarium* 40, no. 1 (2002): 75–102.

Negas, Tina. "Medieval Foliate Heads: A Photographic Study of Green Men and Green Beasts in Britain." *Folklore* 114, no. 2 (August 2003): 247–61.

Neumann, Maike. *Buß- und Bettage: Geschichtliche Entwicklung–aktuelle Situation— Bedingungen für eine erneuerte Praxis.* Göttingen: Neukirchen-Vluyn, 2011.

Nicholl, Charles. *The Reckoning: The Murder of Christopher Marlowe.* London: Harcourt Brace, 1994.

Nicol, David. *Middleton and Rowley: Forms of Collaboration in the Jacobean Playhouse.* Toronto: University of Toronto Press, 2018.

Noble, Louise. *Medicinal Cannibalism in Early Modern English Literature and Culture.* New York: Palgrave Macmillan, 2011.

Norris, Pippa, and Ronald Inglehart. *Cultural Backlash: Trump, Brexit, and Authoritarian Populism.* Cambridge, UK: Cambridge University Press, 2019.

Oakeshott, Ewart. *European Weapons and Armour from the Renaissance to the Industrial Revolution.* Woodbridge, UK: Boydell Press, 2014.

Oates, Joyce Carol. "My Therapy Animal and Me: Identity and Companionship in Isolation." *Times Literary Supplement,* May 15, 2020.

Oates, Rosamund. "Brexit to Bonfire Night: Why the Reformation Still Matters." *Conversation,* October 31, 2017.

Obama, Barack. "Obama: If I Had a Son He'd Look Like Trayvon Martin." YouTube. March 23, 2012.

Oberman, Heiko. *John Calvin and the Reformation of the Refugees.* Geneva: Librairie Droz, 2010.

O'Callaghan, Michelle. "Tavern Societies, the Inns of Court, and the Culture of Conviviality in Early Seventeenth Century London." In Smyth, *Pleasing Sinne,* 37–51.

O'Keeffe, Christopher. "Edinburgh 2019: ROBERT THE BRUCE Himself Angus MacFadyen and Director Richard Gray Discuss the Return of the Scottish King." *Screen Anarchy,* July 8, 2019.

Oldenburg, Scott. *A Weaver-Poet and the Plague.* University Park: Pennsylvania State University Press, 2020.

O'Neill, Stephen. "Finding Refuge in *King Lear:* From Brexit to Shakespeare's European Value." *Multicultural Shakespeare: Translation, Appropriation, and Performance* 19 (2019): 119–38.

———. "Shakespeare's 'Hand,' or 'the Stranger's Case.' Remediating *Sir Thomas More* in the Context of the Refugee Crisis." *Borrowers and Lenders: The Journal of Shakespeare and Appropriation* 13, no. 1 (April 2020): no pagination. Web.

Oppitz-Trotman, George. *Stages of Loss: The English Comedians and Their Reception.* Oxford: Oxford University Press, 2020.

Ormrod, W. Mark. "England's Immigrants, 1330–1550: Aliens in Later Medieval and Early Tudor England." *Journal of British Studies* 59 (2020): 245–63.

Ostovich, Helen, Holger Syme, and Andrew Griffin, eds. *Locating the Queen's Men 1583– 1603: Material Practice and Conditions of Playing.* Farnham, UK: Ashgate, 2009.

Otele, Olivette. *African Europeans: An Untold History.* New York: Basic Books, 2021.

O'Toole, Fintan. *Heroic Failure: Brexit and the Politics of Pain.* London: Head of Zeus, 2018.

Otto, Walter F. *Dionysus: Myth and Cult.* Translated by Robert B. Palmer. Dallas: Spring Publications, 1965.

Outland, Allison. "Ridden with a Welsh Goat: Parson Evans' Correction of Windsor's English Condition." *English Literary Renaissance* 41, no. 2 (Spring 2011): 301–31.

Paris, Jamie. "'Mislike Me Not for My Complexion': On Anti-Black Racism and Performative Whiteness in William Shakespeare's *The Merchant of Venice.*" *Journal for Early Modern Cultural Studies* 20, no. 4 (Fall 2020): 34–61.

Paster, Gail Kern. *The Body Embarrassed: Drama and Disciplines of Shame in Early Modern England.* Ithaca, NY: Cornell University Press, 1993.

———. *Humoring the Body: Emotions and the Shakespearean Stage.* Chicago: University of Chicago Press, 2004.

Pepys, Samuel. *The Diary of Samuel Pepys.* Edited by Robert Latham and William Matthews. London: Bell, 1970–83.

Petherick, Sam. "Synagogue Flooded with Thousands of Donations for Newly Arrived Afghan Refugees." *Metro UK*, August 23, 2021.

Pettegree, Andrew. *Foreign Protestant Communities in Sixteenth-Century London.* Oxford: Clarendon Press, 1986.

———. "'Thirty Years On': Progress toward Integration amongst the Immigrant Population of Elizabethan London." In *English Rural Society, 1500–1800: Essays in Honour of Joan Thirsk*, edited by John Chartres and David Hey, 297–12. Cambridge, UK: Cambridge University Press, 1990.

Pitcher, John. "'Fronted with the Sight of a Bear': *Cox of Collumpton* and *The Winter's Tale.*" *Notes and Queries* 41, no.1 (March 1994): 47–53.

Pittman, L. Monique. *Shakespeare's Contested Nations: Race, Gender, and Multicultural Britain in Performances of the History Plays.* London: Routledge, 2022.

Power, Amanda. *Roger Bacon and the Defence of Christendom.* Cambridge, UK: Cambridge University Press, 2013.

Puar, Jasbir K. *Terrorist Assemblages: Homonationalism in Queer Times.* Durham, NC: Duke University Press, 2007.

Puttenham, George. *The Art of English Poesy: A Critical Edition.* Edited by Frank Whigham and Wayne A. Rebhorn. Ithaca, NY: Cornell University Press, 2007.

Quarmby, Kevin A. "Little Did We Know." *Scene* 3, no. 1 (2019): no pagination. Web.

Rackin, Phyllis. *Stages of History: Shakespeare's English Chronicles.* Ithaca, NY: Cornell University Press, 1990.

Rappaport, Steve. *Worlds within Worlds: Structures of Life in Sixteenth-Century London.* Cambridge, UK: Cambridge University Press, 2002.

Ravelhofer, Barbara. "Henslowe's White Bears." *English Literary Renaissance* 32, no. 2 (Spring 2002): 287–323.

Reynolds, Bryan, and Henry S. Turner. "From *Homo Academicus* to *Poeta Publicus*: Celebrity and Transversal Knowledge in Robert Greene's *Friar Bacon and Friar Bungay* (c. 1589)." In *Writing Robert Greene: Essays on England's First Notorious Professional Writer*, edited by Kirk Melnikoff and Edward Gieskes, 73–94. Aldershot: Ashgate, 2008.

Riech, Alan. "Duncan Petrie, *Screening Scotland*." *Metro Magazine* 137 (2003): 171–74.

Roach, Joseph. "History, Memory, Necrophilia." In *The Ends of Performance*, edited by Peggy Phelan and Jill Lane, 23–30. New York: New York University Press, 1998.

Roberts, Jeanne Addison. "Falstaff in Windsor Forest: Villain or Victim?" *Shakespeare Quarterly* 26 (1975): 8–15.

Rooney, Tom. "Who 'Plaid' the Bear in *Mucedorus*?" *Notes and Queries* 54, no. 3 (September 2007): 259–62.

Rorty, Richard. *Contingency, Irony, and Solidarity*. Cambridge, UK: Cambridge University Press, 1989.

Rose, Jacqueline. "To Die One's Own Death: Jacqueline Rose on Freud and His Daughter." *London Review of Books*, November 19, 2020.

Ross, Cheryl Lynn. "The Plague of *The Alchemist*." *Renaissance Quarterly* 41, no. 3 (Autumn 1988): 439–58.

Rowley, William. *A Critical Old-Spelling Edition of "The Birth of Merlin" (Q 1662)*. Edited by Joanna Udall. London: MHRA, 1991.

Rummel, Erika. "The Theology of Erasmus." In *The Cambridge Companion to Reformation Theology*, edited by David Bagchi and David C. Steinmetz, 28–38. Cambridge, UK: Cambridge University Press, 2004.

Rutter, Tom. *Shakespeare and the Admiral's Men: Reading across Repertories on the London Stage*. Cambridge, UK: Cambridge University Press, 2017.

Ryan, Kiernan. *Shakespearean Tragedy*. London: Bloomsbury, 2021.

Sacks, Jonathan. "Refugee Crisis: 'Love the Stranger because You Were Once Strangers' Calls Us Now." *Observer*, September 6, 2015.

Sager, Jenny. "'Exchange Is No Robbery': Hospitality and Hostility in Robert Greene's *Friar Bacon and Friar Bungay* and *John of Bordeaux*." *Early Modern Literary Studies* 22, no. 1 (January 2021): 1–12.

Salingar, Leo. "The Englishness of *The Merry Wives of Windsor*." *Cahiers Elisabethains* 59 (2001): 9–25.

Sanchez, Melissa. "Bodies That Matter in *Richard II*." In *Richard II: New Critical Essays*, edited by Jeremy Lopez, 95–116. New York: Routledge, 2015.

Sanders, Julie. *The Cultural Geography of Early Modern Drama, 1620–1650*. Cambridge, UK: Cambridge University Press, 2011.

Sandford, Alasdair. "'Brexit Is Delivering' Says Sunka as UK PM Rejects 'Any Alignment with EU Laws.'" *EuroNews*, November 22, 2022.

Santner, Eric. *The Weight of All Flesh: On the Subject-Matter of Political Economy*. New York: Oxford University Press, 2016.

Schalkwyk, David. "Foreword." In *South African Essays on "Universal" Shakespeare*, edited by Chris Thurman, xiii–xxi. London: Routledge, 2016.

Schrickx, William. *Foreign Envoys and Travelling Players in the Age of Shakespeare and Jonson*. Wetteren, Belgium: Universa, 1986.

Schwartz, Rudolf. *Esther im Deutschen und Neulateinischen Drama des Reformationszeitalters: Eine Litterarhistorische Untersuchung.* Oldenburg, Germany: A. Schwartz, 1898.

Schwyzer, Philip. *Literature, Nationalism, and Memory in Early Modern England and Wales.* Cambridge, UK: Cambridge University Press, 2004.

Sedgwick, Eve Kosofsky. *Between Men: English Literature and Male Homosocial Desire.* New York: Columbia University Press, 2015.

———. *Touching Feeling: Affect, Pedagogy, Performativity.* Durham, NC: Duke University Press, 2003.

Selwood, Jacob. *Diversity and Difference in Early Modern England.* Farnham, UK: Ashgate, 2010.

Shakespeare, William. *The Arden Shakespeare Complete Works,* edited by Richard Proudfoot, Ann Thompson, David Scott Kastan, and H. R. Woudhuysen. London: Bloomsbury Publishing, 2021.

———. *The Arden Shakespeare: King Henry IV, Part 2.* London: Thompson Learning, 2001.

———. *The First Part of Henry IV.* Edited by Stephen Greenblatt. New York: Norton and Company, 2008.

———. *King Lear.* Edited by R. A. Foakes. London: Thomas Nelson and Sons, 1997.

———. *The Merchant of Venice.* Edited by John Drakakis. London: Bloomsbury, 2011.

———. *The Merry Wives of Windsor.* Edited by Stephen Greenblatt. New York: Norton, 2008.

———. *The Merry Wives of Windsor.* Edited by R. S. White. New York: Harvester Wheatsheaf, 1991.

———. *The New Oxford Shakespeare.* Edited by Gary Taylor, John Jowett, Terri Bourus, and Gabriel Egan. Oxford: Oxford University Press, 2016.

———. *The Norton Shakespeare,* second edition, edited by Stephen Greenblatt et al. New York: W. W. Norton & Co., 2008.

———. *Othello.* Edited by E. A. J. Honigmann. London: Arden Shakespeare, 2016.

———. *The Second Part of Henry IV.* Edited by Stephen Greenblatt. New York: Norton, 2008.

Shannon, Laurie. "Nature's Bias: Renaissance Homonormativity and Elizabethan Comic Likeness." *Modern Philology* 98, no. 2 (November 2000): 183–210.

Shapiro, James. *Shakespeare and the Jews.* 1996. Rev. ed., New York: Columbia University Press, 2016.

Shell, Marc. *Money, Language, and Thought: Literary and Philosophical Economies from the Medieval to the Modern Era.* Berkeley: University of California Press, 1982.

Shepard, Alexandra. "'Swil-Bols and Tos-pots:' Drink Culture and Male Bonding in England, c. 1560–1640." In *Love, Friendship, and Faith in Europe, 1300–1800,* edited by Laura Gowing, Michael Hunter, and Miri Rubin, 110–30. New York: Palgrave Macmillan, 2005.

Sherman, William H. *John Dee: The Politics of Reading and Writing in the Renaissance.* Amherst: University of Massachusetts Press, 1995.

Shuger, Debora K. "Subversive Fathers and Suffering Subjects: Shakespeare and Christianity." In *Religion, Literature, and Politics in Post-Reformation England, 1540–1688,* edited by Donna B. Hamilton and Richard Strier, 46–69. Cambridge, UK: Cambridge University Press, 1996.

Sidney, [Sir] Philip. *An Apology for Poetry.* Edited by Geoffrey Shepherd. Manchester: Manchester University Press, 1973.

———. *An Apology for Poetry (or The Defense of Poesy)*. Edited by R. W. Maslen. Manchester, UK: Manchester University Press, 2002.

Silcox, Beejay. "Those Who Leave and Those Who Stay: Star-Crossed by COVID-19." *Times Literary Supplement*, May 1, 2020.

Silver, George. *Master of Defence: The Works of George Silver*. Boulder, CO: Paladin Press, 2003.

Sivefors, Per. "Conflating Babel and Babylon in *Tamburlaine 2*." *Studies in English Literature* 52, no. 2 (Spring 2012): 293–323.

Smith, Alan G. R. *The Emergence of a Nation State: The Commonwealth of England, 1529–1660*. Essex, UK: Pearson Education, 1997.

Smith, Anthony D. *The Antiquity of Nations*. Cambridge, UK: Polity, 2004.

Smith, Emma. "May as Polonius, Gove as Cassius: Is Brexit a Shakespearean Tragedy?" *Guardian*, April 12, 2019.

———. "What Shakespeare Teaches Us about Living with Pandemics." *New York Times*, March 29, 2020.

Smith, Ian. "Managing Fear: The Commerce in Blackness and the London Lord's Mayor's Shows." In *Historical Affects and the Early Modern Theater*, edited by Ronda Arab, Michelle M. Dowd, and Adam Zucker, 211–19. New York: Routledge, 2015.

———. *Race and Rhetoric in the Renaissance: Barbarian Errors*. New York: Palgrave, 2010.

———. "The Textile Black Body: Race and 'Shadowed Livery' in *The Merchant of Venice*." In *The Oxford Handbook of Shakespeare and Embodiment: Gender, Sexuality, and Race*, edited by Valerie Traub, 170–85. Oxford: Oxford University Press, 2016.

———. "White Skin, Black Masks: Racial Cross-Dressing on the Early Modern Stage." *Renaissance Drama* 32 (2003): 33–67.

Smyth, Adam, ed. *A Pleasing Sinne: Drink and Conviviality in Seventeenth-Century England*. Cambridge, UK: D. S. Brewer, 2004.

Sofer, Andrew. *Dark Matter: Invisibility in Drama, Theater, and Performance*. Ann Arbor: University of Michigan Press, 2013.

Spenser, Edmund. *The Faerie Queene*. Edited by A. C. Hamilton. Harlow, UK: Longman, 2007.

Stephenson, Charles. *"Servant to the King for His Fortifications": Paul Ive and "The Practise of Fortification."* Doncaster, UK: P and G Military, 2008.

Stern, Elsie R. "Esther and the Politics of Diaspora." *Jewish Quarterly Review* 100, no. 1 (Winter 2010): 25–53.

Stewart, Alan. "'Euery Soyle to Mee Is Naturall': Figuring Denization in William Haughton's *Englishmen for My Money*." *Renaissance Drama* 35 (2006): 55–81.

Stones, E. L. G., ed. *Anglo-Scottish Relations 1174–1328: Some Selected Documents*. Oxford: Clarendon Press, 1970.

Stones, E. L. G. "Introduction." In *Anglo-Scottish Relations 1174–1328*, xiii–xliv.

Strauss-Kahn, Dominique. "L'être, l'avoir et le pouvoir dans la crise." *Politique Internationale* 167 (Spring 2020): no pagination. Web.

Streete, Adrian, ed. *Early Modern Drama and the Bible: Contexts and Readings, 1570–1625*. New York: Palgrave, 2011.

Suckert, Lisa. "Economic Nostalgia: The Salience of Economic Identity for the Brexit Campaign." *Socio-Economic Review* 21, no. 3 (July 2023): 1721–50.

Sullivan, Garrett A., Jr., *Memory and Forgetting in English Renaissance Drama: Shakespeare, Marlowe*. Cambridge, UK: Cambridge University Press, 2005.

Summer, Saralyn Ellen. "'Like Another Esther': Literary Representations of Queen Esther in Early Modern England." PhD diss., Georgia State University, 2005.

Sutton, John. "Spongy Brains and Material Memories." In Floyd-Wilson and Sullivan, *Environment and Embodiment*, 14–34.

Swarbrick, Susan. "Director David Mackenzie on the Making of *Outlaw King*." *Herald*. November 3, 2018.

Taylor, Gary. *Buying Whiteness: Race, Culture, and Identity from Columbus to Hip Hop*. New York: Palgrave Macmillan, 2005.

Thompson, Ayanna. "Did the Concept of Race Exist for Shakespeare and His Contemporaries? An Introduction." In *Cambridge Companion to Shakespeare and Race*, 1–16.

———. *Passing Strange: Shakespeare, Race, and Contemporary America*. Oxford: Oxford University Press, 2011.

Thompson, Ayanna, ed. *The Cambridge Companion to Shakespeare and Race*. Cambridge, UK: Cambridge University Press, 2021.

Thorndike, Lynn. "Roger Bacon and Gunpowder." *Science* 42 (1915): 799–800.

Thorne, Alison. "The Politics of Female Supplication in the Book of Esther." In *Biblical Women in Early Modern Literary Culture 1550–1700*, edited by Victoria Brownlee and Laura Gallagher, 95–110. Manchester, UK: Manchester University Press, 2016.

Tichenor, Austin. "Speaking What We Feel: Shakespeare's Plague Plays." *Shakespeare and Beyond* (blog), Folger Shakespeare Library, August 27, 2021.

Tomasik, Timothy J., and Juliann M. Vitullo, eds. *At the Table: Metaphorical and Material Cultures of Food in Medieval and Early Modern Europe*. Turnhout, Belgium: Brepols, 2007.

Tracy, Larissa. "A Knight of God or the Goddess?: Rethinking Religious Syncretism in 'Sir Gawain and the Green Knight.'" *Arthuriana* 17, no. 3 (Fall 2007): 31–55.

Traister, Barbara. *Heavenly Necromancers: The Magician in English Renaissance Drama*. New York: Columbia University Press, 1984.

Traub, Valerie. *The Renaissance of Lesbianism in Early Modern England*. Cambridge, UK: Cambridge University Press, 2002.

———. *Thinking Sex with the Early Moderns*. Philadelphia: University of Pennsylvania Press, 2016.

Tretiak, Andrew. "*The Merchant of Venice* and the 'Alien' Question." *Review of English Studies* 5, no. 20 (October 1929): 402–9.

Tudeau-Clayton, Margaret. "'The King's English' 'Our English'?: Shakespeare and Linguistic Ownership." In *Shakespeare and Authority*, edited by Katie Halsey and Angus Vine, 113–33. London: Palgrave Macmillan, 2018.

———. "'This Is the Strangers' Case': The Utopic Dissonance of Shakespeare's Contribution to *Sir Thomas More*." *Shakespeare Survey* 65 (January 2013): 239–54.

———. "Shakespeare and Immigration." In *English on the Move: Mobilities in Literature and Language*, edited by Annette Kern-Stahler and David Britain, 81–97. Tübingen: Narr Verlag, 2012.

———. *Shakespeare's Englishes: Against Englishness*. Cambridge, UK: Cambridge University Press, 2020.

Tuerff, Kevin. *Channel of Peace: Stranded in Gander on 9/11*. Austin, TX: River Grove Books, 2017.

Unwin, George. *The Guilds and Companies of London*. London: Frank Cass, 1963.

van Winter, Johanna Maria. *Spices and Comfits: Collected Papers on Medieval Food*. Devon, UK: Prospect Books, 2007.

Vaughan, Rice. *A Discourse of Coin and Coinage*. London: Thomas Basset, 1675.

Vaughan, Virginia Mason. *Performing Blackness on English Stages, 1500–1800*. Cambridge, UK: Cambridge University Press, 2005.

Vaught, Jennifer. *Masculinity and Emotion in Early Modern English Literature*. Aldershot: Ashgate, 2008.

W., J. *The Valiant Scot by J. W.: A Critical Edition*. Edited by George F. Byers. New York: Garland Press, 1980.

Wadell, Brodie. "The Evil May Day Riot of 1517 and the European Union Elections of 2014: Writing about the History of Anti-Immigrant Politics." *Many Headed Monster* (blog), December 7, 2021.

Walsh, Brian. "'Deep Prescience': Succession and the Politics of Prophecy in *Friar Bacon and Friar Bungay*." *Medieval and Renaissance Drama in England* 23 (2010): 63–85.

Washington Post Staff. "Full Text: Donald Trump Announces a Presidential Bid." *Washington Post*, June 16, 2015. Web.

Weaver, Matthew. "'Speak Only English' Posters Racially Aggravated Say Police." *Guardian*, February 2, 2020.

Webb, Henry J. *Elizabethan Military Science: The Books and the Practice*. Milwaukee: University of Wisconsin Press, 1965.

Welch, Ellen. *A Theater of Diplomacy: International Relations and the Performing Arts in Early Modern France*. Philadelphia: University of Pennsylvania Press, 2017.

Whaley, Joachim. *Germany and the Holy Roman Empire*. Vol. 1. *Maximilian I to the Peace of Westphalia, 1490–1648*. Oxford: Oxford University Press, 2012.

White, Paul Whitfield. *Drama and Religion in English Provincial Society, 1485–1660*. Cambridge, UK: Cambridge University Press, 2008.

Wilder, Lina Perkins. *Shakespeare's Memory Theater*. Cambridge, UK: Cambridge University Press, 2010.

Williams, Deanne. "*Friar Bacon and Friar Bungay* and the Rhetoric of Temporality." In *Reading the Medieval in Early Modern England*, edited by Gordon McMullan and David Matthews, 31–48. Cambridge, UK: Cambridge University Press, 2007.

Williams, Kelsey Jackson. *The First Scottish Enlightenment: Rebels, Priests, and History*. Oxford: Oxford University Press, 2020.

Williams, Simon. *Shakespeare on the German Stage*. New York: Cambridge University Press, 2004.

Wilson, Thomas. *Arte of Rhetorique*. Edited by T. J. Derrick. New York: Garland, 1982.

Withington, Phil. "Company and Sociability in Early Modern England." *Social History* 32 (2007): 291–307.

———. *The Politics of Commonwealth: Citizens and Freemen in Early Modern England*. Cambridge, UK: Cambridge University Press, 2005.

Wormell, D. E. W. "Walls of Brass in Literature." *Hermathena* 58 (November 1941): 116–20.

Wright, Louise B. "The Scriptures and the Elizabethan Stage." *Modern Philology* 26, no. 1 (August 1928): 47–56.

Yachnin, Paul. "After the Plague, Shakespeare Imagined a World Saved from Poison, Slander and the Evil Eye." *Conversation*, April 5, 2020.

Yancy, George. *Black Bodies, White Gazes: The Continuing Significance of Race*. Lanham, MD: Rowman and Littlefield, 2017.

———. "Judith Butler: Mourning Is a Political Act Amid the Pandemic and Its Disparities." *Truthout*, April 30, 2020.

Younge, Gary. *Who Are We? How Identity Politics Took Over the World*. New York: Bold Type Books, 2021.

Yuval-Davis, Nira, Georgie Wemyss, and Kathryn Cassidy. *Bordering*. Cambridge, UK: Polity, 2019.

Zombelli, Paolo. *White Magic, Black Magic in the European Renaissance*. Leiden: Brill, 2007.

CONTRIBUTORS

Heather Bailey earned her MA in Renaissance literature from the University of York and her PhD in English from Florida State University. She is an assistant professor of English at Alcorn State University. Publications include "Fletcher's Schoolroom: *Actio* and Dance as Humanist Pedagogy in *The Two Noble Kinsmen*," in *Research on Medieval and Renaissance Drama (ROMARD)* and "'Thou Shalt Be Dido's Son': Surrogate Motherhood in Christopher Marlowe's *Dido, Queen of Carthage*," in the *Journal for Early Modern Cultural Studies*. She has presented at several conferences across the United States and internationally and directed Shakespeare's plays for Uproar Theatre Company (Jackson, Mississippi), including *The Merry Wives of Windsor* and *Much Ado About Nothing*.

Todd Andrew Borlik is professor of Renaissance drama at the University of Huddersfield. He is the author of *Shakespeare beyond the Green World: Drama and Ecopolitics in Jacobean Britain*, *Literature and Nature in the English Renaissance: An Ecocritical Anthology*, *Ecocriticism and Early Modern English Literature*, and over a dozen articles in academic journals such as *Shakespeare Bulletin*, *Shakespeare Quarterly*, *Shakespeare Survey*, and *English Literary Renaissance*. His research interests include Renaissance drama, the prehistory of environmentalism, magic and science, and Global Shakespeares. He is currently coediting an Arden guide to *The Winter's Tale* and *The Oxford Handbook of Shakespeare and the Natural World*.

William Casey Caldwell's research focuses on how Shakespeare and his contemporary playwrights addressed economic issues surrounding citizenship in early modern England. Caldwell is also interested in how these economic aspects of citizenship, including employment, poverty, and urban power, often intersected with social issues related to gender, sexuality, nationality, and race. Caldwell holds a PhD in English literature from Northwestern University, an MFA in directing from the Shakespeare and Performance Program at Mary Baldwin University in partnership with the American Shakespeare Center, and an MA in philosophy from the University of Auckland in New Zealand. He earned his BA in philosophy from the University of Texas at Austin. Caldwell has also worked at several professional theaters and theater programs, including Shakespeare's Globe Theater in London, Austin Shakespeare, the American Shakespeare Center, Chicago Shakespeare, and Shakespeare at Winedale.

Matt Carter is an assistant professor of English at Clayton State University. He is the game designer of Paul's Cross, a board game about the early modern book trade, and has written about the relationship between stage combat and constructions of the self in early modern English drama. His published articles discuss a variety of social justice issues, including constructions of whiteness in the production history of *Othello*, representations of disability in *Richard III* and *The Little French Lawyer*, and constructions of gender in

The Roaring Girl. He coedited *Boundaries of Violence in Early Modern England.* His current research is heavily invested in pedagogical praxis, and he is always looking for new ways to blur the lines between classroom instruction and gaming. His current book project is *Discovering the Kinetic Language of Violence in Early Modern Drama.*

Kevin Chovanec is a data scientist in Marquette University's Office of Institutional Research and Analysis, with interests bridging the fields of natural language processing, data science, and early modern literature. He focuses especially on how transnational religious identification shaped literature during the sixteenth and seventeenth centuries.

John S. Garrison teaches English at Harvard-Westlake School in Los Angeles. His books include *Glass, Shakespeare at Peace* (cowritten with Kyle Pivetti), *Shakespeare and the Afterlife, The Pleasures of Memory in Shakespeare's Sonnets,* and *Red, Hot + Blue.* In 2021 he was named a Guggenheim Fellow.

Scott Oldenburg is a professor of English at Tulane University, where he researches and teaches early modern English literature and culture. He is author of *Alien Albion: Literature and Immigration in Early Modern England* and *A Weaver-Poet and the Plague: Labor, Poverty, and the Household in Shakespeare's London.* He is coeditor with Kristin M. S. Bezio of *Religion and the Medieval and Early Modern Global Marketplace* and *Religion and the Early Modern British Marketplace.*

Matteo Pangallo is an associate professor of English at Virginia Commonwealth University. His monograph *Playwriting Playgoers in Shakespeare's Theater* considers plays by early modern playgoers as a form of fan fiction. His research has appeared in journals such as *Medieval and Renaissance Drama in England, Early Theatre, English Literary Renaissance, Early Modern Literary Studies, Journal of Early Modern Cultural Studies,* and *Review of English Studies,* and in the collections *Early British Drama in Manuscript, A New Companion to Renaissance Drama,* and *The Oxford Handbook of Shakespeare.* He is coeditor of *Shakespeare's Audiences* (with Peter Kirwan) and *Teaching the History of the Book* (with Emily Todd). Currently he is completing his second monograph, *Strange Company: Foreign Performers in Medieval and Early Modern England.*

Jamie Paris (he/him) is a mixed-race scholar (Black, Métis, and Scottish) and an Instructor II in the Department of English, Theatre, Film, and Media at the University of Manitoba. Paris's work on early modern literature is focused on intersectionality, with a specific interest in whiteness studies and premodern critical race studies. He has published on early modern literature, race, and gender with *The Sundial, Early Theatre,* the *Journal for Early Modern Culture,* and *Renaissance and Reformation.* He has also published scholarship about contemporary Black and Indigenous literature with *Canadian Literature* and *Digital Studies.* Paris's next manuscript, *Clothed Villainy,* is interested in the performative nature of whiteness and the role of racial cross-dressing on the early modern stage.

Vimala C. Pasupathi is a professor of English at Hofstra University. She earned her MA from Ohio State University in 1998 and her PhD from the University of Texas at Austin in 2005. Her articles have appeared in a variety of scholarly journals, including *Modern Philology, ELH, Early Theatre,* and *Shakespeare,* as well as in edited collections, among them *Celtic Shakespeare: The Bard and the Borderers* and *Early Modern Military Identities, 1550–1640.* She is currently working on a monograph, *The Militia Theater, 1558–1662:*

Stages of Obligation in English Drama and British History, a study of dramatic representations of a domestic institution whose significance in the history of constitutional rights and military affairs in England has been overlooked by scholars of literature.

Kyle Pivetti is an associate professor of English at Norwich University. His first book is titled *Of Memory and Literary Form: The Making of Nationhood in Early Modern England.* He is also coauthor, with John Garrison, of *Shakespeare at Peace.* His research on adaptation, memory, and political identity has been featured in *Shakespeare, Studies in Ethnicity and Nationalism, Modern Philology,* and *Explorations in Renaissance Culture.*

Margaret Tudeau-Clayton, professor emerita at the University of Neuchâtel, Switzerland, holds a BA and PhD in English literature from King's College, Cambridge. She taught at the Universities of Geneva, Lausanne, and Zürich, before being appointed to the chair in Early Modern English Literature at the University of Neuchâtel in 2006, which she occupied until her retirement in 2018. She is author of *Jonson, Shakespeare and Early Modern Virgil, Shakespeare's Englishes: Against Englishness,* and numerous articles and chapters on English Renaissance literature, especially Shakespeare and translations of classical literature. She has also published work on Jane Austen and Virginia Woolf (a groundbreaking essay on Woolf and Kandinsky was published in the *Times Literary Supplement*). She has coedited four collections of essays: the first with Martin Warner, *Addressing Frank Kermode*; the second, with Philippa Berry, *Textures of Renaissance Knowledge*; the third, with Willy Maley, *This England, That Shakespeare* ; and the fourth with Martin Hilpert, *The Challenge of Change.* Currently in press are an essay on the invention of the English climate and "constitution" and a chapter from her research project on Shakespeare and messianic time.

Index

Abbot, George, 40–43, 46
Abraham and Lot, 67
acrobatics, 65
Act of Union (1707), 171, 172, 175. *See also* Scotland: union with England
Admiral's Men, 81–82, 140, 142
Aeneas, 137
Aeolus, 132
Aethiopia (character), 5–6
"affective turn," in political science, 127
Afghanistan, refugees from, 39
Africa, 9, 10, 12, 90, 91, 97, 100, 137
African Europeans, 100
Agamemnon (character), 34n80
Agincourt, 121, 123–25, 127
agitprop, 193, 195
Ahasuerus, King (character), 68, 70–71, 73, 78, 80
Ahmed, Sara, 112, 118, 127, 128n20
Alba Party, 175
Albion, 5, 20, 144, 147
Alexander III, King, 156
All Fools (play), 18
All's Well that Ends Well, 49
Alleyn, Edward, 152n48
Alonso (character), 12
Americas, 9, 10, 32n40, 86. *See also* North America
Andrewes, John, 146
d'Anghiera, Pietro Martire (Peter Martyr), 8
Anglo-Scottish union, 154, 159, 164, 170, 171, 174
animals, privileged over humans, 53, 56–58
"animot", 53
Anne, Queen, 5–6, 18
anti-Black racism, 5, 6, 30n19 97, 98, 101, 102, 104–5n23
anti-immigrant, 1, 5, 7, 41, 87, 206, 225
anti-Latinx, 87
anti-Muslim, 1, 87. *See also* Islamophobia
antinationalist, 114, 182, 183, 185
Antipodes, The (play), 19

anti-racism, 24, 93, 103
anti-Semitism, 6. *See also* Jews and Jewishness
antitheatrical discourse, 194–95
Antonio (character), 40, 218, 219–20, 226, 227–39, 243n57, 243n70
Apocrypha (Bible), 67, 79
Apollo, 147
Apologie of Raymond Sebond, An, 56, 57
Apology for Poetry, An, 48
apprentices, 19, 89, 217
Aquitania, 5
Arabia, 20, 97
Arabic (people), 94
Arena Stage: *Cymbeline* (1982), 16
Aristotle, 217, 218–29, 236, 240n6, 241n33, 242n37; Aristotelian theory, 49, 202, 218, 219, 225, 228
Arran, James, 168–69
Art of English Poesy, The, 113
Arthegall (character), 134
Arthur, King, 133
Arviragus (character), 14, 15
Asia, 9, 10, 11, 18, 32n40, 34n80
assimilation, 2–4, 5–6, 24, 30n17, 42, 87–88, 184, 194
Assmann, Jan, 74
Assyrians, 136
Atwater, Lee, 86–87
"Auld Alliance," 26, 157, 159, 165–66
Australia, 47, 154
authoritarianism, 2. *See also* neonationalism

Babel, 144, 145
Babylon, 64, 68, 69, 71, 76, 77, 78, 79, 81, 135, 136, 145–46, 152n48
Babylonian captivity/exile, 68, 70, 80, 81
Bacon, Francis, 20, 138
Bacon, Friar (character), 20, 131, 135–38, 140, 142–44, 146, 147, 148, 151, 152
Friar Bacon and Friar Bungay, 20, 25, 131–48, 149n6, 150n23

Bacon, Roger, 132–33, 135, 140, 149n4, 150n19, 151n27
Badiou, Alain, 55
Baker, David J., 6
Baldo, Jonathan, 110
Balliol, John, 157, 158
Bannockburn, 155, 176n8
Bannockburns: Scottish Independence and Literary Imagination, 1314–2014, 155, 176n8
Barbour, John, 155, 161, 177n28
Bartlett, Robert, 8
Bartolovich, Crystal, 12, 33n58
Bassanio (character), 227, 229–31, 235, 236, 243n70
Bastide, Roger, 101
Bastille, 1
Bayer, Gerd, 10, 11
BBC, 2, 108, 112
Beaumont, Francis, 2
Beccarie de Pavie, Raimond de, 151n3
Becoming Christian, 100
Bedford, Duke of (character), 12
Belarius (character), 14, 15
Belgium, 18. *See also* Flemings
Bergeron, David M., 103n5
Berlant, Lauren, 124
Berlin, Adele, 85n47
Berlin Wall, 16
Bernard, Richard, 11, 32n49
Berwick-upon-Tweed, 139, 142, 162, 174
Bilbo (character), 11
Biron (character), 48
Birth of Merlin, The, 147
Bishops' Wars, the, 169
Black Lives Matter (BLM), 102
Black Skin, White Masks, 94
Black Will (character), 19
blackface, 5–6, 10, 90, 92
Blackman, Robert J., 89
Blackwell, Anna, 2, 128n4
Blanks, David, 9
Blind Hary, 177n28
body politic, 21, 27, 54, 120, 123, 198–200, 205–7
Boece, Hector, 157
Boniface, Pope, 157
Bonilla-Silvia, Eduardo, 87
book of prayer (Church of England), 168
Boorde, Andrew, 202
borders, 7, 8, 9, 10, 11, 12, 17, 22, 23, 25, 39, 65, 77, 86, 87, 131–48, 216

Bosworth, 18
Botero, Giovanni, 8
Bottom, Nick (character), 152n48
Bourbon, Duke of (character), 120
Bowyer, William, 168
Boys, John, 57
Brabantio (character), 97
brass, 20, 25, 131, 132–44, 146–47, 149n11, 151n35
Braveheart (film), 154, 155, 161, 171–73
Brazil, 45
Break-Up of Britain, The, 28
Bremo (character), 26, 181–95
Brenz, Johannes, 72
Brexit, 1–3, 5–7, 16, 17, 24, 27, 40, 41, 46, 58, 87, 107–9, 112, 125–27, 153–55, 166, 169–71, 172, 175–76, 216–17, 239; early modern parallels, 5–6, 12, 13, 16, 22, 24, 25, 27–28, 44, 107–9, 112, 125–27, 148, 166–67; and immigration, 28, 40, 41, 43, 58, 87; and identity, 46; Leave, 2, 16, 108; Remain, 16, 33, 108; Scotland and, 153, 155, 169–70, 172
"Brief Report on the New-Found Land of Virginia, A," 91
Brightman, Thomas, 10–11
Britannia/Brittania, 5, 10, 135
British Nationality Act of 1948, 4. *See also* citizenship
Britomart (character), 133
Britton, Dennis Austin, 6, 92, 94, 97, 100–101
Brome, Richard, 19
Bronze Age, 132
Brooke, William, 141
Browne, Robert, 76, 82
Browne, Thomas, 139
Bruce, The (film), 155
Brus (poem), 155
Brussels, 108
Brutus/Brut (legendary founder of Britain), 137, 155–58, 171, 176
Bryant, Chris, 107–8
Buchanan, George, 158
Bunyasi, Tehama Lopez, 96
Burden (character), 135, 136
Burgundy, Duke of (character), 121–22
Burton, Robert, 204, 205
Butler, Judith, 47
Byers, George F., 167

Cadiz, 125

Caesar, Julius, 135
Calais, 136
Caliban (character), 12
California Shakespeare Festival: *Cymbeline*
   (1990), 16
Calvin, John, 70
Calvin, Robert, 4
Calvinism, 4
Camber, 140
Cambria, 14
Camden, William, 150n14
Cameron, David, 1, 154
Campana, Joseph, 1
Campion, Thomas, 9, 32n40
Canada, 102
Candy (Crete), 137
Canterbury, 40, 57
capitalism, 44, 108
CapX, 108
Cardinal's Conspiracy, The, 174
Cardinalis, Hugo, 220
Caribbean, 4
Carlo Buffone (character), 18
Carlson, Marvin, 124
Carmarthen, 133, 147
Carney (character), 163, 165
Carr, Robert, earl of Somerset, 9
Cassidy, Tanya M., 201–2, 203
Castile, 108, 145
Castile, King of (character), 144–45
Catholics/Catholicism, 2, 4, 6, 11, 18, 21–22,
   70–72, 74, 76–77, 79, 80, 81, 132, 139,
   143, 148, 152n53, 183, 196n13, 233
Celtic, 2, 26
Ceres, 147
Chaldeans, 136
Channel Islands, 140
Chapman, George, 18
Charles I, King, 168–69, 171
Charles, Prince, 45
Cheek by Jowl: *The Knight of the Burning
   Pestle* (2019), 2
Cheney, Patrick, 182–83, 185
Chicago, 16
China, 86, 131, 140
Chiverton, Richard, 9
Chrisipus, 9, 19
Christian Testament, 71. *See also individual books*
Christmas (character), 3, 4
*Chronicles of England, Scotlande, and Irelande,
   The*, 114–15, 156

Chryseus, Johannes, 74
Church of England, 4, 44, 101, 168
Cineworld, 153, 172, 175
Cinque Ports, 140, 141
Cipolla, Carlo, 233
citizenship, 4, 27–28, 46, 125, 216–39
Civil Rights Act, 86
Clark, Rachel Ellen, 16
class, 9, 11–12, 23, 26, 38, 41, 46, 54, 58, 69,
   96, 99, 105n23, 181–82, 185–92, 195, 201,
   203, 226
Claudius, Emperor, 135
Claviez, Thomas, 45
Clement (character), 20
Cloten (character), 14
colonialism, 2, 55, 91, 105n23, 184, 185, 190,
   193, 210. *See also* imperialism
Comedy of the Prophet Jonah, A, 67
Comyn, John, 159, 162, 163, 167
Connerton, Paul, 115, 129n34
Connolly, Annaliese, 81
conversion, 4, 23, 90–92, 99, 101, 102, 237–38
Cooper, Frederick, 66
Cordelia (character), 55
Coriolanus, 1, 33n70
Corpus Christi plays, 68
Counter-Reformation, 21, 69, 79
COVID-19, 21, 37–38, 45, 46–47, 48, 49–50,
   54, 55, 174. *See also* pandemic
Craig, Cairns, 172–73
Craig, Thomas, 158, 168
Crawford, Robert, 155, 176n8, 177n28,
   179n61
Critical Race Theory, 87, 105n23. *See also*
   premodern critical race studies (PCRS)
Cromwell, Thomas, 139, 194
Cullen, Jonathan, 1
Curtain playhouse, 152n57
Curth, Louise Hill, 201–2, 203
Cush, land of, 146
Cymbeline, 6, 13–17, 33n70, 143–44, 148, 193
Cymbeline (character), 13, 14, 15, 16, 143

Dainotto, Roberto, 9, 11, 32n40, 32n48
Dale (Pembrokeshire), 139
Damascus, 145–46
Daughters of Niger (characters), 5
Dauphin (character), 120
David and Bathsheba, 67
Davies, Norman, 8
Davison, William, 151n33

Decades of the Newe Worlde or West India, The, 8
Dee, John, 147, 152n53
Defoe, Daniel, 46
Dekker, Thomas, 11, 18–19, 38, 45–46, 49, 89, 103n5
Delanty, Gerard, 8, 9, 22, 32n37
Derrida, Jacques, 53, 57, 58
Desdemona (character), 97
Destruction of Sodom and Gomorrah, The, 67
Devi, Mahasweta, 55
"Device Forts," 139
devolution, 172–73, 175, 216–17, 239
Discourse upon the Booke of Ester, 72
Doctor Faustus, 133, 149n8
Doctor Caius (character), 1, 3, 199–200, 204, 206, 209–10, 211
Doctor Hughball (character), 19–20
Doll (character), 40
Don (river), 17
Douglas, James, 170
Dover, 5, 135, 136, 140
Dover Castle, 140
Dover Harbor, 140
Drakakis, John, 229, 231, 235–36
Drayton, Michael, 133–34, 147
Dudley, Sir Robert, 187
D'Urfey, Thomas, 16
Dutch, 12, 42, 70, 73, 148, 205
Dutch Revolt, 71
Dutch Courtesan, The, 19
Dymchurch Wall, 150n19

Early English Books Online, 103n6
Eastern Europe, 16, 40, 41, 58, 187
East Indies, 91, 184
East Sussex, 135
eco-Marxist, 44
Eddo-Lodge, Reni, 93
Edelman, Lee, 117, 122
Eden, Garden of, 107, 109, 111, 146
Eden, Richard, 8
Edgar (character), 50–54, 57–58. *See also* Poor Tom (character)
Edinburgh Agreement, 175
Edmund (character), 50, 55
Edward II (play), 17
Edward the Black Prince 120, 121, 122
Edward I, King, 25, 138, 154, 155, 156–63, 175, 176n8
Edward I, King (character), 163–65, 167

Edward II, King, 166, 176n8
Edward IV, King (character), 12
Edward, Prince (character), 137, 138
Egypt, 42, 73, 137
Eleanor of Castile (character), 137, 138, 145
eleos, 49
Elizabeth de Burgh (character), 164, 170
Elizabeth I, Queen, 6, 24, 69, 81, 136, 138, 139, 140, 142, 144, 146–47, 148, 193
En Vogue, 86
enclosure, 43, 44, 60n32
Engelische Comedien und Tragedien, 64, 70, 82
English (language), 1, 3, 4, 41–42, 166, 199, 200, 211
English Civil War, 71
English Defence League (EDL), 3, 4
English-Men for My Money, 42
Erasmus, Desiderius, 54–55
erotic melancholy, 200, 203–4, 205
Escobedo, Andrew, 134
Escolme, Bridget, 2
Essayes (Montaigne), 115
Essex, 139
Essex, Earl of, 187
Esther (character), 64, 67, 68–72, 76, 77, 78, 80
Esther (play), 22, 64–82
Esther, Book of (Bible), 67, 68–69, 73, 75, 76, 79, 81, 82, 85n47
Esther, plays of, 23; English, 81; German, 78; neo-Latin, 78
Ethiopia, 5–6, 101, 146, 209
Euphrates, 145
Euriphile (character), 15
Europaeus, 31n34
European Union (EU), 1, 2, 13, 28, 40, 41, 107–8, 126, 169–70, 216
Europensis, 31n34
Evans, Hugh (character), 3, 199–200, 206, 208, 211
Every Man Out of His Humor, 18
Evil May Day, 1
exceptionalism, 5, 6, 14, 20, 24, 25, 107, 144, 181
Exeter, Duke of (character), 122–23, 125
Exodus, Book of (Bible), 42
Eyre, Simon (character), 11–12

Faerie Queene, The, 133–34, 185. *See also* individual character names
Falkirk, 155

Falstaff (character), 1, 13, 27, 190–91, 199–201, 203–11

Famous Historie of Fryer Bacon, The, 133–34, 135, 136, 146, 147

Fanon, Frantz, 94

Faust Book, 149n6

Favell, Adrian, 5

Fawn, The, 143

Ferdinand II, 71, 81

Fernie, Ewan, 110, 125

Ferrand, Jacques, 204, 205, 207

Finch, Henry, 39, 40–43

Finkelstein, Richard, 182

First Charter of Virginia, 91

Fisher, Will, 221

Fitter, Chris, 54

Flanders, 108. *See also* Flemings

Flecknoe, Richard, 10, 12

Flemings, 3, 41, 187, 208. *See also* Belgium

Florence, 148

Florio, John, 50, 56

Fluellen (character), 121, 123

Foakes, R. A., 59

Fool (character), 50

Ford, John, 18, 204

Forest of Dean, 151n35

Fortescue, John, 142

fortifications, 25, 132, 139–41, 145, 147, 150n14, 225

Fortunatus (character), 18

Fortune playhouse, 174

Foucault, Michel, 46

Fough, Mary (character), 19

Fox News, 95

France, 13, 18, 20, 40, 45, 64–65, 68, 70, 71, 73, 79, 120–22, 137, 138, 140, 157, 159, 160, 165–66, 187

France, King of (character), 120, 122

Franciscus (character), 9, 19

Franks, 8

Frégeville, Jean de, 146

French (language), 41, 42, 64–65, 87, 166, 240n6

French (people), 1, 3, 13, 40–42, 46, 58, 73, 76, 118–23, 148, 165, 166, 190, 198–99, 204, 206, 211. *See also* Huguenot

French Revolution, 217

French Wars of Religion, 70, 71. *See also* Thirty Years' War

Freire, Paolo, 6

Freud, Sigmund, 48, 53, 234

Fuller, Nicholas, 4

Gabaldon, Diana, 176nn4–5

Gaelic, 166, 176n4, 194

Galatians, Paul's Letter to the (Bible), 101

Gallagher, Catherine, 117

Gallic uprisings, 8

gender, 77, 98, 101, 105n23, 111, 114–15, 116, 120, 121, 123–24, 219, 225, 240n9

Geneva Bible, 69

Genesis, Book of (Bible), 145, 242n50

Genius (character), 18–19

George, David, 4

German (language), 74, 78, 80

Germans, 64, 70, 73, 74

Germany, 20, 39, 67, 68, 73, 74, 126, 133, 137, 139, 144, 148; British living in, 126

Gerzic, Marina, 2

Gihon, 145–46

Ginzburg, Carlo, 28

Girard, Rene, 45

global South, 21

globalization, 20, 24, 25, 148

Globe playhouse, 112, 113

Gloucester, Duke of (character), 110

Gloucester, Earl of (character), 54, 57

Glyndwr (character), 113, 117

Godly Queene Hester, The, 69

Goitein, S. D., 69

Goldsmith, Robert Hillis, 183, 186

Goneril (character), 50

Goodridge, Leah, 96

Goold, Rupert, 2

Gove, Michael, 1

Graham, Peggy (character), 161, 164

Great Britain, 153, 170

Great Wall of China, 131

Greece, 137

Greeks, 11, 34n80

green man. *See* wodewose

Greenblatt, Stephen, 47, 49, 117

Greene, Jody, 221

Greene, Robert, 19, 20, 25, 131–48, 149n6, 149n8, 149n11, 150n23, 184

Greenstadt, Amy, 229–30, 234, 240n10

Gregorian calendar, 152n53

Greyfriar's kirk, 159, 162

Grieve, Dominic, 108

Guardian, 39, 41, 107, 108

Guiderius (character), 14, 15

Guise, Duke of , 71

gunpowder, 140, 146, 148, 151n27

Habib, Imtiaz, 5, 101
Hadfield, Andrew, 134
Hadrian's Wall, 131
Haekel, Ralf, 66
Hakluyt, Richard, 98
Hal (character), 24, 117–18, 207–8
Hale, John, 8
Hall, Kim F., 5, 97
Haman (character), 68, 71–72, 74, 75, 77, 78, 79–80
Haman. Die schöne und seer tröstlich Histori Hester, 74
Hamanus, 74
Hames, Scott, 173, 175
Hamlet (character), 17, 28, 97
Hamlet, 28
Hanks, Tom, 45
Hannan, Daniel, 108
Hans (character in Esther), 64–65, 73, 76, 78–79
Hans (character in The Shoemaker's Holiday), 12
Hapsburgs, 23, 71, 81
Harfleur, 118–19, 124, 127
Hariot (Harriot), Thomas, 91
Harper, Thomas, 169
Hart, James, 202
Harwich, 139
Haughton, William, 42
Hawkes, David, 221
Haworth, Ben, 2
Hebrew Bible, 40, 43, 67–70, 71, 73, 83n8, 132, 146
Heinemann, Margot, 55
Helen (character), 34n80
Helgerson, Richard, 134, 185, 199
Hénaff, Marcel, 222
Hendricks, Margo, 5, 104–5n23
Heng, Geraldine, 99, 100
Henriad, the, 109, 110, 122, 125, 127
Henrician Reformation, 14. See also Protestants/Protestantism; Reformation
Henry III, King, 140
Henry III, King (character), 20, 137, 144–47
Henry IV, King (character), 113–14, 116
Henry IV, Part One, 1, 12, 112–18, 119, 123, 203
Henry IV, Part Two, 12–13, 190–91, 203, 207–8
Henry V, 109, 110, 118–25

Henry V, King (character), 117–25
Henry VI, Part Three, 12
Henry VII, King, 138–39, 147
Henry VIII, King, 22, 132, 139–40, 142, 150
Henry VIII, (character), 18, 19
Henry, Prince, 18
Henslowe, Philip, 142
Hercules, 152n48
Herodotus, 136
Heroic Failure: Brexit and the Politics of Pain, 109
Hester and Ahasuerus, 81, 82
Hey for Honesty, Down with Knavery, 11
Heywood, Thomas, 18, 34n80, 89, 203
Higgins, Katie W., 126
Higson, Andrew, 173–74, 177n27
Hill, Christopher, 46
Hill, Tracey, 103n5
Hirsch, Afua, 3
Hiscock, Andrew, 7
Historie of the Raigne of King Henry the Seventh, 138
Historie of Scotland, 156, 158
History of Great Britanie, The, 13
Hobbes, Thomas, 20, 191
Hochschild, Arlie Russell, 93
Hoenselaars, A. J., 150n23
Holinshed, Raphael, 114–15, 156, 158
Hollow Crown, The, 2
Holy Roman Emperor (character), 144
Holy Roman Empire, 22, 70, 71, 77, 79, 82
Homer, 132
Hopkins, Lisa, 16, 132
Horace, 132
Horatio (character), 17
Hotspur (character), 24, 116–17, 118, 125
Howard, Jean E., 193, 194
Howard, Lord Admiral Charles, 142
hübsch und Christlich Spiel des gantzen Buchs Ester, Ein, 78
Huguenot, 4, 146
Hutson, Lorna, 232, 240n10
Hyland, Peter, 180–81, 182
Hythloday, Raphael, 43, 44

Iachimo (character), 13
Iago (character), 97
iconographic personification, 32n40
Ida (character), 19
identity politics, 46, 58–59
immigrants, 2, 19, 27, 28, 39–42, 75, 148,

198–211, 218, 225, 238; blamed for infection, 41–42; children of, 238; citizen immigrants, 27; House of Commons debate about (1593), 4; immigrant labor, 1 and 12; internal, 43 and 44; and native poor, 43–44; nonnaturalized, 27; petition against (1571), 4; racialized, 41–42, 46; restrictions on, 12, 86–87; welcomed, 39–40, 42–43. *See also* Brexit; refugees
imperialism, 10, 24, 26, 138, 147, 181, 190, 192. *See also* colonialism
inclusion, 1, 3, 27, 28, 77, 200, 207, 217
India, 20, 55, 70
"IndyRef," 153, 155, 173, 175. *See also* Scotland: independence referendum
Injured Princess, or, The Fatal Wager, The, 16
Innogen (character), 14, 15, 17, 148
Instructions for the Wars, 151n33
international trade, 8, 90–91, 98–99, 102, 137, 148, 210, 224–25, 226, 236
Ireland, 26, 133, 184, 187, 194, 195
Irish, 4, 181, 184, 187
Iron Age, The, 18, 34n80
Isabella, Queen (character), 17
Isin, Engin, 218, 226, 237
Islam, 3, 149n4
Islamophobia, 3. *See also* anti-Muslim
isolationism, 14, 24, 25, 69, 108, 126, 138, 143, 144
Israel, 42, 69, 71, 72, 75, 76
Italian (language), 41, 151n36, 152n57
Italy/Italians, 8, 12, 16, 20, 42, 137, 139
Ive, Paul, 140–41, 142, 146, 147, 151n33
Iver (character), 163, 164

James I of England and VI of Scotland, King, 4, 5, 18–19, 44, 55, 144, 170–71, 193
Janssen, Geert, 70
Jeremiah, Book of (Bible), 146–47
Jerusalem, 69, 76, 77
Jesuits, 74
Jew of Malta, The, 82
Jews and Jewishness, 6, 11, 22, 39, 40, 41, 42, 68–69, 70, 72–73, 75–77, 79–81, 82, 85, 98, 101, 227–31, 238, 242n51,
John of Bordeaux (play), 142
John of Fordun, 157
John of Gaunt (character), 12, 24, 28, 107–9, 111–12, 125–26, 143–44
Johnson, Boris, 1, 28, 87, 174
Johnson, W. R., 183

Jones, John Henry, 133, 149n6
Jonson, Ben, 4, 5, 18, 38, 103n5
Jonah, Book of (biblical), 40
Judah, Kingdom of, 85n47
Judea, 137
Juliet (character), 47
jus soli, 4
Justice Suresby (character), 45

Kaethler, Mark, 103n5
Karim-Cooper, Farah, 91
Karremann, Isabel, 112
Katherine, Princess of France (character), 121–22
Kearney, James, 51
Kent, 135, 139
Kent, Earl of (character), 50, 55
Kerrigan, John, 169
Killeen, Kevin, 68
King Lear, 2, 13, 21, 38–39, 45, 49–59
"King's Device" strategy, 139
Kipling, Rudyard, 91
Kirwan, Peter, 1
Kitzes, Adam, 205–6
Kläger, Florian, 10, 11
Knapp, Jeffrey, 134
Knave in Grain, The, 9, 19
Knowsley House, 3–4
Kolb, Laura, 231
Kuntzel, Wolffgang, 74
Kyd, Thomas, 132

Lacy (character in *Friar Bacon and Friar Bungay*), 137
Lacy (character in *The Shoemaker's Holiday*), 12
Laird, Fiona, 1–2
Lamis, Alexander, 86
Lanchester, John, 37, 131
L'Anglois, Abraham, 3–4
language, 3, 7, 41–42, 58, 65, 199, 211
Latin, 8, 74, 78, 158
Laud, Archbishop William, 168, 174
Lear, King (character), 45, 50–51, 52, 53, 56–57. See also *King Lear*
Le Pen, Marine, 87
Lee, Maurice, 168
Leiden, 71
Leith, Murray Stewart, 172
Lévi-Strauss, Claude, 58
Leviathan, 20

Levin, Carole, 184, 192
Leviticus, Book of (Bible), 42
Libel of 1593, 41, 42, 44, 148
linguaphobia, 3
Lipsitz, George, 95
Little, Arthur L., 99
"Little Englander," 137
livery companies, 89, 90, 92, 217, 226, 235
London, 18, 19, 33, 34, 44, 89, 138, 148, 153, 174, 184, 216–17, 226; attitude to strangers, 41, 42–43, 46; Dutch immigrants of, 148; theater, 67, 76, 81–82, 113, 140, 181; wall around, 143
London Review of Books, 37, 48
Loomba, Ania, 90
Lord of the Isles, The, 155
Lord Mayoral Shows, 89–91, 92
Loudoun Hill, 170
Love, Heather K., 125
Love's Labor's Lost, 48
Love-sick King, The, 132
Lawrence, Friar (character), 47
Lucius (character), 15
Lucrece (Shakespeare), 120
Lupton, Julia, 234, 236, 238
Lusitania, 5
Luther, Martin, 67, 70, 74
Lutheranism, 32n49, 66
Lyne, Raphael, 114

Macbeth, 154, 155, 233
Macbeth (character), 233
Macedonian, 79
Macfadyen, Angus, 172, 174, 175, 178n47
MacFerchard, Fergus, 157
Mackenzie, David, 171–72, 177n29
Maid of Honour, The, 18
Mair (Major), John, 158–59, 161
Majumdar, Nivedita, 55
Manning, Roger, B., 190
Manchester, 216–17, 239
Map of Early Modern London, 104n14
Mardell, Mark, 108–9
Mardocheus, 72–73
Margaret (character), 137
Marlowe, Christopher, 17, 133, 141, 143, 145, 149n8, 182–83, 184–85, 197n44
Marriage of Oceanus and Brittania, The, 10
Marston, John, 19, 143
Martin, Trayvon, 95–96
Marx, Karl, 55

Marxism, 55
Mary, Queen, 42
Mason, Roger A., 25, 156
Masque of Blackness, The, 5–6
Massinger, Philip, 18
Massumi, Brian, 120
Matthew, Book of (Bible), 43
Mauritania, 5, 20
Maynard, Robyn, 102
McAdam, Ian, 234
McEachern, Claire, 134
McEwen, Nicola, 169, 175
McKeown, Adam, 134, 147, 150n14
McNeill, William, 38
memory, 25, 43, 70, 74, 84n34, 101–27, 204
Mendelsohn, Everett, 201
Mentith, Earl of (character), 167
Merchant of Venice, The, 6, 27–28, 40–41, 42, 97, 192, 216–39
Mercutio (character), 47
Meres, Francis, 220
Merlin, 133–34, 147
Merlin, Pierre, 70, 71, 76, 79
Merry Devil of Edmonton, The, 11
Merry Wives of Windsor, The, 1–2, 3, 27, 198–200, 203–11
Mesopotamia, 20, 146
Metro, 39
Mexico, 86, 87
Middle East, 16
Middleton, Thomas, 2, 23–24, 88–92, 94, 101, 102, 103n5, 142
Midsummer Night's Dream, A, 2, 152n48, 193
migration, 37, 39–41, 66, 70, 75, 81–82
misogyny, 6, 105n23
Montaigne, Michel de 50–51, 52, 56, 57, 58, 115
Moors, King of the (character), 88, 90–96, 98–100, 102
Moors, Queen of the (character), 102
Morag (character), 163, 164
Mordecai, 68, 70, 76, 77, 78, 80. See also Mardocheus
More, Sir Thomas, 43
More, Sir Thomas (character), 40, 43, 44, 45, 46, 51
Morocco, Prince of (character), 97
Morris, Ian, 22
Moryson, Fynes, 75, 85n59
Moscow, 17

Moss, Jonathan, 127
Mosse, Miles, 220
Most Famous History of the Learned Fryer Bacon, The, 149n6
Motoko, Hori, 201
Mucedorus (character), 26, 181–87, 189–94, 197n44
Mucedorus, 26, 180–195
Much Ado About Nothing, 2
Mullaney, Steven, 113
multilateralism, 16, 138, 147
Munday, Anthony, 88, 89, 103n5
Munt, Sally R., 111
Muslims, 3, 11, 32n37, 94, 98
Myddelton, Thomas, 88–89, 91

Naeogeorgus, Thomas, 74
Nairn, Tom, 28
Nardizzi, Vin, 151n35
Nashe, Thomas, 207
National Covenant (Scotland), 155, 168
National Front, 87
national identity, 2, 5, 7, 11, 12, 17, 20, 21–23, 26, 27, 28, 41, 46, 115, 126–27, 145, 147, 172, 185
national sovereignty, 1–2, 7, 22, 26, 27, 164
nationalism, 2, 17, 24, 25, 69, 87, 109, 112, 115, 122, 132, 134, 137, 138, 143, 147, 148, 153, 155, 167, 171–73, 175, 183, 184, 185, 199. *See also* neonationalism
nationhood, 2, 3, 6, 7, 110, 112, 120, 122, 123, 127, 128n20, 134, 136, 139, 182
necrophilia, 114
Nederman, Cary, 226
neonationalism, 2, 3, 6–7, 20, 28. *See also* Brexit; nationalism; Trump, Donald J.
Neptune, 143, 144
Netflix, 25
Neville's Cross, 155
New Atlantis, 20
New Historicism, 6
New Oxford Shakespeare, 51
New York Times, 45
Newfoundland, town of Gander, 39
"News from Graves-End," 45
Nichol, David, 103n5
Nicholl, Charles, 141
Nicodemism, 76
Nimue, the Lady of the Lake, 134
9/11, attacks of, 39
Ninus, 135, 152n48

Noah, 59
Noble, Louise, 209
"Norman Yoke" myth, 46
North Africa, 137
North America, 184. *See also* Americas
Norwich, 41, 42
nostalgia, 2, 109, 110, 112, 116
nuclear disarmament, 16

Oates, Joyce Carol, 47
Obama, Barack, 39, 95–96
Obermann, Heiko, 70
O'Callaghan, Michelle, 201
occupatio, 113–15, 117, 118–19
Oceanus (character), 5, 10, 144
Odyssey, The, 132
oeconomie, 222–23, 232, 234, 241n33
Of a Rich Man and Lazarus, 67
Old Fortunatus, 18
Olivia (character), 48, 62n55
O'Neill, Stephen, 2, 39–40
Opus Majus, 151n27
Orbe Novo, De, 8
Original Practices, 6
Orleans, Duke of (character), 120
Ormrod, W. Mark, 12
Otele, Olivette, 100
Othello (character), 6, 97
Othello, 97
otherness/alterity, 4, 22, 28, 58, 87, 99, 181, 185, 186, 190, 192, 211, 217, 218, 224, 225, 227, 237–38, 239
O'Toole, Fintan, 109
Ottoman Empire, 11, 22. *See also* Turk/ Turkish
Outlander, 154, 176n4
Outlaw King, The, 25, 26, 153–79, 177n29
Ovid, 182–83, 185
Oxford, 132, 135, 137

"Palae Albion," 13
Pallas Athena, 147
Pamlico, 91
pandemic, 21, 37–38, 45, 46–48, 49–50, 54–55, 59, 174. *See also* COVID-19; plague
Paphlagonia, 20
Paraphrases, 54
Parliament (European), 1
Parliament (Scottish), 154, 170, 172, 174, 175
Parliament (UK), 1, 12, 39–40, 43, 46, 55, 107, 108, 142, 169

Passion plays, 68
Passions of the Minde in Generall, The, 127
Pax Eliza, 142–43
Peasant Revolt of 1381, 3
Pedlar's Prophecy, The, 42
Peele, George, 67
Pembrokeshire, 139
Pepys, Samuel, 202
Performing Blackness, 91
peripeteia, 21, 37–39, 45, 52–59
Perkin Warbeck, 18
Persia, 9, 20, 68, 73, 79, 137, 145
Pettegree, Andrew, 42
Pfeilschmidt, Andreas, 74, 78
Philip IV, King, 165
phobos, 49
Pilgrimage of Grace uprising, 139
Pitcher, John, 193
Pittman, L. Monique, 2
Pius II, Pope, 31n34
plague, 38, 41, 45–50, 54, 202. *See also*
    pandemic
Play of the Prophet Daniel, A, 67
players, English traveling, 22, 64–66, 68, 70,
    74–75, 81, 82
Poland, 8, 11, 137
polearms, 186–90
Politique Internationale, 47
Poly-Olbion, 133
Poor Tom (character), 50–54, 56, 57. *See also*
    Edgar (character)
Portia (character), 97, 231, 236–38, 243n70
Portsmouth, 142
Portugal/Portuguese, 8, 42, 203
Posthumus (character), 13
poverty, 43–44, 50–52, 53–58
Practice of Fortification, The, 140–41
pragmatism, 76
Precopites, 8
premodern critical race studies (PCRS), 5,
    62n74, 91, 104–5n23
Prince Palatine's Men, 146
Prodigal Son, The, 67
Prospero (character), 33n58
Protestants/Protestantism, 18, 21–22, 66,
    67–78, 80, 81, 82, 91, 92, 98, 132, 136, 138,
    141, 143, 146, 148. *See also* Henrician Ref-
    ormation; Reformation
Principal Navigations, 98
Psalms, Book of (Bible), 57
Puar, Jasbir, 114
Purchas His Pilgrimage, 98

Purchas, Samuel, 11, 98
Puttenham, George 113–15
Pyramus (character), 152n48
Pyrenees, 145

Quarles, Francis, 78
Quarmby, Kevin A., 2
quarterstaff, 186–90
Queen (character in *Cymbeline*), 14, 143–44
Queen Anne's Men, 76
Queen's Men, 140, 141, 142–43

race, 4–5, 7, 10, 12, 23–24, 28, 58, 86–102,
    105n23, 157, 181; Black actors, 1; Black
    Christians, 23, 88, 90, 98–99, 101, 102;
    Blackness, 97; climate theory of, 127;
    whiteness, 5, 88, 97, 99; Windrush gen-
    eration, 4. *See also* premodern critical race
    studies (PCRS); racism
racism, 2, 3, 5, 6, 14, 40, 41–42, 46, 58–59,
    86–102, 190, 216. *See also* anti-Black rac-
    ism; race; xenophobia
Randolph, Thomas, 11
Rappaport, Steve, 226
Ravelhofer, Barbara, 180
Reagan, Ronald, 6
Redcrosse Knight (character), 185
Reformation, 21, 22, 54, 66, 67, 68, 146, 183,
    196n13. *See also* Henrician Reformation;
    Protestants/Protestantism
Reformed Politicke, The, 146–47
refugees, 14, 37, 39–40, 46, 77, 148. *See also*
    immigrants
religious identity, 11, 22, 23, 66, 67, 70, 74,
    75–77, 82
respectability politics, 93–98, 101–2
Revelation of the Apocalypse, A, 10–11
Revenger's Tragedy, The (2017 production), 2
Reynolds, Brian, 138
Rhee Wall, 150n19
Richard II, 12, 24–25, 107–12, 116–17, 126,
    143–45
Richard II (character), 25, 108–9, 110–11,
    116, 125, 126
Richard III, King, 12
Richard III (2016 production), 2
Ridpath, George, 158, 168
Rivera, Geraldo, 95–96
Roach, Joseph, 114
Rob Roy, 154, 173
Robert the Bruce, 154, 155, 157, 158–59, 168,
    169, 170, 171, 176

Robert the Bruce (character), 159–67, 170, 174, 175, 177
Robert the Bruce, 153–55, 158, 159–60, 162–64, 165, 169, 171–72, 174, 175
Robert I, 155, 171, 176n8
Robinson, Emily, 127
Roderigo (character), 97
Roe, Sir Thomas, 11
Roman Empire, 8, 15, 89–90, 143, 150
Romani, 4
Rome, 2, 8, 13, 14, 15, 18, 22, 34n80, 37, 70, 74, 79, 135, 137, 140
Romeo (character), 47
Romeo and Juliet, 38, 47–48
Romney Marsh, 150n19
Rooney, Tom, 180
Rorty, Richard, 43
Rose, Jacqueline, 48
Rose playhouse, 142, 152n48
Rowley, Samuel, 19
Rowley, William, 103n5, 147
Royal Shakespeare Company (RSC); *Cymbeline* (2016), 16; *The Merry Wives of Windsor* (2018), 1, 2
Rudolf II, 81
Russia, 8, 11, 187
Rye, 135, 136, 139, 140

Sachs, Hans, 74, 78
sack, 27, 198, 200–11. *See also* wine
Sacks, Jonathan, 39
Sager, Jenny, 152n57
Salingar, Leo, 198
Salkeld, Duncan, 101
Salmond, Alex, 153–54, 172, 175, 178n49
Salusbury, Sir Thomas, 3
San Diego Repertory Theatre production of *Cymbeline* (1990), 16
Sanchez, Melissa, 110
Santner, Eric, 234
satire, 77, 85n47, 226
Schacter, Daniel, 115
Schalkwyk, David, 55
schöne und seer tröstlich Histori Esther, Die, 74
Schwyzer, Philip, 134
"Scotching the Brut," 25, 156, 158
Scotland, 19, 25–26, 28, 32, 138, 139, 153–76, 176n5, 187; independence referendum, 153–54, 155, 169–70, 172, 173–75; union with England, 154, 159, 164, 170, 171
Scott (character), 163
Scott, Sir Walter, 155

Scottish (people), 116
Scottish Constitutional Convention (SCC), 154
Scottish History of James the Fourth, 19, 20
Scottish kirk, 155
Scottish National Party (SNP), 172, 174, 175
Scottish War of Independence, first, 155
Sea of Azov, 17
Sebastian (character), 12
Second Discovery by the Northern Scout, A, 174
Sedgwick, Eve Kosofsky, 112, 240n10
Sedgwick, Obadiah, 71, 75
Semiramis, 135, 136, 145
Sermon on the Mount, 43
Seven Sins of Memory, The, 115
"Seven Types of Forgetting," 115
Shakespeare Repertory Theatre production of *Cymbeline* (1993), 16
Shakespeare, William, 1–2, 6, 12–13, 14, 15, 17, 24–25, 27, 33, 37, 39–40, 41, 43–46, 47, 48–49, 51, 53, 54, 56, 58, 90, 97, 103, 107–8, 110–16, 120–21, 124, 125, 127, 129, 143–44, 152, 154–55, 180, 181, 192, 193, 198–200, 204, 205, 206, 208, 210, 217, 220, 229, 230, 233, 234, 235, 236. *See also individual plays and characters*
shame, 24–25, 107–27, 128n20, 129n34, 129n38, 181
Shapiro, James, 238
Shepard, Alexandra, 206
Shepherd, Geoffrey, 49
Shift (character), 18
Shirley, J. S., 202
Shoemaker's Holiday, The, 11–12
Shrewsbury, field of, 118
Shuger, Debora K., 54
Shylock (character), 6, 28, 40, 192, 217–21, 225–39, 242n49, 243n70
Sidney, Sir Philip, 21, 37, 38, 48–49, 50, 55–56, 98
Silcox, Beejay, 47
Silver, George, 186
Sir Thomas More, 21, 38, 39–42, 43–45, 51, 54, 58
Sivanandan, A., 46, 55
Slatyer, William, 13
Smith, Alan G. R., 193–94
Smith, Candis Watts, 96
Smith, Emma, 45–46, 54, 108
Smith, Ian, 5, 23, 92, 97, 99
Smug / Smug the Smith (character), 11, 33n55

Snout (character), 152n48

Socrates, 232

sodomy, 220–21

Sofer, Andrew, 233

Sogliardo (character), 18

solidarity, 12, 39, 40, 42–44, 51, 54–56, 58, 79, 81, 124

Sonnet 147 (Shakespeare), 114, 117, 124

Sony Pictures, 154, 176n5

Southern Strategy, 87. *See also* Atwater, Lee

Spain/Spanish, 8, 18, 20, 24, 137–39, 140, 148, 151n35, 203, 208

Spanish (language), 152n57

Spanish Armada, 25, 125, 131, 132, 134, 138, 139, 141, 142–44, 148, 151n35

Spanish Flu, 48

Spanish Tragedy, The, 132

speciesism, 56–59

Speed, John, 150n14

Spenser, Edmund, 3, 133–34, 147, 183, 184, 185. See also *Faerie Queene, The*, and *individual characters*

St. Bartholomew massacre, 40

St. Giles Cathedral (Edinburgh), 168

St. Paul's Churchyard, 90, 92

St. Peter's Basilica, 37

staff fighting, 26, 186, 188, 189

Stanley, James, Lord Strange, 3

Stationers' Register, 168

stereotypes, 14, 22, 97, 150n23, 181, 184

Stern, Elsie, 76, 85n47

Stewart, Alan, 238

Still, Melly, 16

Stockwood, John, 72

Stonehenge, 133

Stones, E. L. G., 156

Strange's Men, 142

strangers. *See* immigrants

Stratford Festival production of *Cymbeline* (1986), 16

Strauss-Kahn, Dominique, 47

Sturgeon, Nicola, 169–70, 174

Sullivan, Garrett, 119

Sunak, Rishi, 28

Susanna, 67

Sutton, John, 209

Swetnam, Joseph, 186, 187, 188, 189

sword fighting, 19, 26, 186

Syria, 20

Tamburlaine, 145

"Tamburlaine" (libel author), 148

Tamburlaine the Great, Part II, 141, 149n8

Tamil, 46, 55

Tanais, 17

Tartars, 8, 149n4

Tatham, John, 9–10, 12

Taylor, Gary, 92, 102

Tempest, The, 12

Thames, 204, 208, 209

Thessalia, 20

Thirty Years' War, 23, 71, 72, 73, 79, 81. *See also* French Wars of Religion

Thisbe (character), 152n48

Thompson, Ayanna, 101

Thorndike, Lynn, 151n27

Three Ladies of London, The, 17

Tichenor, Austin, 48

Times Literary Supplement, 47

Titus Andronicus, 82, 90

Tory Party, 175

Tracy, Larissa, 183

tragedy, purpose of, 38–39, 48–49, 55–56, 108

tragic irony, 21, 37

Traister, Barbara, 134–35, 137–38

transnational, 7, 8, 12, 19, 21, 22, 24, 65–67, 71, 72, 79, 82

Travellers Breviat, The, 8

Treasurie of Auncient and Moderne Times, 10

Treaty at Berwick, 155

Treaty of Edinburgh-Northampton, 155

Treaty of Paris, 165

Treaty of Rome, 108

Trémoille, Charlotte de la, 4

Trémoille, Claude de la, duke of Thouars, 4

Trigge, Francis, 44–45

Trinculo (character), 12

Triumphs of Truth, The, 23–24, 88–102, 103n5

Troy/Trojans, 18, 34n80, 132, 157

True Tragedie of Richard the Third, 18

Trump administration, 7

Trump, Donald J., 86–87

Truthout, 47

Tudeau-Clayton, Margaret, 60n24, 199–200

Tuerff, Kevin, 39

Turk/Turkish, 10, 11, 22, 101, 208. *See also* Ottoman Empire

Turner, Henry, 138

Twelfth Night (holiday), 3, 184

Twelfth Night, 48

Twitter, 153–54

typology, 22, 66–70, 73–75, 79, 81

Ubaldini, Petruccio, 148
Ukraine, 8
Ulster, Earl of (character), 164
Union of Crowns, 170. *See also* Scotland: union with England
Union Jack, 1
"Unite the Clans" ad campaign, 175
United States of America, 6, 7, 39, 45, 86–87, 101, 109, 148, 154
universalism, 18, 37–38, 46–49, 50–52, 54, 55–56, 58–59, 62n74, 154
usury, 217, 218–29, 233–34, 242n37, 242n49, 242n51
Usury (character), 17
Utopia, 43–44

Valerio (character), 18
Valiant Scot, The, 25, 155, 158, 160–61, 163–65, 167, 168, 169, 170–71, 174–75, 176, 177
Vandermast (character), 137
Vandermast, Tarquatus, 149n11
Vaughan, Rice, 220
Vaughan, Virginia Mason, 91
Vaughan, William, 203, 205
Venice/Venetians, 8–9, 40, 152n57, 227, 237, 238
Venice, Duke of (character), 97
Venus, 147
vice figure, 80
Viola/Cesario (character), 48
Virgil, 184
Virginia, 91

Wadell, Brodie, 1
Wales, 131, 134, 138, 139, 156, 166, 170, 175, 181, 184, 187, 195
Wallace, 177n28
Wallace, William, 159–64, 167, 168, 177n29
Wall, The, 131
Walsh, Brian, 135, 142–43
Walsingham, Sir Francis, 72, 141, 142–43, 151n33
Wars of the Roses, the, 129n37
Washington, DC, 16
Waterson, John, 169
Watkins, John, 184, 192
Watts, Jake, 127

Webster, John, 89
Welch, Ellen, 17
Welsh (people), 26, 113–17, 119, 120, 123, 181, 184, 187, 198–200, 206, 208, 211
"Welsh hook," 187, 188
West Indies, 91, 210
Westminster, 90, 154, 169, 175, 216
Westmoreland, Earl of (character), 113–14, 116
When You See Me, You Know Me, 19
Whitaker, Tobias, 201–2
white gaze, 88, 92, 93–95, 98, 102
White, R. S., 199, 208
Whitehall, 175
WikiLeaks, 154
Williams, Deanne, 135, 137
Wilson, J. Dover, 235
Wilson, Robert, 17
Wilson, Thomas, 220
Wily Beguiled, 132
Windrush scandal, 4–5 30n19
Windsor, 27, 198–99, 200–1, 206, 208–9, 210
wine, 27, 68, 198, 200–8, 209, 211; Rhenish, 137, 202. *See also* sack
Winter's Tale, The, 180
Withington, Phil, 217–18
wodewose, 26, 181, 183–84, 186, 189–90, 195, 195–96n12
World War II, 16, 38, 39, 124
Worshipful Society of Apothecaries (the Pepperers), 89
Worshipful Company of Grocers, 89
Wright, Thomas, 127
xenophobia, 1, 3, 5, 14, 42, 126, 148, 150n23, 152n57, 187, 195, 199–200, 206, 216, 217, 239. *See also* anti-Black racism; anti-immigrant; racism
Xenophon, 232

Yachnin, Paul, 49–50
Yancy, George, 94
York, Duke of (character), 12
York plays, 84n34
Younge, Gary, 46, 55
Yousaf, Humza, 174
Ypres Tower (Rye), 140

Zimmerman, George, 95